Modern Occultism

Also by Mitch Horowitz

Occult America

One Simple Idea

The Miracle Club

Uncertain Places

Daydream Believer

The Seeker's Guide to the Secret Teachings of All Ages

The Miracle Habits

The Miracle Month

Secrets of Self-Mastery

The Miracle of a Definite Chief Aim

The Power of the Master Mind

Magician of the Beautiful

Mind As Builder

Cosmic Habit Force

Happy Warriors

Practical Magick

MODERN OCCULTISM

History, Theory, and Practice

MITCH HOROWITZ

Published 2023 by Gildan Media LLC
aka G&D Media
www.GandDmedia.com

First Edition: 2023

Front cover design by Tom McKeveny.
Interior design by Meghan Day Healey of Story Horse, LLC.
Author photo by Yoshino.

Library of Congress Cataloging-in-Publication Data is available upon request

ISBN: 978-1-7225-0626-1

10 9 8 7 6 5 4 3 2 1

In memory of Jacob Needleman
1934–2022

"Fight, Arjuna"

CONTENTS

CHAPTER ONE

The Age of Hermes

With usual restraint, a *New York Post* headline of June 19, 2018, announced: "This sex-crazed cultist was the father of modern rocketry." The occasion was a TV series dramatizing the life of pioneering rocket scientist Jack Parsons (1914–1952).

Parsons, cofounder of NASA's Jet Propulsion Laboratory—some say its initials JPL mythically stand for *Jack Parsons Lives*—was among the brightest intellects in rocketry in the immediate post-war era. He was handsome, deeply read, and well liked. "Jack is one hell of a nice guy and a number-one rocket engineer," science-fiction writer Robert Heinlein wrote in a 1949 letter.

Parsons was also a dedicated occultist who collaborated with figures from British magician Aleister Crowley to Scientology founder L. Ron Hubbard. Jack's heterodoxy placed him on the wrong side of the nation's defense establishment, which sidelined the energetic scientist and denied him coveted security clearances.

Although obscure when he blew himself up at age thirty-seven in his Pasadena home laboratory while mixing pyrotechnics for a Hollywood special effects company, Parsons and his wife, artist and occultist Marjorie Cameron (1922–1995)—who believed he was murdered—have grown considerably in reputation since. As of this writing, Wikipedia's article on Parsons surpasses in length (and visits) many pieces on major inventors, scientists, and statesmen.

How did such diffuse and seemingly contradictory thought currents galvanize within one person? In actuality, Parsons, for all his remarkable individualism, was a direct product and exemplar of the culture of magick, experiment, and search that sprang from modern occultism.

The passions that moved Jack touch many of us in modern life. Like him, we employ a vocabulary, outlook, and sense of possibility that emerged from the birth, rebirth, and winding path of occult spirituality. To trace the influence of that obsidian thread—its origin, entanglements, frictions, points of contact, key figures, and catalytic role in modern life—is the aim of this journey.

This book is as much the history of an idea as it is of people and events. The *idea*, simple in concept yet seismic in impact, is that there exist unseen dimensions or intersections of time, all possessed of their own events, causes, intelligences, and perhaps iterations of ourselves; the influence of these realms is felt *on and through* us without mediation by any religion or doctrine.

Since relatively early in the revival of the search for ancient spiritual concepts during the Renaissance—by spiritual, I mean extraphysical—the outlook I describe has been broadly, though not exclusively, known by the English term *occult* from Latin *occultus* for *secret* or *hidden*.

In strictest terms, occultism is a Western concept. Although there exist esoteric (Greek *esoterikós* for "inner") teachings within Vedic, Buddhist, Animist, Taoist, Confucian, and Shamanic traditions around the world, the occult rose from the West's rupture with its own religious past during the rise of the Abrahamic religions, Christianity in particular. Occultism differs from esotericism insofar as the esoteric usually corresponds to an exoteric or outer counterpart, generally a traditional religion of which esotericism reflects the inner core. The occult is independent of religion while not necessarily rejecting of it.

When I write of the West, I mean the Abrahamic sphere of influence, i.e., regions defined by traditions of Judaism, Christianity, and, to a degree, Islam. Hence, I am chiefly referencing territories occupied first by the Greek armies of Alexander the Great (356–323 BC) and later by the Roman Empire, extending from Ancient Egypt and Constantinople to the Mediterranean Basin, Persia, and much of Europe, as well as colonial and migratory offshoots, including the Americas.

Modern Occultism explores the roots, people, ideas, aesthetics, and practices that have shaped our conception of the occult, as we have been shaped by them. This book began, and is significantly expanded from, a twelve-part course I delivered with the Theosophical Society in America. Our hundreds of online participants covered almost all fifty U.S. states, Canada, Mexico, and ranged overseas to Taiwan, Dubai, Singapore, Uganda, Turkey, Slovenia, Macedonia, Cyprus, Britain, Monaco, Australia, and the Netherlands. Our exchanges helped me reckon with much of the history I explore.

I describe myself as a critical but "believing historian" and I participate in many of the movements I consider. Hence, I am dedicated to documenting metaphysics in history and practice. Most historians of religion and spirituality are, in fact, believing historians. Many enduring books on both traditional and new religious movements are by writers who emerge from the congregations they document or adjacent ones. This is true, for example, of histories of recent religious movements like Christian Science and Mormonism just as it is of the historicism of Jewish sages and Catholic saints.*

Authors and scholars rarely reference themselves as critical believers to avoid the appearance of a gap in judgment. Indeed, some scholars and historians of esotericism take umbrage at being asked about the nature of their beliefs. But, in a sense, such questions are natural. People are generally *born into* Judaism, Christianity, or any number of traditional faiths. Occultism or esotericism, however, is something *sought after*. It does not readily present itself. Hence, scholarly attitudes often reflect a chronicler's private outlook.

I venture that the participating querent can, with proper measure, stand at the center of the movements studied, at least those of a contemporary nature, and more fully perceive the values emanating from them, as well as fissures between ideal and practice.

---

* Examples include the work of Robert Peel (1909–1992), Richard Lyman Bushman (b.1931), D. Michael Quinn (1944–2021), Gerhsom Scholem (1897–1982), and John W. O'Malley (1927–2022).

One of the scholars of esotericism I most admire, Wouter J. Hanegraaff, sees it differently: "Students in the fields of religion, philosophy, and science must make up their minds about whether they want to be gardeners or biologists. If they prefer the former, then the study of esotericism is not for them."* I dissent from this framing. To follow the agrarian metaphor, there exists another option (at least), which is to be a scientific agriculturist. "Objectivity, in fact, is not just a single standpoint," wrote philosopher Mary Midgley.**

In that vein, I am inspired by a passage from historian of esotericism and musicologist Joscelyn Godwin from the journal *Theosophical History* in July 1990: "My own mind is open to the possibility of events for which materialistic science, and the historical scholarship modeled on it, has no place; consequently, I do not automatically dismiss the idea of immaterial influences . . . Henry Corbin coined the valuable term of 'hierohistory' (hiérohistoire): the superior or sacred history that gives meaning to earthly events."

We who live in the West occupy a peculiar situation regarding our religious past. With respect to religious history, our storyline differs from the development of religions in many of the Eastern cultures.

In the East, including China, India, Japan, and a variety of Asian societies, there prevails an ancient religious continuum. Vedism or Hinduism is one of the oldest continuously observed faiths in the world. The same is true of Buddhism. In Persia, although dominated by Islam, this is the case with Zoroastrianism. While certain societies, like mainland China, are officially atheistic there persist Taoist, Confucianist, and Animist traditions, which have timelines extending millennia.

In the West, including many parts of the Mediterranean and Near East, a different story prevails. The ancient cultures of Greece, Rome, Egypt, Mesopotamia, and the so-called Biblical lands, for hundreds and in some cases thousands of years maintained distinct religious traditions, often polytheistic, nature-based, and seasonal in practice, frequently possessed of an esoteric core, and steeped in varied obser-

* *Western Esotericism: A Guide for the Perplexed* (Bloomsbury Academic, 2013).

** *The Myths We Live By* (Routledge, 2004).

vances we now call sacrificial, petitionary, ceremonial, astrological, divinatory, alchemical, ritualistic, and initiatory. Deity veneration was a common thread. Such traditions, extending across Europe and the Near and Middle East, commanded the dedication of millions of people for thousands of years.

Yet with the fall of Rome in the West and the spread of Christianity in the West and East these traditions, to a very great extent, disappeared for centuries. With the rise of Islam, further discontinuity swept away Persian and Arab faiths, ancient and more modern, two notable exceptions being Zoroastrianism and Yezidism.* Their priesthoods, temple orders, social systems, liturgies, parables, sacred texts, and lexicon of gods were wiped out or transmuted. Many of their books were destroyed in warfare or conflict, pillaged and pirated, or sequestered in monasteries or by private collectors; in other cases, they were buried and forgotten—and sometimes unearthed.

The unraveling of the ancient West began, more or less, following the reign of Roman Emperor Constantine, who converted to Christianity in 312 or 313 A.D. and in 330 A.D. relocated the locus of the empire to Constantinople, today Istanbul. Rome continued to wield dominant power in the West for about another 200 years; the Byzantine Empire itself staggered to a finish in 1453 when the Ottomans entered its last stronghold.

Current historians avoid the term Dark Ages. That phrase has fallen into disfavor because it implies that, other than subsistence living and feudal warfare, little civilizational activity occurred for hundreds of years between the fall of Rome in the West in 476 A.D. and the dawn of cathedral building in the mid-1100s A.D. followed by the Renaissance around 1300 A.D. Past generations harbored the unspoken generalization that between Rome's collapse and reemergence of learning traditions, seminary orders, and reasonably stable monarchies beginning in the 1100s, there existed a cultural ice age. That is, of course, inadequate. But it is also true that religious traditions of Western antiquity, later called *occult*, were to a very great extent obliterated by the dominance of Christianity, dissolution of Rome, and later advent of Islam in the early seventh century A.D.

---

* The Yezidis practice an esoteric tradition dating to the Middle Ages. They are today among the world's most oppressed religious minorities. There is no shorthand for Yezidi practice, which involves worship of a rebellious angel. For background, I recommend Peter Lamborn Wilson's *Peacock Angel: The Esoteric Tradition of the Yezidis* (Inner Traditions, 2022).

Hence, when I use the Latin term *occultus*, it bears remembering that its adoption grew from an effort to identify, reference, and in some cases revive traditions that suffered decline and banishment in the West due to the schismatic discontinuity of our religious past.

Discontinuity, however, conceals hidden bonds. In many cases, when ancient Greco-Roman temples were demolished or buried, their foundations were turned into building sites for the Notre Dame cathedral (construction beginning 1163 A.D.) and other expressions of Christianity throughout the Middle Ages. Although he effectively rendered Christianity into Rome's state faith, Constantine himself combined Christianity with worship of the sun god, Sol Invictus, a practice continued by pilgrims on the steps of St. Peter's Basilica into the mid-fifth century A.D.* The Emperor Julian (331–363 A.D.), sometimes called Julian the Apostate, attempted to rollback Christianity as the official state religion. He began restoring some pagan and Jewish temples. But his reign was brief, from 361 to 363 A.D., so his program was not universally felt. Hence, there are no neat "starts and stops" in religious history; changes, even when overwhelming, proceed in an uneven or combinative manner.

In late antiquity, specifically the generations immediately preceding and following the death of Christ, we find formative—if indirect—connections to themes regarded as occult, esoteric, alternative, Gnostic, or, for that matter, New Age. The term New Age is often used as an epithet for everything considered trendy, fuzzy-headed, and fickle in modern spirituality. I reject that usage and believe it fails to capture the experience of millions of seekers. I define New Age as a radically ecumenical culture of therapeutic spirituality.

Because many of our connections or parallels to ancient spirituality emerge from late antiquity, I want to take us back to the world of Alexandria in the era of Cleopatra. The name Cleopatra (69–30 B.C.) is, of course, as widely recognized as Caesar or Napoleon. Such figures can appear as impersonal memes like the visage of Washington gazing out from a dollar bill. But she was, of course, a full-blooded figure with a life marked by ideals, missteps, and pathos.

---

* *The Early Church* by Henry Chadwick (Penguin Books, 1967, 1993).

Cleopatra was the final leader of what could be considered an independent Ancient Egypt. She ruled from 51 to 30 B.C., when she took her own life following naval defeat to the Roman fleet at Actium, suicide of her partner Mark Antony, and Rome's siege of Alexandria. Cleopatra was not Egyptian but Greek by descent. Egypt's ruling class had been Greek extending to the founding of Alexandria in 331 B.C. by Hellenic conqueror Alexander the Great. Thereafter the pharaonic system was revised and the Egyptian throne occupied by rulers stemming from the lineage of Alexander's generals, called Ptolemies.

Cleopatra proved unique within the Ptolemaic lineage. Overall, the Alexandrian era spelled gradual decay of Egypt's temple orders and religious systems. In one sense, the Greek administrative and ruling class was Philo-Egyptian; rulers often admired and adopted Egyptian culture. But they intermarried to strictly preserve their Hellenic bloodline. As a result, and despite cultural affinity, Greek rulers often had a distant relationship to the millions who made up Egyptian civilization. Their concerns were chiefly economic and military versus religio-cultural. Cleopatra differed. She was more than a Philo-Egyptian installed on a Hellenic throne. Although entangled in her own military campaigns, domestic crises, and geopolitical intrigues, she valued and sought revival of Egypt's esoteric tradition. The leader did so primarily from the cultural and economic seat of Alexandria where she funded restoration of monuments, priesthoods, and temple orders.

For a time, she revived Egyptian mystery tradition while managing to protect the empire from excessive encroachment by Roman forces. Following Cleopatra's reign, however, Egypt became a Roman military province and agricultural redoubt. But thanks in part to Cleopatra's influence, religious practices endured in Alexandria. Following her death, the city continued to function as a cultural hub. In generations ahead—and this is vital to our concerns—a cohort of urban-dwelling, Greek-Egyptian scribes, many of them part of the administrative class, began writing down aspects of Egyptian esoteric philosophy in Greek.

This undertaking proved enormously significant in future centuries because it served to preserve and translate some of Egypt's esoteric philosophy into an expository literary form that modern Westerners, who had little understanding of hieroglyphs or Demotic (a hieratic script used for official business), could grasp. Indeed, the

West did not even begin to decipher hieroglyphs until after the discovery of the Rosetta Stone by Napoleon's invading armies in 1799.

These Greek scribes wrote down ideas that were previously passed on through *oral tradition*, or almost certainly so. Most of the ancient religious and philosophical ideas that reach us today began in oral form and were only later committed to writing by figures who we call Homer or Plato or Pythagoras, or in the last case by his students. In actuality, we know little about the identity or even the verity of such figures. It was common in the ancient world that scribes—we wouldn't consider them distinct authors in our modern sense—affixed the name of a venerated or legendary figure to their writings in order to lend them gravity. What are the gospels themselves but oral tradition, written by evangelists, Luke, Mark, etc., whose personhood is undetermined? It is a modern innovation that a writer or author has an individual identity.

In Ancient Egypt, the Mediterranean, the Biblical lands, Hindustan or Ancient India, China and Japan, it was common that a scribe functioned on behalf of a government, army, empire, academy, or royal court. In many cases, we do not know if authorial names represent single, demarcated personas. For example, we do not know the identity of Lao Tzu, the legendary author of the *Tao Te Ching* (c. 400 B.C.). We do not know with any certainty the identity of Sun Tzu, author of *The Art of War* (c. 500 B.C.) who was not credited until about 100 B.C., which would be four centuries after the death of Zhou dynasty general Sun Tzu (c. 544–496 B.C.), an honorific title meaning "Master Sun." Very little is understood about the author other than historical consensus that such a figure existed as a commander in the dynastic emperor's army.

One of humanity's oldest forms of writing—and also an oracular tool—is the ancient Chinese *I Ching*, or Book of Changes, a pictogrammatic alphabet of sixty-four hexagrams. First published in the late-ninth century B.C., the oldest attributed author is Fu Tsi or Fuxi, a mythical ruler, somewhat like King Arthur, said to command China during the third millennium B.C. Nor do we know the identity of Homer (c. eighth century B.C.) or if he was a singular being. Indeed, most of the ideas and mathematical formulas attributed to Pythagoras (c. 570–495 B.C.), who tutored students at an academy reputed to be in Croton, Italy, were not written down, in this case by his students, until centuries after the Greek sage died around 495 B.C.

Such is the case with the late-ancient Greek-Egyptian literature I've referenced, which was often attributed to Hermes or *Hermes Trismegistus*, an appellation of honor that Greek-Egyptians bestowed upon Thoth, Egypt's god of writing and intellect. They saw the ibis-headed god as "three-times greater" than their own god of intellect, communication, and writing, Hermes, later the Roman god Mercury. Hence, late-ancient Greek scribes and builders termed this being Thrice-Greatest Hermes or Hermes Trismegistus.

I've noted all this to frame the vintage and sourcing, sketchy and uncertain, for our antecedents of the occult. The timing of this record later became a source of controversy, to which we return. But for now, I want to note that our references to history often pay too little acknowledgment to the complexities of what the recorded past, as it reaches us, consists of.

"The earliest that Hermes attains the actual epithet 'Thrice Greatest,'" writes scholar of religion M. David Litwa in *Hermetica II* (Cambridge University Press, 2018), "it seems, is with Thrasyllus of Alexandria, famous astrologer of the emperor Tiberius (reigned 14–37 A.D.)." Earlier references to Thoth as three-times great extend to the 2nd century B.C.*

To lend gravity to their work, as we've seen was customary in many ancient traditions, as well as to honor the source of their ideas, anonymous Greek-Egyptian scribes often affixed this title to their transcripts. Hence, their literature came to bear the name of the mythical being Hermes Trismegistus. In later centuries, this oeuvre was called Hermetic literature or *Hermetica*, a term that entered English in the early seventeenth century.

There exist many diffuse and, as they have survived, disorderly Hermetic tracts. Some were ceremonial and magical in nature, oriented toward specific spells, prayers, or alchemical operations; these are generally called technical Hermetica. Others were more philosophical and existential. Within these tracts appears a discernable core. The outlook animating the philosophical Hermetica can more or less be distilled this way: all of creation emanates from one great higher mind, which the Greeks called *Nous*. This higher mind creates

* *Hermetica* translated by Brian P. Copenhaver (Cambridge University Press, 1992).

through the exercise of thought. Creation expands outward through concentric circles or planetary spheres of reality—humanity appears within one of these concentric circles.

A key remnant of philosophical Hermetica (some would argue for it being technical but it conveys an existential outlook), produced in very late antiquity is *The Emerald Tablet*. The magical text was first translated from Latin into English by Sir Isaac Newton (1643–1727). In this work appears the famous dictum, "as above, so below," which I believe parallels the Western Scriptural precept, "God created man in his own image."*

As it happens, Newton's interest in late alchemy, which did not fully come to light until the mid-twentieth century, was stoked by the writings of a mysterious Eirenaeus Philalethes, the pseudonym of Harvard-educated colonial-era alchemist and medical practitioner George Starkey (1628–1665). "Both Starkey and Philalethes wrote about the properties of matter as well as its structure," noted Michael Meyer of the Science History Institute, "and these ideas influenced Newton's thinking and practice, including perhaps his thinking about light and how white light could be broken down and recombined in ways similar to matter."**

Newton's magical interests were revealed by none other than seminal economist John Maynard Keynes (1883–1946), whose analysis of boom-and-bust cycles did much to stabilize market economies in the twentieth century. In 1936, Keynes purchased Newton's dust-gathering papers and discovered, to his surprise, the mind not of a hardened materialist but a learned mage. Ten years later, Keynes announced in a posthumously read speech, "Newton, the Man," delivered at the Royal Society as part of the tricentennial of Newton's birth (postponed due to World War II):

> Newton was not the first of the age of reason. He was the last of the magicians, the last of the Babylonians and Sumerians, the last great mind which looked out on the visible and intellectual world

* From Newton's translation: "Tis true without lying, certain and most true. That which is below is like that which is above." Litwa (2018) provides an annotated translation from Latin: "True it is, without falsehood, certain and most certain: that which is above is like that which is below, and that which is below is like to that which is above, to accomplish the wonders of a single reality."

** "Isaac Newton and the American Alchemist," *Distillations*, July 14, 2016.

with the same eyes as those who began to build our intellectual inheritance rather less than 10,000 years ago. Isaac Newton, a posthumous child born with no father on Christmas Day, 1642, was the last wonderchild to whom the Magi could do sincere and appropriate homage.

Returning to the philosophical Hermetica, its recurrent ideal is that just as humanity was created by an infinite mind, *Nous*, so can we create within our own sphere of existence. The secret of human development is discovering the psyche's causative dimensions and the expansion to which they point.

In a key Hermetic tract, translated from Greek to Latin during the Renaissance, man is urged toward awareness of how his mind, through its ability to visualize all things, originate new concepts, and surpass physical boundaries, reflects innate divinity:

> See what power you have, what quickness! If you can do these things, can god not do them? So you must think of god in this way, as having everything—the cosmos, himself, (the) universe—like thoughts within himself. Thus, unless you make yourself equal to god, you cannot understand god; like is understood by like. Make yourself grow to immeasurable immensity, outleap all body, outstrip all time, become eternity and you will understand god. Having conceived that nothing is impossible to you, consider yourself immortal and able to understand everything, all art, all learning, the temper of every living thing.*

Yet there also exists tension between man's self-actualization—a process that makes him greater than the gods who are fixed in existence—and physical limitations man suffers in his sphere of existence. This parallels Psalm 82:6–7, "Ye are gods . . . but ye shall die like men."

Hence, within the cosmic framework you occupy, you, too, are capable of thought causation. But the Hermetic literature cautions that the individual, although possessed of faculties of this higher mind, is restricted by physical parameters of the concentric circle he dwells in. That is not cause for despair or fatalism; again, one of the central

* *Hermetica*, book XI, translated by Copenhaver (1992).

principles of Hermeticism is that the individual is *ever in the process of becoming*, of growing closer in nature to the gods. In Book I of the *Corpus Hermeticum*, often called "Poimandres" (a Greek-Egyptian term of unknown origin, possibly meaning *man-shepherd*), the individual rises through the planetary spheres *shedding vices* picked up earlier when descending through the spheres. Each planet rules a vice, a schema that scholar of esotericism Richard Smoley calls the origin of the Seven Deadly Sins.

Hermeticism posits what we might call a theory of reincarnation or eternal recurrence, which holds that the individual occupies a physical form that dissipates but the psyche is rejoined to universal life stuff, which could be considered thought. Psyche is then reprocessed into life (which does not necessarily mean that the personality remains intact) where it may traverse circles of existence that approach nearer to the center of being.

Although book XII of the *Corpus Hermeticum* expounds on "cyclical recurrence," the role of reincarnation is ambiguous. Souls "are dissolved not to be destroyed but become new," Hermes tells his disciple Tat.* The late-ancient Hermeticist Stobaeus (c. early fifth century A.D.) heads a section of his *Anthology* "On the Incarnation and Reincarnation of Souls," with Isis telling Horus, "Those sent down to rule, Horus my child, are sent from the upper zones. When released, they return to the same regions or ascend even higher unless some of them did something <against> the dignity of their own nature and the precept of divine law."**

In his 2022 study *Hermetic Spirituality and the Historical Imagination*, Wouter J. Hanegraaff issues an important caution to interpreters of the Hermetica: these texts have undergone immense shuffling, rewriting, and copying even in their late-ancient environs. "This means," he writes, "that precisely those elements in the Hermetica that strike us as familiar (those that make us feel comfortably 'at home' in our own mental world, surrounded by concepts and ideas that we readily know and understand) are most likely to lead us astray."

This is because material that appears "familiar" or, I would venture, parallel to modern concepts, seems so because ancient scribes

* My reference to "cyclical recurrence" is from *Hermetic Spirituality and the Historical Imagination* by Wouter J. Hanegraaff (Cambridge University Press, 2022). Translation of Hermes to Tat is Copenhaver (1992).

** Litwa (2018).

were adapting source material to which they had access to reflect rising norms, conceptions, or vernacular of the day, which also populated the more canonical literature to which we're accustomed. There was the further issue of their own religious outlook and preferences. From our modern vantage point, there exists no *pure* Hermeticism.

Another of the ways the Hermetic seeker discovers his capacities as a creator is through what came to be called alchemy, a term shrouded in etymological mystery. Although the word alchemy appears in Arabic in the centuries following Christ, we do not know precisely where it comes from. It is tantalizing and important to understand the possible origin of the word and what it means for modernity's connection to Ancient Egypt.

Alchemy was practiced in Persia, North Africa, and later different parts of the Mediterranean and Western world; it was an effort on the part of ancient and early modern seekers and proto-scientists to transform gross into fine matter. Or, as is typically heard, lead into gold. There was a physical dimension to alchemy as there was a psychological and mystical dimension. *Every thought system in the ancient world intermingled.* There wasn't a difference between so-called science (not yet extant) and spirituality. Astrology and astronomy were adjoined; art, mathematics, and sacred geometry or use of numbers to unlock the code and system of the universe were adjoined; architecture and worship were adjoined; chemistry and mysticism, in alchemy, were adjoined.

Alchemy is the root of the modern term chemistry but, as noted, its etymology is unsettled. The likelihood is that alchemy is a Latin-Anglicized version of Ancient Egypt's name for itself. The term *Egypt* is Hellenic in nature. Ancient Egyptians referred to themselves through the hieroglyphic characters K M T or *Kemet*. The term means *Black Land*. Egypt referred to itself as the Black Land to connote the rich soil and fertility that the Nile River brought to Central Egypt. The desert, the outlying regions, were called the Red Land, where life was harsher and less fertile. *Al* is Arabic for "the," hence there's every possibility that *alchemy* is an Arabic and later Hellenic version of Ancient Egypt's name for itself. We are uncertain about the phonetic pronunciation Ancient Egyptians used. In Hebrew, one of several neighboring languages, the sounds for S and T were sometimes transliterated—in similar vein an early Greek phonetic pronunciation of Kemet is *Chemi*. Hence, *Al-Chemi* or alchemy.

Modern people speak of *black magic* or *black arts* with sinister connotation. But if the etymology I'm describing is correct, the sinister connotation is culturally conditioned. Black arts or black magic—used as a persecutory epithet in the West starting in the fifteenth century—would, in its purest form, reference the origin of alchemy: the Black Land and its arts of transformation.

Alexandria is also the birthplace of Western astrology, although the concept's antiquity runs deeper. Astrology as practiced today in the West does not reflect the astrology of the early ancients although it springs from it foundationally. Astrology itself dovetails with the Hermetic worldview: "as above, so below." All is interconnected, including psyche and cosmos.

Astrology's earliest origins are traceable to 2,000–1,600 B.C. in Mesopotamia, sometimes referred to as Babylon, but the Babylonian Empire was only one later phase that Mesopotamia or modern-day Iraq passed through. Extending to deep antiquity, at least the second millennium B.C., we find the earliest threads and stirrings of astrological forecasting. Moving forward to the second and third century B.C. in Mesopotamia, we see greater formality and codification of astrological principles. Greek scribes and thinkers in Alexandria took a mélange of Mesopotamian and Egyptian ideas and curated them into the earliest form of what we consider astrology in the West.

One of the key episodes in the codification occurred in Alexandria around 150 A.D. At that time, Hellenic astrologer and mathematician Claudius Ptolemy issued a work called *Tetrabiblos* ("four books") in which he took strides devising the system of astrology adapted in the modern West. Here is Alexandria, almost 200 years following the death of Cleopatra, still serving as a springboard for concepts that modern people call occult. Regarding Ptolemy's codification of astrological principles, he was not the only Hellene attempting this; but his authorial voice survived time and marked a critical turning point in formulating the modern philosophy.

Ptolemy argued that the signs of the zodiac, e.g., Aries, Taurus, Sagittarius, Capricorn, Gemini, are *keyed to the seasons*. This reflected a subtle and important standard, which fostered two divergent systems: Vedic or sidereal astrology and tropical or seasonally based astrology. The former prevails in the East and the latter in the West. (The Chinese zodiac is based on the lunar calendar and has little in common with either.) The division of the two systems can be understood by considering that the night sky looks differently to us today than it did to dwellers of antiquity. The location of celestial objects remains constant but our *vantage point* has shifted due to a slight wobble in earth's axis. This results in the *precession of the equinoxes*, in which the zodiac wheel appears to cycle gradually backwards, a phenomenon first detected by Greek astronomer and mathematician Hipparchus (190–120 B.C.).

A dweller of ancient Mesopotamia who walked outside at dawn on March 21 or 22 would, like us, observe the vernal or spring equinox. This occurs when the sun rises in the crisscross of two imaginary lines: the celestial equator and the ecliptic. Earth's equator "pushed out" into space is the celestial equator. If you positioned earth at the center of the solar system with the sun tracing an arc throughout the sky, that forms the ecliptic, which is also the zodiac wheel. Hence, on the morning of the vernal equinox, you see the sun rising in this crisscross of the celestial equator and the ecliptic, heralding the dawn of spring.

In the centuries before Christ, the sun rose in that crisscross in the sign of Aries. The ram, symbolizing fertility, birth, boldness, and new beginnings, naturally suits the advent of spring. Due to earth's wobble on its axis, however, the appearance of the vernal equinox recedes one degree every seventy-two years. Each zodiac sign contains 30 degrees. In about 2,160 years, the vernal equinox recedes through an entire zodiac sign. It then enters a different sign. The equinox recedes around the zodiac wheel once every 26,000 years, sometimes called a Platonic year.

In the Christian era, after the Emperor Constantine converted in 312 or 313 A.D., and Christianity began its rise to dominance, the vernal equinox entered Pisces, the fish. Christ was said to be a "fisher of men" one of whose miracles was creation of "loaves and fishes" to feed a crowd. The vernal equinox lingered in Pisces for centuries, again to the eye receding one degree every seventy-two years, so that in our era the vernal equinox now falls in Aquarius. Hence the term Aquarian Age or "dawning of the Age of Aquarius," as went the popular song from the sixties-era musical *Hair.*

Aquarius is traditionally represented as the water bearer and a sign of mysticism, revolution, innovation, and change. As such, the Aquarian Age is considered one of spiritual and social experimentation. In certain Gnostic teachings, Aquarius marks the ascent of the zodiac (with Leo commencing descent). There also exist lower iterations of Aquarius, such as mechanical, insincere virtue. A wide range of spiritual writers in the early twentieth century spoke of this dawning Aquarian Age. A channeled reinterpretation of Christ's philosophy called *The Aquarian Gospel of Jesus the Christ* by retired Civil War chaplain Levi H. Dowling (1844–1911) appeared in 1908 and helped popularize this notion.

Returning to Alexandria around 150 A.D., Ptolemy contended he was aware of the precession of the equinoxes. But he argued that this fact does not alter the basic principles of astrology, which are keyed to the seasons and function as compass points or windows onto the cosmos. His reasoning prevailed and most Westerners use the Ptolemaic system with its fixed seasonal or tropical coordinates. Western astrologers also use star-based or sidereal coordinates, reflecting the *actual position* of the stars and planets vis-à-vis earth's vantage point, when referencing *epochal ages* like Aquarius.

As centuries passed, Vedic or Eastern astrologers, who are part of Hindu religious tradition, determined that the *sidereal system* is simply more accurate. They calculated precession into their forecasts. Hence, Vedic astrologers, unlike their Western counterparts, use the *actual physical position* of celestial objects apropos earth's vantage point. Astrology remains part of Hindu religious tradition. Before marriage, modern Hindu couples often consult an astrologer to determine when or whether to have a child, buy a home, set the wedding date, and so on.

Ptolemy instigated a series of debates that have never been settled because they go to the heart of what reality is if one takes seriously occult and esoteric traditions. In addition to questions of precession, there is debate over whether celestial objects are causative or correlative. In dominant Mesopotamian and Egyptian perspectives, the zodiac reflects synchronistic pictures of what is occurring on earth, i.e., correlative. But Ptolemy, in a perspective that gained sway within the Hellenic world, maintained that the position of celestial objects are causes; not just correlations but actual influences. Hence, in the Ptolemaic view, Mars, Venus, Jupiter, and so on, do not just *symbolize* what the individual experiences upon first breath—the starting point of life in the astrological schema—but *instigate* or influence it.

Among those who engage astrology, it has been argued that the ancient craft is less determinative of life today than in antiquity because life is now more flexible than it was in an era when an individual was all-but-certain to die in the same caste or status into which he was born.

I am delving into some of this material because I want to elucidate the foundations (or one might say fissures) that modern occultism stands on. When considering themes like alchemy, astrology, and Hermeticism itself, it is important to realize that we do not have uninterrupted, uniform connections.

It is also important to recall, as alluded earlier, that during the early Middle Ages, or what used to be called the Dark Ages, many of these ideas were either adapted into Christianity (especially for seasonal festivals and feast days) or simply vanished from view. For example, Halloween is rooted in the ancient Celtic festival of Samhain (pronounced *saa'wn*), which marked a seasonal change; observers often lit bonfires throughout the night to honor and consort with spirits of dead relatives. It is a period when the veil between the seen and unseen world is considered thinnest. By the early Middle Ages, the church incorporated the enduring pagan ceremony into its calendar as All Soul's Day on November 1, although adaptations, of course, survive. Historians eschew the term Dark Ages because, again, it connotes a period of dormancy and immobility; but there was, in fact, discontinuity of tradition and belief.

If one considers how ancient religious ideas fell into disuse, suppression, and prohibition during the years in which Christianity progressed throughout Western, Middle Eastern, and Near Eastern life—although certain retentions linger in folk traditions (nothing totally vanishes)—you can see why there exists no neat thread of connection to any of these ancient practices. Sometimes within modern life, we reach parallel insights, which correlate with ancient ideas. Modern people occasionally re-embrace antique ideas and revive or remake them, as has been attempted within traditions from Freemasonry to witchcraft. But we rarely experience uninterrupted connection.

This is at the heart of why *occult* connotes hidden or secret. Occultism is, in effect, a revivalist movement. It is a reclamation and adaptation of spiritual themes and methods that once flourished and were later suppressed by a cultural order that remains dominant. Hence, there is a perpetual outsider quality to occultism.

As with "black magick," many modern people consider occultism sinister. That is cultural conditioning. Was humanity more sinister in Cleopatra's era than in modern centuries? Who could witness the mass carnage of the twentieth century—Stalin, Hitler, Mao—and even suggest as much? Rather, it is simply that victors generally classify vanquished on their own terms. As pagan and Christian powers clashed for control in late antiquity, Christendom was eventually able to classify nature-based religions and mystery traditions as heretical and thus evil. Had paganism triumphed, its dominant culture would have classified Christianity the same way. It is human nature. There are no "good guys" and "bad guys" in this historical drama. I should mention that I use the term pagan fitfully since it is actually a Latin-derived (*paganus*) epithet used by early Christians to denote people who lived in outlying areas or backwater villages who were slow to learn of, and thus adopt, Christianity. The term pagan entered English in the seventeenth century.

Obviously there's nothing intrinsically sinister about the occult—but is there something secret? If ideas that are suppressed, unseen, or neglected for centuries connotes hidden, then the answer is approximately yes.

Another variant of belief that persisted in the late-ancient world, suffered brutal suppression, and experienced modern rediscovery is Gnosticism. This term, too, was first used as a pejorative at its scholarly inception in the seventeenth century. Within Gnosticism—from Greek *gnosis* for higher knowing—certain doctrines of the ancient occultic or esoteric worldview were combined with notions emanant from Judaic Scripture and early Christianity into a compelling and original mélange of thought and practice, which has reemerged today within scholarly and spiritual subcultures.

The basic outlook of Gnosticism, broadly speaking, is that among deific energies of creation there exists a cosmic clash between forces of material malignance versus spiritual harmony. In one variant of

Gnostic belief, our world is ruled by a vengeful and maleficent God sometimes called by the Greek-Latin term *demiurge*. The demiurge is based on Hebraic Scriptural concepts of a punitive and "jealous God" referenced in Exodus, Deuteronomy, Isaiah, and elsewhere. In the Gnostic mythos, *Sophia*, or divine wisdom, grew impregnated with negative emotions and birthed the earthly demiurge who usurped her power.

This ersatz deity placed men and women into a so-called Garden of Paradise, which was more a veil of shadows keeping them from knowledge of their true spiritual selves. In some narratives, the wisdom-proffering serpent is considered heroic. Men and women are spiritual beings imprisoned in flesh and kept in darkness in this world of illusion and appearances, or what in Vedic tradition is sometimes called *maya* or *samsara*. In Gnostic thought, there exist governors, known by the Greek term *archons*, who function as deputy rulers of our corrupt physical world.

The false God, or demiurge, is at once demanding, punishing, and covetous of loyalty, like a cruel parent. In some Gnostic texts, the figure of Christ is an authentic, liberating, freeing counter to the demiurge, a force of creation, beneficence, and spiritual evolution intended to vanquish forces of illusion and malevolence. These themes reemerge in modern conspiracist culture.

Some Gnostic groups—their beliefs varied widely—emphasized so-called *Apocrypha* or "hidden things," writings roughly contemporaneous with Scripture that ecclesiastical authorities deemed unacceptable, of questionable legitimacy, and noncanonical, although acceptance differs by denomination. Another class of non-canonical books is called *pseudepigrapha* ("false writings"), late-ancient books of dubious authorship that often feature biblical figures. One is the "Testament of Solomon" (c. first century A.D.) a Greek text in which the archangel Michael gives Solomon a ring with a pentagram on it that allows the king to command demons and enlist their aid in construction of the temple. Some pseudepigraphic works have commonalities with biblical and rabbinic texts.

One of the most enduring and influential works of Apocrypha is the Hebraic Book of Enoch, produced around 300–200 B.C. The name Enoch appears several times in Scripture, including as the son of Cain and also as the descendant of Seth, the third and final son born to Adam and Eve after the fratricide. The latter Enoch—who we reencounter when meeting Renaissance magician John Dee—is considered Noah's great-grandfather. Referencing the latter Enoch, Genesis 5:24 remarks enigmatically: "And Enoch walked with God: and he was not; for God took him" (KJV).

The Book of Enoch, which actually consists of five distinct tracts, tells the story of a biblically aged figure, thought to be the latter Enoch to whom it is attributed. In an act of gnosis, the patriarch bursts through the world of illusion and experiences the unseen world. The narrative also tells of a class of angels called Watchers, a subset of which descended to earth as fallen or rebellious angels, who then instruct humanity and mate with mortal women, giving birth to the *Nephilim*, a marauding race of giants. To some interpreters, this triggered the flood.

Mediterranean Gnostic sects often combined elements of Christianity and Judaism with retentive practices from paganism, hence assembling a syncretic faith that honored the Christian salvific message but maintained initiatory and esoteric practices of pre-Christian antiquity; some included Persian gods, such as the sun deity Abraxas (sometimes also an archon). These sects and groupings were often violently suppressed or eradicated by Christian troops and governments. This persecution culminated in 1209 with the Crusader massacre of thousands of men, women, children, and refugees attached to the Gnostic Cathar sect in Southern France. Strands of the movement survived another century.

Although the Book of Enoch has circulated in various forms since the early 1700s (though not in English until 1821), it is important to note that many Gnostic texts we know today, including some of the Gnostic gospels, such as Thomas and Philip, did not come to light until discovery of a cache of ancient Gnostic texts in the wake of World War II in 1945 at Nag Hammadi in Upper Egypt. A local farmer discovered thirteen leather-bound papyri manuscripts buried in a sealed jar—an event that reignited interest in Gnosticism and opened new vistas on the ancient practice.

Indeed, Gnosticism as both revival movement and adapted retention has, over the past eighty years or so, attained considerable popularity in the West. Prior to the Nag Hammadi discoveries, other forms of Gnostic literature were available and Gnosticism was discussed but largely within academic and esoteric niches. Since then, Gnostic texts have grown far more widely disseminated within popular and public circles. Within the Nag Hammadi cache were also partial or complete Hermetic and Platonic texts.

Hence, we in the twenty-first century occupy an unusual position vis-à-vis Gnosticism, not entirely unlike what our forebearers in the Renaissance found themselves facing with Hermeticism, whose manuscripts were rediscovered in the mid-to-late 1400s, as explored in the next chapter. It will be fascinating to see how modernity's reencounter with Gnosticism develops.

With regard to Hermeticism and astrology, modern people are likewise recipients of new discoveries, translations, adaptations, and understandings. The famous *Emerald Tablet*, mentioned in connection with Isaac Newton, is a case in point. Until the 1920s, *The Emerald Tablet* was widely deemed a medieval fakery written in Latin. But since then, scholars have discovered progressively earlier fragments and translations of the work.* The earliest source we now have of *The Emerald Tablet* is from the eighth century A.D. in Arabic. German scholar of alchemical texts Julius Ruska (1867–1949) estimated the composition of *The Emerald Tablet* to sometime between 600 and 750 A.D., with the original possibly in Greek.** (Hermetic works got translated not only into Latin but also Arabic, which likewise served as a source of retention.)

Until recently, Hermeticism itself was widely considered an ersatz philosophy, which many scholars of religion considered a faux antique "mutt" of pseudo-Egyptiana and Neoplatonism. But as we've uncovered other texts of contemporaneous and deeper antiquity, we find correspondences between Hermeticism and Ancient Egypt. This turnaround began, in part, through a remarkable book, *The Egyptian Hermes* by Garth Fowden, published by Cambridge University Press in 1986. Since then, and also dated to the discovery of earlier Coptic texts in the 1970s, the view has shifted with Hermeticism now

---

* This history is well summarized in "Historical Note Concerning the Emerald Tablet" in *Meditations on the Tarot* written anonymously by Catholic scholar and Traditionalist Valentin Tomberg (1900–1973). The posthumous work is itself something of a mystery, thought to date to 1967 with its first publication in French in 1980 and its English publication five years later. I published a 2002 edition at Penguin Random House, which includes the translator's corrections and an afterword by Traditionalist theologian Cardinal Hans Urs von Balthasar.

** *Tabula Smaragdina. Ein Beitrag zur Geschichte der hermetischen Literatur* [*Emerald Tablet. A contribution to the history of Hermetic literature*] (Heidelberg: Carl Winter, 1926).

better understood as an authentic retention of aspects of Egyptian antiquity.

What's more, our generation possesses the first truly serviceable English translations of the Hermetic literature most especially Brian P. Copenhaver's 1992 *Hermetica* from Cambridge University Press. Another important translation is from Clement Salaman, who with a team of collaborators published *The Way of Hermes* in 2000 with Inner Traditions. And there exist other translations, including of technical Hermetica, such as the notable *Greek Magical Papyri in Translation* (Volume 1) by Hans Dieter Betz published in 1996 with University of Chicago Press. All of this scholarly and highly readable material opens doors closed to recent generations.

I must add a word about a historically important 1906 translation by G.R.S. Mead (1863–1933), *Thrice-Greatest Hermes*, a then-exhaustive three-volume set. Mead, a brilliant scholar and translator who was secretary to Russian occultist and Theosophy cofounder Madame H.P. Blavatsky (1831–1891) in London during the final three years of her life, created a translation that filled a yawning historical gap since the prior significant translation was from John Everard (c. 1584?–1641), posthumously published in 1650. The Everard translation is, along with Walter Scott's (1855–1925) 1920s-era efforts, widely considered historically unreliable. For its part, Mead's work, although a key resource, is rendered in almost leaden Victorian prose, which seems to echo the language of the King James Bible. I think Mead miscalculated that this literary device would bring gravity to his text. Nonetheless, his work is a widely credited influence on Carl Jung, Hermann Hesse, and W.B. Yeats and provided a generation of modern seekers with an entry point to Hermeticism. Wouter J. Hanegraaff made an important note in *Hermetic Spirituality and the Historical Imagination*: "While G.R.S. Mead's edition and translation was universally ignored by scholars because of the author's Theosophical commitments . . . he sometimes saw more clearly than his learned despisers . . ."

Similar developments are occurring through Project Hindsight and other efforts relating to new translations of previously unknown or untranslated Hellenic works of astrology.

Hence, our generation is experiencing a petite Renaissance of rediscovery and reengagement with primary occult and esoteric writings. Seen in a poetic light, the ancient esoteric traditions could be said to have prophesized their own revival. One of the most moving works of Hermeticism is a dialogue called *Asclepius* named for the disciple to whom Hermes Trismegistus speaks. At this point, we do not possess the original Greek but know the full work only in Latin and some fragments in Coptic. (Scholars have been discovering progressively earlier fragments and references so that situation, too, may change.) In *Asclepius*, the unknown writer forecasts the division and fall of Ancient Egypt. In achingly melancholic language the tract intones,

> Oh, Egypt, Egypt, there will remain of your religion only fables. Those who follow your ideas will be thought mad. Those who disparage your ideas will be celebrated, will be extolled, will be uplifted. The world will be turned upside down, but oh, Egypt, Egypt, there will come a day when the gods are returned to their thrones and you are praised in your glory once again.

This is my adaptation. The *Asclepius* prophecy corresponds in tone to the Vedic description of the present Hindu cycle of *Kali Yuga*, considered an age of spiritual degeneration: "These will all be contemporary monarchs, reigning over the earth; kings of churlish spirit, violent temper, and ever addicted to falsehood and wickedness . . . Wealth and piety will decrease day by day, until the world will be wholly depraved."*

The Library at Alexandria (c. 285 B.C.–275 A.D.) underwent several catastrophes during its existence, including fires and conflagrations among warring forces. But a final confrontation between Egypt, then a Roman protectorate, and invaders from Palmyra in 270 A.D. apparently resulted in its ultimate devastation. Some of its scrolls and manuscripts may have already been safeguarded and moved elsewhere.

One of the last Hermeticists, the Macedonian writer Stobaeus, whose birth and death dates are unknown, wrote in the early fifth century A.D. at the outer cusp of classical antiquity. In 529 A.D., the Roman Emperor Justinian closed the Platonic academy in Athens, leaving figures like Stobaeus nowhere to write and teach; they would be marked heretics throughout the West and Near East. Many his-

* *The Vishnu Purana* translated by H. H. Wilson, 1840.

torians consider the closing of the academy, once headed by one of the last Neoplatonic philosophers Proclus (412–485 A.D.), the coda of classical antiquity.

About thirty years before the abolishment of this last pagan redoubt, Stobaeus, echoing *Asclepius*, wrote: "Up, Up O ye gods! . . . the dawn of a new day of justice invites us."*

The voices of *Asclepius* and Stobaeus prophesized their imminent end. But also, a day of renewal. Part of the gambit of this book is that the Hermeticists and their cohort were, whether by accident or insight, not wholly wrong.

---

* *Giordano Bruno and the Hermetic Tradition* by Frances A. Yates (University of Chicago Press, 1964).

CHAPTER TWO

Renaissance Revival

Although esoteric ideas of late antiquity were overshadowed and suppressed, threads of these beliefs and practices experienced revival, rebirth, and renewed relevance during the Renaissance, the flowering of arts and culture in Europe that flourished from about 1400 to the early 1600s.

It is deceptively easy to reference vast ideas and shifts, empires and the rise and passing of historical epochs. One can forget, of course, that there existed countless and diffuse populations. The Roman Empire itself encompassed nations from Central and North Africa, the Mediterranean, Near East, Persia, Western and Eastern Europe, British Isles—people spanning from African to Celtic lands, all seeking stability, survival, meaning, commerce, culture, worship, methods of agriculture, building, and hunting. So little about their lives reach us, as little about ours will reach people a thousand years hence. I try to take a moment whenever leaping over swaths of history, which I must as a necessity of space, to acknowledge the vast personas, different languages, dispersed regions united by day-to-day survival and some sense of connectedness that lent meaning—and perhaps provided help—in navigating existence.

Cleopatra committed suicide rather than become a prize of the Roman Emperor Augustus (63 B.C.–19 A.D.), who eventually succeeded the assassinated Julius Caesar (100–44 B.C.). The ruler took her own life in August of 30 B.C., following the suicide of her lover and collaborator Mark Antony by several days. That symbolically and effectively marked the end of Egypt as a freestanding empire. It was dominated thereafter by Roman troops. Although Rome could rule with a brutal hand militarily and economically, the Empire generally permitted a reasonable degree of religious freedom.

Competitive and sometimes syncretic religious cultures within the Empire led to frictions of their own, occasionally exploited by authorities. Eventually, Christian forces were in conflict with long-established pagan and nature traditions. As noted previously, the scales tilted militarily, economically, and culturally in favor of Christendom when Emperor Constantine converted to a version of Christianity in 312 or 313 A.D.

For generations, many people in the Roman Empire, like Constantine, combined facets of the newly ascended religion with ceremonies and local worship of pantheistic deities. Following Constantine, Rome endured for generations but eventually was so pressed by corruption, fraying outer frontiers, and invasion that by 476 A.D., the city of Rome fell and the Empire was largely extinguished in Western Europe.

Rome, however, persisted for several hundred years as a military and economic power ruling from Constantinople, today Istanbul. By 529 A.D., the Emperor Justinian (482–562 A.D.) reclaimed parts of Western Europe. But that year, as noted, the ruler also closed the Platonic academy in Athens, which for centuries sustained study of Pythagoreanism, Hermeticism, and Neoplatonism. The edict dealt a death blow to formalized study and promulgation of classical and esoteric philosophy.

In centuries ahead, Western life was marked by a fraying of power structures that once reflected the military, economic, and cultural dominance of Rome. Many people struggled to maintain agricultural existence and eventually assembled into clusters we know as feudal states or duchies ruled by local potentates or strong men. Tribes and clans formed into different groups, further fraying power structures. Indeed, local clashes broke up many parts of Western and Eastern Europe. There was plague, smallpox, banditry, and hunger, along with breakdown of highways, waterways, trade and shipping routes, and economic centrality. One way that historians detect economic and cultural decline from 600 to 800 A.D. is lack of shipwrecks. Maritime skills hadn't improved; maritime activity had declined.

In the early Middle Ages, the Christian monastic system, already in practice from late antiquity, developed more fully. The preservation of many ancient and esoteric works, sometimes in the form of books but often in scrolls, papyri, parchments, or canvases, is due to monastic enclaves. Monks organizing themselves into monasteries, sometimes Coptic, Byzantine, Roman Catholic, or Eastern Orthodox, structured libraries where records not destroyed in chaos, persecution, piracy, or warfare were maintained.

The Dark Ages saw new efforts at civilization, religiously, culturally, agriculturally, and militarily. But it was nonetheless an epoch marked for centuries by quest for survival rather than development of civic culture. This began to change by the late 1200s with the writings of Dante and flowering of arts, poetry, painting, religious statements, and Christian architecture—most notably the growth of cathedrals, which often incorporated esoteric and sacred geometric principles.

"In quantitative terms," wrote Joscelyn Godwin in his 2007 *The Golden Thread* (Quest Books), "the Gothic cathedrals are as astonishing as the Pyramids. In France alone, the ninety years from 1180 to 1270 saw the building of eighty cathedrals and nearly five hundred abbeys. The whole country's economy was dominated by it." Godwin continued:

> How would you go about building a cathedral in a paperless and largely illiterate society? . . . The 'mason's secret' of the ancient architect was that he was trained to construct an entire building in his imagination . . . Also, given that the ancient architects, from Stonehenge to Chartres, were primarily engaged with sacred buildings, it is certain that their imaginations were suffused with religious myths and symbols. The mental construction of temples and churches was inseparable from meditation on the meaning of those myths, while the intense effort of imagination could pass over into visionary experience.

The historian's observation comports with the meaning of the Greek term *adytum* for "inner temple"—and provides a valuable hint of the merits of modern Freemasonic practice of memorization, a topic we revisit.

The artistic and intellectual dawning grew dynamically in Florence, Italy, inaugurating a period considered the early Renaissance. With the leadup to the 1300s, life grew stabler, trade routes reopened, and commerce expanded. The longstanding series of wars called the Crusades, from 1095 to 1291, in which Western armies campaigned to retake Jerusalem and other holy sites from the forces of Islam, wound to a close. Economic, military, and familial burdens that the Crusades placed on individuals, communities, and nations eased. Returning Crusaders brought home tales of myth, wonder, and ruins of ancient lands.

The end of the Crusades also brought backlashes. The Catholic military order of the Knights Templar played a major role in the conflicts, both financially and martially. But when the Crusades ended in the late thirteenth century, the Knights' purpose as a combat and financial institution was unclear. The French monarchy and Vatican, both in debt to the order, considered the Templars a potential rival. In a push to solidify control over banking and military mechanisms, the papacy decimated the Knights with accusations of heresy, leading to forced confessions, jailing, and, in many cases, torture and death.

Coerced witnesses sometimes recalled the Knights worshipping a disembodied head called "Baphomet," possibly an Old French corruption of *Mahomet* (Mohammed), prophet of the opposing forces. The figure may have also been associated with Banebdjedet an Ancient Egyptian ram god with its cult center at Mendes. As will be seen, French occult writer Eliphas Lévi (Alphonse Louis Constant) in 1855 associated Baphomet with the Sabbatic Goat or "goat of the Sabbath," a popular pagan retention.

The church developed its own fissures between Western and Eastern branches. From 1438 to 1445, the Council of Ferrara-Florence convened to seek reconciliation between Latin and Greek divisions. The years-long conference drew together a wide range of clerical thinkers, scholars, and philosophers. Much of their business centered on liturgical minutiae. But Florentine leader Cosimo de' Medici (1389–1464) grew inspired by florid and vivid lectures on ancient wisdom delivered by Byzantine Neoplatonic philosopher Georgios Gemistos (c. 1355/1360–1452/1454), known by his self-chosen appellation Plethon, a name resonant of Plato's.

Cosimo and others remarked on how the eighty-year-old expounded on Hellenic philosophies as though he had been present for their making. Plethon, or "second Plato" to some students, considered himself the last of the classical Hellenists, a claim not without merit. Indeed, the philosopher purposefully muted his true beliefs, which would have amounted to a crime of heresy: replacement of Abrahamic monotheism with revived Hellenic polytheism merged with wisdom from Persian prophet Zoroaster (c. seventh or sixth century B.C.) at least as interpreted through the lens of Greek antiquity. A rival at the conference wrote in scandalized tones:

> I myself heard him at Florence . . . asserting that in a few more years the whole world would accept one and the same religion with one mind, one intelligence, one teaching. And when I asked him "Christ's or Muhammad's?," he said, "Neither; but it will not differ much from paganism."*

Listening to this dramatic and self-styled figure, Cosimo yearned to inaugurate a new Platonic academy in Florence.

One of the animating passions of the early Renaissance, spurred in part by Plethon, was a revival of interest in the ancient past, something also glimpsed by Crusaders. Indeed, some Renaissance thinkers, theologians, and translators began to speak of a *prisca theologia*, an ancient or primeval theology. The term appears in the work of scholar-translator Marsilio Ficino (1433–1499), who we soon meet, but began conceptually—and possibly in specific usage—in Plethon's lectures at the Council of Ferrara-Florence. Thinkers began to speculate over the existence of an antique, foundational, pre-Christian theology. Where to find it?

Vestiges of ancient esoteric philosophy and religion survived in Greek, Coptic (which employed a Greek-style alphabet), and Arabic, sometimes translated into Latin, providing a tantalizing scent trail. But, often, these were just fragments. The great libraries, academies, and temple orders were irreversibly gone. Some precious shards were preserved in monasteries, but the splendor of Ancient Egypt was a faintly retained memory, spoken of by an occasional traveler, tradesman, or Crusader who might have glimpsed some of Egypt's

---

* *Esotericism and the Academy* by Wouter J. Hanegraaff (Cambridge University Press, 2012).

monuments. Consider how distant this must have seemed to Renaissance thinkers. When Greek historian Herodotus (c. 484–c.425 B.C.) encountered the pyramids, they were as ancient to him as he is to us. Renaissance intellects, or at least idealists among them, held to the belief that some undiscovered source contained this *prisca theologia*, vessel of cosmic secrets.

Permitting a modern tangent, this is not wholly different from the animating spirit that drove Madame H.P. Blavatsky, cofounder of the Theosophical Society, to produce her two-volume cosmology *The Secret Doctrine* in 1888. Blavatsky, too, believed that there existed a forgotten primeval philosophy from which all modern religions emerged. H.P.B.'s timeline was considerably vaster and involved deeply antique civilizations and stages of spiritual development, a topic to which we return.

All of this reached a head of sorts around 1462, or it may have been 1460 because historical dates conflict. On or around 1462, there occurred a small but tectonically influential event that considerably shaped the Renaissance—and gave us many of our modern concepts of the occult. As the story is often recounted, a Byzantine monk from Macedonia, one Leonardo da Pistoia, entered the royal court of Florentine ruler Cosimo de' Medici, who had previously thrilled to the talks of Plethon.*

The monk Leonardo, who may have been in Cosimo's employ as an antiquity seeker, presented the ruler with a cache of papyrus manuscripts. Expressing an esoteric philosophy narrated by Egyptian-named figures, the scrolls were signed by Hermes or *Hermes Trismegistus*. Hermes Trismegistus was, as noted, a Greek honorific title for Thoth, Egypt's god of writing and intellect, meaning "thrice-greatest Hermes." As the signatories meant it, Thoth, a figure often depicted as a man with the head of an ibis pressing a stylus onto a clay writing tablet, was three-times greater than Hermes, god of intellect, writing, culture, and commerce.

The Greek manuscripts thrilled Cosimo, who thought this might be a core sample of the lost primeval theology. The treatises, originally

---

* Leonardo's and his manuscripts' vintage are recorded in Marsilio Ficino's Latin introduction to his *Corpus Hermeticum* translation as "having been brought from Macedonia to Italy by the diligence of Leonardo da Pistoia, a learned and honest monk." From "Marsilio Ficino and His Translation of *Corpus Hermeticum* VI" by Maurits Van Woercom, final thesis, CSW Van de Perre in Middelburg (Netherlands), December 29, 2021.

fourteen as translated, had been unseen for at least a thousand years.* He instructed his court translator, scholar and philosopher Marsilio Ficino, to suspend work on translations of Plato and turn attention to these manuscripts. Cosimo was desperate to read this material before his death, which occurred in 1464, about two years after the monk entered his court and one year from when Ficino completed his effort.

Ficino translated the manuscripts into Latin, which remained the lingua franca among educated classes. As was seen, the philosophical Hermetica presented a vision of humanity emergent from a great mind of creation, in Greek called *Nous*. This infinite intelligence created or projected humanity and all things through a series of concentric circles. It stood to reason, in the Hermetic outlook, that as a figment of the great over-mind of creation, the created being also possesses causative mental abilities. Moreso, through a process of eternal recurrence, the soul, psyche, or essential self, transmigrates through these concentric circles and over a period of lifetimes grows closer to the central mind of creation, until the individual becomes as the gods.

Each of these translated tracts was relatively brief, what we would now consider a pamphlet. Eventually, this cache of manuscripts grew to seventeen and became known as the *Corpus Hermeticum*, literally "Hermetic Body."** In most translations of the *Corpus Hermeticum*, the tracts are numbered one to eighteen—but one tract, number fifteen, is missing. The "lost tract" is a passage from a tenth-century Byzantine encyclopedia of antiquity called the *Suda*, coupled with three passages from Macedonian Hermeticist Stobaeus. The *Suda* ventured a Christian interpretation of Hermes as a pagan who foresaw Christianity: "He was called Trismegistus on account of his praise of the trinity."*** Several early Christian writers sounded this theme. Some Christian writers were sympathetic toward Hermes as a precur-

---

* *The Bookseller of Florence: The Story of the Manuscripts That Illuminated the Renaissance* by Ross King (Atlantic Monthly Press, 2021).

** Ficino in 1463 originally translated fourteen of seventeen tracts, which he printed in 1471. In 1482, Italian scholar and Hermeticist Lodovico Lazzarelli (1447–1500) translated "three extra treatises which he had apparently discovered in a separate manuscript (apparently not preserved)," writes Antoine Faivre in "Hermetic Literature IV: Renaissance-Present" in *Dictionary of Gnosis & Western Esotericism* (Brill, 2006). "Lazzarelli," notes Wouter J. Hanegraaff in his article on the scholar in the same source, "is important as the first Latin translator of the three final treatises of the *Corpus Hermeticum*." One of the questions of Hermetic history is the nature and vintage of the manuscript discovered by Lazzarelli. As Hanegraaff notes, Lazzarelli discovered the additional three tracts "in a manuscript different from the one used by Ficino, and which had not been translated into Latin."

*** Copenhaver (1992).

sor to Christ while others, including Saint Augustine (354–430 A.D.), were more dismissive. Added in 1574, the *Suda* passage was later dubbed pseudo-Hermetica and removed. But the *Corpus Hermeticum* remained traditionally numbered one to eighteen, with the fifteenth entry absent to keep the number system consistent.

In many regards, Ficino's Latin translation represents the literary reintroduction of ancient esoteric philosophy into the modern world. Many Renaissance thinkers regarded Hermes Trismegistus as a kind of prophet or even man-god, a figure who might have been an instructor to Abraham and Moses, hence an ur-teacher, soul guide, psychopomp, and, to some, an *actual being* who belonged to deepest antiquity. As enthusiasts saw it, this possibly deific being had written, transmitted, or inspired these manuscripts, which reflected humanity's primaeval theology. This ideal later hit the rocks of disappointment and, in a sense, produced a second stage of obscurity for Hermeticism.

For now, though, we remain within the period of highest hopes.

As often happens at a defining epoch, many related writings began to appear or reappear. Other works, later called technical Hermetica, dealt with spells, alchemy, astrology, divination, prophecy, talismans, and spirit conjuring. This material arose from Greece, Egypt, Mesopotamia, the Middle East, and Western and Eastern Europe. What to call these ideas and methods? There existed a term in Latin, *occultus* or *occulta*, meaning hidden or secret. These ancient practices and theologies, in many cases pre-Christian and sometimes even pre-Judaic, came to be known in English as *occult*. The term entered the Oxford English Dictionary in 1545.

German polymath and theologian Heinrich Cornelius Agrippa (1486–1535) proved pivotal in establishing the concept of an occult body of knowledge. In 1510, Agrippa, writing by hand in Latin, produced a three-volume set of books, *De Occulta Philosophia* ("On the Occult Philosophy"), in which he labored to unite vast strands of this rediscovered philosophy or at least portions that he felt amounted to a philosophy. In an act of great fortitude, Agrippa, biding time with the religiously controversial material, waited until 1531 for his first volume to appear. All three volumes did not see print until 1533, two years before his death.

The author and curator also demonstrated exquisite care in navigating church strictures, sometimes winning the imprimatur of ecclesiastical authorities to publish this pre-Christian religious philosophy, which Agrippa diplomatically framed with prayers and prefatory material of an explicitly Christian nature. The scholar shrewdly opened his volumes with an admiring letter from Johannes Trithemius (1462–1516), a German Benedictine abbot with his own deep interests in the occult.

The first English translation of Agrippa's *Three Books of Occult Philosophy* appeared in 1651. The Latin books were translated by an unknown (and probably self-protective) writer who used the initials J.F. Sources dispute whether the initials belonged to antiquarian James Freake or chemist John French. In any case, 1651 marked the appearance of an English translation that would, in various forms, endure and serve as a reference for more than 350 years. In 2021, a scholar of esoterica, Eric Purdue, published with Inner Traditions the first translation since J.F. from Agrippa's original Latin into English. As such, it is a significant resource. (I should note that there exists a popular and creditable annotation of Agrippa issued in 1992 by Donald Tyson with publisher Llewellyn, which is based on the 1651 original.)

As translated into English, Agrippa occasionally used the term *demon*. Here I must add Purdue's clarifying note from volume one of his 2021 translation:

> Agrippa is following the Renaissance understanding of the term daemon. The modern usage of "demon" typically implies an evil spirit. The Greek root, *daimon*, is more complex. Sometimes it could mean a deity or sometimes a spirit. By the Renaissance, the Latin *daemon* often referred to a lower-level spirit, one that was more terrestrial. Some daemons were good, some evil. Later in book three, Agrippa quotes Iamblichus at length, showing that daemons could be attending spirits for people, places, and various activities of life. Some support life and happiness, others do not.

This is a case in point of how occultic terms are sometimes reprocessed in a uniformly negative light due to centuries of cultural conditioning. At its root, the term demon was a neutral reference to spirit.

To give a flavor of how ideas travel, among Agrippa's formulas are instructions for creating a silver amulet with symbols of Jupiter to draw power from the god and planet. That same amulet was found around the neck of Mormon prophet Joseph Smith (1805–1844) following his death by mob violence in Carthage, Illinois in 1844. Raised in Central New York's "Burned-Over District," a time and place we later visit, Smith probably did not derive the design directly from Agrippa but rather an 1801 popularization by Englishman Frances Barrett, *The Magus*. I wrote in my 2009 *Occult America*:

> Magic and myth were part of the firmament of the Smith household. According to historian D. Michael Quinn in his monumental [1997] study *Early Mormonism and the Magic World View,* Joseph Smith's family owned magical charms, divining rods, amulets, a ceremonial dagger inscribed with astrological symbols of Scorpio and seals of Mars, and parchments marked with occult signs and cryptograms popular in eighteenth- and nineteenth-century English and American folklore. In her 1845 oral memoir, the family matriarch, Lucy Mack Smith, recalled the Smiths' interest in "the faculty of Abrac"—a term that might have been lost on some. In fact, *Abrac,* or *Abraxas,* is a Gnostic term for God that also served as a magical incantation. It forms the root of a magic word known to every child: *abracadabra.**
>
> For his part, Joseph Smith venerated the powers of the planet Jupiter, which was prominent in his astrological birth chart. According to Quinn, Smith's first wife, Emma, reported that Smith carried a protective Jupiter amulet up to his death. The surviving silver amulet displays markings that derive from the work of Renaissance mage Cornelius Agrippa and that were spread among British and American readers by the English occultist Francis Barrett in his 1801 book *The Magus,* a popularization (and partial copycat) of Agrippa. Smith's occult interests closely reflected those that traveled through Central New York.

Since we are exploring how texts morph and migrate, it is important to note that Agrippa himself drew upon certain ideas from a medieval *grimoire* (an Old French-derived term that attained popularity following Barrett) or spell book known in Latin as the *Picatrix*.

* Genesis 41:43: "Pharaoh had Joseph ride in the second chariot and the crowds yelled before him 'Abrak!'" This Egyptian word of unknown meaning may be the origin of *abracadabra*.

The volume seems to have been written in the mid-eleventh century in Arabic, although some scholars argue for earlier vintage.

The *Picatrix*, whose original Arabic title was roughly *The Goal of the Sage*, is a book primarily, though not wholly, of astrology. The author of the *Picatrix* is unknown but the work is sometimes attributed to Arab scholar Maslama ibn Ahmad al-Majriti (d. 1005–1008). It was translated into Latin and Spanish in the mid-thirteenth century, with its name perhaps a mangling of the earlier Arabic title. Again, Hermetic volumes tended to get translated into Arabic, Latin, and Coptic. In broad terms, the *Picatrix* might be considered a work of technical Hermetica. Among its concepts are *decans*, a method of dividing astrological signs by 10 degrees. This seems to have influenced Agrippa, making the *Picatrix* an important work in the development of modern astrology.

Among key mystical systems that gained prominence during the Renaissance is Kabbalah, specifically in the form called Christian Kabbalah. The cosmological Jewish thought system aroused a wide range of thinkers, including those who populated the start and close of the Renaissance: Catholic theologian and artist Ramon Llull (c. 1232–c.1315);* philosopher Giovanni Pico della Mirandola (1463–1494); Catholic scholar of Greek and Hebrew Johann Reuchlin (1455–1522); mathematician, astrologer, and magician John Dee (1527–1609); and physician and philosopher Sir Thomas Browne (1605–1682).

These figures and others comported insights of late ancient or medieval Jewish mysticism with belief in the divinity of Christ, seeing Kabbalah as a precursor to Christian practice. Rendering Kabbalah into a Christian framework was also a means of eluding church persecution. Again, Agrippa waited more than twenty years before he finally saw publication of his *Occulta Philosophia*. A great deal of diplomacy and cat walking were required for Renaissance thinkers interested in Kabbalah, Hermeticism, and occult philosophy. Christianizing a thought system, winning the imprimatur of a local bishop, and declaring fealty to Christ in a preface were standard practice.

* Lull created a highly complex visual language of letters, symbols, and geometric shapes imposed within concentric circles, the turning of which is intended to reveal truths about the universe. Lull's "language" is among the earliest forms of computation.

Two primary works of Kabbalah were translated into Latin and gained currency among Christian thinkers. The first was the *Sefer Yetzirah* or *Book of Formation*. The *Sefer Yetzirah* was probably written in Mesopotamia in Hebrew between the third and sixth centuries A.D., considered the Talmudic era. The work was likely assembled from a variety of insights among disparate rabbinic sources. The other key repository of Kabbalistic thought was the *Zohar* or *Book of Splendor*. This was written in Aramaic in Spain, arguably by Spanish rabbi Moses de Leon (c. 1240–1305) around 1275.

Both the *Zohar* and *Sefer Yetzirah* are elliptical works written in Hebrew and Aramaic and thus very difficult for Latin thinkers to translate and grasp. These works and commentaries on them, which exist in various forms today, are challenging, offering facets of the Jewish mystical schema, which in certain respects comports with Hermeticism's ideal that all of creation is an expression of one great source of intellect fragmented into different aspects. Within Kabbalah, and specifically the *Zohar*, one of these models of creation is called the *sefirot*, or ten units of creation that compose reality. The searching individual is charged with working his way up through these ten expressions of creation—comparable to rising through the planetary spheres in Hermeticism—to understand the mechanics of life, including power, intellect, justice, love, harmony, and empathy.

As the individual rises through the ten *sefirot*, which in traditional Kabbalah are sometimes arranged in a pattern called the Tree of Life (first drawn by Johann Reuchlin), he grows closer to the Godhead or what might be called the great intellect, *Nous*. Like Hermeticism, Kabbalah contains teachings about transmigration of souls, as one lifetime is scarcely considered sufficient, even for the dedicated mystic, to rise up through the *sefirot*.

Within Kabbalah are also magical uses of names and numbers. There exist seven names for God within traditional Judaism—the holiest of these, signified by consonants Y H V H, is considered lost to time in pronunciation. Alchemists believed that all matter went back to one primal substance. It is sometimes said that this substance was codified in the ancient Hebrew name for God, Yod Hey Vav Hey, or Y H V H. We sometimes pronounce it *Yahweh* or *Jehovah*. Religiously observant Jews use the term *Adonai*, acknowledging that pronunciation of Yod Hey Vav Hey is lost to history. According to Jewish lore, whoever learns the pronunciation grows all-powerful. For some alchemists, Yod Hey Vav Hey signifies the basic stuff of creation, which in Hermeticism is thought.

In a teaching from the *Zohar*, the name of God consists of a sequence of 72 Hebrew characters. The Hebrew alphabet contains 22 letters but a formation of 72 devise the magical name and encode the fragments into which divinity dispersed itself in creation. This knowledge forms the "spiritual technology" Moses is said to have used to part the Red Sea. Hence, Christian Kabbalists and magicians believed they were encountering a system through which the seeker could identify and wield constituent parts of creation. The ideal was to transcend the bonds of existence and advance toward the one true power and grace—or *as above, so below.*

Christian Kabbalah flowered throughout the sixteenth century. This opening was, of course, limited to those who had access to education, books, patrons, and financial resources, much of which were stationed in and around church structures. Certain wealthy families like the House of Medici funded translations and printings of books, often by hand. Hence, for all the influence of occult ideas, they were available in real time to a small cluster of clerics, translators, mathematicians, tutors, courtiers, and nobility. But the flowering was authentic so that such ideas were written about, discussed, and vouchsafed to later generations, including ours.

For all that, a backlash began to grow. Some church authorities and local parishes revolted against occult, Hermetic, Kabbalistic, alchemical, and astrological experimentation. There was, most severely, an uptick of violence against accused witches. Although this brutality extended to the early Middle Ages it erupted anew in the late 1500s.

The Witch Craze was not limited to rural areas but traversed Western and Eastern Europe where various victims, usually isolated, unmarried, or older women, were sometimes caught up in paranoid finger-pointing and accused of spell casting or curses. Not infrequently, women unprotected by family structures (and sometimes even then) were considered practitioners of the old nature ways, now heretical, and blamed when animals died, crops failed, or plagues or other sicknesses erupted. The search for a hidden foe nearly always results in one being found. And the enemy is almost invariably defenseless.

The numbers are difficult to track but historical consensus holds that from 1450 to 1750, roughly 40,000 people, and possibly more, were killed, with tens of thousands more subjected to brutal and terrifying trials.* What was notable about the Salem witch trials of 1692–93 in the American colonies, which claimed twenty-five lives in hanging, pressing, or death in jail, is that they did not persist (although episodes of mob violence against religious outliers, such as the Shaker founder Mother Ann Lee, who is later met, certainly did).** The last witch trial recorded in the Western world occurred in Switzerland in 1782, which resulted in the torture and beheading of a rural housemaid, Anna Goldi. Consider that Switzerland was a relatively prosperous nation deep into the Age of Enlightenment. Acts of mob violence against accused witches continued sporadically throughout the world, flaring up in economically pressed regions even in the twentieth and twenty-first centuries.***

The late-Renaissance backlash was also felt within aristocratic and church-based environs. Shortly before his death, English playwright Christopher Marlowe (1564–1592) expressed anti-occult themes in his *Doctor Faustus*, written in 1592 or 1593. The dramatist died under mysterious circumstances, stabbed to death in London in 1593 soon after he completed his most famous work. Based on folkloric sources, *Doctor Faustus* is the classic tale of a man who attempts to sell his soul to the devil and is thus conscripted to damnation. Marlowe's statement was considered a satire of figures like Cornelius Agrippa and John Dee who had been the court magician and astrologer to Queen Elizabeth and to whose remarkable career we soon return. As such, *Doctor Faustus* proved an ominous bellwether to late-Renaissance occultists.

There was likely a real Faust. He was probably alchemist, Hermeticist, and magician, Johann Georg Faust, who lived in German-speaking Central Europe, dying around 1540. Central European legend held that the mysterious figure made a pact with Satan for knowledge and power. This Faust is likely Marlowe's model but the matter is unsettled; several

---

* E.g., see "Case Study: The European Witch-Hunts, c. 1450–1750 and Witch-Hunts Today" at gendercide.org.

** It should be noted that witch trials also occurred in the American colonies before Salem: "The first hanging of a witch in New England occurred in Connecticut in 1647; a number of other cases came to court in the 1640s to 1680s, and there were hangings at Providence in 1662." From *A New History of Witchcraft* by Jeffrey B. Russell & Brooks Alexander (Thames & Hudson, 1980 and 2007).

*** See my "Persecution of Witches, 21st-Century Style," *The New York Times*, July 4, 2014.

magicians, philosophers, and physicians in the mid-to-late Renaissance also bore the name.

A more modern and highly regarded iteration of *Faust* came from philosopher, novelist, and dramatist Johann Wolfgang von Goethe (1749–1832), completed from 1772 to 1775. Goethe's *Faust* is subtler than Marlowe's. The philosopher's version also tells the story of a sorcerer, alchemist, and Hermeticist who makes a pact with the devil or Mephistopheles, as named in Goethe's play, to serve him for eternity in exchange for infinite knowledge. But Goethe's Faust does not fully trust Mephistopheles. And the feeling is mutual. The two do a kind of intellectual dance around one another with Faust skeptical that Mephistopheles will deliver the happiness, knowledge, and fulfillment he promises. So, Mephistopheles proposes an odd bargain. He tells Faust that he'll do everything he says in exchange for the mage's eternal service, but with a wrinkle: in order to prove that he's being on the level with Faust, Mephistopheles vows that *only when a moment arrives in the sorcerer's life that's so sublime that he would be willing to live eternally within it will he die* and be claimed by the Dark Emperor. It's a strange wager—a *Faustian bargain*—and the magician agrees.

At the end of Goethe's *Faust*—this being a spoiler alert—Faust never quite reaches that moment of sublimity. Rather he keeps thinking that it's *off in the future*. He dies thinking of the ultimate moment—but not from it. Mephistopheles finds himself unable to claim Faust because while he ponders euphoric ultimacy he does not experience it. Hence, if anybody tells you that you're never satisfied, you can respond neither was Faust—and it saved him. It could also be argued that worldly pursuits leave one perpetually unsatisfied. But perhaps it's worth never being satisfied.

Marlowe's drama was a morality tale and broadside against Renaissance occultism. But Goethe's, which I think is the far greater of the two, more subtly and sympathetically probed human striving. Regardless, in its timing Marlowe's *Doctor Faustus* mirrored and abetted the reversing tides against occultism. Even prominent figures were unsafe. This is typified by the fate of Italian philosopher and scientist Giordano Bruno (1548–1600), burned at the stake in Rome. After seven years of Bruno's trial and imprisonment, the Vatican's court of inquisition convicted the philosopher-scientist of multiple heresies, including practice of magic, teaching reincarnation or transmigration of souls, and endorsing "cosmic pluralism," or existence of other worlds and beings.

What seems to have most disturbed church authorities was Bruno's doctrine of a decentered cosmos. In 1584, the heretic wrote in his treatise *On the Infinite Universe and Worlds*, "There are therefore innumerable suns; there are infinite earths that equally revolve around these suns, in the same way as we see these seven (planets) revolve around this sun that is close to us."* The prevailing view was geocentric or earth-centered, with our planet at the heart of the cosmos and the sun and planets revolving around it.

This perspective was already upended in 1514 by the work of astronomer Nicolaus Copernicus (1473–1543) but suppressed by church authorities. The well-traveled Bruno cast a powerful shadow across Western Europe and argued for heliocentricity with renewed vigor. Amid mounting tensions between Bruno and his inquisitors, the scientist paid the price of burning at the stake in 1600. Bruno was, in many regards, the consummate Renaissance mage. He was so deeply steeped in Hermeticism that even today you can find online sources that actually misattribute to Bruno variations of the Hermetic passage quoted in chapter one: *See what power you have, what quickness! . . .*

This misunderstanding derives from—but is in no way attributable to—pioneering British historian Frances A. Yates (1899–1981), who wrote monumental works on the occult revival of the Renaissance. Yates, particularly in her *Giordano Bruno and the Hermetic Tradition* (University of Chicago Press, 1964)—an invaluable text and source of personal inspiration—argued elegantly that Bruno emerged from a Hermetic-Egypto milieu in which the sun is the central force of cosmic creation and Hermeticism bears markings of an Egyptian esotericism that views the sun not only as a life-giving entity but positions it at the center of the known cosmos. Bruno was also influenced, of course, by the astronomical work of Copernicus. But his interiorized worldview was intellectually, philosophically, and aesthetically Hermetic. As Yates saw it, there existed a marriage within Bruno of revived Hermeticism, Renaissance occultism, and Copernican astronomy. Hence, there is no easy sorting out of magical and enlightenment insight; the two are not only bound but the earlier functions, at times, as antecedent to the latter.

* Translated from the original Italian by David Barrado Navascués at "Giordano Bruno: the Philosopher of Astronomy," July 23, 2015, bbvaopenmind.com.

English magician John Dee suffered a far less brutal fate than Bruno but his career nonetheless tells an elegiac story. Dee was titular court magician and astrologer to Queen Elizabeth (1533–1603). Although Dee astrologically selected her coronation date, Elizabeth at times kept the controversial scholar-mage at arm's length.

Dee, who signed his letters to Elizabeth with the numerical sigil 007, is sometimes fancifully depicted as an occult secret agent and coded namesake to Ian Fleming's James Bond. That's a considerable stretch. There exists no evidence of Dee functioning in an espionage capacity (which to some observers confirms its secrecy) and his signature was possibly an alchemical symbol of eyes and the sacred numeral seven.

The "occult agent" and James Bond connection got launched in a 1968 biography, *John Dee, Scientist, Geographer, Astrologer and Secret Agent to Elizabeth I* by journalist and popular historian Donald McCormick writing under the pseudonym Richard Deacon. McCormick had made other controversial claims about various figures working as spies. A more reliable and esoterically informed record appears in Jason Louv's *John Dee and the Empire of Angels* (Inner Traditions, 2018).

None of this is to say that Dee's career lacked controversy: in 1555, the police of Queen Mary (1516–1558) arrested and imprisoned Dee in the Tower of London for conjuring or "calculating." His specific crime was casting horoscopes of the royals. Dee may have placed himself in legal jeopardy by sharing Mary's horoscope with the younger Elizabeth. He was eventually cleared of treason and released that year.

When Elizabeth took the throne in 1558, Dee was more or less protected and elevated as occasional court philosopher and magician. Artists, occultists, and aesthetes sometimes called the queen *diva Elizabetta* or "divine Elizabeth" for her cultural liberalism. It would be going too far to say that Elizabeth embraced Dee but she granted him a stipend and held audiences with him. In that vein, Dee typified the late-Renaissance magician in a fitful age: sometimes feted, sometimes condemned.

During his period of relative safety, Dee proved uniquely important to the development of Renaissance occultism. Among his accomplishments was creation in 1564 of a symbol called the *Monas Hieroglyphica*. It consisted of a simple cross surmounted by an astrological sun and crescent moon, with the rams-horn glyph of Aries at its base. Dee's *Monas Hieroglyphica* was designed to unite the zodiac and alchemy. He felt the symbol unlocked all of occult philosophy. "Dee belonged to a generation that searched passionately for the right key to reading nature's language," notes historian Egil Asprem. "Variously, he found cues in optics, kabbalistic hermeneutics, emblematics, mathematics, astrology, and magic."*

For nearly thirty years of his highly productive life, Dee, in a journey that probably began in 1581, attempted to consort with angels or spirits. In his intimate collaboration with occultist Edward Kelley (1555–1597/8), Dee in about two years worked out a twenty-two-glyph "angelic language," corresponding to letters of English. Future writers dubbed it *Enochian* based on Dee's observation that the pre-flood patriarch Enoch was the last figure to know elements of the cryptic tongue, which Dee and Kelley believed was used in Eden. For this reason, Dee also called the language "Adamical." He believed it man's primordial, universal idiom. Dee and Kelley employed the "Celestial Speech" in "angelic conversations" with spirits.

Kelley was among several scryers with whom Dee worked—probably four had preceded him—but their partnership, which commenced in 1582, was by far Dee's most fruitful and fractious. Under the dictate of angels, the two swapped wives for a time, a practice instigated by Kelley whom most biographers felt played on Dee's ingenuousness and bouts of credulity. Kelley was a scryer or seer who prophesizes by peering into a reflective surface like a mirror, crystal, or bowl of water. Dee himself owned a black obsidian "spirit mirror."

It is often difficult to reconstruct exactly how classical magicians performed their rites since explanations and diary installments frequently prove obscure; the seeker can be left as though mentally trying to reconstruct Plato's description of the cave. In this case, however, magician-scholar Stephen Skinner, in his 2012 republication of *Dr. John Dee's Spiritual Diaries* (Llewellyn), performed yeoman's work of reassembling the Dee-Kelley operations. I quote from (though substantially abridge) Skinner's reconstruction not only for its descriptive

---

* *Arguing with Angels: Enochian Magic & Modern Occulture* (State University of New York Press, 2012).

value but also to capture the arduous effort and patience of the classical practitioners:

> Essentially Dee and his skryer Edward Kelley sat in front of a 'Table of Practice' in a chamber of practice reserved specifically for these sessions which they referred to as 'Actions' (with spirits/angels). The table was referred to as the Holy Table, and the top of the table was engraved with a design . . . The purpose of this design was the same as the floor inscribed magical circle of the grimoires, which was to ensure that the spirit/angel was restrained spatially to the table top, and constrained to tell the truth. The 22 letters on the border (and in the centre of the Table) are from the Enochian alphabet also transmitted earlier to Dee and Kelley by the angels (similar to the 22 letters of the Hebrew alphabet reflected in the Four Worlds of the Kabbalists . . .) . . . The table stood upon four wax insulating discs, which also had engraved upon them the Sigillum Dei Aemeth ('Sigil of Truth') . . . These had a similar function to restrain and constrain the spirit/angel. The same design made in wax was placed upon the Holy Table, insulated by a silk cloth . . . Upon the wax disc is the crystal skrying stone, described by Dee as 'natural Diaphanite' . . . Each session began with long and earnest prayers, plus often the recitation of some of the Penitential Psalms by Dee, designed to ensure the purity of the following operation. Kelley would then seat himself in front of, and gaze into the crystal. After a varying length of time (between a few minutes and more than an hour) Kelley would see a veil within the crystal, which then parted to reveal a spirit or angel, often seated upon a throne. I say 'spirit or angel' because one of their long running problems was to decide if the entity which appeared was a spirit (who might convey bogus information) or an angel. Dee (and indeed many grimoires) developed tests and questions for determining this. Kelley then reported what he heard and saw in the crystal, and Dee painstakingly recorded it in amazing detail, as accurately as any scientific record. Dee would hastily write the record on rough (sometimes light blue) paper and then make a fair copy afterwards. During the communication, Dee interjected with questions, and Kelley conveyed the (often evasive) answers of the spirits/angels . . . These angels/spirits often delivered prophecies or answered Dee's questions relating to Central European politics, as well as providing alchemical advice, and a number

> of tedious sermons and rants about the wickedness of Dee, Kelley or their several potential patrons. Dee was particularly interested in the possibility of an immanent Second Coming and the setting up of a new Kingdom of God. Although Dee had introductions to some of the most powerful men of his time (including the King of Poland and Rudolph, Emperor of Bohemia) he wasted these opportunities by allowing himself to convey these sermons and fire and brimstone rants unmodified to these potential patrons, rather than using his considerable knowledge to secure a regular source of patronage and pension, or at least to promote the religious reformation that he so vehemently desired. It is rather perplexing that a man of Dee's intellect did not tire much earlier of these unfulfilled prophecies and evasive answers. It may be that his overwhelming piety and belief in the intrinsic goodness of the angels kept his disbelief at a distance.

Scrying, it should be noted, was the method also used by world famous seer Michel de Nostradamus (1503–1566) who employed the practice—although, again, details are sketchy—to produce his prophetic books of quatrains, or four lines of verse, organized into sets of one hundred or *centuries*. Nostradamus produced ten centuries across four works (with some quatrains missing and others of questionable provenance).

Writing in Middle French, Nostradamus, too, was occasionally feted by royals including Catherine de' Medici, wife of King Henry II of France. An astrologer and self-styled physician, Nostradamus is famous today primarily because his prophecies experienced renewed scrutiny during World War II due to quatrains concerning "Hister," later interpreted as Hitler though it is also an ancient name for the Danube River in Austria. Scholar of esotericism Richard Smoley writes, "A more likely interpretation would equate 'Hister' with the Austria of Nostradamus's time, thus predicting a bloody engagement in which much of Europe is pitted against the Hapsburg monarchy. In fact, this happened during the Thirty Years' War (1618–1648)."*

I quote from *The Essential Nostradamus* by Richard Smoley (2006). I published this edition and recommend it for Smoley's typ-

* During World War II, both the Axis and Allies sought to use the prophecies of Nostradamus for propaganda purposes. According to declassified intelligence papers, occult scholar Manly P. Hall was asked to participate in an MGM propaganda documentary in which Nostradamus prophesied Allied victory. Although the studio produced four Nostradamus shorts, this one to my knowledge was never made.

ically precise translation and historical notes. I commissioned the work because I wanted readers to have a textually faithful and historically accurate rendering of Nostradamus following the instructive experience of encountering an author, now deceased, who falsified a Nostradamus quatrain. The passage, from Century X, quatrain 72, is sometimes related to the terrorist attacks of 9/11 ("The year 1999, seven months . . ."). The quatrain uses the Middle French word *ressusciter,* which means to revive or resuscitate. But the author rendered it as *devastate*, its near opposite. When I called him out, he refused to acknowledge mishap or fakery. He finally conceded, saying: "You must understand that there is an entertainment quality to this." I replied, "I do understand. But not here." My dedication is to see that readers receive accurate material. As it happens, most interpretations of Nostradamus's reported foresight of 9/11, as with other historical landmarks, are made by pointing to his elliptical passages after the fact. Popular renderings of Nostradamus in tabloid and adjacent media are often invented from whole cloth.

In any case, absent perceived confluence between Nostradamus's quatrains and World War II, the prognosticator, a household name and staple of tabloid and video exploitation (not to mention a bevy of ongoing popular books), might well be a footnote of the magical Renaissance. Unlike Nostradamus, Dee is recalled as a virtuosic astronomer, polymath, mathematician, and proto-scientist. In addition to fluency in Latin, Skinner notes, "Dee was an acknowledged expert, in his own time, on a number of 'hard' sciences including mathematics, geometry, astronomy, optics, geography, navigation, on all of which he wrote substantial works."

But the mage died in ruin. Following Elizabeth's death in 1603, Dee suffered vandalism and destruction of his home and library in southwest London at the hands of a pious mob presumably reflecting the judgments of Marlowe. Elizabeth's successor, James I—for whom the King James Bible is named—had little of the queen's tolerance. Stripped of court dignities and stipends, Dee lived quietly with his daughter and caretaker Katherine, selling possessions to survive. He died in poverty in late March 1609. Even his grave marker went missing, eventually replaced by a commemorative plaque in 2013. In a final indignity, depending on one's point of view, Dee was posthumously denounced in 1659 for consorting with the devil—a Middle English term—by popular translator and literary critic Meric Casaubon (1599–1671).

"In 1659," wrote Egil Asprem, "the magical workings of Dee and Kelley were canonized by the publication of Meric Casaubon's *A True and Faithful Relation* [*of what passed for many yeers between Dr. John Dee . . . and some spirits*]—an account brought to the public with the intention of showing how a good but gullible man was lured into damnation by a cunning nigromancer [the black magician Kelley]. The book at first caused a stir, tempting others to try what Dee had done rather than keeping them away from magic." In fairness, it must be noted that Meric Casaubon's account provided scholarly curation and preservation of Dee's work and diaries from this significant phase of the mage's career. The work is the basis for the 2012 republication by Skinner. Casaubon, as it happens, was the son of philologist Isaac Casaubon to whom we now turn.

I noted earlier that the Renaissance intellect was animated by the ideal of a *prisca theologia*, or primeval theology, a thought system considered older than any other. When the Hermetic literature was rediscovered in the court of Cosimo de' Medici, there burned a hope that this was the primeval theology eagerly sought.

But there occurred a decisive and peculiar revelation in 1614, which shook and eventually dashed the ideal of Renaissance Hermeticists that this ancient literature harbored the grail-like primal theology. This episode, although critically important, indirectly contributed to an intellectual error in the Western mind from which I personally believe we are only beginning to recover.

The incident was a groundbreaking textual analysis of the *Corpus Hermeticum* by linguist Isaac Casaubon (1559–1614). In a work published in 1614, Casaubon determined through vernacular, textual, and historical references that the Hermetic literature was produced in *late antiquity*, specifically in the generations following Christ. It should be noted that—as with much of intellectual history—Casaubon's analysis was preceded by decades of fragmentary effort by other linguists who made related notes. The voice of Hermes, at least in these hallowed works, did not share vintage with Abraham and Moses or belong to the mists of deepest antiquity. This revelation gradually proved deflating to many educated people of the era and in decades ahead. Yet herein lies a strange historical wrinkle, which ripples into the present day.

As noted, dreams of a recovered *prisca theologia* faded after Casaubon's textual analysis. Along with these withered hopes, however, another kind of viewpoint settled over the Western cultural scene in the dawning Age of Enlightenment. The viewpoint held that because the wished-for vintage of these philosophical tracts had been dispelled, there was something compromised, fraudulent, and corrupt about the Hermetic literature itself. Other theological statements, both Abrahamic and Eastern, were spared this verdict. This intellectual leap represented an error in the development of Western thought.

In my estimation, the summary judgment of the Hermetica's "illegitimacy" grew from an ingrained malady of the Western intellect, which is habituated "either/or" or "take it or leave it" thinking based, in part, on the absolutist formulas of Aristotle. This might also be called black-and-white or binary thinking. Author, researcher, and clinician Raymond A. Moody, M.D., who coined the term Near-Death Experience (NDE) in his 1975 study *Life After Life*, makes the valuable observation that most Westerners are educated to think in opposites but a third option exists: there is true, there is false—and there is *unintelligible*.

This is a critical insight, especially in our era when we are, for example, witnessing the mainstreaming of the UFO thesis, throwing modern culture into an indeterminant and uncertain place. Yet we experience hobbled intellectual capacities, often with "believers" off to one side and rejectionist "skeptics" off to another. Reaction to the Hermetic literature was a primary case. Because the Hermetica, so the reasoning went, proved not as old as acolytes and historians believed, it follows that the project of its revival, and the even literature itself, is compromised, sullied, and counterfeit.

Left out of this debate was a historical principle that proves as critical to our understanding of the value of the Hermetica as to contextualizing nearly any ancient text. Simply because we determine the date when a text was produced—sometimes through contemporaneous comparisons, analysis of lexicon, and other historical markers—*does not mean that the text's ideas started then.*

Not only were texts copied and recopied, sometimes among different languages, but, as alluded earlier, *the story of humanity is itself that of oral tradition.* The human story mirrors itself on both a macro and micro scale. When a baby is born that child possesses only the expressive ability of sound. The infant can cry to indicate he or she is hungry or that something is wrong. Eventually, the child develops motor skills and later speech. Later still, speech becomes writing. What else is writing but approximation of speech? The development of human history echoes that of the individual. It is a fact of historicism that much of our religious and parabolic literature began as oral tradition. This is so whether referencing Scripture, Homer, or teachings of Pythagoras.

As noted, most of the ideas attributed to Pythagoras were not written down, in this case by students, until centuries after the Greek sage died. Why would the cultural scene differ for Greek-Egyptian antiquity? Hence, I view the Hermetic literature as a deeply valuable time capsule of a very ancient past to which we possess a frayed thread of connection; that thread has gotten broken, it has intermingled with other related or unrelated ideas, it has been interrupted. But it persists. To assume that classical Hermetic literature is not reflective of older oral tradition is to assume that it is an exception to the history of ideas itself.

In any case, as the Age of Enlightenment proceeded, the Hermetica was written off and, at times, even mocked. Natural philosopher Sir Thomas Browne was left to write in his 1643 *Religio Medici*, "The severe Schools shall never laugh me out of the Philosophy of Hermes, that this visible World is but a Picture of the invisible wherein . . ." In Mary Shelley's *Frankenstein*, published about two centuries after Casaubon, some of her characters—this was not Shelley's attitude—debase Hermetic tradition and ridicule the tragic figure of Victor Frankenstein for reading its tracts.

As I was writing this chapter, I encountered a blog that studies the anthropology of texts whose writer, while offering many erudite insights on early Christian works, reflected on "Casaubon and the exposure of the Hermetic corpus," noting that, "I knew that the 'Hermetic corpus' was bogus, but not why"—conflating the redating (and contending the texts themselves intentionally clouded the matter) with a revelation of philosophical or textual illegitimacy.*

This argument is not entirely unfair so much as unsettled. The books of the *Corpus Hermeticum* emerged from multiple hands and cannot be referenced monochromatically. To the critic's point, Book XVI does, indeed, proffer the conceit that it was written in Egyptian:

* https://www.roger-pearse.com/weblog/2011/05/12/casaubon-and-the-exposure-of-the-hermetic-corpus/.

> When the Greeks will later wish to translate [my books] from our language into their own, the result will be very great confusion in the texts and unclarity. For when it is expressed in its native language, the discourse retains the clear meaning of its words. And in fact the nature of the sound and the power of the Egyptian words contains in itself the force of what is said.*

I do not wish to make a fig-leaf intellectual justification on behalf of texts for which I feel obvious affinity. In this matter, I consider myself in sympathy with the semi-famous lament of mathematician Warren Weaver speaking on psychical research in 1960: "I find this whole field [parapsychology] intellectually a very painful one. And I find it painful essentially for the following reasons: I cannot reject the evidence and I cannot accept the conclusions."

In essence, dating does not always determine vintage of ideas. Nor can all *Corpus* tracts be classed together. What of the Egyptian conceit of Book XVI? Scholar Garth Fowden, who did much to restore Hermeticism's legitimacy as a neo-Egyptian expression, wrote of its unknown author: "Clearly we have to do here with an Egyptian who, desiring to convey the impression that his work is but a translation from his native tongue, acts on the principle that attack is the best form of defence. He may himself have had no choice but to write in Greek, but he shared with many Hellenized oriental intellectuals a suspicion of the debilitating effect of translation—understood in the broadest sense—on the distinctive essence of his own tradition."** This might be called a virtuous conceit.

Arguments and counterarguments aside, the redating brought with it general judgment of fraud. Due to this leap in thinking, the Hermetic literature was mostly excluded from the ancient philosophical and spiritual corpus. Eventually, the Hermetica, this oeuvre so seminal to Renaissance thought, fell into near obscurity. Indeed, after the 1650 English translation and some errant literary references, the trail goes largely cold. No direct Hermetic literature is included, for example, in Harvard's canonical Loeb Classical Library. There appeared, thanks to the late nineteenth century occult revival

* From "Protestant versus Prophet: Isaac Casaubon on Hermes Trismegistus" by Anthony Grafton, *Journal of the Warburg and Courtauld Institutes*, 1983, Vol. 46.

** *The Egyptian Hermes* (1986).

instigated by Madame Blavatsky, some less-than-satisfactory Victorian translations, along with a monumental effort by G.R.S. Mead, described earlier. It was only in 1992 when Brian P. Copenhaver's translation emerged that we came to possess what I think is the first truly serviceable English translation.*

I believe that dismissal of the Hermetica cost us centuries of progress in our ability to study the existential philosophy of a critical phase of antiquity. This was due, in large measure, to a misunderstanding of how ideas get passed on and to the thought-habit of absolutism. Yet here we encounter an example of just how strange life is, of its discursive and tantalizing compensatory measures.

In 1614, the same year that Hermes Trismegistus was dethroned, a year that could symbolically be considered the close of Renaissance occultism, there began circulating in Central Europe an enigmatic text written in German called the *Fama Fraternitatis*, roughly "The Story of Our Brotherhood."

The work, in existence as early as 1610 but aboveground for the first time, purported itself the manifesto of a secret brotherhood, or "invisible college" as it was sometimes later termed. The fraternity was *Brothers of the Rosy Cross* or *Rosicrucians*. As Hermes was exiled, the *Fama Fraternitatis* heralded an unseen order of adepts intent on instigating a new era of learning, mysticism, esoteric study, radical ecumenism, and decentering of the church from political power and regulation of the spiritual search.

Had the occult moment passed—or was it just dawning?

---

* An important adjunct to Copenhaver is the previously referenced *Hermetica II: The Excerpts of Stobaeus, Papyrus Fragments, and Ancient Testimonies* in an English Translation with Notes and Introductions by M. David Litwa (Cambridge University Press, 2018).

CHAPTER THREE

Secret Brotherhoods

The question of secret societies is probably the most contentious in the occult. As I write these words, we occupy an age of suspicion. The notion that a group called the *Illuminati* or some other secret organization is manipulating and depriving us of power is common fare on podcasts, late-night radio, YouTube videos, below-the-radar bestsellers, and so on. One hears the term Illuminati so frequently that the very familiarity of its repetition serves as a point of validation.

Once on a streaming television show, I made laudatory remarks about the Illuminati as a historical group—and a veritable defender of principles and values that many people now embrace, such as separation of church and state, freedom of search, belief in individual potential, and perpetuation of initiatory religious experience. I received a swath of hate email. Of all the topics I've probed, from ESP to Satanism, I've never gotten such voluminous blowback. The advocate of any point of view, by nature, always perceives him or herself as part of the "Light realm," as Gnostic teachings put it. My correspondents certainly did.

Although it is important to note current mood, my aim in this chapter is not to dwell on social or psychological triggers behind the present culture's fascination with, and feelings of emotional intensity toward, secret societies, particularly Freemasonry and the Illuminati. Nor is it my purpose to consider exclusive fraternities in general, such as Yale's storied Skull and Bones, Bohemian Grove, or related groups that, rightly or not, are deemed clandestine power centers. Rather, I consider the historical foundations and veritable purpose of the secret society in occultism. By studying history, we are studying the present because human nature remains constant. Indeed, many issues surrounding the question of early modern secret societies are not dissimilar to those we face today.

What are secret societies? It's a given across human history that we have always organized into communities of interest and mutual aid, clubs, fraternities, pressure groups, and lobbies. But the secret society played a distinct role in the history of modern esoteric and occult spirituality. To a significant extent, what is historically called the secret society has often been a response to the backlash against the occult and esoteric search; the secret society represents a vessel, of greater and lesser quality, for occult ideas that may have been socially endangering to the seeker.

When I write of danger to the seeker, that is in no way abstract. As considered, deep into the Age of Enlightenment in Europe, witch trials and persecution of occultists persisted. In 1790, Italian magician, self-styled Freemason, and occult adventurer Alessandro Cagliostro (1743–1795) was lured under false pretenses to Rome, where he was arrested by the Vatican's Office of the Inquisition. Sentenced to death in 1791, he received a stay of execution but died of disease four years later in the dungeons of the Inquisition at the brutal Fortress of San Leo. His crimes? Heresy and Freemasonry.

I've noted the fates of Bruno and Dee. Today, these may seem like once-upon-a-time nostrums but that depends where you live. In most contemporary nations of the Middle East, for example, Freemasonry is outlawed. If you embark on organized or group study of Freemasonic practices of initiation, occult and esoteric symbolism, passion plays or dramas, and you happen to live within most nations of the Middle East, you're violating the law. Application or severity of punishment varies. It is no minor aside to note that the occult search is not something modern people should take for granted. In 2021, a still-at-large arsonist burned down the historic home of members of the Church of Satan in Poughkeepsie, New York, in the Hudson Valley. Two residents sleeping inside narrowly escaped alive.*

Relatedly, witch hunts, denunciations, arrests, jailings, loss of life, privilege, and property were basic realities in a Europe that had seen a flowering of and backlash against occult spirituality. The continent itself entered a generation of warfare in 1618 with the outbreak of the Thirty Years' War. The conflict ravaged Central Europe, the German-speaking region bordered by the Rhine Valley in the West and Prague or Bohemia in the East. For three decades, Catholic and Protestant armies clashed across this vast swath of land, once home to some of the most radical experiments growing from the Reformation and occult Renaissance.

Long after the Thirty Years' War ended in 1648 that area of Central Europe suffered devastation, famine, and terrorism by brigands, often demobilized soldiers. Although the war had many causes, it was, in part, a reaction against religious liberalism and occult spirituality by the papal Habsburg Empire. The devastation brought dire consequences for religious radicals, some of whom migrated from Central Europe, crossed the Atlantic, and reached the American colonies, the subject of our next chapter. I am going to set aside, for now, the migratory impulse, and the need (or urgency) for religious innovators to travel. Rather, we are going to consider the fate of those who stayed behind.

For some who remained, the response to oppression, warfare, and outlawing of heretical ideas was not to stop searching or take the dangerous and uncertain journey across the Atlantic. The response was the secret society. It was to study, seek, learn, develop, initiate, and reform self and others within a closely guarded atmosphere. My contention is that the secret society was necessary, both spiritually and, in closed societies, politically. It is a near-universal truth of human nature that we harbor affinity for rank, drama, symbol, and pageantry. The secret society held some of that appeal, too. But to a great extent, the secret society, as it developed in late-Renaissance Europe, and sometimes exported itself to other parts of the world, grew in response to oppression.

---

* See "Church of Satan's 'Halloween House' Gutted by Arsonist" by Corey Kilgannon, *New York Times*, January 19, 2021, and "The upstate occult: An interview with writer Mitch Horowitz" by Will Solomon, Albany *Times-Union*, October 25, 2022.

One of the many historical dramas that ignited the Thirty Years' War involved clusters of people dedicated to esoteric spirituality, including monarch Rudolph II (1552–1612). Rudolph himself was an emperor within the Habsburg Empire. The Habsburgs were a long-running, land-holding cluster of royals closely, although not exclusively, allied with the Vatican. Rudolph II, however, was also an acolyte of alchemy, astrology, and occult sciences. He was specifically interested in the work of Christian Kabbalist Johann Reuchlin; magician John Dee; and alchemists Michael Maier (1568–1622), who was a court counselor, and the legendary Paracelsus (c. 1493–1541).

Swiss alchemist Paracelsus was among the most celebrated physicians of the sixteenth century, pioneering important aspects of occupational illness, modern medical theory, toxicology, and pharmacology. As a Hermeticist, Paracelsus believed in correspondences, not only between mind and cosmos but also mind and body, mapping early awareness of mind-body medicine and the mental factor in illness. Paracelsus' career was hampered only by his bombastic and cantankerous temperament, which resulted in his assailing the reputations—and even burning the books—of perceived historical and contemporaneous medical rivals. He was, nonetheless, a figure of national pride in Switzerland later known as the "Hermes of the North" and the "Trismegistus of Switzerland." Today, a Swiss pharmacy chain bears his name.

Returning to Rudolph, in 1583 the monarch relocated the Habsburg capital from Vienna to Prague, which was then part of Bohemia, already a center of occult study. Bohemia grew into a hub for Hermeticists, Pietists (a mystical wing of Lutheranism), alchemists, and Kabbalists. In 1609, Rudolph issued a document called the "Letter of Majesty" that extended religious freedom to residents of Bohemia, acceding to concerns of Protestants. Among the Habsburgs, this was considered outrageously radical.

As noted, much of the Habsburg line allied with the Vatican. Naturally, they wanted to push back against Protestantism, radical Lutheranism, the Reformation, and religious experimentation. Many Habsburgs bristled that one of their own backed almost unprecedented religious liberalism. Rudolph died in early 1612 before any formal moves were made against him. After his death, he was replaced for about five years by his brother, Matthias (1557–1619), a more conservative but passive and conciliatory figure who, to the dismay of the Habsburgs, did little more than preserve the status quo.

By 1617, the House of Habsburg had enough. The aging and childless Matthias was effectively replaced by a more iron-fisted ruler and strict counter-Reformist, Ferdinand II (1578–1637). In 1618, Ferdinand revoked Rudolph's "Letter of Majesty," igniting tensions with Protestant forces in Bohemia. In May, this resulted in Protestant partisans throwing three of Ferdinand's advisors from a third-floor castle window in Prague, an episode called the Defenestration of Prague. The men survived but weeks of unrest followed. This served as the ignition point of the Thirty Years' War.

Within Bohemia, Protestants, Pietists, occultists, and esotericists had grown accustomed to a fair degree of religious freedom. Under Ferdinand, this vanished. A cohort of partisans moved against Ferdinand, appealing for help to yet another aristocrat from the Habsburg family. Their hoped-for savior was young Frederick V (1596–1632), a Calvinist married to Elizabeth Stuart. Elizabeth was the daughter of James I, who in 1603 succeeded Queen Elizabeth. The rebels essentially asked Frederick and Elizabeth to enter Bohemia and serve as their new rulers. They counted on Elizabeth receiving military support from her father's English throne. Frederick, like Rudolph, was steeped in the occult, esoterica, and religious liberalism. He accepted the rebels' entreaties and secured enough electors—Bohemia was an elective monarchy—to replace Ferdinand in late summer of 1619. But disaster ensued.

The Habsburgs, seeking to reassert Vatican control over religious life in Europe, amassed an army to depose Frederick and Elizabeth. After a year of rule, Frederick and Elizabeth's forces were routed in fall 1620 outside Prague at the Battle of White Mountain. James I refused to enter the conflict and left his daughter and son-in-law to languish and flee. Ferdinand was restored—yet the Thirty Years' War, a series of continual and bloody skirmishes, plodded on for decades.

Religious freedom in Bohemia, meanwhile, ended and occult experimentation all but vanished. Bohemia previously hummed with studies into philosophy, the arts, alchemy, astrology, divination, number symbolism, the magical uses of hymn—igniting the Bohemian mind. Indeed, the term *bohemian* came to denote one who is offbeat, outspokenly artistic, a renegade or freethinker. This approach to life was publicly erased in the territory from which the term arose.

Although the Bohemian mosaic withered, some surviving experimenters, seekers, intellects, heretics, reformers, and religious radicals did not fade away. In certain instances, they, like other persecuted seekers, went underground to form a community of ideas. As historian James Webb memorably put it in his 1974 *The Occult Underground*, "Bohemia is a land without a geography: but its capital is Paris." And its outposts abound.

As noted in the previous chapter, in 1614 a mysterious manuscript circulated in Central Europe. Authored anonymously in German, it was called the *Fama Fraternitatis*. This document, which had been passed around in private since at least 1610, now emerged aboveground.* It proclaimed the existence of a hidden fraternity of seekers dedicated to social polity, radical ecumenism, individual development, separation of political and aristocratic power from religion, and the possibility that the developed individual, who rose up through systems of esoteric initiation, could govern himself and required no outside power, whether church, aristocratic, military, or judicial, to mediate life for him.

The response was shock and enthrallment. Who was this mysterious fraternity calling itself *Brethren of the Rosie Crosse* or *Rosicrucians*? They were sometimes deemed an "invisible college." The following year, 1615, excitement grew when there appeared another anonymously written Rosicrucian manuscript. This time written in Latin, it was called the *Confessio Fraternitatis* or *Confessions of Our Fraternity*. In the *Confessio*, which included John Dee's *Monas Hieroglyphica* in a conjoined tract, the mysterious Rosicrucians revealed more of their story. The work described the birth and journeys of the group's leader, Christian Rosenkreuz, who traveled the world, including the Middle East, studying man's religions. The legendary pilgrim was said to have lived for 106 years and was entombed in secret.

In the most alluring part of the tract, his esoteric brothers located the tomb of Christian Rosenkreuz, which they discovered was

* Historian Tobias Churton has done important work on the pre-history of the *Fama* in his *Invisible History of the Rosicrucians* (Inner Traditions, 2009). For translations and valuable introductions to the primary Rosicrucian literature, the seminal work is *Rosicrucian Trilogy* by Joscelyn Godwin, Christopher McIntosh, and Donate Pahnke McIntosh (Weiser Books, 2016).

alchemically lit—not by the sun but an unknown force within. The seven-sided tomb or vault was encrypted with symbols and a layout communicating principles of initiation. The *Fama* and *Confessio* forecast the dawning of a new age of spirituality in which everyday people would be educated, hospitals would open to the public, and privileges would be granted not on bloodline but merit.

In 1616, there appeared the third and final of the original Rosicrucian documents, a religious allegory called the *Chemical Wedding of Christian Rosenkreuz,* once more written in German. This work is attributed to Johann Valentin Andreae (1586–1654), a Protestant reformer and Hermeticist. Andreae's views shifted at various points in life, either out of changes of heart or self-protection. The *Chemical Wedding* included references to John Dee (his *Monas Hieroglyphica* appeared on the title page and adjoined the wedding invitation) and principles of alchemy, specifically joining masculine and feminine energies to create the divine hermaphrodite, a perfected individual, neither masculine nor feminine but a being of universal energies, qualities, and possibilities. This alchemical parable was a religious allegory about a young seeker, Christian Rosenkreutz, called to assist in a royal wedding, a joining of male and female energies. In essence, the story told the progress of an esoteric pilgrim.

Other Rosicrucian-themed manuscripts included the 1618 *Mirror of the Wisdom of the Rosy Cross*, authored pseudonymously by Theophilus Schweighardt, believed to be alchemist Daniel Mögling (1596–1635). The book featured a delightful symbolic illustration of an "invisible college"—a university tower on wheels.

Were these the works of an authentic hidden brotherhood—or just a philosophical provocation from one or more individuals? Seekers yearned to know. Some wished to join. We have no evidence that the Rosicrucians, if real, were ever located. History records no physical lodge with membership rolls, meetings, rosters, books, or fraternal rules.

Perhaps the Rosicrucian manuscripts were, as suggested by Frances A. Yates, an avengement by disgruntled followers of John Dee.* Or, as is likelier, by radical Lutherans, deeply disappointed with the slowed progress of the Reformation and how religious freedom

---

* See Yates's *The Rosicrucian Enlightenment* (Routledge, 1972) and *The Occult Philosophy in the Elizabethan Age* (Routledge, 1979).

was granted and rescinded in Bohemia. The authors may have been Hermeticists and occult experimenters let down by how prevailing regimes, including England after the death of Queen Elizabeth, failed to defend religious liberty and abandoned Frederick and Elizabeth Stuart in Bohemia. There existed any number of people who harbored good reasons to present themselves as Rosicrucians.

In any case, it is probable that the order itself was more thought movement than actual fraternity. But it was a thought movement igniting of hopes among people deeply dejected—and even moved to arms—over anti-Reformist aristocracies and reasserted Vatican power in Europe.

For clarity, I must note that many later groups claimed lineage with the Rosicrucians, which we will consider in connection with the nineteenth century occult revival. Several orders and individuals, starting in the mid-1800s through the early twentieth century and beyond, declared themselves Rosicrucians and quarreled over authenticity with contemporaneous groups. As suggested, Rosicrucianism was more thought movement than identifiable brotherhood. No one, according to any records considered sound and evidentiary, ever identified a Rosicrucian order, hence claims of lineage are romantic at best.

Modern orders in the U.S. include AMORC, or Ancient and Mystical Order Rosæ Crucis, founded in 1915 by Harvey Spencer Lewis (1883–1939) and the Rosicrucian Fellowship, founded in 1908/1909 by Max Heindel (1865–1919). In summer 1989, the then-leader of AMORC in an interview with *Gnosis* magazine acknowledged that the group had no fraternal or historic bond to an ancient or Renaissance-based Rosicrucian society. That noted, I think every seeker in every generation can identify with Rosicrucian ideals, including civic equality, the search, and ecumenism. I discourage doting upon pageantry, secrecy, or claims of ancient bloodlines. Esoteric history gets terribly interrupted and very few direct retentions exist between our world and antiquity. But there can exist parallel insights and values.

For some, the ideals of the occult Renaissance could be kept alive only by inner light, like the alchemically illuminated tomb of Christian Rosenkreuz. It was the light of the search, which was the essential point of Rosicrucianism. Interestingly, in the wake of the Rosicrucian literature, we begin to detect the existence of another organization that is very real, that does have members, meeting places, rosters, rules, bylaws, and elected officers. That is Freemasonry. Freemasonry is almost unique in modernity insofar as there exists no consensus, including within its own organizational structures, about the nature of its founding.

Masonry has produced from within its ranks first-class historians, a topic to which I return when considering the mystic history of America. And yet there is no firm consensus within Freemasonry, either among rank-and-file members, leadership, or its roster of homegrown historians, as to the order's origins. There exists a mythos about Freemasonry extending to the building of King Solomon's temple. Others more literally discuss Freemasons emerging from the stone guilds that built the Gothic cathedrals and abbeys of the Middle Ages. There may be some hardcore legitimacy to that. Stone building was a form of *operative masonry*, which necessarily integrated religious and symbolic understanding because its members were developing sacred architecture. But in order for historicism to be definitive, we require accounts and records, which must be weighed for trustworthiness and corroboration. Circumstantial connections and theories, however sensible, are insufficient.

Among the early evidence we possess for the establishment of Freemasonry, not just as an operative art but as a spiritual and esoteric path, is a work of epic verse composed in Scottish English in 1638 by Edinburgh poet and historian Henry Adamson, *The Muses Threnodie; or Mirthful Mournings on the death of Mr. Gall.* A sprawling, early Romantic work, Adamson's elegy to a lost friend depicts the nature of life in rural Scotland. It contains this intriguing passage:

> For we be brethren of the Rosie Crosse;
> We have the *Mason word* and second sight,
> Things for to come we can foretell aright,

In his original, Adamson highlights the term *Mason word* and attaches it to "second sight." It is among the earliest references we possess of Freemasonry as a speculative craft.

One of the few surviving records of early initiation into Freemasonry is from 1641 involving British statesman and scientist Robert Moray. Hold his name in mind. As will be seen, Moray was later a founder of the British Royal Society, which was considered one of the bastions of Enlightenment Era thought. Minutes survive of Moray's induction into the Lodge of Edinburgh at Newcastle. He signed the document, as he did future correspondence, *with a pentagram*, the Pythagorean five-pointed star used by Masons, adjoining his name.

Another early record of initiation dates to 1646. It is from the diaries of British antiquarian and esotericist Elias Ashmole, who writes of being initiated into a Freemasonic lodge and identifying another inducted with him: "I was made a Free Mason at Warrington in Lancashire, with Coll: Henry Mainwaring of Karincham." Related entries appear in 1682. Ashmole was sufficiently enamored with Rosicrucianism that he copied English translations of the *Fama Fraternitatis* and *Confessio Fraternitatis* by hand. His private papers show that he wrote out his own petition to join the Rosicrucians. It is unknown what, if anything, he did with his petition or if he ever came into contact with any actual Rosicrucians.

These dates are critically important because the Grand Lodge of England did not emerge aboveground until 1717. Thereafter, we begin seeing lodges proliferate and migrate to the American colonies, Spain, France, and Italy. Only in recent centuries has Masonry emerged as a visible organization. But these references demonstrate that lodge-based Masonry was operative in the wake of Rosicrucianism.

Rosicrucianism and Masonry share outlooks: that all religions are valid and equal; that the individual can self-develop through initiation and study; that illumination is handed down not by ancestry or central authority but through self-refinement; that ties between religious officialdom and state power must be severed; that rank and privilege are earned through peer election versus bloodline. Both Rosicrucianism and Masonry embraced alchemical and esoteric symbolism. What Rosicrucianism endorsed in principle Masonry enacted in practice.

The backlash came quickly. In 1738, Pope Clement XII issued a papal bull—the most solemn form of announcement and considered infallible—against Freemasonry. The edict prohibited church members from participating in Masonry and named it a heretical order antithetical to the church. Several related bulls and encyclicals appeared in generations following. In 1884, Pope Leo XIII issued an encyclical reasserting that Catholics could not be Freemasons. This same encyclical was reaffirmed in 1983 by Cardinal Ratzinger who later became Pope Benedict. (There are many Catholic Masons.) Speaking with reporters on July 28, 2013, the usually temperate Pope

Francis condemned "Masonic lobbies."* The church has maintained persistent opposition to Freemasonry. Many forces within the Vatican view any kind of religious order or initiatory spiritual body outside its structures with suspicion. As will be seen, Masonry and the Vatican have also occupied opposing sides of political conflicts in Europe.

In sum, I think it is fair to argue that Masonry, the most widespread clandestine spiritual thought movement, the prototypical modern secret society, developed out of three factors: 1) the ideas of Rosicrucianism; 2) the ashes of the Thirty Years' War; and 3) the disappointments of post-Elizabethan reaction against esoteric spirituality. Masonry was, in a sense, the final outpost of the occult Renaissance.

I must add a further word about the speculated origins of Freemasonry and the suppressed Knights Templar. A connection is often posited and warrants consideration.

As noted, the Knights Templar was a banking and martial order that proved powerful and influential within the Catholic Church during the Crusades. When the Crusades ended in 1291 and into the early 1300s, questions arose about the role and purpose of the Knights Templar. The order represented a power center of its own, stoking anxieties within the conjoined French aristocracy and Vatican hierarchy. In addition to its combat readiness, the Knights Templar was a financially powerful institution to which members of the French monarchy and Vatican administration were in debt. Hence, it was not difficult to imagine a scenario in which the Knights could become a competing institution.

In late 1306 or early 1307, Pope Clement summoned the grand master of the Knights, Jacques de Molay, to Avignon in France—soon the temporary home of the French-aligned papacy—under pretense of discussing a new Crusade. In 1307, on a dawn raid of Friday the thirteenth of October, secret agents of King Philip IV arrested Molay and all of his fellow Knights in France. Their property was seized and in months ahead Molay and members of the Knights Templar were imprisoned, interrogated, tortured, and coerced into confessions of

* "Pope Francis: 'Masonic Lobbies . . . This Is The Most Serious Problem for Me'" by Michael W. Chapman, CNSNews.com, August 2, 2013.

heresy. The former Crusaders were accused of idolatry, specifically of worshipping a disembodied human head—later conflated with a goat-headed god and identified with Baphomet—defiling the cross, and having sex with men. Some members of the order made confessions, including Molay who later rescinded his. Fifty-four Templars, but not yet Molay, were burned at the stake in May 1310.

The Vatican formally dissolved the order in March 1312. Molay was condemned to the stake in March 1314. All of this was done with the utmost cynicism, not because the Knights Templar were engaged in occult or heretical activity but because they were a martial and banking order that held debts and threatened the primacy of monarchic and Vatican forces. It's a story as old as human nature. Rumor held that a lost fleet of the Templars made its way to Scotland and fought on the side of Robert the Bruce in his war of independence against England, also leaving its symbolic markings on Rosslyn Chapel, built in 1456.

In 1989, English historians Michael Baigent and Richard Leigh, famous for their *Holy Blood, Holy Grail,* which informed some of Dan Brown's *The Da Vinci Code,* considered in *The Temple and the Lodge* whether the surviving Knights formed the basis of Freemasonry. I noted in a 2020 introduction to the book (with some of my references further explored in the next chapter):

> Although I write as a historian who shares the authors' Masonic sympathies, I believe that Baigent and Leigh placed too much stock in secret historical retentions, by which I mean concealment and preservation of hidden bloodlines and traditions within highly placed families and social cliques.
>
> Frankly, I detect little direct inheritance of esoteric traditions within the contemporary world. History is messy and family trees—especially family trees of ideas—rarely reach us intact. More common are self-styled "secret societies," which pretend to ancient ties and whose acolytes sometimes unknowingly rely on hidden wisdom of no greater vintage than the occult revival of the mid-to-late nineteenth century.
>
> None of this means that Baigent and Leigh were wrong about lingering and even seismic effects of occult philosophies. Ideas, symbols, practices, and insights not only endure across time but sometimes form unseen foundations. This is especially true of Freemasonic influences. Do you doubt that? Just look at the back of

a dollar bill. The eye-and-pyramid is not a direct leaf from Masonry but reflects Masonic philosophy to the core: material life (the pyramid) is incomplete without the eye of providence.

In *The Temple and the Lodge*, Baigent and Leigh creditably explore Freemasonic influences on America's framers and revolutionists, a fact of history that most mainstream historians until recently underappreciated or overlooked. In the American colonies, fraternity outweighed philosophy. "Most colonists did not actually read Locke, Hume, Voltaire, Diderot, Rousseau, any more than most British soldiers did," Baigent and Leigh write. But a significant number of thought leaders, including Washington, Franklin, and Hancock, took vows to Freemasonry. In the agrarian world of the colonies—a landscape largely limited to church, home, and farm—fraternal ties carried outsized influence.

Freemasonic ideals—which included religious inclusivism, separation of church and state, and belief in the sanctity of the individual—forged a powerful bond and shared outlook among some of the founders, including a wide range of generals and signers of the Constitution. Baigent and Leigh (in what I consider a stretch) even suggest that Masonic sympathies blunted British commanders' fighting resolve against the colonists.

Because the suppression of the Templars began Friday the thirteenth in 1307, it is sometimes bound up with the mythos of Friday the thirteenth as a day of bad luck.

Fear of the number thirteen is actually one of humanity's oldest superstitions. The earliest known origin appears in ancient India, where it was considered unlucky for thirteen people to sit together at a meal. Nordic mythology holds that Loki, deity of mischief, is the thirteenth guest at a banquet of gods, which ends in argument and violence. The same narrative element—a nefarious thirteenth guest at a dinner—hangs over the story of Judas Iscariot, the so-called traitor apostle and thirteenth man at the Last Supper.

Another ancient source, a work of technical Hermetica, describes a formula of "sympathetic magic" for getting a lover to submit to you by crafting a wax doll and piercing it with thirteen needles. Some modern practitioners of Wicca and neopaganism postulate that ancient Celtic Druids organized their ceremonial circles in orders of thirteen and replicate the practice today.

Historically, Jesus is said to be crucified on Good Friday, also linked to the number. Hence, the Templar connection is one of many in this intriguingly widespread piece of folklore.

I mentioned earlier the British Royal Society, formed in 1660 to further the study of the arts and sciences. It was considered a bastion of Enlightenment Era culture and remains active.

One of the key founders of the Royal Society was chemist Robert Boyle, who in his letters of 1646 and 1647 lauded an "invisible college" and the work of an unseen community of thinkers, philosophers, and seekers. His term was sometimes associated with the Rosicrucians.

Another founding member of the Royal Society was John Wilkins, who had been chaplain to Frederick V, the ruler who, with his wife Elizabeth Stuart, was the ill-fated leader of Bohemia before his military loss to Habsburg forces. Wilkins quoted admiringly from the *Fama Fraternitatis*, the founding document of the Rosicrucians.

Another of the founding members of the Royal Society was Elias Ashmole who recorded being inducted into Freemasonry in 1646, copied the *Fama* and *Confessio* by hand, and wrote his private petition to join the Rosicrucians.

Robert Moray, who was inducted into the Freemasons in 1641, was also a founding member of the Royal Society. These are among the critical figures at the group's foundations.

What I write is inconclusive—but noteworthy. Consider the family tree of ideas, the reformists of Bohemia, the unseen voices of the Rosicrucian manuscripts, the early initiates into Freemasonry, and the founding names of the Royal Society. The search weaves above and below ground. Sometimes light must be taken underground. But that light nurtured, kept, and stoked can reemerge to influence broader society, which rarely understands esoteric sources behind some of its ideals.

Finally, I must consider the short life of the most controversial secret society in Western history, the Illuminati. European monarchies and church hierarchies retained control of Europe into the late 1700s. Although reforms occurred, the progress of Enlightenment Age activity was stalled in the political reaches of public life. Ruling structures, and the privileges and laws they maintained, remained largely intact. Monarchies ruled Bavaria, Spain, France, England, Prussia, and the duchies of Italy. Religious and intellectual freedom was limited; the "invisible college" had gone only so far.

Among the dissatisfied was a Bavarian law professor and philosopher named Adam Weishaupt (1748–1830). On May 1, 1776, Weishaupt and four confederates founded an organization called "League against the enemies of reason and humanity" or Order of Perfectibilists. In 1778, they began calling themselves Order of Illuminati. The handful of seekers believed that neither Rosicrucianism, Freemasonry, the Royal Society or any other organizations invested in reform and human potential were sufficiently radical or effective. And certainly, the outer structures of political life held little promise for change.

Weishaupt and his collaborators believed that Europe needed a clandestine society that reasserted the earliest ideals of Masonry and the occult values of the Renaissance, namely that the individual himself is an extension of the cosmos and that through reclaiming ancient wisdom and passing through initiatory ranks, the individual could grow perfected or illumined. The illumined individual has as his birthright liberty from church, state, and narrowly prescribed judicial systems or doctrines imposed from above. Members of the Illuminati, as led by Weishaupt, believed, finally, that Europe required revolutionary movements echoing the goals of revolutionists in the American colonies.

Indeed, the Illuminati was founded about two months before the Continental Congress on July 4th, 1776, declared emancipation from the British crown. For Weishaupt and his collaborators directly challenging the aristocracy could result in imprisonment, banishment, or death. Hence, they organized their so-called illumined lodges with hopes that in secret, in the self-lit tomb of Christian Rosenkreuz, they could incubate ideas that would produce revolutionary consequences in outer life and forge a new legion of European leaders who were esoterically aware and had sufficient political power to loosen the bonds of church and aristocracy.

At the Illuminati's height, according to existing records, the lodge counted 600 to 650 followers. For a secret order, the Illuminati proved prodigious at recordkeeping. Some initiates were figures of influence, including a member of lesser nobility and Freemason named Adolph Knigge, who joined in 1780 and did a great deal to help with recruitment and formalization of ceremony and ritual. Knigge and Weishaupt never fully got along and Knigge quit of his own volition in 1784.*

Philosopher and dramatist Goethe, a Mason, joined in 1783. As seen earlier, Goethe several years prior crafted the definitive stage version of *Faust*. There is some question whether the composer Mozart, himself a Mason, belonged to the Illuminati. Mozart joined Freemasonry in late 1784 and remained a Mason until his death in 1791. His father, Leopold, was also a Mason. The year of Mozart's death saw the first performance of his opera, *The Magic Flute*, which is suffused with Masonic themes. Some of its music is based upon Masonic ceremonies. Mozart also wrote compositions for Masonic pageants and festivals.

Regarding the possible Illuminati connection, the composer belonged to an Austrian lodge called Beneficence Lodge. The head of Beneficence Lodge, Otto von Gemmingen, was part of the Illuminati. Many members of Beneficence Lodge likewise appeared on Illuminati membership rosters. Mozart attended lectures at another lodge of which he was not a member, True Concord, which likewise had a strong contingent of Illuminati. There is no evidence that Mozart joined the Illuminati but he was in proximity to some of its key figures.

Part of the Illuminati program was to recruit from, infiltrate, and remake Masonic lodges, Lenin-style, as vehicles for revolution. In that sense, the Illuminati could be regarded as a renegade Masonic movement. Several orders calling themselves Masonic lacked formal ties to Masonry but used the label independently, a practice that continues today. Since renegade lodges rarely advertise themselves as such, many members are personally unaware of being outside the traditional fold.

The Bavarian government's secret police intercepted the Illuminati's writings and branded them dangerously subversive—with that the order quickly fell under suppression. In 1784, the Duke of Bavaria, Charles Theodore, unilaterally passed a law outlawing all non-approved societies, whether intellectual, academic, scientific, or religious. This 1784 edict is often called a ban on secret societies,

---

* Among the most useful sources for this section are Katherine Thomson's unjustly rare *The Masonic Thread in Mozart* (Lawrence & Wishart, 1977) and a groundbreaking 2022 English translation by Jon E. Graham of French historian René Le Forestier's 1914 study, *The Bavarian Illuminati* (Inner Traditions).

which is true enough, but it was actually a ban on all groups lacking monarchic approval. The following year, 1785, the Duke established another law that specifically disbanded the Illuminati, targeting the order directly. In 1787, another law authorized the monarchy to seize property belonging to Illuminati lodges and members. And finally, in 1790, the Bavarian aristocracy issued its final edict, prescribing death for members of the Illuminati. No members or activity are evident since.

No executions are recorded but there were banishments. Targeted members were stripped of job, property, rank, privilege, and sometimes expelled from the nation. A wave of banishments occurred in January 1791, although this practice had been underway for several years. I want to put a human face on this for a moment because when we talk of these movements and figures, the various names, Knigge, Weishaupt, Goethe, Mozart, can seem as distant and impersonal as visages on Mount Rushmore.

Who were the victims? What did they experience? What motivated them? I do not mean to paint an idealized picture of the Illuminati. They were figures possessed of the same foibles and hunger for power and prestige that motivate many people. Indeed, some in proximity to the Illuminati, including Leopold Mozart, the composer's father, disdained the group due to its program to infiltrate Freemasonry and transform lodges into covert vehicles. Centuries later, Gandhi, who had esoteric associations of his own, wrote that any kind of secrecy runs counter to the ethos of democracy. Although the nonviolent revolutionary professed admiration for Madame H. P. Blavatsky and the Theosophical Society, something we soon consider, he never joined. In a letter published in the newspaper *Young India* in 1926, Gandhi noted, "What has been a bar to my joining the society . . . is its secret side—its occultism. It has never appealed to me. I long to belong to the masses. Any secrecy hinders the real spirit of democracy."

For his part, Weishaupt was prepared to use secrecy and subterfuge. The Illuminist considered Freemasonry, at least in its current form, as weak tea. He experimented with Masonry before founding the Illuminati but found the larger group too passive, too exclusive, and too expensive. His one-time deputy Knigge also considered Masonry insufficient to the task of developing individuals who could take on the monarchy and extol classically liberal principles. Although the Illuminati's leadership were disaffected with Freemasonry, they nonetheless sought to infiltrate its structure. That is ethically questionable.

But it is also important to understand something about what life becomes when you are targeted by the full power of the monarchical state with its laws, edicts, courts, and prisons. It is profoundly difficult to hang onto the existence you knew and the property and position you held. In that vein, I want to quote from a letter written to Weishaupt on November 29, 1785, by a former member named Ferdinand von Meggenhofen, It was soon after the first round of anti-Illuminist laws were issued. Meggenhofen wrote Weishaupt from a Franciscan monastery in Munich, where he was banished and imprisoned:

> My teacher, my friend,
>
> Here am I sitting in this lonely cell, my dear friend, to which superstition and fanaticism have condemned me, and my first thought is for you; my desire is to inform you of the amazing story of my inquisition. Could you, my teacher, ever have supposed, a few years ago, when we were rejoicing among ourselves at the progress made in our Institute, and at the tremendous advances which our country was making in enlightenment and culture—could you ever have believed that the reward for our labours would be, for you, banishment to a foreign country with your wife and children,* and for me, imprisonment in a monastery, by way of punishment because we attempted to enlighten our fellow-countrymen and to dam the strongly-flowing stream of spiritual despotism?—But a weak government allowed the evil against which we fought to grow strong roots, and we were defeated.
>
> O friend! I should like to lament, like Jeremiah, about the destruction of our country, and to shed bitter tears over the ruins of our fine work. But why ruins?—The oak still stands firmly rooted.—The lightning of fanaticism has struck down a few branches, divided them, and enabled them to be planted in other districts, where they may grow more peacefully into trees . . .
>
> The hardest task lay before me: that of informing my parents. At the end of the court-martial I went to see them, and eventually, after many devious approaches, I informed them of my suspen-

* In 1784, Weishaupt was fired from his position at the University of Ingolstadt and fled Bavaria.

> sion and dismissal.—O friend! never did I have greater need of my philosophy than at that moment. Let us draw a veil over that cruel scene or my heart will break and I shall go mad. Then I went on parade . . .
>
> First they set before me letters from my friends, and made me answerable for certain expressions . . . I explained the passages in question in such a way as to do no harm to my correspondents, without denying the truth . . . O despotic suspicion! how petty, ridiculous and cruel can you be? In your blind eyes the slightest expression of friendship, and the free utterances of a blameless heart signify treachery and insult . . .
>
> Then my examiner had the effrontery to ask why I had not handed in all my friends' letters in which the Order was mentioned. "Because", I answered, with a look of supreme contempt, "His Excellency cannot possibly suppose that I would betray my friends and act against all obligations of honour and righteousness."

Historian Katherine Thomson, who reproduced Meggenhofen's letter in full, notes in a postscript: "After his release Meggenhofen kept his resolve to live quietly and humbly. On 26 October 1790 he was drowned in the river Inn, when a boat in which he was travelling was overturned. Since his body was not immediately found a priest declared that he had been carried straight to hell as a member of the Illuminati. (His body was eventually found over a year later, thus dispelling the legend.)"

Over the course of the letter, Meggenhofen goes on to say how, even in his imprisonment, he did everything possible to practice and propagate the teachings that they studied together and live by their principles. He had been stripped of livelihood and property, removed from family, and was effectively imprisoned in a monastery where he was supposed to undergo religious reeducation. As noted, upon his release in 1790, he drowned and his body was not immediately found. A priest announced that because he had been a disciple of the devil, a member of the Illuminati, his body had ethereally gone straight to hell. The body later turned up. This is what families were subjected to.

Weishaupt lived out the remainder of his life in Gotha, another part of the German-speaking region, and continued his writing on Illuminism. He struggled to earn a living until his death in 1830.

I ask that we remember the human beings behind these stories. When people talk about the persistence of the Illuminati today, as some kind of a shadowy sinister group, return to the passage by Ferdinand von Meggenhofen and be reminded what a real member of the historical Illuminati experienced—and the human cost and pathos when thought movements are suppressed.

The Illuminati, of course, persisted in legend. The fictional strand of Illuminism began soon after the French Revolution in 1789. In less than ten years, apologists for the bygone regime issued conspiratorial tracts that reassessed the revolution not as a foreseeable reaction to absolutist power, political and economic suppression, and a caste system in which the individual would almost certainly die in the same strata into which he or she was born, but, rather, as the result of a hidden campaign by a suppressed sect.

The notion that the aristocratic structure could vanish so quickly and completely, with little retention of the familiar order, struck some observers with disbelief. One could examine the social causes of revolution and reach an orderly set of reasons why a suppressed population after centuries erupts in political ferment. It is no great stretch. But for some who were emotionally and financially attached to the aristocratic and church order, and who witnessed the life they knew so quickly upended, it proved more digestible and intriguing to posit the hand of a hidden foe.

So was born a branch of conspiratorial literature that has echoed into the twenty-first century. This is why the vanquished order, in fantasy versus fact, remains known. The first revisionist work, *Proofs of a Conspiracy*, arrived in 1798 from Scottish writer, inventor, and natural philosopher John Robison. It is a long, belabored, and muddled tract in which Robison concludes that certain revolutionary branches of Freemasonry (seen as a cocoon to Illuminism) were founded by the Jesuits, another longstanding canard. This heightens the irony that another such tract appeared contemporaneously from *Jesuit priest* Abbé Barruel, *Memoirs Illustrating the History of Jacobinism* (1797/98, translated to English 1798/99).

Barruel contended that the Illuminati, this vanished group of a few hundred artists, intellectuals and religious freethinkers, was the hidden hand behind the French Revolution. In a letter of January 31, 1800, Thomas Jefferson praised Weishaupt and called Barruel's work "perfectly the ravings of a Bedlamite." Jefferson wrote, "Wishaupt

[sic] believes that to promote this perfection of the human character was the object of Jesus Christ. That his intention was simply to reinstate natural religion, & by diffusing the light of his morality, to teach us to govern ourselves." The third president and author of the Declaration of Independence further noted, "if Wishaupt had written here, where no secrecy is necessary in our endeavors to render men wise & virtuous, he would not have thought of any secret machinery for that purpose."

Did these esoteric rebels change anything? Were they more than fodder for rumors and histrionic theories echoed centuries later on digital media?

On July 4, 1776, two months after the founding of the Illuminati in Bavaria, the Continental Congress of the United States authorized a committee, chaired by Benjamin Franklin, a Freemason, to design a seal for the new nation. The Great Seal of the United States was ratified in 1882. The front of the Great Seal shows the familiar American Eagle, clutching olive branches in its right talon and arrows in its left. On the reverse of the Great Seal is the alluring eye-and-pyramid. The pyramid is completed by the All-Seeing Eye, the eye of inner knowing associated with the Ancient Egyptian Eye of Horus. The juxtaposition posits that material progress is incomplete without gnosis or greater understanding.

Surrounding the eye-and-pyramid, which today appears on the back of the dollar bill, is the Latin slogan, *Annuit Coeptis Novus Ordo Seclorum*, roughly translated "Providence Smiles on Our New Order of the Ages." The esoteric imprimatur was neither Freemasonic nor Illuminist. But it reflected like values and imagery. We next explore how some of the occult and esoteric threads of the Old World extended to the new.

CHAPTER FOUR

Mystic America

This chapter is meaningful to me because it marks the subject matter that began my career as a historian. My first book, *Occult America*, was published in 2009 but, like many books, it had a backstory. Several years earlier, I consumed a work by a British historian whose name I have mentioned previously, Frances A. Yates.

Yates wrote several wonderful and significant books about the influence of occultism and Hermeticism on early modern life. One of her books that particularly impacted me was *The Occult Philosophy in the Elizabethan Age* (1979), her last full-length work before she died in 1981. The book was so revealing, meticulous, and capturing of the human spirit: the wish to know, to search, and to ask the basic but neglected question, what's around the next corner?

I was deeply affected by Yates's combination of idealism and seriousness: her gravitas and yet absence of embarrassment at having *ideals*. There exists so much cynicism in our culture, hastened by social media, yet Yates demonstrated how you can combine idealism with intellectual substance. You can believe in something, stand for something, and still possess the tools, critical outlook, scholarly bona fides, and discrimination of a historian. I told myself that I wanted, in my own way and as I am best able, to do that for modern occult spirituality.

In summer 2005, a man who was then president of the Philosophical Research Society in Los Angeles, Obadiah Harris, said to me, as a New Yorker, if you're ever in the neighborhood our podium is open to you. I got off the phone and determined immediately that I was going to be "in the neighborhood." I emailed him to say that I would be there in September. When someone offers you the opportunity to hone your craft, say yes; fill in the details later. On a September afternoon in 2005, I spoke at the Philosophical Research Society's Egyptian-Mayan-art deco campus in Griffith Park, one of the under-recognized jewels of American architecture, designed by Robert Stacy-Judd. I titled my talk in homage to Yates, "The Occult Philosophy in America." That served as the basis for my first book, *Occult America*, which I worked on in proposal form for a year before I began to write it in earnest.

Hence, this subject means a lot to me personally. It means a lot historically, too, because the United States, for all the flaws and catastrophes that have marked its history, has served as a springboard for much of what is novel, experimental, and alternative on the global spiritual scene, including the rebirth of occultism. When Madame H.P. Blavatsky, co-founder of the Theosophical Society, reached New York City in 1873 the world traveler said that she approached America as "the cradle of Modern Spiritualism" with "feelings not unlike those of a Mohammedan approaching the birthplace of his Prophet."* She later said America was the ideal place to organize her explorations without harassment by legal authorities, as she experienced back home in Tsarist Russia. For all its contradictions, the U.S. occupies a unique space within this study. From the colonial era onward, it often served as a safe harbor for religious experimenters from the Old World, which is where we pick up our thread.

The previous chapter on secret societies considered the backlash against the occult revival of the Renaissance. This was felt with particular fury in Central Europe, an area bordered by the Rhine Valley in the West and Bohemia and Prague in the East, which during the later stages of the Renaissance was, due to the

* Letter to *The Spiritualist*, December 13, 1874.

influence of Rudolph II, suffused with seekers interested in alchemy, astrology, divination, number symbolism, Hermeticism, and the theories of Pythagoras and Paracelsus. This was birthplace to the Rosicrucian thought movement and the Bavarian Illuminati. This German-speaking region of Central Europe was devastated between 1618 and 1648 by the Thirty Years' War, which had many factors but essentially pitted Habsburg Catholic armies against Protestant armies. The conflict began in a church-based backlash against the occult and esoteric religious experimentation of the Renaissance and general religious toleration. The war's aftereffects, including famine, fires, agricultural and economic devastation, destruction of villages and cultural centers, and marauding bandits (often former soldiers), were suffered for decades. At its end, with the 1648 Peace of Westphalia, resurgent church powers clamped down on religious life.

The Rhine Valley and surrounding regions were carved up into different aristocratic duchies or municipalities. The atmosphere was oppressive and barren. Whenever possible, pilgrims, monks, experimenters, heretics, and intellectuals, who decades earlier had known relative freedom in Bohemia, departed the area and, in some cases, made the dangerous and arduous journey across the Atlantic. Word spread that in the nascent American colonies a liberal degree of religious freedom prevailed.

In summer 1693, a young monk named Johannes Kelpius (1667–1708) led a band of about 40 pilgrims out of the Rhine Valley, sojourned west across Europe, got steerage to England, and from London departed on an extremely perilous journey of about six months across the Atlantic. In June 1694, they reached the City of Philadelphia, which then consisted of about 500 houses. The Hermetic pilgrims made Philadelphia—"City of Brotherly Love"—their destination because of its reputation for religious tolerance. The town was founded in 1682 by William Penn (1644–1718), a British convert to Quakerism who was discriminated against at Oxford and finally imprisoned in the Tower of London in 1668 for his heterodox religious writings.

Unlike many religious radicals, Penn came from a wealthy family to whom the British crown owed money. To get out of debt, the monarchy gave Penn a land grant in 1681 of what is now the State of Pennsylvania. Penn not only became the founder of Pennsylvania, but his ideal was to establish the City of Brotherly Love, a place where people could worship freely. I do not intend to leave the misimpression that Penn's 1682 Frame of Government created a religiously egalitarian society. Jews and other non-Christians could live and practice in the territory but could neither vote nor hold office. Penn made it clear that atheists were unwelcome. Rhode Island alone extended full religious freedom at the time. It was only in 1777, when Thomas Jefferson wrote, but had not yet presented, his Virginia Statute for Religious Freedom, later ratified as the First Amendment in 1791, that religious favoritism was on its way to statutory prohibition, a principle requiring persistent re-judication. The radicalness of Jefferson's religious vision should not be underestimated.

"Even John Locke," wrote historian Henry Wilder Foot in *Thomas Jefferson* (Beacon, 1947), "advocating separation of church and state, had not gone so far as to advocate religious freedom for Catholics or atheists. The Virginia Statute for Religious Freedom, therefore, went far beyond anything hitherto dreamed of in Europe."

Kelpius and his followers formed a monastic colony along the banks of the Wissahickon Creek, just outside town. The woods-dwellers studied astrology, scanned the heavens for apocalyptic portents and signs—according to some accounts they brought with them a telescope which they mounted to the roof of a forty-foot-square log tabernacle—studied the magical uses of hymn and music, and produced botanical remedies and talismans. The Kelpius circle settled a harsh, rocky landscape, but they found what they had risked their lives for: ability to live in a Hermetic, communal setting without molestation; and freedom to study alchemy and number symbolism, heavenly signs, uses of botanical spells and remedies, and practice monastic worship. They traded the world that they knew for a tough, knotty, and weather-beaten terrain. For nearly fifteen years they made it work. In 1708, Kelpius died, probably of tuberculosis. But a seed was planted.

Word spread of the Kelpius colony, sometimes called the Woman in the Wilderness. Revelation 12:14: "And to the woman were given two wings of a great eagle, that she might fly into the wilderness, into her place, where she is nourished . . ." Some termed them the Tabernacle in the Forest. Even across the Atlantic, news traveled of this little colony of Hermetic pilgrims, prompting others to make the arduous journey to attempt what Kelpius and his followers had accomplished.

In 1720, another Rhine Valley mystic, Johann Conrad Beissel (1691–1768), migrated to Philadelphia to join Kelpius's colony. On arrival, he discovered that his inspiration had died twelve years earlier. Undaunted, Beissel started his own, larger mystical colony in Ephrata, Pennsylvania, in 1732. The Ephrata colony, some of whose buildings remain, proved more thriving, stable, and economically self-sufficient. The Ephratans likewise studied the magical uses of hymn, music, and sound. They lived under what could be considered primitive Christianity or biblical communism (to which Penn, as it happens, was personally sympathetic). The Ephrata colony became a more permanent fixture on the American landscape.

Again, word trickled to the Old World that heretical religious movements could find a relatively safe harbor in the American colonies. This caught the attention of a devout Quaker woman living in Manchester, England, where she was persecuted for witchcraft in the early 1770s. Her name was Ann Lee (1736–1784). Ann belonged to a sect known as the Shaking Quakers, so called because devotees were known to writhe and gesticulate in ecstasy of the spirit.

Local authorities accused Ann of witchcraft and sorcery. She was jailed, harassed, and beaten. But Ann was not to be another casualty of religious violence. She escaped with eight followers, including an unfaithful husband. In 1774, Ann and her band of Shaking Quakers journeyed across the Atlantic to New York City. They worked menial jobs throughout most of 1775, sweeping chimneys, scrubbing floors, and cleaning chamber pots. Ann's husband abandoned her. Undeterred, she and a group grown to twelve left the city in 1776. With money they had scraped together, Ann and her followers traveled up the Hudson Valley where they formed their own religious colony outside Albany in a town then known by its Native American name, Niskayuna. Today it is Watervliet.

In the fall of 1776, the woman called Mother Ann Lee and her twelve pilgrims inaugurated the nation's first Shaker Village. The group now known as Shakers broke ground in a root-ridden, marshy, and mosquito-infested landscape. Celibate and pacifist, they refused to fight in the War of Independence, arousing local suspicions that they were British spies. Through swampy summers and mud-frozen winters, the band endured and grew, sprouting other villages in New Lebanon, New York, and Hancock, Massachusetts. To admirers and followers, Mother Ann was a spiritual avatar. The buildings of her village stand today—as does Mother Ann's spare headstone nearby.

Mother Ann did more than found a sect. She set the migratory pattern of a profoundly important geographical area and artery in the spiritual development of America and the modern world. It became known as the Burned-Over District. The Burned-Over District is a snaking stretch of land about 25 miles wide and 300 miles long, extending from Albany in the east to Buffalo in the west. It became one of the main passages through which Americans flowed West, bringing commerce, settlement—and beliefs. Historian Carl Carmer called it "a broad psychic highway, a thoroughfare of the occult."*

In many regards, the Burned-Over District replaced the devastated Rhine Valley as the springboard of religious experiment in modern life. Ann Lee and the Shakers anchored the beginning of the Burned-Over District, a place considered "burned over" by the fires of spirit (although the origin of its name has never been definitively settled). Fatefully, the Burned-Over District was traversed by a carriage path, which today is Route 20. It is the longest continuous road in the United States, extending from Boston, where it is called Boston Post Road, to Eugene, Oregon. Along its trail, Mother Ann's movement later migrated as far north as Maine and as far south as Kentucky.

Other seekers, both in the new nation and across the Atlantic, heard about this growing group of Shakers, who described contacting voices and figures of the spirit world, including vanquished Native American tribes. The Burned-Over District itself had been home to the Iroquois, an amalgam of six nations: Mohawk, Oneida, Onondaga, Cayuga, Seneca, and Tuscarora. Self-described as "People of the Long House," the Iroquois were ruled over by 50 chiefs, a civic system studied by Benjamin Franklin. The Iroquois are sometimes characterized as one of the world's oldest democracies. Some nations, including the Mohawk, sided with the British during the War of Independence, giving the colonial government pretext it had long sought to push the Iroquois off the lush farmland and forest, opening Central New York to land speculation and settlement from New England. Throughout the eighteenth century, "the native tribes were dragged into the rivalries of French and English colonists, themselves the reflection of wars in Europe," notes Joscelyn Godwin in *Upstate Cauldron: Eccentric*

---

* *Listen For a Lonesome Drum: A York State Chronicle* (Farrar & Rinehart, 1936, 1950).

Spiritual Movements in Early New York State (State University of New York Press, 2015).

The neutral Shakers carried on, abstaining from sex, wine, and tobacco. They were ascetic and self-sufficient. Some observers casually hold that celibacy spelled the inevitable end of the Shakers. But ostensibly celibate monastic orders persist around the world. The Shakers built their movement by taking in seekers, widows, orphans, ex-convicts, and others who had difficulty finding structure or resources. By the late nineteenth century, as American society grew more varied and flexible in living and working arrangements, such retreats from outer life became less necessary. Broad social changes rather than celibacy alone contributed to their demise.

Though Mother Ann died in 1784, her influence extended further in death than life. The late 1830s saw the dawn of a feverish and profoundly influential period of Shaker activity called "Mother Ann's Work." The departed leader appeared as a spirit guide directing a vast range of supernatural activity and instruction.

The devout received ghostly visions and songs, which they turned into strangely beautiful paintings and haunting hymns, many of which survive. Villagers spoke in foreign tongues, writhing and rolling on the floor in meetings that lasted all night—some even getting intoxicated on "spirit gifts" of wine or Indian tobacco. In an America that had not yet experienced the Spiritualist wave of séances, table tilting, or conversing with the dead, the Shakers prophesied that soon spirits would appear in every house and hamlet in the land—that America was poised for a renaissance of contact with the invisible world.

I often say that migratory waves foretell new religious movements. Migrants generally leave behind churches, congregations, and family attachments back home. They open to new religious voices and commitments. Again, this is among the reasons the place was called the Burned-Over District. Not only was it burned over by the fires of spirit but it was said that *everybody belonged to something*, not infrequently a breakaway church or metaphysical club, sect, or commune. As far as converts went, one itinerant minister supposedly told another, that place had been *burned over*. As we'll see, this pattern repeated in California in the early twentieth century.

One of the most unusual figures to populate the Burned-Over District emerged as Mother Ann and the Shakers were establishing their communities. A strange drama played out in the life of another woman, a New Englander named Jemima Wilkinson (1752–1819), who grew up on a prosperous Quaker farm in Cumberland, Rhode Island.

In 1770, when Jemima was seventeen years old, she encountered the last wave of the Baptist religious revival movement called the Great Awakening. That year, charismatic British minister George Whitefield was making his last traverse through New England as part of the final leg of the Great Awakening. Whitefield died in late September. Jemima, this young woman raised in a liberal Quaker household, experienced a religious conversion of deep intensity. Her habits changed. She sat alone in her room poring over Scripture. When someone is ignited with the spirit of the search, there's no telling where things are headed.

In fall 1776, Jemima was struck with typhus fever. On October 4, she took to her bed and slipped in and out of a coma, experiencing fever dreams of heavenly realms and other worlds. The slender, emaciated young woman was not expected to survive. Her family sat bedside in a death vigil. But about thirty-six hours later, Jemima shockingly sprang up from bed. This woman who had been on the brink of death appeared ruddy and filled with life. She announced to her speechless onlookers that the woman they knew as Jemima was, in fact, dead. The being standing before them, she said, was an avatar of the divine spirit and would answer only to the name *Publick Universal Friend*.

The Sunday following her revival, the Publick Universal Friend marched to a local churchyard and began delivering a homily under a tree. Locals were aghast—not only was Jemima "back from the dead" but this was the first time that neighbors had seen a woman deliver a talk in public. The Friend began speaking in Rhode Island, New York, and Philadelphia. She soon crisscrossed between British and American military lines, one of the only figures capable of doing so.

Followers of the Publick Universal Friend came in contact with members of Johann Conrad Beissel's commune at Ephrata, Pennsylvania. They were influenced by some of the Ephratan practices, including holding sabbath on Saturday. The Friend's supporters decided to establish their own commune for their avatar. In 1788, these New Englanders followed the flow into the Burned-Over District; they moved deeper west onto the shores of Crooked Lake, today called Keuka (Iroquois for "canoe landing.") They settled two towns, both of which still stand, one called Penn Yan and the other Jerusalem. In the latter, they built a mansion for their spirit guide, where she resided until her death in 1819. The dwelling today is a private family home.

Jemima and her circle did a great deal to settle that part of New York State, prompting historian Herbert A. Wisbey, Jr., to dub her the "pioneer prophetess."* Ancestral names of the Friend's followers still appear in the local phone directory. On the tidy main street of Penn Yan, you can encounter residents who trade stories about the Public Universal Friend. As one folktale goes, the Friend led followers to a local body of water—some say a canal off main street—where she declared her intention to walk on water. "Have ye faith that I can do this thing?" she demanded. "Yea, we believe!" followers replied. "Then if ye have faith," the Universal Friend said, "there is no need for any vulgar spectacle." With that, she got into her carriage monogrammed with initials U * F (a real vehicle) and rode off.

Not only were all of these seekers among key settlers of Central New York but they further opened Americans to the validity of intentional communities and women as religious leaders. I hope what I'm describing gives an idea of the centrality of the breakaway colony in the development of religious experimentation. In that vein, I want to recommend a 2021 documentary directed by Kier-La Janisse, *Woodlands Dark and Days Bewitched*, in which I participated in a small way. (I also met my partner, Jacqueline Castel, on set.) It is a magisterial movie that surveys folk horror, which often rests on fictionalized but culturally grounded stories of "strange colonies." This theme animates movies like *The Wicker Man, Children of the Corn, The Dark Secret of Harvest Home, The Village,* and *Midsommar.*

Recent to this writing, a successful commune and retreat center stood in New Lebanon, New York, on the site of the second Shaker Village. Founded in 1975, its future grew uncertain in 2022 following the financial crisis of the lockdown. Called the Abode of the Message, it was based in the teachings of Sufism, the mystical variant of Islam. One of the Abode's longtime members told me that when they were scouting land for their community in the early 1970s, the founders—filled with flower-power idealism and the same intrepid spirit that

* *Pioneer Prophetess* (Cornell University Press, 1964).

sustained earlier colonies—visited the remaining Shaker Village at New Lebanon. Two elderly practitioners still lived there.

"The spirits told us you were coming," a Shaker woman told her Sufi guests. "We've been expecting you." To the longhaired youths, it was the passing of a baton.

The Burned-Over District further gave birth to the religions of Mormonism and Seventh Day Adventism and to movements in perfectionism, biblical communism, and, most significantly, suffragism.

Indeed, this narrow stretch of land in Central New York was, for about two generations in the first half of the 1800s, the springboard for nearly everything novel and radical in American life. This can be difficult to understand because if you visit the Burned-Over District today, including some of the towns I've mentioned—Jerusalem, Pen Yann, Niskayuna—and those I'll be mentioning—Palmyra, Batavia, Hydesville—you'll see beautiful, lush farmland interrupted by occasional sprawl. Strip malls crop up here and there but the area remains one of lush greenery, lakes, and meadows. A visitor could justly ask, "What's so magical about this place?"

I've provided some cultural and social background. There exist Native American legends: in particular, the Iroquois considered the area ancestral home to an ancient Indian tribe older than any known. Mormon prophet and Burned-Over District son Joseph Smith considered it a lost tribe of Israel, a theme integrated into *The Book of Mormon*, published to the world in 1830. Some locals felt that the voices and spirits of this tribe endured as a world within a world. In 1811, New York's seventh governor, DeWitt Clinton, delivered a talk to the New York Historical Society in which he affirmed his belief in this unknown tribe:

> There is every reason to believe that, previous to the occupancy of this country by the progenitors of the present nations of Indians, it was inhabited by a race of men, much more populous, and much further advanced in civilization. The numerous remains of ancient fortifications, which are found in this country . . . demonstrate a population far exceeding that of the Indians when this country was first settled.

Clinton and others reported esoteric fraternities among nineteenth century Iroquois, which some considered a form of "ancient Freemasonry." These speculations were heightened when Seneca leader Red Jacket and other New York–area Indians were seen wearing Freemasonic-style medals in the shape of the square and compass, a fact well documented in a 1903 New York State Museum monograph, *Metallic Ornaments of the New York Indians* by archaeologist William M. Beauchamp.

Interpretations abounded. Smith himself, known as a local treasure hunter, said he received ancient golden plates buried in the Hill Cumorah near his home in Palmyra. The plates, he said, were written in "reformed Egyptian hieroglyphics" and translated by the young seeker through a pair of ancient seer stones, Urim and Thummim, matching those worn in the breastplates of ancient Hebrew priests.

Smith's *Book of Mormon* revealed a vast alternate history, involving a tribe of Israel fleeing the Holy Land for America, experiencing the gospel directly from Christ, and later suffering fracture and vanquish in a "great and tremendous battle at Cumorah . . . until they were all destroyed." (Mormon 8:2) The scale and scope of the *Book of Mormon* were extraordinary—seen by followers as buttressing the lore of Smith's home district rather than built upon it.

Smith was also inspired by the rites and rituals of Masonry, which he considered fragments once practiced by Hebrew priests. He aligned with Masonry in a surprising manner, marrying the widow of Masonry's most famous apostate. It began in the mid-1820s, sparked by a violent episode that played out not far from Smith's home. In 1826, a disgruntled Mason living in Batavia, New York, William Morgan, threatened to expose Masonry's secret rites in a manuscript he was readying for publication. Morgan was soon kidnapped and never seen again—possibly murdered at the hands of Masonic zealots.

The presumed homicide and dead-end legal investigation raised suspicions about Masonry's influence in law enforcement and the courts. The episode unleashed a torrent of anti-Masonic feeling stoked by a general mood of discontent over corruption in high places. In time, 52 anti-Masonic newspapers sprang up in the nation, with dozens of anti-Masonic representatives sent to state legislatures. While the waters soon calmed, Freemasonry would never again command the same level of prestige in American life.

Morgan left behind a widow, Lucinda. She eventually met a new husband with whom she trekked west to join Smith in his aim of relocating Mormonism. Around 1836, Lucinda, though remarried, became one of Smith's multiple "spiritual wives."

As the Mormons wandered the nation in search of a safe home, Smith founded a Freemasonic lodge at his large community at Nauvoo, Illinois. In the early 1840s, he introduced into Mormonism the symbols of Masonry, such as the rising sun, beehive, and square and compass. Smith conducted initiation ceremonies in a makeshift temple over his Nauvoo store. He also studied Hebrew and possibly elements of Kabbalah with a French-Jewish Mormon convert named Alexander Neibaur. It was a period of tremendous innovation within the nascent movement. It reached a sudden end.

In 1844, Smith surrendered to authorities at Carthage, Illinois, where he sat in a jail cell to await trial on charges arising from the destruction of an opposition newspaper at Nauvoo. Smith had sanctioned the burning of a critical news sheet. Although his act was indefensible, it served as an excuse for the state government to finally get its hands on the religious leader. Illinois' frontier towns were increasingly wary of Mormon newcomers, who maintained their own militia and formed a political power bloc.

While the prophet and his closest colleagues waited in a two-story jailhouse in Carthage, they found themselves without protection that the state's governor promised. Armed bands roamed the area. In early evening of June 27, a mob stormed the jail. Before diving from a window to escape, Smith was reported by witnesses to issue the Masonic distress signal, lifting his arms in the symbol of the square and beginning to shout, "Oh, Lord my God, is there no help for the widow's son!" Musket balls tore through his falling body. As noted, descendants testified that on the prophet's body appeared his old amulet of Jupiter derived from the occult philosophy of Cornelius Agrippa.

In 1784, the Burned-Over District attracted an unusual visitor: the French hero of the revolutionary war, the Marquis de Lafayette. He was both a Freemason and student of someone we explore in the next chapter, occult healer Franz Anton Mesmer (1734–1815).

In short, Mesmer believed that all of life is animated by an invisible etheric fluid, which he called "animal magnetism." The experimenter taught that if a magnetizer or Mesmerist places an individual into a trance, he can then manipulate or realign the subject's animal magnetism, healing the patient of physical or emotional maladies. Lafayette arrived to tour the area and study whether the dances and ecstatic states of the Shakers related to Mesmer's theories of animal magnetism.

In the early 1940s, a story began circulating in American historical literature claiming that shortly before Lafayette departed for the U.S., he had an audience with King Louis XVI. The King teased him for being apprenticed to Mesmer and wondered what Lafayette's close friend General Washington would think of all this. I could find no source for the tale and wondered, as one must in these instances, whether it really happened. And if Louis XVI said this, who overheard him?

The story turns out to be true. Following the French Revolution and Reign of Terror, a military officer who had spent years in Louis XVI's court, Le Comte D'Allonville, wrote a ten-volume series on court intrigues published from 1838 to 1841, *Mémoires Secrets, de 1770 à 1830.* And there, in volume one, is Louis teasing Lafayette: "Que pensera Washington en apprenant que vous êtes devenu le premier apothicaire de Mesmer?"—*What will Washington think when he learns that you have become Mesmer's chief apothecary apprentice?* Lafayette was undeterred. While visiting, he handed Washington a personal letter from his occult mentor in which Mesmer requested Washington's support to open an American branch of his Society of Harmony, the organization that taught the healer' methods.

In his dispatch of June 16, 1784, preserved in the Library of Congress, Mesmer told Washington: "It appeared to us that the man who merited most of his fellow men should be interested in the fate of every revolution which had for its object the good of humanity." Mesmer was venturing a loaded point, attempting to place himself in league with democratic revolutions. It wasn't entirely farfetched. As will be seen, some supporters interpreted Mesmer's trance sessions or séances—a term he used—as revealing *a deeper and common aspect of humanity;* every entranced subject, from slave to noble, possessed an ethereal or inner self beyond rank or label, and, thus, was naturally equal. This interpretation united occult, revolutionary, and Enlightenment thought.

Toward the end of Lafayette's tour on November 25, 1784, Washington replied to Mesmer, diplomatically if guardedly:

> The Marqs de la Fayette did me the honor of presenting to me your favor of the 16th of June; & of entering into some explanation of the Powers of Magnetism—the discovery of which, if it should prove as extensively beneficial as it is said, must be fortunate indeed for Mankind, & redound very highly to the honor of that genius to whom it owes its birth. For the confidence reposed in me by the Society which you have formed for the purpose of diffusing & deriving from it, all the advantages expected; & for your favourable sentiments of me, I pray you to receive my gratitude, & the assurances of the respect & esteem with which I have the honor to be Sir,
> Yr most obedt humble servt

Part of the basis of Washington and Lafayette's friendship was their bond as Freemasons. The founders included many Masons, such as Benjamin Franklin, John Hancock, and Paul Revere. Among Signers of the Declaration of Independence, nine out of fifty-six were Masons, as were thirteen out of thirty-nine signers of the Constitution, and thirty-three out of seventy-four of Washington's generals. As explored in the last chapter, Freemasonry grew parallel to the radically ecumenical and esoteric thought movement called Rosicrucianism, as well as the fading but still-active occult experimentation of the Renaissance. Following on the Grand Lodge of England in 1717, the first Masonic lodge in the American colonies appeared in 1731 in Philadelphia.*

Fraternal affiliation with an esoteric society was significantly defining of a person's life in the colonies. For generations following the Philadelphia lodge, and well into the nineteenth century, America remained a largely rural environment. Dominant institutions were farms, granges, trading posts, forts, taverns, ports, and churches. There were few venues to get books, exchange ideas, and be educated. Church life was dominant and notions of heresy very much alive.

To join Freemasonry meant undertaking a singular social bond. It was all-the-more remarkable to join a fraternal order that used occult and esoteric symbols as keys for ethical development, including the skull and crossbones, obelisk, all-seeing eye, serpent, ladder of wisdom, and pyramid—symbols that populated the ancient reli-

---

* This date is based on lodge minutes. Since informality occasionally prevailed among nascent colonial lodges, the start date is sometimes set a year or more earlier while other lodges, including in Massachusetts and Virginia, claim precedence.

gious imagination and were now reconfigured, along with passion plays and initiatory rites, within Masonry. Freemasonry validated the basic validity of all faiths, including pre-Christian religions. I cannot emphasize how radical a break that was. The basic bylaws and documents of Freemasonry, even in the colonial era, while extolling the existence of a Creator, stopped short of elevating Christianity as the sole means of salvation. This indirectly validated occult philosophy.

The religious neutrality codified in the Declaration and Constitution grew from the Enlightenment philosophies of Locke, Voltaire, and Rousseau. But, as noted, how many in rural America read them? How many have today? Colonials, at least those of means, had the capacity to participate in a fraternal order that enshrined and protected the individual spiritual search—and believed that the search was not the property of any congregation, doctrine, or dogma. That was the radicalism of Freemasonry. That is also why Masonry has historically been considered threatening to established religious order.

On July 4, 1776, the Continental Congress formed a subcommittee chaired by Benjamin Franklin charged with designing the Great Seal of the newly declared nation. As alluded, the Great Seal, ratified in 1782, displays on its front the familiar American eagle grasping olive branches in its right talon and arrows in its left. But the reverse of the Great Seal tells a more esoteric story. It appears today on the back of the U.S. dollar bill, where it was not actually placed until 1935, as explored later. The image shows the pyramid and all-seeing eye or, classically, Eye of Horus, hovering above it. The incomplete pyramid is capped by the eye of providence to suggest that material work is incomplete without higher knowing. Surrounding it is the Latin maxim, *Annuit Coeptis Novus Ordo Seclorum*, roughly translated, *Providence Smiles on Our New Order of the Ages.*

It is not a Masonic symbol. But I think it fair to venture that the symbol is inspired by Freemasonry, which used the eye of providence in its lexicon. The symbolism is Masonic philosophy defined: earthly works are incomplete without the light of wisdom. As the more idealistic founders saw it, the new nation was part of a revived chain of great civilizations, including Egypt, Greece, and Rome, which saw their purpose intertwined with the eternal search and imprimatur of creation. This is also reflected in the Hellenic-Egyptian architecture that later characterized the U.S. capital.

I want to note a strand of Freemasonry that is important to American history but poorly understood. That is Prince Hall Masonry, a Black Masonic order. In the 1770s, a freed man of color named Prince Hall, who was a Boston leatherworker, assembled with fourteen Black colleagues to form a Freemasonic lodge. Refused entry to mainline Masonry, the men organized themselves into African Lodge No. 1.

The historicism of Prince Hall Masonry has, until recently, been marred by mistakes stemming from documents of the late eighteenth century. Much of traditional history records that Prince Hall Masonry was founded in 1775. It was not. That error got inserted into records of the Massachusetts Historical Society in 1795 and was thereafter widely repeated. Hence, even materials of significant vintage and familiar sourcing can be wrong. Two impeccable Masonic historians, John L. Hairston Bey and Oscar Alleyne, produced a clarifying monograph in 2016, *Landmarks of Our Fathers*. Revisiting original records, the authors determined that the founding of Prince Hall Masonry, or African Lodge No. 1, was not 1775 but 1778.

Prince Hall was the lodge's first Grand Master and his branch of Freemasonry later took his name as a Black Masonic movement. Prince Hall Masonry is today increasingly recognized within traditional Masonry. Importantly, Prince Hall's name appeared on two petitions opposing slavery in the American colonies: one in 1777 and one in 1778, the founding year of African Lodge No. 1. These are among the earliest anti-slavery petitions in the colonies. In effect, *the first Black-led abolitionist movement in America was Freemasonic*. I am not saying that abolitionism arose from Freemasonry. Abolitionism had many thought-streams, including Quakerism. But with discovery of Prince Hall's signature on these early petitions, and understanding when Prince Hall Masonry was founded, the confluence is important to note.*

---

* Freemasonry is a traditionally male order. There are recognized co-ed lodges, including in an ongoing movement called Co-Freemasonry, which originated in France in 1890. There is also a men's and women's adjunct group called The Order of the Eastern Star founded in Mississippi in 1850.

One of the most significant American movements in occultism is the magical system called hoodoo. "The way we tell it," wrote novelist and folklorist Zora Neale Hurston in her 1935 *Mules and Men*, "hoodoo started way back there before everything . . . Nobody can say where it begins or ends."

Hoodoo is sometimes confused with Vodou. Vodou is an Afro-Caribbean religion with its own deities, priesthood. and liturgy, properly spelled Vodou in Haiti and Voodoo in the American South. Hoodoo has a lineage all its own. It was and remains a syncretic, spell-working system originated by enslaved people in the U.S.

Hoodoo began as a retention of traditional religious ideas from West and Central Africa which were combined with practices that embondaged people found in America, from Pennsylvania Dutch folklore to Catholic saint veneration to variants of Kabbalah. Hoodoo is spelled lowercase. Its etymology is unclear. But hoodoo may come from *huduba*, a term used among the Hausa people of West and Central Africa meaning to arouse resentment against someone. In blues songs, singers would sometimes lament being "hoodooed"—i.e., crossed and tricked by spellcasting. In practice, hoodoo draws heavily upon botanical and household items—roots, plants, soaps, minerals, animal parts, perfumes, nails, pins—objects that a displaced people adapted to retain ties to old rituals and spirits.

Abolitionist hero Frederick Douglass (c.1818–1895) placed hoodoo at the center of what he called the defining moment of his life. Douglass did not use the word hoodoo. But the episode, which he recounts in all three of his memoirs across nearly fifty years,* is marked by telltale occult references, for generations unnoticed by (and of little concern to) mainstream historians until I first documented its significance in *Occult America*. As I began researching Douglass's life, including the cultural touchstones and language of his magical incident, it was as though a light switched on; and this neglected chapter began to emerge.

Douglass was born into slavery in 1817 or 1818, he did not know which. As a young child, he was separated from his mother—a woman

* *Narrative of the Life of Frederick Douglass, an American Slave* (1845); *My Bondage and My Freedom* (1855); and *Life and Times of Frederick Douglass* (1893).

who walked miles from another plantation for the rare occasion of rocking him to sleep or giving him a handmade ginger cake—and enslaved by a family in Saint Michael's, Maryland. They later uprooted the adolescent Frederick to their home in Baltimore. Once more, in Frederick's adolescence the family rearranged its household and took him back with them to the plantation fields in St. Michael's.

But the man who headed Frederick's household felt that a youth who tasted city life could no longer be counted on to work the fields. So, in January of 1834, Frederick, on the eve of his sixteenth birthday or thereabouts, was shipped off to work for a farmer in the Maryland countryside named Edward Covey, known as a "breaker of slaves." Covey was a sadistic slaveholder, proud of his reputation for beating and tormenting his charges. Covey subjected Frederick to regular whippings and harassment for any trumped-up reason. The beatings grew so severe that one night Frederick escaped Covey's farm and returned to his old household in St. Michael's, begging them to take him back in. He was refused. Terrified, bloodied, starving, and beaten, the youth trudged back to Covey's farm. He hid in the woods outside Covey's property, not knowing what to do.

Just at that time, Frederick wrote, he was happened upon by a local man named Sandy Jenkins. Frederick wrote that Sandy, also a slave, was known locally as a wise African spiritual advisor, a man who still retained some of the old ways.

Sandy "was not only a religious man, but he professed to believe in a system for which I have no name," he wrote in 1855. "He was a genuine African, and had inherited some of the so-called magical powers, said to be possessed by African and eastern nations." Sandy took Frederick back to his cabin, cleaned him up, fed him—and something more. Douglass wrote in 1845:

> He told me, with great solemnity, I must go back to Covey; but that before I went, I must go with him into another part of the woods, where there was a certain root, which, if I would take some of it with me, carrying it *always on my right side*, would render it impossible for Mr. Covey, or any other white man, to whip me. He said he had carried it for years; and since he had done so, he had never received a blow, and never expected to while he carried it. I at first rejected the idea, that the simple carrying of a root in my pocket would have any such effect as he had said, and was not disposed to

> take it; but Sandy impressed the necessity with much earnestness, telling me it could do no harm, if it did no good. To please him, I at length took the root, and, according to his direction, carried it upon my right side.

There is no record to bear the matter out, but the object Sandy pressed upon Douglass was very likely a rock-hard, bulbous root known within hoodoo as *John the Conqueror* or sometimes *High John. John de conker* is the pronunciation in oral records and song. It is the ultimate protective object, used for everything from personal safety to virility, traditionally carried by a man rather than a woman. In the magical lore of "like bestows like" (conceptually echoing *as above, so below*), the dried root is shaped like a testicle. There is historical conflict over the root's species; botanical drawings differ among catalogs of old hoodoo supply houses. But most careful observers and practitioners of hoodoo today agree that the likeliest source is the *jalap root*, which dries into a rough, spherical nub.

Armed with what he warily called "the magic root," Douglass set off for Covey's farm. On arrival, he received a shock. Covey was downright *polite*. "Now," wrote Douglass in his first memoir, "this singular conduct of Mr. Covey really made me begin to think that there was something in the *root* which Sandy had given me." But then it struck him: it was *Sunday*; ever the upright Christian, even Covey took a day of rest. Come Monday, things darkened. "On this morning," Douglass continued, "the virtue of the *root* was fully tested." Covey grabbed Douglass in the barn, tied his legs with a rope, and prepared to beat him.

"Mr. Covey seemed now to think he had me, and could do what he pleased; but at this moment—from whence came the spirit I don't know—I resolved to fight." Here began the historic turnaround in Douglass's life: "I now resolved that, however long I might remain a slave in form, the day had passed forever when I could be a slave in fact."

Douglass was no believer in magic. But in both his earlier and later memoirs, he proved resolutely unwilling to slam shut the door on the matter or to qualify the veneration he felt for Sandy. "I saw in Sandy," he wrote in 1855, "too deep an insight into human nature, with all his superstition, not to have some respect for his advice; and perhaps, too, a slight gleam or shadow of his superstition had fallen upon me."

Sandy, the "clever soul," the "old adviser," and the "genuine African," provided a rare measure of counsel in brutal world. His authority was grounded in an occult tradition that no slaveholder could enter.

The "magic root" episode framed the inner revolution of Douglass's life. He knew that even though he was, for the time being, a slave in fact, he would never again be a slave in spirit. As he liberated himself in spirit, he determined to free himself physically at the first possible opportunity. In 1836, Frederick attempted to escape and was captured. Two years later, he made a second attempt and succeeded. He fled Baltimore to New York City and from New York to upstate New York, not far from the Burned-Over District. He became one of the critical voices of abolitionism in America and around the world.

In a sobering and sorrowful coda, Douglass noted in his latter two memoirs that Sandy Jenkins himself might have betrayed Douglass and his would-be escapees during his first attempt. He surmised in 1893:

> Several circumstances seemed to point Sandy out as our betrayer. His entire knowledge of our plans, his participation in them, his withdrawal from us, his dream [foreseeing the capture] and his simultaneous presentiment that we were betrayed, the taking us and the leaving him, were calculated to turn suspicion toward him, and yet we could not suspect him. We all loved him too well to think it possible that he could have betrayed us. So we rolled the guilt on other shoulders.

In a rare and valuable 1904 book, *Shakerism, Its Meaning and Message*, authors Anna White and Leila Sarah Taylor note a wave of spirit visits at the second Shaker Village at Mount Lebanon, New York: "In 1842, there came at Mount Lebanon, and then through the other societies, a strange epoch of visitation by representatives of all nationalities. Indians, Arabs, Ancient Jews, Chaldeans, Persians, Hindoos,—people of remote lands and ancient times, thronged to the City of Zion." About ten years later, "the spirit visitors announced to the people that they were about to leave them and go out into the world. They would visit every city and hamlet, every palace and cottage in the land."

Already in early 1848, some felt this prophecy coming to pass in a Burned-Over District village called Hydesville, outside Rochester. That winter, the log cabin of the Fox family was riddled with weird bangs, cracklings, and knocks. Two of the adolescent daughters of the household, Kate, eleven, and Margaret, fourteen, told their shocked Methodist parents that the noises were *spirit raps*. Moreover, the girls explained that through the rapping they had worked out a system of communication with the invisibles.

Various clergy, journalists, jurists, and scientists descended on the Fox family cabin to investigate Kate and Margaret. They included New York State Supreme Court Justice John W. Edmonds, abolitionist William Lloyd Garrison, and newspaper editor and publisher of the *New-York Tribune* Horace Greeley—all of whom validated the girls' claims. In 1850, Greeley hosted the Fox family at his New York City home. Later that year, the reformist editor installed the younger Kate to spend four months with his wife at the Greeleys' gloomy, rambling house in Chappaqua, New York, where the lonely and unhappy adolescent made nightly efforts to contact the couple's departed five-year-old son.*

So was born the age of Spiritualism or talking to the dead. Many Americans embraced the phenomena of midnight raps—they organized séance circles and Spiritualist clubs, eventually expanding into newspapers and a wide array of newsletters and journals. The movement's reigning dean and prophet emerged from the modest environs of Poughkeepsie, New York, in the Hudson Valley, southwest of the Burned-Over District. A young farmhand and cobbler's apprentice, Andrew Jackson Davis (1826–1910), at age seventeen, with the help of an itinerant Mesmerist, began entering trances from which he produced voluminous lectures on unseen dimensions and "Summerland," his term for the afterlife. Dubbed by the press the "Poughkeepsie Seer," Davis popularized the word séance, the same used by Franz Anton Mesmer. In Davis's 1851 book, *The Philosophy of Spiritual Intercourse*, the Poughkeepsie Seer taught Americans how to join hands around tables in kitchens and parlors to seek communication with the spirit world, just like Kate and Margaret.

---

* Not all newspapermen were as taken with the Fox sisters. Some of "the New York press accused the girls of 'jugglery' and 'fraud,' and declared all who believed them were idiots, lunatics, or knaves," wrote Ernest Isaacs in "The Fox Sisters and American Spiritualism," *The Occult in America* edited by Howard Kerr and Charles L. Crow (University of Illinois Press, 1983).

Davis's visions didn't impress everyone. Edgar Allan Poe, then a struggling journalist and short-story writer, sat in on some of the seer's New York trance sittings. Poe came to regard Davis with a mixture of intrigue and contempt. In 1849, Poe used one of his last short stories, *Mellonta Tauta* (Greek for "Things of the Future"), to poke fun of Davis by mangling his high-sounding name as "Martin Van Mavis (sometimes called the 'Tougkeepsie Seer')."*

At the same time, Poe contributed to the popularity of Mesmerism by using themes from Davis's trance sittings in one of his most popular stories, *The Facts in the Case of M. Valdemar.* It told of a Mesmerist who keeps an ill man from slipping into death by holding him in a magnetic trance. Poe completed the story in New York the year he met Davis. Never explicitly billed as fiction and written like a medical case study, the story was initially taken as literal reportage by some in the U.S. and Britain. The *Sunday Times of London* reprinted it without comment in January of 1846 under the banner "Mesmerism in America: Astounding and Horrifying Narrative."

Davis was not without significant defenders. Among them was a Rev. George Bush (1796–1859)—a first cousin, four and five times removed, to Presidents George H.W. and George W. Bush. Though long forgotten, the Rev. Bush was a respected religious scholar and speaker who shared podiums with Ralph Waldo Emerson. Bush stirred enormous controversy in 1845 when he left the Presbyterian pulpit to become a minister in the Church of the New Jerusalem, a congregation based on the mystical ideas of Swedish scientist Emanuel Swedenborg (1688–1772), more of whom is soon heard. Bush was one of the Swedenborgian faith's most prominent converts—and a stalwart defender of Davis.

"Indeed," the bible scholar wrote of Davis in 1857 in his book *Mesmer and Swedenborg*, "if he has acquired all the information he gives forth in these Lectures, not in the two years since he left the shoemaker's bench, but in his whole life, with the most assiduous study, no prodigy of intellect of which the world has ever heard would be for a moment compared with him."

---

* Poe's crack appears in an epigraph that is often omitted from anthologized versions of his story. Poe is referencing President Martin Van Buren, who in 1837 succeeded Davis's namesake, Andrew Jackson.

Given Spiritualism's nationwide range of clubs and publications—including a peak of sixty-seven newspapers—it is reasonable to estimate that the population ran into hundreds of thousands and, depending on how stringently one defines a follower, possibly a million or higher. In a nation that counted its overall population at thirty to thirty-five million in the mid-nineteenth century, it is likely that almost one in ten adults considered themselves believers, of one degree or another.

The numbers proved so large that, by the close of the 1850s, the Burned-Over District was eclipsed by the movement it spawned and no longer served as the engine of mystical religion in American life. Chicago, Boston, New York, Philadelphia, and many towns and cities had Spiritualist societies, newspapers, and congregations and soon produced innovations of their own. Spiritualism was not a regional sensation but a national movement.

Part of Spiritualism's appeal is that figures like Kate and Margaret Fox and Andrew Jackson Davis emerged from the ordinary environs of life. Kate and Margaret came from a poor farming family. Davis was a cobbler's trainee. And yet they claimed to have parted the veil, to have broken through to the other side, to have worked out systems of communication with the unseen world. This appealed to the do-it-yourself instincts of everyday people who felt enthralled with the possibility that not only was the age of biblical prophecy more than a bygone past, but it was available within the trappings of familiar life. To people who suffered the staggering losses of childhood diseases—in New York City in 1853, nearly half of all reported deaths were children under five—the prospect of communication came as a salve within the strict environs of Calvinist Protestantism.

The world witnessed a different expression of occultism taking shape in America. It did not rely on illumined teachers, secret societies, or esoteric studies. It involved a young slave receiving a magic root. A local treasure hunter heralding a new scripture. The Publick Universal Friend showing the face of a reanimated—and female—avatar. A migrant fleeing charges of witchcraft to launch a new movement. Teenage girls claiming to work out a code with the spirit world. A cobbler's apprentice entering psychical trances. To a significant extent, it was landless and working people seizing a greater life through their ability to claim compact with the unseen.

Spirit raps were soon heard at séance circles in the drawing rooms of Paris and London, where fashionable classes took a deep interest in things that went bump. Spiritualism, this movement that started in a log cabin, became, in effect, the nation's first religious export.

Meanwhile, as Americans organized séances and consorted with mediums, it grew apparent that most spirit mediums were women. With Spiritualism's development into a national movement with its own lecture clubs, newspapers, and eventually churches, there appeared, for the first time in modern life, a framework in which women could function as religious leaders, of a certain sort. Spiritualism, already developing a progressive politics, attracted a wide range of women who desired a voice in the civic culture.

In July 1848, about six months after Kate and Margaret Fox introduced the Rochester rappings, the gavel fell on the watershed Seneca Falls Convention for women's rights, about forty miles east of the Fox home down Route 20, the "psychic highway." Indeed, for about two generations in the nineteenth century, you could not find a suffragist activist who had not spent some time at the séance table or a séance habitue who was not active in or at least sympathetic toward suffragism. Insecure in her public speaking abilities, the usually skeptical Susan B. Anthony wrote to her colleague Elizabeth Cady Stanton in 1855, "If the spirits would only just make me a trance medium and put the right thing into my mouth. You can't think of how earnestly I have prayed to be made a speaking medium for a whole week."* In 1853, suffragist Mary Fenn Love convened the first New York State Women's Rights Convention. "Spiritualism has inaugurated the era of woman," she announced. Two years later, Mary married the movement's reigning prophet, Andrew Jackson Davis.**

Validating Fenn's declaration, Spiritualism provided a unique springboard for women to enter politics in an era before suffrage. On January 11, 1871, Congress hosted the first woman to address a joint

---

* *Radical Spirits* by Ann Braude (Indiana University Press, 1989, 2001). See Braude's pioneering history of Spiritualism and suffragism for this and the following quote.

** In 1885, after thirty years of marriage and public collaboration with Love, Davis divorced her, saying his spirit guardians told him that the couple's "'central temperaments' do not harmonize" (from Davis's 1885 memoir, *Beyond the Valley*). Davis remarried (his third time), and left Mary to raise four grandchildren placed in her care by her deceased daughter. Mary died of cancer the following year in West Orange, New Jersey.

committee. That winter day, free-love advocate—and avowed trance medium—Victoria Woodhull (1838–1927) took the floor. Poised and handsome, Woodhull delivered a rousing brief in defense of voting rights, known as The Woodhull Memorial. The medium, famous for her sittings with magnate Cornelius Vanderbilt, told journalists that the address was dictated to her in a dream by a ghostly, tunic-wearing Greek elder—a spirit guardian who guided her since she was little.

In 1872, the Equal Rights Party, a consortium of suffragists and abolitionists, named Woodhull the nation's first female presidential candidate. That year, the proto-feminist found herself mocked as "Mrs. Satan"—complete with reptilian wings—by cartoonist Thomas Nast in *Harper's Weekly* who depicted her holding a scroll reading, "Be Saved by Free Love."

Woodhull's protest campaign proved short-lived, eclipsed by her twin passions for publicity-mongering and political chicanery. The medium–activist selected Frederick Douglass as her running mate—but without asking him. "I never heard of this," the abolitionist hero said.* Days before the election, Woodhull, along with her sister and second husband, were arrested on trumped-up obscenity charges and held for a month, preventing her from attempting to vote.

* *Other Powers* by Barbara Goldsmith (Knopf, 1998).

CHAPTER FIVE

The Occult Revival, Part I

In the Age of Reason, one of the most powerful esoteric voices belonged to a scientist: Emanuel Swedenborg (1688–1772), a Swedish engineer, inventor, and mystic whose works were widely translated for the first time in the mid-1840s, including into English. Swedenborg's visions spoke to the modern yearning for connection to an invisible world, a perceived greater world whose forces and events function as antecedents to our own.

Beginning in 1749, Swedenborg wrote of entering into a kind of illumined trance and through out-of-body projection, traveling to other realms, dimensions, and planets. He explored these realizations over the course of dozens of books, articles, and lectures—teaching that everything experienced in your everyday world is mirrored by events, personas, and activities that occur in an invisible multidimensional world.

His works held the promise that thought itself is like a bidirectional, infinite ray of light into the unseen. Thought affects things not only in the world we occupy but also throughout infinite creation. Humanity did not yet possess the concept of a radio wave, which goes on forever. Swedenborg taught that thought itself does so. Moreover, the individual not only projects thoughts into the infinite but receives thoughts from the greater cosmic world. Such things enter your psyche based on your ethical and personal sympathies. In this way, the individual might experience psychical events and extraphysical communication. When you sleep, for example, and enter a state of reduced stimuli and alternative consciousness, you may experience receptivity. Your dreams, memories, emotions, appetites, morals, and attitudes, all of these things are not just locally produced phenomena arising from cognition and automatism, Swedenborg taught, but rather extend from an infinite cosmic network.

Although Swedenborg recorded his own flights to heavenly realms, he warned that spirit communications should never be attempted casually. The seer cautioned in his 1758 opus, *Heaven and Hell:*

> At the present day to talk with spirits is rarely granted because it is dangerous . . . evil spirits are such that they hold man in deadly hatred, and desire nothing so much as to destroy him both soul and body, and this they do in the case of those who have so indulged themselves in fantasies as to have separated from themselves the enjoyments proper to the natural man."*

Although Swedenborg discouraged most mediumistic phenomena, he spoke of a "Divine influx" that could permeate the individual and reorganize one's persona. It was generations later that American philosopher William James spoke of a "conversion experience" or what might be called an epiphany or moment of clarity. Contemporary people commonly talk of higher realization, illumination, vibrations, or frequencies. Swedenborg's *divine influx* came to define the individualistic esoteric spiritual ideals of the burgeoning industrial age: the principle that the individual could be penetrated by cosmic forces—or, as a psychological correlate, could experience profound self-knowing.

This idea gripped the religious (and even to a degree materialist) imagination. Vital forces, whether metaphysical or subconscious, could rework one's existence, went the popular hope; and these invisible forces are no less palpable than electricity, magnetism, gravity, and radio waves. In fact, from antiquity to modernity, invisible currents were posited before humanity understood these physicalist counterparts.

---

* Swedenborg wrote in Latin. This passage is from the 1900 translation by John C. Ager.

Contemporaneous to Swedenborg lived a figure we have briefly met—and whose impact was felt more directly: Swiss-Viennese occult healer Franz Anton Mesmer (1734–1815).

In 1778, Mesmer entered Paris with his own theory of vital, invisible forces. Mesmer contended that all life is animated by an etheric fluid, which he called *animal magnetism*. The theorist proved capable of placing individuals into suggestive "magnetic" trances. This is the practice redubbed "hypnotism" in the early 1840s by Scottish physician James Braid (1795–1860). In short, Mesmer theorized that physical or emotional disorders stem from an imbalance in animal magnetism. By placing the subject in a magnetic state, i.e., a Mesmeric or hypnotic trance, the operator or Mesmerist could manipulate and realign the patient's animal magnetism—and, hence, cure him of disease, discomfort, anxiety or melancholia. Some correspondents in letters and journals did describe cures this way.

As noted, some advocates of social reform in France took interest in Mesmerism. To these enthusiasts, the susceptibility of all people, from peasants to noblemen, to enter a Mesmeric trance validated the ideal of innate equality within human beings. Indeed, in pre-revolutionary France every advance in science or industry took on political overtones. To Mesmer's supporters, efforts to discredit Mesmerism amounted to the ploy of entrenched aristocratic interests, such as the French Academy of Sciences, to suppress a medical practice beyond its purview. A not dissimilar attitude prevails in some American environs today with regard to alternative healing.

Benjamin Franklin, who was then serving as America's ambassador to France, considered Mesmer a dangerous fraud and questioned whether sexual liberties were taken while subjects were entranced. In March 1784, King Louis XVI asked Franklin to chair a royal committee to investigate Mesmer's methods. The Franklin commission, composed of members of the French Academy of Sciences and the Paris Faculty of Medicine, conducted a series of trials to test the healer's theories.

Franklin's shaky health kept the elder statesman from witnessing most of the trials firsthand. And Mesmer himself departed Paris in the lead-up to the investigation. One of Mesmer's students, physician Charles d'Eslon, consented to work with the commission, though somewhat contentiously. In trials, the investigators discovered that magnetic treatments could move patients to convulsions, or Mesmer's "crises," and other kinds of violent bodily effects, from coughing blood, to temporarily losing the power of speech, to sensations of heat or cold, and, in a few limited cases, claims of comfort or cure.

The investigators noted that many patients, when blindfolded, could be induced to convulsions if they merely *thought* they were being subjected to Mesmeric methods. Hence, the panelists concluded in August 1784 that Mesmer's "cures" were all in the imagination, induced either by the charisma of the healer or the copycat effect of convulsions that occurred en masse in séances. In their report to the king, commission members wrote that their "decisive experiments" had proved "that the imagination alone produces all the effects attributed to magnetism; & when the imagination does not act, there are no more effects."

Left unaddressed was the question of *why* the subject's imagination should produce any results at all. Content to dispel notions of etheric magnetism, commission members left dangling what may have been their most significant observation. Regardless, the panel's conclusions irreversibly sullied Mesmer's reputation. He never again resided in Paris. Mesmer eventually returned to the German-speaking Swiss region where he was born and lived out a mostly quiet existence, corresponding with supporters and seeing patients until his death in 1815.

Mesmer's keenest students came to feel that perhaps the master was wrong about the existence of an invisible fluid, this etheric life force he called animal magnetism, but maybe what *was* happening when people entered deeply suggestive states, when their conscious thoughts and cognizance were stilled, was the revelation of a deeper, unknown territory of mind. D'Eslon, the late-eighteenth century Paris physician, wrote: "It may indeed be entirely imagination. And if it is? Then imagination is a force as potent as it is little understood. Let us work with this mysterious imagination, let us use it to cure, let us learn more about it."* Or, as it was put to Franklin's committee by a patient of Mesmer: "If it is to an illusion that I owe the health which I believe that I enjoy, I humbly beg the scholars who are seeing so clearly, not to destroy it; let them enlighten the universe, but let

* *Doctors of the Mind: The Story of Psychiatry* by Marie Beynon Ray (Little, Brown, 1942).

them leave me to my error; and let them allow to my simplicity, to my weakness, and to my ignorance, the use of an invisible force, which does not exist, but which heals me."*

Current concepts of the subconscious or unconscious mind did not exist throughout the eighteenth and even much of the nineteenth centuries. The notion of a subliminal, subconscious, or unconscious mind did not spread until the 1890s, thanks in part to the efforts of philosopher-scientists F.W.H. Myers and William James.

Prior generations shared no common idea that there exists a glacial mind below the surface of conscious life. And that this repository of unacknowledged memory, desire, and trauma is, perhaps, the secret engine driving events and relationships. Contemporary to Mesmer, the mind was seen as an instrument to calculate, analyze, enumerate, and communicate—but the notion that there existed a great undercurrent of thought of which we are largely unaware, and which harbors hidden assumptions, fears, and needs, and further that this mind is suggestible and manipulable, did not then exist, at least in any widespread manner. In effect, the search for vital energies, divine influx, and animal magnetism, was a reach to identify *some force* instinctively sensed in life but that moderns lacked the vocabulary to describe.

A bridge of sorts emerged in the work of Idealist philosopher Arthur Schopenhauer (1788–1860). In 1836, Schopenhauer produced one of his key works, *On Will in Nature*. In this book, which helped cement Schopenhauer's reputation as one of the most renowned philosophers of the age, the thinker buttressed and supported his earlier philosophical assertions about the role of mind and imagination in representing and shaping our experience of reality.

In *On Will and Nature*, Schopenhauer came as close as any modern figure to equating ancient magic and directed thought: "Man had not learnt to direct the *light of speculative thought* towards the mysterious depths of his own inner self." [emphasis added] And further, "those who are more deeply initiated into ancient Magic, derive all its

* "Mesmerism and Revolutionary America" by Helmut Hirsch, *American-German Review*, October 1943.

effects from the magician's *will* alone." [emphasis in original] "The Metaphysical in general, that which alone exists apart from representation, the thing-in-itself of the universe is nothing but what is known to us within ourselves as the *will*." [emphasis in original] He quoted German mystic Jakob Böhme (1574–1624): "Magic is action in the *will's spirit*." [emphasis in original] And finally he noted, "The zealous cruelty with which Magic has always been persecuted by the Church and to which the papal malleus maleficarum bears terrible evidence, seems not to have for its sole basis the criminal purposes often associated with the practice of Magic or the part assumed to be played by the Devil, but rather to proceed partly from a vague foreboding and fear lest Magic should trace back its original power to its true source . . ." [i.e., will].*

Schopenhauer called this source "the light of speculative thought." The reader was encouraged to cultivate realization of how deeply this *light of speculative thought* could define his experience of self and world, not only in image but in fact.

Hence, many searching moderns embraced the idea that there exists an unknown life force. It was insufficient to call it merely soul or spirit. That was too vague, pedantic, and ill-defined. Some edged toward the concept of an unseen mind, whether biologic, metaphysical, or perhaps both, for which the individual functioned as an outlet and medium of projection; not just as a branch sprouting from a tree but a receptive organ with powers of its own.

A similar passion animated a thirty-one-year-old Ralph Waldo Emerson. He wrote in his journals of December 8, 1834:

> Why not strengthen the hearts of the waiting lovers of the primal philosophy by an account of that fragmentary highest teaching that comes from the half fabulous Heraclitus, Hermes Trismegistus, and Giordano Bruno, and Vyasa, and Plotinus, and Swedenborg.

* 1903 translation by Jessie Hillebrand aka Madame Karl Hillebrand (1827–1905). In citing the *Malleus Maleficarum* (Latin for "Hammer of Witches"), Schopenhauer references one of the most feared and reviled works of the Inquisition. Written by German Catholic clergyman Heinrich Kramer in 1486, the *Malleus* instructs how to identify and try suspected witches, including use of torture and deception to win confessions, as well penalties of death, such as burning at the stake.

> Curious, now that first I collect their names, they should look all so mythological.

The artistic school called Romanticism responded to this hunger. Romanticism was an outlook in painting, drama, poetry, and storytelling that sought to reconnect the individual to the mythical—to remythologize existence, to compare the individual to the heroes who populated parabolic myths of antiquity, not just in strictly metaphorical fashion but in a manner that reclaimed the "something missing" in self since the disappearance of primeval, nature-based, and esoteric spirituality. The term occult had, for the time being, fallen from favor; but the Romantics breathed new life into it, at least conceptually.

The Romantics found inspiration in figures including Schopenhauer, poet-mystic William Blake (1757–1827), and literary force John Milton (1608–1674). This was especially so with Milton's 1667 epic *Paradise Lost* in which Satan, in its two opening chapters, is reimagined as a great rebel, icon of defiance, usurper, and revolutionary. Milton's Satan is, in a sense, a protean being—not just a branch or object but one who seeks self-creation and mutability. Milton presented the Dark Lord, unbowed following his defeat and ejection from heaven, as a fiery optimist: "The mind is its own place, and in it self/ Can make a Heav'n of Hell, a Hell of Heav'n." Satan's collaborators mirror his formidability. The demon Mammon at one point declares, "Hard liberty before the easy yoke."

A distant echo of Hermeticism sounds in their dialogue. The vanquished angels yearn for reclamation of birthright to create, produce, be causative rather than caused, subject rather than object. In some of the most famous lines of Western literature, Milton's Satan says, "Here we may reign secure, and in my choice/ To reign is worth ambition though in Hell:/ Better to reign in Hell, then serve in Heav'n."

In actuality, the precursor to Milton's famous lines may be Julius Caesar (100–44 B.C.), at least as posthumously recorded by historian Plutarch (c. 46–119 A.D.):

> We are told that, as he was crossing the Alps and passing by a barbarian village which had very few inhabitants and was a sorry sight,

> his companions asked with mirth and laughter, "Can it be that here too there are ambitious strifes for office, struggles for primacy, and mutual jealousies of powerful men?" Whereupon Caesar said to them in all seriousness, "I would rather be first here than second at Rome."*

As noted, Goethe, writing from 1772 to 1775, produced a vivifying version of the Faust myth, exploring the sorcerer who makes a bargain with Mephistopheles, with neither quite getting the better of the other. In 1789, Goethe wrote a poem "Prometheus" in which he celebrated the ancient Titan of myth who stole fire from the gods and brought it to humanity, allowing them to cook, practice metallurgy, forge jewelry—and weapons. Creativity and friction go hand in hand.

The Romantic imagination took new interest in Prometheus who defied the gods. Was this mythically the same force that encouraged Eve, primeval woman, to eat from the Tree of Knowledge of Good and Evil? In that sense, the parabolic snake is not corrupter but emancipator; proto-feminists, including Mary Wollstonecraft Shelley (1797–1851), were fascinated with this image and the possibility that the Satanic or Promethean figure could be seen no longer as a being of maleficence but rather could be read according to a counter-narrative in which this force *emancipated*. Albeit, sometimes with tragic results. Wollstonecraft Shelley subtitled her 1818 *Frankenstein*, "The Modern Prometheus." Her heterodox hero Victor wanders into a library containing books of occultism: "In this house I chanced to find a volume of the works of Cornelius Agrippa. I opened it with apathy; the theory which he attempts to demonstrate, and the wonderful facts which he relates, soon changed this feeling into enthusiasm. A new light seemed to dawn upon my mind; and, bounding with joy, I communicated my discovery . . ."

We're apt to view Frankenstein, not wrongly, as a deeply tragic tale. It is also a story of heroic creation gone awry, a mythos found in the tale of the Golem in which, in varying permutations, rabbis create a being from clay who protects them but eventually turns against them. For those with ambition, the Kabbalistic *Sefer Yetzirah* contains elliptical instructions on how to animate a golem; the explanatory

* *Plutarch Lives*, Vol. VII, Loeb Classical Library, translated by Bernadotte Perrin (Harvard University Press, 1919).

commentary is complex, probably purposefully obfuscatory, and the operation requires two to three Jewish scholars—it is forbidden to attempt it alone, a warning that eluded Victor.

In any case, the Romantic *Frankenstein* is no simple narrative of human hubris, of the wish to create gone mad, a la Marlowe's *Faust*; it is likewise a tale of the innate imperative of creating and its intrinsic danger because, again, friction and creativity, life and destruction, possibility and risk, knowledge of good and evil, are innate to being human, if we deserve the title.

William Blake, the central literary figure of the Romantic movement, in 1790 wrote his enduring work *The Marriage of Heaven and Hell* in which he contended that life is one whole and that we cannot sustain neat divisions between "above" and "below." For Blake, the principles of heaven and the "Proverbs of Hell" are necessarily complementary. He wrote, "One Law for the Lion & Ox is Oppression." And further, "Opposition is true Friendship." Blake's entry into the Western literary and ethical mind left a profound impact on the rising generation of Romantics, including Lord Byron (1788–1824), who sharpened the image of Lucifer as a misunderstood radical.

In perhaps the most alluring and underappreciated work of "Romantic Satanism," Lord Byron used his 1821 drama *Cain* to retell the Genesis narrative from Cain's point of view, audaciously asserting the that scorned brother had a legitimate perspective. Lord Byron depicts Cain as an inspired malcontent who refused religious conformity, who did not wish to render sacrifices to what he saw as a questionable and jealous God (a view at home in Gnosticism), and who rejected scripted piety.

Reacting from anger, Cain committed a tragic act of fratricide, for which he suffered the rest of his life. But, again, he was not without a point of view, a theme Lord Byron beautifully and outrageously pursued. In so doing, the poet drew calumny from critics and defenders of probity. Perhaps speaking to himself, Lord Byron in this "closet drama" depicts dialogues between Cain and Lucifer in which the latter tells the son: "I know the thoughts/ Of dust, and feel for it, and with you."

In this literary revolution appeared the principle that life proves unsusceptible to simplistic doctrine; but rather the individual possesses capacity for, and right to, measurement, evaluation, creation—and destruction. Humans are not kept beings in a primeval aquarium but are gods in potential, as told in Hermeticism.

Nowadays, we love the rebel, or profess to. We're enthralled with screen depictions of Loki, Darth Vader, and Maleficent. These archetypes appear in hip hop, punk, and in personas like Marlon Brando, Elvis Presley, and James Dean. But the rebel ideal didn't fully exist in the modern Western mindset until the Romantics stoked notions of anti-heroism, usurpation, and nonconformity. They did so against the backdrop of Schopenhauer, Swedenborg, and Mesmer, all reasoning that there exist vital forces for the individual to use in acts of Promethean alchemy to establish self in the world.

The primeval world and its secrets cracked a bit more open in 1799. It was through a discovery in Egypt made by the teams of artists, draftsmen, historians, stenographers, and archeologists that Napoleon Bonaparte brought with him on his ill-faded invasion of the Black Land. The emperor's incursion ran from 1798 to 1801. Following a string of decisive victories over Egypt's Mamluk armies, Napoleon suffered defeat by British armed and naval forces, one of his few invasive failures. He also marched armies into Syria, with similar results. But through his misadventure, Napoleon, ironically, instigated the modern field of Egyptology.

Some of the invader's artisans and scholars discovered what came to be called the Rosetta Stone. It was an ancient handwritten carving in black granite-like stone, standing about three-and-a-half feet high. Produced in 196 B.C., the stele featured a decree heralding the reign of Ptolemy V (210–180 B.C.), among the last of the Ptolemaic line. The tribute is carved triply in traditional hieroglyphs; Demotic, a phoneticized variant of hieroglyphs used for official business; and Greek, language of the ruling class. Suddenly the mysteries of the ancient hieroglyphs, previously indecipherable to moderns, were opening.

New passion arose to understand the primeval world, not just through Hermetic literature, but through the symbolic-phonetic tongue of Ancient Egypt.* Like the tripartite Rosetta Stone, all of the developments explored to this point intermingled: hunger to discover

* Classical Mayan civilization, which existed contemporaneously to latter Egyptian antiquity, was not rediscovered by the Modern West until about a generation later when in 1839 American explorer John Lloyd Stephens and English draftsman Frederick Catherwood explored overgrown Central American ruins that had survived Spanish conquest.

vital forces; romanticization of antiquity; and the wish to reclaim mythical or magical insight.

Among the areas where this remythologizing played out, albeit fancifully, was the deck of onetime playing cards, possessed of archetypal and intriguing images, called Tarot. Tarot has two parts to its history. One is inception and one is reintroduction as an occult tool. There exists a modicum of continuity between the two but it is vital to understand the difference in these conceptions.

The first Tarot decks, not yet bearing that name, emerged in Northern Italy in the early 1400s. That is the first physical, empirical existence of Tarot that we possess. It is also important to note that paper was not in general circulation until post-antiquity. Paper was invented in China and did not enter European use until about 1150 A.D. Hence, the medium of cards appeared on the European scene in the early medieval period. The first Tarot cards were called *carte de trionfi*, or cards of triumph or trump cards. The deck was often called *Tarocchi* in the early 1500s. Around 1530, the center of production shifted away from Northern Italy to Marseilles, France. Late in the century, the French term *Tarot* gained prominence. We possess variants of the Marseilles Tarot today.

The images of Tarot—the pope, priestess, death, lovers, the juggler, the tower—had some continuity with the archetypes of Hermeticism but visibly emerged from passion plays, carnivals, and stained glass of the early medieval period. That said, Tarot possesses alluring images. The visuals themselves convey allegorical meaning—they are recognizable in almost any culture. I venture that you could go almost anywhere in the world, at almost any time, show people the cards for the lovers or emperor or devil, and you would likely find some common conception of meaning. But equally important to understand historically, is that Tarot at its inception was not used for divination—that usage did not develop until more than three centuries later.

Rather, Tarot began as a household game. It was a precursor to our modern bridge. In some parts of the world, including France and Italy, it is still played as a game. Yet to say it was a *game* doesn't quite get at the depths of what that concept meant in the Renaissance period. In 1616, late-Renaissance alchemist Michael Maier (1568–1622) published an allegorical work called *Lusus Serius*, Latin for a "serious game." The concept connotes the creativity and profundity that arises from playfulness. We speak of "playing" an instrument but that doesn't mean musicianship is frivolous. We refer to a drama as a "play." That does not reference a minor charade. Something deeper is at work. People possessed few domestic objects in the medieval and Renaissance period; hence, everything was imbued with significance. To term something a "game" does not debase it; any more than to speak of a "passion play," which is to say a medieval or Renaissance-era religious drama, means an ordinary entertainment. Even a household object with obvious utility was, at least for the wealthy, decorative, purposefully designed, and valued—not frivolous or disposable.

The oldest near-complete Tarot deck we possess today dates to the mid-1400s. It is called the Sforza-Visconti deck, named for the aristocratic Milanese family that commissioned it. There are about fifteen surviving copies of the Sforza-Visconti Tarot in various degrees of completion around the world. The fullest version known contains 74 of 78 cards and is housed in the Pierpont Morgan Museum and Library in New York City.

It should be noted that various playing decks were, at times, also used for divinatory purposes; so, it cannot be ruled out that Tarot was likewise used privately in this manner. But the explicitly occult conception of Tarot emerged in 1781. That year marked publication of the eighth volume in a nine-part series of books produced by speculative historian, Freemason, and French nobleman Antoine Court de Gébelin (c. 1725–1784).

In 1773, Court de Gébelin began issuing his nine-volume series called *Le Monde Primitif* or "The Primeval World." In volume eight of his 1781 edition of *Le Monde Primitif*, Court de Gébelin deemed Tarot an arcane work of wisdom emanating from Ancient Egypt. Court de Gébelin believed, as many Renaissance philosophers did, in the existence of the *prisca theologia*. He identified its source as Egypt, which was probably right in broadest strokes. Yet he also identified Tarot, romantically and fancifully, as a book of high secrets, key to the mysteries, and encrypted guide to esoteric philosophies. For this he had no sources beyond his keen and idealistic imagination. "It would not be an exaggeration," writes scholar of esotericism Donald Tyson," to say that the occult Tarot owes everything to France, and that it originated from the pen of a single man, Antoine Court de Gébelin."*

* *Essential Tarot Writings* edited and annotated by Donald Tyson (Llewellyn, 2020). Tyson has performed the important service of publishing his complete English translations of the Court de Gébelin and Comte de Mellet essays—a remarkably neglected task until his effort.

Court de Gébelin explained his epiphanic knowledge arriving one day when he witnessed a French-Swiss noblewoman and friends "playing the game of Tarots." He fatefully gazed upon the World card:

> I there cast my eyes, and at once I recognize the allegory: everyone leaves off their game and comes to see this marvelous card in which I apprehend what they have never perceived: each one asks me to expound another of the cards: in one quarter of an hour the cards were comprehended, explained, declared Egyptian: and since it was not the play of our imagination, but the effect of the deliberate and significant connection of this game with all that is known of Egyptian ideas, we promised ourselves to share the knowledge some day with the public . . .

It is notable, apropos of earlier consideration, that the author continues to call Tarot a "game" throughout his essay.

Court de Gébelin invited a co-author, the Comte de Mellet, to contribute a short essay on Tarot. This essay, Tyson reckons, may have predated and influenced Court de Gébelin's effort. In homage to Hermeticism, Comte de Mellet, calls Tarot the "Book of Thoth," pairing it to divinatory meanings and instructions for a spread. Comte de Mellet also made the first connections between Tarot and the Hebrew alphabet. The writer associated the 22 trumps with the commensurate number of Hebrew characters, a previously unknown device. Hence, in 1781 *Le Monde Primitif* inaugurated explicit interpretation of Tarot as an Egyptian-derived book of secrets and allegorical key to the seen and unseen worlds. For occultism, the moment cannot be underestimated.

Another Frenchman adopted and expanded this innovation: Jean-Baptiste Alliette (1738–1791), an occultist who used for his *nom de plume* the reverse spelling of his surname: *Etteilla*. An aficionado of Christian Kabbalah, the cartomancer elected to read his name from right to left, in the style of the Hebrew alphabet. In 1789, Etteilla produced the *Grand Etteilla Tarot*. It was the first Tarot deck explicitly designed for divination. Westerners now encountered the rebirth and remaking of Tarot as an occult device connected to Ancient Egypt and Kabbalah, associations that got ramped up in future years.

With the advent of the *Grand Etteilla Tarot*, querents experienced a deck more fully illustrated, vivid, and dramatic, laced with early Romantic and anglicized Egyptian imagery. Older decks from Marseilles and Northern Italy tended toward sparser illustrations. Indeed, beyond the 22 trumps, the suit cards or minor keys, which included variations of staffs (wands), coins (pentacles), cups, and swords, were mostly utilitarian in style. The late-fifteenth century Sola Busca deck was more fully and alluringly (even hauntingly) illustrated; but the popular Marseilles decks tended to be more ascetic.

Seekers wouldn't start to encounter richly illustrated decks until the late-nineteenth and early twentieth centuries, culminating in the ur-deck designed by English artist Pamela Colman Smith (1878–1951) and Brooklyn-born British occultist Arthur Edward Waite (1857–1942), issued in late 1909. I return to this development because it is key to Tarot's growth as a popular tool.

Understanding occult history requires accepting history as it really existed not as I might want it to romantically exist. That does not imply that novelty is wrong. Nor does it mean that because an idea is old and widely repeated it is necessarily true—or because an idea is new, novel, or reformed it is necessarily trifling. Religion has always been combinative and syncretic. Religion is drawn from a great variety of sources and ideas, which are shaped and reshaped across centuries. Very often meaning is found by reading new stories into an object, idea, or practice—or reviving a theme or idea that has perhaps reached us in fragmentary ways. New forms are not illegitimate expressions. But it behooves us to understand their lineage.

For example, Pope John Paul II (1920–2005) canonized 482 saints, far more than his modern predecessors combined, who canonized about 300 saints in the previous *six centuries*.* John Paul viewed saint veneration as a practice that would draw people closer to Catholicism. That is a legitimate point of view. The process of opening new doorways and possibilities, fostering new definitions, and venturing new uses is always aided by reworking prior ideas or using them in fresh ways. Hence, I encourage people to find *balance* in these histories. To get at the essence of something, it is vital that we not excessively project backward our own ideals, wishes, and preconceptions; just as we must not decry or invalidate novelty and adaptation.

* Sainthood is not a merely declarative process. It entails four steps: 1) candidate is named Servant of God, 2) candidate is named Venerable, 3) candidate is deemed Blessed or beatified (requires 1st verified miracle), and 4) candidate is Canonized (requires 2nd verified miracle).

In that vein, we encounter a figure of extraordinary intellectual vigor and contradiction. Through his efforts, occultism found new life and expression, which reverberate to the present. He was a French ex-seminarian, political reformer twice jailed for this beliefs in "neo-Catholic communism," and self-taught occultist born Alphonse-Louis Constant. He became known throughout modern life as Eliphas Lévi (1810–1875).

Constant was a deep aficionado of Christian Kabbalah. He adopted the name *Eliphas Lévi Zahed* in a manner that he believed phonetically reproduced his given name in Hebrew. Lévi entered seminary as a young man, discovered quickly that the priesthood was not for him—his mystical, sexual, and social impulses proved too independent—and he morphed into an early Christian socialist. In 1841, Lévi published *La Bible de la liberté* ("The Bible of Liberty"), which the government seized upon its publication in August. Convicted on charges of insurrection, Lévi languished eight months in prison.* The one consolation of brutal Parisian prison conditions was Lévi's discovery of the work of Swedenborg. Even during his later magical phase, the seeker-radical suffered another six-month prison sentence in 1855 for opposition to Napoleon III.

Lévi was a perpetually struggling outsider. He chaffed against the doctrinal limits and vows of celibacy required for the priesthood. He proved willing to sacrifice his freedom for his political views. He found satisfaction on neither path. He was casting about for an *idea*. From where did power arise? Where is meaning vested?

It struck Lévi that the crisscrossing currents of his era—revival of ancient ideas, or in some cases, dramatization and recreation of antique doctrine; the search for hidden forces; the burning for personal liberty—could be unified into one whole. Lévi, the radical, Kabbalist, and ex-seminarian, found his answer in a reintroduction of ceremonial, practical magic into modern life. American contemporary Edgar Allan Poe could have been describing Lévi when he grumbled in his 1849 collection of aphorisms "Fifty Suggestions": "The world is infested, just now, by a new sect of philosophers, who have not yet suspected themselves of forming a sect, and who, consequently, have adopted no name. They are *the Believers in Everything Old*."

* Conflicting accounts record Lévi's sentence as either eight or eleven months; the discrepancy may be due to a conflation of his sentence with the three months that his publisher, Auguste Le Gallois, was also jailed. Both men were also fined 300 Francs each.

From within the old, Lévi found the new. Under his reformed name (which also helped distance him from his political activities), he announced in 1854,

> Beyond the veil of all hieratic and mystical allegories of the ancient doctrines, beyond the shadows and strange rituals of all initiations, under the seal of all sacred writings, in the ruins of Nineveh and Thebes, on the eroded stones of the ancient temples and upon the darkened sides of the sphinxes of Assyria or of Egypt, in the marvelous or monstrous paintings which express the sacred pages of the Vedas for Indian believers, in the strange symbols in our books on alchemy, in the initiatory ceremonies practiced by all mystery cults, we find the traces of a doctrine which is the same everywhere and everywhere is carefully hidden. Occult philosophy seems to have been the wet nurse or the godmother for all religions, the secret lever of all intellectual powers, the key to all divine enigmas, and the absolute queen of society in the eras in which it was reserved exclusively for the education of priests and kings.*

It formed the beginning of *The Doctrine of High Magic*. In 1855, Lévi wrote a sequel, *The Ritual of High Magic*. The following year, 1856, Lévi combined them for a landmark volume called *The Doctrine and Ritual of High Magic*. Lévi's *Doctrine and Ritual of High Magic* became the founding document for an occult revival. It was the equivalent of a modern occult codex handed down on a rediscovered Sinai. In short, *The Doctrine and Ritual of High Magic* reintroduced and remythologized occultism as a practical path.

Lévi adopted Court de Gébelin's thesis and deemed Tarot an allegorical key to the mysteries, a book of wisdom concealing humanity's inner truths. "The Tarot, that miraculous book," he wrote, "the inspiration for all the sacred books of the ancient peoples, is, because of the analogical precision of its figures and its numbers, the most perfect instrument for divination, which can be used with complete confidence." Taking a further leaf from Comte de Mellet, Lévi drew detailed correlations between Tarot and Kabbalah. He correlated the

---

* Lévi is quoted from *The Doctrine and Ritual of High Magic* translated by John Michael Greer and Anthony Mikituk (TarcherPerigee, 2017), which I published. It is an authoritative and now flagship translation that presents the first full English rendering of Lévi's work since Arthur Edward Waite's 1896 *Transcendental Magic*.

major trumps and suits to the Sefirot, the 10 forces of life in Kabbalah. He further matched the 22 characters of the Hebrew alphabet to the 22 major trumps and synced elements, numbers, and zodiac signs to the trumps and suits.

It was Eliphas Lévi, finally, who cemented the perceived connection between Tarot and Kabbalah. This included his connection between the trumps and the 22 paths of the "Tree of Life," an illustration of Kabbalistic cosmology. The earliest widely acknowledged illustration of the Tree of Life first appeared in philosopher and German-Jewish Catholic convert Paolo Riccio's 1516 Latin translation of Rabbi Joseph ben Abraham Gikatilla's (1248–c.1305) Kabbalistic study, *Sha'are Orah* or *Gates of Light*, written about 1290 in Spain, although the Tree's design has been traced back to Johann Reuchlin who had been in contact with Riccio's son. Several variations of the Tree of Life illustration followed.

Lévi's most lasting interpretation was correlation of the trumps to the 22 letters of the Hebrew alphabet, Aleph, Beis (Beit), Gimel, and so on. Classically, each Hebrew character corresponds to a numeral in the Hebraic system of numerology called *gematria*.* Likewise, he devised connections to the zodiac and matched the suits to the classical elements (fire, water, air, earth), alchemical essences (sulfur, mercury, salt, azoth—the last considered an "animating spirit"), and the four characters of the Hebrew Tetragrammaton, *Yod Hey Vav Hey*, the unpronounceable name of God. Lévi's admirer Gérard Encausse (1865–1916), or Papus, furthered this practice in his sometimes dense and confounding 1889 *Tarot of the Bohemians.*

Hence, in Levi's interpretation, an alchemical key runs through the Tarot-Kabbalah correlation. It is not always clear what Levi's sources were. To allay any confusion, I must note that there is no reference, directly or indirectly, to Tarot in traditional Kabbalah. Everything that appears in Kabbalistic texts predated Tarot by centuries.** In

* The Golden Dawn later modified Lévi's ordering, moving the Fool from the penultimate position, associated with *shin*, the twenty-first letter of the Hebrew alphabet, to first place, *aleph*, which in *gematria* is one but counted as zero by the Golden Dawn. Admittedly, these correspondences are confusing: although each system has its own internal logic, there also exist loose ends and sui generis judgments.

** In a rhetorical bow to this fact, modern occultists sometimes use the terms *Hermetic Qabalah*, *English Qabalah*, or, more commonly, just *Qabalah*, a disambiguation that began in the late nineteenth and early twentieth centuries. A series of "English Cabala" correspondences appeared in Willis F. Whitehead's 1899 *The Mystic Thesaurus*. Conceptually, though without the alternate spelling, this adapted system was referenced in Aleister Crowley's 1904 *The Book* his 1946 *Major Trends In Jewish Mysticism*—a book that reignited the study of classical Kabbalah in the twentieth century—German Israeli historian and philosopher Gershom Scholem (1897–1982) referred to "the brilliant misunderstandings and misinterpretations of Alphonse-Louis Constant, who has won fame under the pseudonym Eliphas Lévi, to the highly colored humbug of Aleister Crowley, and his followers . . ."

Scholem's critique should not be read as a blanket dismissal. The scholar also took to task contemporaneous Jewish religious authorities for neglecting study and texts of Kabbalah; he recognized occultists for at least sustaining their visibility. Scholem noted ruefully:

> It is not to the credit of Jewish scholarship that the works of the few writers who were really informed on the subject were never printed, and in some cases were not even recorded, since there was nobody to take an interest. Nor have we reason to be proud of the fact that the greater part of the ideas and views which show a real insight into the world of Kabbalism, closed as it was to the rationalism prevailing in the Judaism of the nineteenth century, were expressed by Christian scholars of a mystical bent, such as the Englishman Arthur Edward Waite of our days and the German Franz Josef Molitor a century ago. It is a pity that the fine philosophical intuition and natural grasp of such students lost their edge because they lacked all critical sense as to historical and philological data in this field, and therefore failed completely when they had to handle problems bearing on the facts.

To many seekers, Tarot-Kabbalah correspondences are sacrosanct. But this model was, in fact, an interpretation and innovation devised largely by Lévi. That does not mean it is intellectually dismissible. Familiarity is not truth; novelty is not falsehood. Many people detect meaning in that system. But it behooves us to know its background and vintage.

---

of the Law: "Thou shalt obtain the order & value of the English Alphabet; thou shalt find new symbols to attribute them unto." The first work to popularize the spelling Qabalah seems to have been 1912's *The Kabbalah Unveiled* by S.L. MacGregor Mathers (1854–1918), a British occultist who cofounded the Hermetic Order of the Golden Dawn c. 1888. "The term 'Unwritten Qabalah,'" Mathers wrote in a typically cryptic passage, "is applied to certain knowledge which is never entrusted to writing, but communicated orally. I may say no more on this point, not even whether I myself have or have not received it."

Pursuant to that, I recommend a 2005 book *The Tarot* by Robert M. Place. An artist and interpreter of Tarot, Place laid out both mystical and historically accurate dimensions of Tarot. For historiography, the vital sources are *A Wicked Pack of Cards: Origins of the Occult Tarot* by Ronald Decker, Thierry Depaulis, Michael Dummett (Duckworth, 1996) and *A History of the Occult Tarot, 1870–1970* by Ronald Decker and Michael Dummett (Duckworth, 2002). Artist Place wisely cautioned that if one gets excessively concerned with memorizing, charting out, and configuring all the correlations in the systems of Lévi and magical orders such as the Golden Dawn, which is later encountered, it can form a closed-circuit that distracts from the deck's allegorical symbolism, which is the basis of its fascination. That said, these are individual choices. Lévi was an extraordinary and original interpreter. I simply believe that we should understand the foundations we stand on. In that vein, the Kabbalist should know something about Hebrew, the astrologer something about astronomy, and the Tarotist its authentic history. Understanding lineage does not demythologize or detract from meaning but expands it.

In addition to Tarot, Lévi brought new life and exposed the general culture to arcane or esoteric symbols including the pentagram; the six-pointed Star of David; the Tetragrammaton or four-lettered name of God: Yod-Hey-Vav-Hey, יהוה; and the goat-headed god referenced as Baphomet, the deity with whom the Templars were (probably spuriously) accused of consorting.

An alluring and now-immortal illustration of this cross-legged, goat-headed hermaphrodite—which Lévi alternately called the Goat of Mendes for Banebdjedet, deity of the Egyptian ceremonial city; the Sabbatic Goat (or "goat of the Sabbath"); and, finally, Baphomet—serves as the frontispiece of part two of *The Doctrine and Ritual of High Magic*. Lévi's hand-drawn figure, so widely familiar and readapted, extends its right arm above and left arm below; the forearms bear the alchemical terms *solve* and *coagula*, Latin for *dissolve* and *conjoin* or *solve et coagula*. Lévi was expressing the principle of balance: life is not divided among higher/ lower, heaven/ hell, inner/ outer—it is a whole. The "Great Work," or *Magnum Opus* in alchemy, is to unify and occupy that paradox.

Since the image of Baphomet and ceremonial goats are bound up with the modern occult, I want to venture some historical background. In book II of his *Histories*, Herodotus (c. 484–425 B.C.) wrote about his encounters in Mendes:

> This is the reason why the Egyptians of whom I have spoken sacrifice no goats, male or female: the Mendesians reckon Pan among the eight gods, who, they say, were before the twelve gods. Now in their painting and sculpture the image of Pan is made as among the Greeks with the head and the legs of a goat; not that he is deemed to be in truth such, or unlike to other gods; but why they so present him I have no wish to say. The Mendesians hold all goats sacred, the male even more than the female, and goatherds are held in especial honour: one he-goat is most sacred of all; when he dies it is ordained that there should be great mourning in all the Mendesian province. In the Egyptian language Mendes is the name both for the he-goat and for Pan. In my lifetime a monstrous thing happened in this province, a woman having open intercourse with a he-goat. This came to be publicly known.*

Since the Middle Ages, goats were associated with the so-called witches' sabbath, probably originating with the ceremonial goats of the Canaanites and Egyptians, as just explored. In any case, a revival of interest in Baphomet was already underway in France before Lévi, due to Napoleon's invasion of Egypt and ensuing fascination with Eastern mysteries.

Among Lévi's core insights was "astral light" as the vital energy behind magical operations. Lévi theorized "astral light" as the core of magic and key to the Great Work. This comports with contemporaneous references to invisible or vital forces such as Edward Bulwer-Lytton's (1803–1873) "Vril" in his 1871 novel, *Vril, The Power of the Coming Race*. And, more significantly, Arthur Schopenhauer's view of imagination: "Man had not learnt to direct the *light of speculative thought* towards the mysterious depths of his own inner self." [emphasis added] And, eventually, Aleister Crowley

* Translated by A.D. Godley, Loeb Classical Library, 1920.

(1875–1947): "Magick is the Science and Art of causing Change to occur in conformity with Will."*

In his reference to "astral light," Lévi was echoing but not exactly copying Schopenhauer's "light of speculative thought." The occultist *metaphorically named* directed thought—and yet it was not wholly metaphorical if one thinks of the neurological pathways through which electrical impulses travel in the brain. It was a dramatized articulation of a force that humanity had not yet come to understand: inner workings of mind and existence of a glacial subconscious or subliminal mind.

In ways both profoundly affecting and dynamic, Lévi interpreted this astral light as inner will. Magical operations were a means of arousing and enlisting this inner force, which Levi also compared to the "serpent of Genesis." Such a force, he further wrote, could be raised through the sexual urge and directed via *focused imagination.* This force could be termed *emotionalized thought, sexually charged thought, willpower,* or all these. Lévi believed that the ancient symbols—Tarot (in his reading), alchemical sigils, the pentagram, the serpent, Baphomet, the parabolic myths and ancient fables—were at once reflections of and methods toward arousing awareness and use of this elemental force: *sexuality-thought-will*, symbolized by the serpent and united toward one goal.

Aleister Crowley's later definition of ceremonial magick as *Will projected* was pioneered by Lévi. Lévi, in his way, also gave new voice to what Mesmer was reaching for, as well Schopenhauer's description, and what the Romantics alluded to literarily. The exercise of causative, extraphysical *thought force* could be aroused through desire, want, need, focus, symbol, and sexuality. This, finally, was the ancient and elusive *Philosopher's Stone.* This was the alchemical key. The *Open Sesame.* The means of enacting the *Great Work.*

"Prime matter had no 'pattern,'" wrote Andrew Ede and Lesley B. Cormack in *A History of Science in Society*:

* Crowley is quoted from his 1929 *Magick In Theory and Practice.* Spelling "magick" with a "k," as I often do in this book, is derived from early modern English and was popularized by Crowley to distinguish ceremonial magick from stage magic, a usage I abide.

> so the alchemists thought it could be made to take on the pattern of terrestrial matter. The key to this transmutation process was often thought to be a kind of catalyst. This agent was known by a number of names, but the most common was the 'philosopher's stone,' which was mentioned as early as 300 CE in the alchemical collection *Cheirokmeta* attributed to Zosimos.* Whether the philosopher's stone was an actual object, the product of alchemical processes, or a spiritual state depended on the theory of the alchemist.

In an empowering innovation, Levi explained how this *élan vital*, this vital force, for which the era had been searching, dwells within the individual where it can be aroused by desire, symbol, ceremony, image, and allegory. Power is retained by reserve and focus; it is diluted by excess and dispersal. Hence, Lévi gave the dawning magical culture its motto:

> One must KNOW in order to DARE.
> One must DARE in order to WILL.
> One must WILL to have the Empire.
> And to reign, one must BE SILENT.

Offshoots are often unintended and unsupported. This, too, is part of Lévi's legacy. The occultist made several references to Lucifer in *Doctrine and Ritual*, sometimes reading an alternate meaning into the rebel angel as the ultimate servant of God and sometimes in a more baleful manner.

Entire papers and volumes have been written, and justly so, on how the Hebrew-derived name Satan, or *adversary*, or the Latin-derived term Lucifer, or *light-bringer*, culturally morphed, in the centuries following Scriptural historiography into synonyms for the God-opposing force. The traditional Hebrew term for Satan is השטן, literally "The Satan," pronounced *ha-sa-taan*, sometimes also described as the *prosecutor.*

---

* *Cheirokmeta* is ancient Greek for "things made with hands." (It is the root, by way of Middle French chiromancie, or chiromancy, a modern term for palmistry. Palmistry was popularized to modern audiences by William John Warner (1866–1936) known Cheiro.) Zosimos of Panopolis or Zosimus Alchemista was a Greek-Egyptian alchemist thought to live in the late third and early fourth centuries A.D. *A History of Science in Society: From Philosophy to Utility*, 2nd edition, was published in 2012 by University of Toronto Press.

Relatedly, Lévi produced an 1860 sequel of sorts to *Doctrine and Ritual* in *The History of Magic*, translated into English in 1913 by Arthur Edward Waite. In his introduction, Lévi intoned:

> Lucifer—Light-Bearer—how strange a name, attributed to the spirit of darkness! Is it he who carries the light and yet blinds feeble souls? The answer is yes, unquestionably; for traditions are full of divine disclosures and inspirations. Satan himself is transformed into an angel of light, says St. Paul. And Christ Himself said: "I beheld Satan as lightning fall from heaven." So also the prophet Isaiah: "How art thou fallen from heaven, O Lucifer, son of the morning."*

This passage was adapted, uncredited, along with much else, into American Freemasonic leader Albert Pike's (1809–1891) massive compendium *Morals and Dogma of the Ancient and Accepted Scottish Rite of Freemasonry* in 1871. Pike wrote:

> The Apocalypse is, to those who receive the nineteenth Degree, the Apotheosis of that Sublime Faith which aspires to God alone, and despises all the pomps and works of Lucifer. LUCIFER, the *Light-bearer*! Strange and mysterious name to give to the Spirit of Darkness! Lucifer, the Son of the Morning! Is it *he* who bears the *Light*, and with its splendors intolerable blinds feeble, sensual, or selfish Souls? Doubt it not! for traditions are full of Divine Revelations and Inspirations . . .

Pike's passage became a flashpoint, enduring into the twenty-first century, for conspiracists and anti-Masons to proclaim a spurious Masonic connection to Luciferianism. This connection was further linked with Baphomet—proclaimed a shadowy secret deity within Masonry's inner circle by French writer and provocateur Léo Taxil in the 1890s. Taxil's fictions gained sufficient traction so that they reappear today in an illustrated tract *That's Baphomet?* issued by rightwing Christian pamphleteer Chick Publications, with source references to Pike and Lévi.** Read with any degree of care, however, it is plain that Pike, and his uncredited source Lévi, were writing

* Lévi is citing, respectively, Luke 10:18 and Isaiah 14:12.

** The inimitably illustrated pamphlet can be viewed at Chick.com.

in a condemnatory fashion of the rebel spirit. Clarifying the matter, Masonic historian Arturo De Hoyas wrote in 2011 in his authoritative annotated edition of *Morals and Dogma*:

> . . . why does it say that "Lucifer, the light-bearer" is a strange name for the spirit of darkness? Simply because the name Lucifer *means* "light-bearer." The name derives from the Latin genitive [or modifier] *lucis* (light) and *ferre* (to bring *or* to bear); hence *lucis-ferrer* becomes *Lucifer*, the "light-bearer." It is thus ironic that the "spirit of darkness" should be called "light bearer." The notion that the Adversary uses light to deceive people was accepted by the Apostle Paul, who wrote that Satan disguises himself as an angel of light (2 Cor. 11:14), and this scripture may have helped connect the Adversary with the name Lucifer.
>
> *Lucifer, Son of the Morning.* But why is Lucifer called "the Son of the Morning?" This alludes to older translations of Isaiah 14:12 (e.g., KJV) which read, "How art thou fallen from heaven, O Lucifer, son of the morning!" According to Biblical commentators this verse is actually a condemnation of an ancient king of Babylon, who had persecuted the Israelites, and does not refer to the devil at all.

Whatever one's theological outlook, this is a clear exegesis of the meaning behind both texts. It also signifies how early occult-revival expressions often stood, sometimes pedantically, on a traditional Abrahamic foundation, regardless of the authors' use of esoteric and pre-Christian symbology.

It would fall to later generations, seeking to revive and adapt a perennialist worldview, or their own version of the *prisca theologia*, to create a departure from the traditional Western outlook. In any case, the Pike-Lévi passage became, and remains, a favorite of anti-Masonic writers who, through misreading and polemic, mischaracterize Freemasonry as a proxy for Satanic dogma of their own conception. What's more, the sometimes-dense and elusive formulas adopted by Lévi, and those orders and individuals he later influenced, began to foster a kind of magickal formalism from which later innovators, including chaos magickians, as will be seen, struggled to liberate themselves.

By the mid-to-late nineteenth century, modern occultism drew upon ideals, imagery, and drama of antiquity—remade in light of humanity's hopes, wishes, and strivings in the Industrial Era. Seen from one perspective, mechanistic forces appeared to rule the world. Darwin's theories on the orderly biologic development of life were published in 1859. But to a cohort of rebels, seekers, occultists, and esotericists, there existed a substory. To them, the individual was an unruly being possessed of self-determining qualities. One of the great figures on the modern scene to explore this view was American ceremonial magician Pascal Beverly Randolph (1825–1875).

Randolph, a free man of partial Black descent, was born in 1825 in the notorious and dangerous Five Points neighborhood on Canal Street in lower Manhattan. His father abandoned the family leaving Randolph and his mother to enter a poor house when he was six or seven. His mother soon died, probably of typhus, and he was left orphaned, raised variously by foster parents and a half-sister. Seeking to escape street life and pissant labor, the adolescent Randolph became an itinerant sailor. He was able to leave New York City and travel to the near-East and Europe.

He took immediate and burgeoning interest in the occultism of Eliphas Lévi and any related teachings he could find. Here was a Black man, alive during slavery, orphaned since age six or seven, left to fend for himself in often-brutal surroundings. In his occult studies, he sought power, selfhood, and possibility. Randolph wrote, perhaps fancifully, of his journeys:

> One night—it was in far-off Jerusalem or Bethlehem, I really forget which—I made love to . . . a dusky maiden of Arabic blood. I of her and that experience learned . . . the fundamental principle of the White Magic of Love; subsequently I became affiliated with some dervishes and fakirs by whom . . . I found the road to other knowledges . . . I became practically . . . a mystic and in time chief of the lofty brethren . . . discovering the elixir of life, the universal Solvent . . . and the philosopher's stone.*

* *Eulis!* (1874), with thanks to Hugh B. Urban.

Starting at about age twenty-one, and extending across his career, Randolph founded, folded, and then re-founded his own occult orders. One was the Brotherhood of Eulis, which had its earliest roots in 1846. Randolph reconstituted it in 1874. The name was drawn from the Greek god Eos, a personification of the dawn. This formed the basis for one of Randolph's key books, *Eulis!*, published in 1874, a magickal discourse on the "Philosophy of Love."

Another of his groups, founded in 1858, was *Fraternitas Rosae Crucis* or Fraternity of the Rosy Cross, first based in San Francisco and later in Quakertown, Pennsylvania, where it was eventually led by American occultist R. Swinburne Clymer (1878–1966). This led to a drawn-out series of feuds and disambiguation among American Rosicrucian orders over who represented the "real" tradition and hierarchy. For his part, Randolph claimed the term Rosicrucian from its Renaissance-era roots and remade it. He identified the Rosicrucian brotherhood not as a thing but an idea and named himself its titular head.

"Power cannot be bought with money," Randolph wrote in his 1867 *Guide to Clairvoyance*, "I *want the best souls to come to me. Such may be admitted to the Rosicrucian Brotherhood!*"

He produced his own books, eventually more than twenty, receiving some of his insights through clairvoyant perception, trance states, and drug use. Randolph was among the first modern Westerners who employed drugs, notably hashish, to gain visions, insights, and alternate perspectives. He also participated in Spiritualism, séances, and—most importantly—became a pioneering teacher of sex magick or, as he called it, *Affectional Alchemy*.

Randolph also used the term (or his followers did) *Magia Sexualis*—the title of a posthumously published book, which seems to have surfaced in 1931. He taught that sex magick heightens the capacity to impose your will over events by *focusing and concentrating intensely on what you desire at the point of mutual climax*. Unlike later systems, Randolph's sex magick was prescribed expressly in partnership and preferably marriage. (Even still, Randolph was spuriously accused of disseminating "obscene" materials, for which he was briefly jailed—and severely financially strained—in 1872.) This is one of the ways in which what is called sex magick emerged on the modern occult scene. Today, this method is commonly used in connection with sigil magick whereby the seeker turns a desire into an abstract drawing or symbol—as will be seen, a practice pioneered in its earliest form by British artist and occultist Austin Osman Spare (1886–1956)—and reaches an ecstatic state or climax while viewing the symbol, thus "charging" it as a representation and conduit of will.

In addition to sexuality, drugs, and his efforts at clairvoyance and séances, Randolph sought to employ the magickal uses of mirrors, a thread from John Dee. He believed that gazing intently into a mirror and focusing on your desires could turn that mirror, at least within the psychology of the exercise, into a channel for the *light of speculative thought* and hence a means of projecting your wish, similar to the climax of sex magick. (For a modern iteration of this, see Claude M. Bristol's 1948 book, *The Magic of Believing.*) In his quest to discover *amplifiers* of unseen forces, Randolph brought a do-it-yourself ethic and simplicity to magick.

Like many Spiritualists and mediums, Randolph was impassioned and active as a voice for abolitionism. "In September 1866," writes scholar of religion Hugh B. Urban, "the Southern loyalists convened in Philadelphia to support the republican cause, to seek recognition for their loyalty and to urge extending the ballot to the 'loyal Negro.' Randolph went there to deliver a fiery and famous speech that was widely reproduced throughout the newspapers of the day:"

> I am not P.B. Randolph; I am the voice of God crying, "Hold! Hold!" to the nation in its mad career! The lips of the struggling millions of the disenfranchised demanding Justice in the name of Truth—a Peter the Hermit, preaching a new crusade against Wrong—the Genius of Progress appealing for schools; a pleader for the people . . . mechanic for the redemption of the world.

"Arguably," Urban notes, "the most important contribution Randolph made to modern esotericism was his system of magical eroticism, or affectional alchemy. In sexual love, Randolph saw nothing less than 'the greatest hope for the regeneration of the world, the key to personal fulfillment as well as social transformation and the basis of a non-repressive civilization.'"*

---

* *Magia Sexualis: Sex, Magic, and Liberation in Modern Western Esotericism* by Hugh B. Urban (University of California Press, 2006). Urban's latter quote is from Franklin Rosemont's foreword to *Paschal Beverly Randolph: A Nineteenth-Century Black American Spiritualist, Rosicrucian, and Sex Magician* by John Patrick Deveney (State University of New York Press, 1997), the sole biography of Randolph and a valuable resource.

Randolph produced his writings and formed his oprganizations in a spirit of anarchistic self-determination. He had never attended seminary. He had no formal schooling, literary background, or credentialed pedigree. This was not Schopenhauer, Mesmer, Blake, or Shelley but a self-made man from the streets who felt that no license, training, or approbation (other than perhaps his own) was required to practice magick. There was a daring to this man, an uncontained rebelliousness—yet also a deep sorrow. Randolph took his own life by gunshot wound to his head in 1875 at age forty-nine in Toledo, Ohio. The circumstances are sketchy and sometimes disputed but Randolph apparently believed that his wife was cheating on him. In any case, Randolph, the unsettled seeker, was plagued by grief, betrayal, and debt.

Randolph left a considerable legacy. In addition to his magickal work, this self-invented seeker had a simple motto: *TRY.*

In his book *Dealings with the Dead*, written in 1861 or 1862, he wrote that an unseen intelligence named Thotmor told him: "Our motto—the motto of the greater order of which I was a brother on earth,—an order which has, under a variety of names, existed since the very dawn of civilization on the earth is 'Try'."

Randolph adopted it as his personal slogan. He further defined the principle "Try" through his term *Volantia* in *Eulis!*: "the quiet, steady, calm, non-turbulent, non-muscular exertion of the human *Will.*"* The motto echoed the simple command issued to the hero of the *Bhagavad Gita*: *"Fight, Arjuna."* It traced a strange and winding path of its own.

Although Randolph took his life in Toledo on July 29, 1875, a different, and perhaps related, drama played out in New York City in the preceding May. A New Yorker and former staff colonel for the

---

* This is sometimes rendered alternately, possibly through elaboration of another writer: "It is simply a *quiet* power, and requires no muscular or nervous, but simply a still, mental force, to urge it into play, when it is feeble, as in most it is; it should be cultivated by thinking determinedly, at intervals, of *one thing only* at a time to the total exclusion of every thing, topic, or subject besides." I encourage parallel study of the volume *Meetings with Remarkable Men* by G.I. Gurdjieff (1866–1948) in which the teacher refers to "the law-conformable result of a man's unflinching perseverance in bringing all his manifestations into accordance with the principles he has consciously set himself in life for the attainment of a definite aim." Gurdjieff is further encountered in chapter eight, "Secret Teachings, Old and New."

Union Army, Henry Steel Olcott, had recently met and befriended an extraordinary, world-traveled Russian noblewoman, Madame H. P. Blavatsky, with whom he was embarking on a series of occult experiments and studies.

In May of 1875, Henry pulled together a small circle of seekers into a group called the "Miracle Club." Their plan was to study hidden forces, clairvoyance, Kabbalah, Egyptian geometry, Eastern spirituality, and reincarnation. The club, Blavatsky later wrote in one of her massive scrapbooks, was formed "in consequence of orders received from T*** B***"—or Tuitit Bey, one of the hidden adepts under whom she claimed tutelage.

Henry fretted that his fledgling group wasn't getting very far. He believed the Miracle Club would not work out. The same month, he received a mysteriously timed letter. It was signed by the same Tuitit Bey writing "From the Brotherhood of Luxor, Section the Vth." The unknown mentor told him:

> Brother Neophyte, we greet thee.
>
> He who seeks us finds us. TRY.
>
> Rest thy mind—banish all foul doubt. We keep watch over our faithful soldiers. Sister Helen [Blavatsky] is a valiant, trustworthy servant. Open thy Spirit to conviction, have faith and she will lead thee to the Golden Gate of truth. She neither fears sword nor fire but her soul is sensitive to dishonour and she hath reason to mistrust the future . . .
>
> Thou hast many good mediums around thee, *don't give up thy club.* TRY. [emphasis added]

It was Henry's first of several phenomenally produced or "precipitated" letters received from unseen masters, teachers, adepts—or Mahatmas—from the East who Madame Blavatsky called her tutors. In what is referred to as "Mahatma Letter No. 5," dated around November 26, 1880, the master called Koot Hoomi told Theosophist A.P. Sinnett: ". . . bear in mind, that these my letters, are not written but *impressed* or precipitated and then all mistakes corrected." Historian Michael Gomes, who has personally examined some of the archived letters, reports to me that this description is physically accurate, i.e., the penmanship left no indent on the page.

The message reached Henry in May of 1875, the same month that Eliphas Lévi died and about two months before P.B. Randolph's death. As instructed, Henry *did try.* His struggling Miracle Club formed the nucleus of a larger organization launched later that year, the Theosophical Society. It is no exaggeration to say that the occult group changed the world, spiritually, artistically, and politically.

CHAPTER SIX

The Theosophical Dawn

Historical controversies embroil Madame H.P. Blavatsky (1831–1891). In 2012, during my publishing days, I issued an excellent biography of the Victorian icon by historian Gary Lachman, *Madame Blavatsky: The Mother of Modern Spirituality.*

The book received scrutinizing and critical reviews in places we had not sent it, including the *Paris Review* and *Harper's Magazine*. I was surprised that organs of lettered opinion, without myself, Gary, or anyone having solicited them, felt driven to comment on the life of an occultist who died in 1891.

They criticized her in binary terms and dedicated significant space to doing so. As is typical, Blavatsky was depicted as a purveyor of fake mysticism, manufactured mediumistic tricks, and charlatanry.

Indeed, the world-traveled Russian writer and seeker attracts unending umbrage and debate. To tell the story of Blavatsky is almost to enter a "hall of magic mirrors," as historian and Theosophist Victor A. Endersby titled his 1969 biography. For all the contention, however, it is difficult to imagine our modern world without her.

An extraordinary range of cultural and social figures crisscross Blavatsky's legacy, from composers Igor Stravinsky and Alexander

Scriabin to political leaders Mahatma Gandhi, Jawaharlal Nehru, and Henry A. Wallace to poets W.B. Yeats, George Russell (AE), and T.S. Eliot to artists Agnes Pelton, Hilma af Klint, Nicholas Roerich, Piet Mondrian, and Wassily Kandinsky to novelist L. Frank Baum (*The Wonderful Wizard of Oz*) to modern artists such as musician Todd Rundgren, filmmaker David Lynch, and Elvis Presley (an avid reader) to movements ranging across the alternative spiritual spectrum, including those adapting Eastern spirituality in the West and variants of Wicca and witchcraft.

Blavatsky's earliest collaborators proved remarkable in their own right, including Theosophical Society co-founder Henry Steel Olcott (1832–1907). It is with their partnership that we begin.

In winter 1877 there stood a squat, redbrick tenement on the West Side of Manhattan at Eighth Avenue and 47th Street, what is today considered Hell's Kitchen or the Theater District. The five-story brick building still stands as an Econo Lodge, part of the discount hotel chain. But in winter of early 1877 it was a walkup dwelling.

On the second floor sat a cramped warren of rooms, which the New York press jokingly dubbed "the Lamasery" for the religious monasteries of Tibet. Within the Lamasery dwelt Madame H.P. Blavatsky, a world-traveled Russian noblewoman who arrived in New York City in 1873. She came, she explained, because she yearned to visit the birthplace of Spiritualism. Moreso, she felt that the free religious winds in the U.S. made the nation a propitious launch pad for her reignition of occult spirituality.

About a year after arriving, she met her roommate, Henry Steel Olcott a retired staff colonel from the Civil War. During Henry's twenties, he was considered a wunderkind of scientific agriculture. As an officer, he was among the first investigators of the Lincoln assassination. Henry later grew interested in Spiritualism and researched various mediumistic claims. His efforts led to an 1875 book, *People from the Other World*, an illustrated investigation.

The two met on a porch in Chittenden, Vermont in 1874. Henry was on assignment for one of New York's dailies to investigate a "ghost farm" run by two brothers, William and Horatio Eddy. The siblings claimed they were able to conjure ghostly phenomena and otherworldly spirits.

As Henry stepped onto the veranda the sunny midday of October 14, he encountered and chivalrously lit the cigarette of the commanding, imposing woman who arrived that day. She was oddly garbed in a puffy red shirt, known as a Garibaldi shirt. It was named for Italian revolutionary and Freemason Giuseppe Garibaldi (1807–1882) who popularized its style while fighting to unify a fragmented Italy into a single democratic republic. Garibaldi's struggles led him into military conflict with the Vatican, which until 1870 maintained its own militia. Although not widely remembered, Garibaldi was considered a dramatic, romantic, and idealistic revolutionary challenging Western Europe's waning aristocracies.

Blavatsky told her new friend that she had fought at Garibaldi's side—she lifted her shirt to reveal to a wide-eyed Henry bullet wounds from their campaigns. He was enthralled. They did not become lovers but, for a time, inseparable though fractious friends with a shared passion for the unseen.

Their vehicles were first the short-lived Miracle Club formed in May 1875 and soon after the Theosophical Society, which they founded in New York City that November. Henry installed the two of them in the cluster of rooms called the Lamasery in late summer or early fall of 1876.

One winter night at the Lamasery in 1877, Henry experienced perhaps the formative episode of his life. Madame Blavatsky had gone to sleep and he was seated alone in his room reading by the flicker of gas lamp. Henry was poring over explorer John Lloyd Stephens' memoir of scouting Mayan ruins in Yucatan, with the only noises the hiss of steam heat. Reading and smoking, Henry was suddenly startled to attention. There appeared before him, with no footsteps, creaking floorboards, or sound of an opening door, a massively tall, turbaned man later identified as Master Morya, an adept from the East.

"All at once," Henry wrote in his memoir *Old Diary Leaves*, "as I read with my shoulder a little turned from the door, there came a gleam of something white in the right-hand corner of my right eye; I turned my head, dropped my book in astonishment, and saw towering above me in his great stature an Oriental clad in white garments, and wearing a head cloth or turban of amber-striped fabric, hand-embroidered in yellow floss silk."

It was one of the "hidden masters" that Madame Blavatsky said had been tutoring her since adolescence—and from whom Henry had begun receiving letters during his efforts with the Miracle Club. Now, standing before Henry in resplendent white garb with a silk turban encircling his head, was this Eastern mystery teacher, Morya, who, Henry later recounted, reassured the acolyte that he was on the right path.

Morya encouraged him in his investigations, his close partnership with Madame Blavatsky—and something more: he told Henry that he wanted the pair to relocate to India, which was then under the yolk of colonial machinery. The Hindu religion was being eaten away by well-funded and military-backed missionary campaigns dispatched from England and Western Europe.

As proof of their encounter, and to persuade Henry he wasn't dreaming, Morya removed his *fehta* or turban and left it on the table for the stunned onlooker.* With that, Morya vanished.

As it happened, about eighteen months later in December 1878, Henry and Madame Blavatsky did leave New York City for Bombay, now Mumbai, arriving in January. The pair reestablished themselves in a nation then as unfamiliar to most Westerners as the surface of another planet. They had limited finances; no command over language, culture, or custom; few personal contacts; and both were well into middle age and not in robust health. Blavatsky was obese and had some difficulty getting around. Henry suffered from a gouty leg.

They uprooted themselves from the relative comforts of Victorian-era New York where reasonably well-established dwellers could have domestic servants, ice in their drinks, and enjoy a coal-heated and gaslit home. You could taxi around town in a horse and carriage, go to the theater, or take a train to Coney Island; restaurants abounded. Moreover, the couple were widely known personalities about town accustomed to jousting with the tabloid press. In September 1877, Blavatsky had published her first book, *Isis Unveiled*, a sprawling work of occult philosophy and history. Henry was respected as a lawyer and journalist who had covered the execution of abolitionist John Brown and made some of the first arrests of suspected collaborators in Lincoln's assassination. Although considered eccentric in their partnership in occult studies, they were eminent if notorious figures.

---

* The garment is archived at the Theosophical Society's international headquarters at Adyar on the southeast coast of India. As of this writing, I have not personally viewed the item.

Leaving all that behind, they established themselves in the ancient nation where they and followers helped inaugurate the nascent Indian National Congress, the policymaking arm of the independence movement, the helm of which was later taken by Mahatma Gandhi. The anti-colonial leader spoke admiringly of the influence that Blavatsky's philosophy of religious universality had on him during his student years, an episode to which we return.

Indeed, in a remarkably overlooked facet of twentieth century history, Gandhi openly credited Theosophy with returning him to Hinduism and its holy book, the *Bhagavad Gita,* which became the guiding text of the leader's life. Blavatsky's *Key to Theosophy*, Gandhi wrote in his autobiography, "stimulated in me the desire to read books on Hinduism, and disabused me of the notion fostered by the missionaries that Hinduism was rife with superstition."* Theosophy, he later told biographer Louis Fischer, "is Hinduism at its best. Theosophy is the brotherhood of man."** Gandhi partnered (and sometimes feuded) with the Theosophical Society during India's independence movement, crediting it with easing relations between Hindu and Muslim delegates to the Indian National Congress.

So prominent was Theosophy in India's political life that even the Congress's founding in 1885 was instigated by an early Theosophist, A.O. Hume, a retired Anglo-Indian government secretary who said that he was acting under "advice and guidance of advanced initiates."*** In 1973, Hume, seen as a founding light of the independence movement, appeared on a commemorative Indian postal stamp. In 1917, Blavatsky's successor, Annie Besant, was elected president of the Congress, making the Theosophist the first woman and last European to hold the title.

For his part, Henry made speaking tours of India, Japan, Ceylon (now Sri Lanka), Burma (now Myanmar), and helped instigate a vast Buddhist revival. In Sri Lanka, an Anglican bishop groused in a letter home that "the Secretary of an obscure society" had been encouraging Buddhist monks, "hailing them as brothers in the march of

* *Autobiography: The Story of My Experiments with Truth* (Public Affairs Press, 1948).

** *The Life of Mahatma Gandhi* (Harper & Brothers, 1950).

*** Hume's encounter with "advanced initiates" appears in Edward C. Moulton's introduction to *Allan Octavian Hume: 'Father of the Indian National Congress' 1829–1912* by Sir William Wedderburn (Oxford University Press, 1913, 2002).

intellect."* Olcott used the missionaries' own methods against them: He wrote *The Buddhist Catechism*—still read in Sri Lankan classrooms today—to codify the native faith as missionaries had the Christian one.

He successfully lobbied English authorities to permit the national celebration of Buddha's birthday, during which worshippers rallied around an international Buddhist flag Olcott helped design. He raised money for schools and educational programs. The Buddhist revival ignited. Within twenty years of Olcott's first visit, the number of Buddhist schools in the island nation grew from four to more than two hundred.** In recognition, Henry's death, February 17, 1907, is today nationally celebrated as "Olcott Day." In 1967, Henry's visage, too, was memorialized on a Sri Lankan postal stamp.

As alluded, the notion of Westerners making a spiritual sojourn to India had not yet entered the Western psyche. Most Victorians did not see India as a fount of religious wisdom. Rather, the nation was widely considered a cultural boondocks that the British Empire used as a base for mercantilism and military command. It was not until decades later that writers like W. Somerset Maugham or Paul Brunton wrote about spiritual journeys to India—and nearly a century later that the Beatles visited in 1967, joining Maharishi Mahesh Yogi at his ashram in Rishikesh. The tracks for such journeys were laid by Blavatsky and Olcott.

What, if anything, happened that winter night in the gaslight of Henry's room on the West Side of Manhattan? Did he invent the story? Did he imagine it? I am hardly about to advocate for a mysterious turbaned man materializing in front of Henry. At the same time, I also reckon that the strange and outwardly spiraling history of this couple expands in directions that shouldn't be possible. If the critics are right, Blavatsky and Olcott ought to be a forgotten novelty of the nineteenth century occult revival, their names an afterthought. And yet, what they and

* *The Dawning of the Theosophical Movement* by Michael Gomes (Quest Books, 1987).

** See biographies of Olcott, *Yankee Beacon of Buddhist Light* by Howard Murphet (Theosophical Publishing House, 1972, 1988) and *The White Buddhist* by Stephen R. Prothero (Indiana University Press, 1996). Olcott left a vast record of his affairs, most usefully his six-volume *Old Diary Leaves* (G. P. Putnam's Sons, issued 1895–1935).

their closest colleagues created, widely acknowledged or not, was history itself.

And who, in essence, *was* Madame Blavatsky? It is a question that we will never fully answer. Forensically, she was born to minor Russian nobility in 1831, involved in a coerced and unhappy marriage (she later had another short-lived marriage in Philadelphia), and began to travel as a young woman. Since girlhood, she had dreams about figures from the East who wished to tutor and help her. As she entered her early twenties while touring England, Blavatsky said that she experienced her first encounter with a hidden master at the International Exhibition at Hyde Park's Crystal Palace in 1851—a hugely tall man who accompanied the royal Nepalese delegation. There abound records and controversies around her traveling to Tibet, Egypt, Persia, and the Far East. She said she was guided in her studies and travels by the adept Morya and others such as Koot Hoomi (also spelled Kuthumi), Serapis Bey, and Tuitit Bey—flesh-and-blood beings who she maintained were unbound by certain dimensional or material realities and thus able to materialize at will.

Under tutelage to the masters, she spurred a spiritual revolution to save the Western world from domination by philosophical materialism, or belief that matter creates itself and nothing exists beyond flesh and bone, motor skill and cognition—that one's psyche is an epiphenomenon of the brain, like bubbles in a glass of carbonated water, and when the water is gone, so are the bubbles. As seen, she said she was charged with rescuing the Eastern philosophies from dissolution under colonial rule.

Her stories of hidden masters of wisdom from Persia, the Himalayas, Egypt, and India, wielded an unusual effect on the West. Although earlier Transcendentalist thinkers, such as Ralph Waldo Emerson, Henry David Thoreau, and Bronson Alcott, were versed in some of the Vedic literature available to English speakers, and they wrote about such things in their journals, poetry, and essays, their work did not necessarily reach the everyday individual, the kind of person who hadn't read British poet Edwin Arnold's 1879 epic "The Light of Asia" on the life of Buddha.

Indeed, we have an overdeveloped sense of the availability of ancient or Eastern literature in translation prior to the late nineteenth century. In 1841, when Emerson published his first series of essays, there were probably just four or five copies of the *Bhagavad Gita* in

English throughout all of America. One was in the library at Harvard, one was in Emerson's personal library. Emerson lent his copy to Thoreau and some of his contemporaries. The remaining two or three, according to best estimates, were in private libraries. The first Latin and French translations of the Chinese ethical classic the *Tao Te Ching* were not available until 1838 and the first English version in 1868. (Catholic missionaries circulated partial Latin translations starting in 1788). I've already mentioned the paucity of Hermetic translations. Hence, it's important to recall these limits.

It was the fantastical and theatrical quality of Madame Blavatsky, and the manner in which the press took to her, that began to spread the idea in the popular mind that there existed gurus, swamis, and masters of wisdom in the nations of the East, a world that many Americans barely knew existed, or if they thought of such places at all were likely to consider them holdouts of superstition and burlesque tribalism. Blavatsky's stories of tutelage by these masters gave Westerners an alternate point of reference.

Hence, Americans were able to understand what it meant when the first gurus ventured West, such as Swami Vivekananda (1863–1902) who visited the Chicago World's Fair in 1893 and spent the next two years touring America, speaking on karma, nonattachment, and reincarnation.* Or the monk Paramahansa Yogananda (1893–1952) who came to America in 1920 and taught Kriya Yoga, a practice encompassing both spiritual and physical techniques. When Maharishi Mahesh Yogi, founder of Transcendental Meditation, visited Southern California in 1959, modern Westerners had a way to contextualize him.

"In a tiny room on the fourth floor of the Central Y.M.C.A.," wrote the *Honolulu Star Bulletin* on Maharishi's stopover, "a remarkable man sits cross-legged on a deer's pelt. His eyes remind you of the innocence of a puppy's eyes. He has no money. He asks for nothing. His

---

* From *Occult America*: "At once friendly and exotic-looking in his turban and robes, Vivekananda—a serious purveyor of Hindu ideas—seemed to enjoy his contact with the refreshingly unpretentious, caste-free Americans. He discussed reincarnation with cowboys, chided Americans for their materialism, and teased Spiritualists for showing more interest in conjuring up 'creepy things' than the higher goal of self-knowledge. In good humor, the swami repeated the story of a husband–wife team of spirit mediums with whom he shared a kitchen at a New York rooming house. The couple performed a stage show together and would often get into domestic spats. Vivekananda recalled that after one of their arguments the wife turned to the Eastern master and complained: 'Is it fair of him to treat me like this, when I make all the ghosts?'"

worldly possessions can be carried in one hand. Maharishi Mahesh Yogi is on a world odyssey . . . In the meantime, he sits quietly in room 424. He sleeps three hours a night, eats one vegetarian meal a day, and does not think of tomorrow." *

This process expanded in the U.S. with the passage of the 1965 Immigration Act, which allowed greater Asian immigration, permitting entry to a new cohort of gurus and yogis, including Swami Prabhupada (1896–1977) that year. Again, when John, Paul, George, and Ringo visited Maharishi at Rishikesh in 1967, the notion of a Westerner sojourning East, and vice versa, had a touch of familiarity. That acclimation began largely through Madame Blavatsky.

Aside from her narrative about spiritual masters, Madame Blavatsky taught that there exists an occult philosophy, or "secret doctrine," as she titled her vast cosmological opus in 1888. This secret doctrine, in her telling, is a primeval "hierohistory," using Henry Corbin's term. We explored the concept of a *prisca theologia* in the Renaissance. Blavatsky conveyed a similar theme. This occult or secret doctrine was deeply, almost unthinkably, ancient and unknown. It was far older than all modern faiths and, in fact, underscored them.

What's more, she taught that humanity itself is millennia upon millennia older than modern authorities understood. And, further, that humanity spans vast evolutionary cycles of development, through which it eventually evolves finer sensory abilities and exists under fewer restrictions of physical law. Blavatsky described this in terms of epochs of evolving "root races"—not races in the ethnic sense but pertaining to spiritual development. In the fetid atmosphere of Darwinian misapplications, Blavatsky, on occasion, made racial generalizations that were at once conventional to the Victorian era and shabbily conceived, a subject of future controversies, as considered in chapter nine, "Politics and the Occult."

In *The Secret Doctrine*, Blavatsky described *seven root races*, which span vast millennia, and are older than anything understood in terms of human history, some emanating from supposed "lost continents" of Atlantis and Lemuria. Each of these seven root races, in turn, divides

* "Indian Yogi Offers Meditation to All," December 31, 1958.

into *seven subraces*, with humanity working its way up this scale of spiritual development.

She wrote that current humanity is the *fifth subrace* of the *fifth root race* and that the early twenty-first century would see emergence of the *sixth sub-race*. This developmental process requires 700 or 800 years. And another 25,000 years before commencement of the seventh subrace.

It is important to clarify that Blavatsky counted evolutionary cycles in millions of years. As Pablo Sender helpfully summarized in "The Dawn of Civilization: An Esoteric Account of the First Three Root Races" in Fall 2019 in *Quest* magazine:

> According to *The Secret Doctrine*, the First Root Race, nonphysical beings lacking in consciousness, began to develop over 1.5 billion years ago. The first self-conscious humanity resembling what we know today was the Third Root Race, which started over 18 million years ago. The anthropological records, historic and even prehistoric, belong to our current Root Race, which is the fifth (out of seven).

Blavatsky's cycles are correspondingly vast in nature to the Vedic cycle of *yugas* or world ages. The four recurrent cycles require 4,320,000 earth years to complete and then recommence. Humanity's current cycle of *Kali Yuga*—considered an era of conflict and spiritual degradation—began in 3,102 B.C. and concludes in 428,899 A.D., lasting 432,000 conventional years (a number with surprising congruences in other religious systems). Using esoteric calendrics of his own, Traditionalist philosopher René Guénon (1886–1951) calculated stage four, the Kali Yuga, at a more compact 6,480 years, running 4,481 B.C. to 1999 A.D. This means that present humanity has returned to the first stage of Krita Yuga or the Golden Age: "But it is hard to imagine the author of *The Reign of Quantity* [Guénon] if he were living now, agreeing with that," Joscelyn Godwin notes in *Atlantis and the Cycles of Time* (Inner Traditions, 2011).

Back to more easily grasped measures of time, Blavatsky wrote in 1888 that the current process of transformation from the fifth to sixth subrace would begin in the United States. "It is in America that the transformation will take place," reads *The Secret Doctrine*, "and has already silently commenced." Signposts in *The Secret Doctrine* and later interpretation by Blavatsky's protégé and successor, British political reformer Annie Besant, point to the change originating on the West Coast in California.

This bears pausing over. In 1888, California was a place of orange groves, ranches, mines, desert climate, and seashore. Although the 1840s Gold Rush brought a wave of migrants, the coastal state remained, in essence, a ranch town and agricultural hub. It wasn't until an economic boom brought on by the shipping industry around World War I that California began to develop into the economic powerhouse and migratory magnet it is today. People arrived for myriad reasons, including commerce and health, as the climate was considered a tonic. California not only became home to the nascent movie business but started to develop into the epicenter of alternative spirituality, which it has remained. As with the Burned-Over District, population flows presage religious innovation. Hence, the Southern California coast became the capital of everything radical and breakaway in spirituality.

None of that was especially foreseeable in 1888 when Blavatsky published *The Secret Doctrine* in which she wrote: "Occult Philosophy teaches that even now, under our very eyes, the new Race and races are preparing to be formed, and that it is in America that the transformation will take place, and has already silently commenced." She specifically referenced humanity's transformation from its current role as the fifth subrace of the fifth root race into a sixth subrace (again, seven subraces appear within each root race) in the Pacific Rim, a process that would unfold in "some few hundred years more." As alluded, Besant interpreted the quoted passage referencing Southern California, which I consider accurate to Blavatsky's outlook.

In the opening page of *The Secret Doctrine*, Madame Blavatsky tells the reader she is viewing and writing down stanzas of wisdom from *The Book of Dzyan*, a mythical Tibetan Buddhist text not known to physically exist. The author leaves open the question of whether she's perusing a physical work or viewing its passages in a phenomenalistic or clairvoyant manner: "An Archaic Manuscript—a collection of palm leaves made impermeable to water, fire, and air, by some specific unknown process—is before the writer's eye."

In an 1895 article, "The Sources of Madame Blavatsky's Writings," Spiritualist writer William Emmette Coleman tracked Blavatsky's antecedents and maintained that she clipped-and-pasted many of her ideas from a handful of contemporaneous books; I don't think that covers all the bases but it is a critique with which scrutinizing readers should be familiar.*

I offer this comment from Blavatsky's secretary G.R.S. Mead, whose scholarship I noted earlier. In *The Theosophical Review* of April 15, 1904, Mead wrote:

> Let me then speak of a subject of which I presumably know as much as even the most industrious adverse critic of H.P.B.'s work—her literary remains. I have carefully read all she has written; much of it I have edited, some of it I have read many, many times. I think I may say without any undue boasting that no one knows better than I do the books from which she quotes and the use she makes of quotations. She was, indeed, more or less mediaeval, or even, at times, Early-Christian, in her quotation work; let us grant this fully in every way—though perhaps we are a little inclined to go too far in this nowadays. But what I have been most interested in, in her writing, is precisely that which she does not quote from known sources, and this it is which forms for me the main factor in the enigma of H.P.B. I perpetually ask myself the question: Whence did she get her information—apparent translations of texts and commentaries, the originals of which are unknown to the Western world?

In the last chapter I mentioned Henry Olcott's efforts to sustain his Miracle Club in New York City. As seen, in May 1875 he received a mysteriously timed letter. Addressing Henry as "Brother Neophyte," the missive came from a group calling itself the Brotherhood of Luxor signed by Tuitit Bey. The order of Eastern adepts said it was watching over him and felt encouraged by his progress. The letter

---

* The Coleman charges are judiciously reviewed in "Roots of the Oriental Gnosis: W. E. Coleman, H. P. Blavatsky, S. F. Dunlap" by Jake B. Winchester, University of Amsterdam, thesis for MA in Western Esotericism. For a further response to Coleman, see "Plagiarism and the *Secret Doctrine*" by Darrell Erixson, *Theosophical History*, July 2006.

concluded by telling Henry, in odd vernacular at once colloquial and portentous, "don't give up thy club. TRY."

Henry continued with the Miracle Club but also felt that a greater vehicle was needed, something more ambitious and formal. A September 17 gathering at Blavatsky's apartment at Irving Place, where Henry had installed her, attracted Spiritualist thinker Emma Hardinge Britten (1823–1899) and others to hear a lecture on Egyptian geometry. An impressive figure in her own right, Britten was an early Theosophist and political reformer who stumped for Lincoln's candidacy.* She saw Spiritualism, with its female leadership and alternative social structure, as the basis of a new religious order.

That evening, Olcott proposed to his peers forming another organization to study ancient and contemporary spiritual mysteries. On November 17, Olcott, Blavatsky, and their collaborators inaugurated the Theosophical Society, not just an ad hoc club of the curious but a structured group with three stated aims: "1) To form a nucleus of the universal brotherhood of humanity, without distinction of race, creed, sex, caste or color. 2) To encourage the comparative study of religion, philosophy, and science. 3) To investigate unexplained laws of nature and the powers latent in humanity." Olcott was named its first president.

Within the three principles appeared the nascent language of a spiritual revolution that in the next century swept the world: civic, social, and spiritual equality (echoing the Rosicrucian manifestos); defense of all religions without necessary fealty to any, presaging the now-popular stance "spiritual but not religious;" freedom to select among varying spiritual practices; and comparative study of extraphysicality and human potential. All of this was summarized in the organization's future motto, at once idealistic and defiant: "No Religion Higher Than Truth."

Young inventor Thomas Edison (1847–1931) joined the Theosophical circle. Olcott recounted Edison describing an elaborate instrument he constructed—with one end attached to his forehead and the other to a pendulum—to test kinetic powers of the mind. Major General Abner Doubleday, posthumously (though spuriously) credited with inventing baseball, also entered their world. Doubleday, a Civil War veteran who led a crucial command at Gettysburg, created

* For an account of séances in the Lincoln White House, see my *Occult America*.

one of the first English translations of Lévi's *Doctrine and Ritual of High Magic*, which was serialized for several years in a Theosophical monthly *The Word* starting in 1912. Doubleday spoke with his new colleagues about karma, which he said gave him courage under fire (he had been wounded several times). Other early members of the Theosophical Society included kabbalists, clergy, journalists, social reformers, activists, and academics interested in exploring the occult.

When Olcott first met Blavatsky, the charmed bourgeois in him marveled over her tales of "traveling in most of the lands of the Orient, searching for antiquities at the base of the Pyramids, witnessing mysteries of Hindoo temples, and pushing with an armed escort far into the interior of Africa."

During her evident wanderlust, Blavatsky met a married couple of seekers, Emma and Alexis Coulomb, in Egypt in 1871. They contacted her again in 1879 to say they were stranded in Sri Lanka and financially destitute. The following year, H.P.B. relocated the couple to Bombay and employed them as "man Friday" workers for the transplanted Theosophical Society. But frictions flared and the Coulombs, whom Blavatsky accused of blackmail, were dismissed in May 1884. In September, the Coulombs sent a series of letters to Christian missionary friends impugning Blavatsky as a fake conjuror and fraud.* To compound matters, in December, the formidable psychical investigator Richard Hodgson arrived in Madras to investigate these and other charges for the British Society for Psychical Research. As Tuitit Bey had cautioned Henry in 1875, "her soul is sensitive to dishonour and she hath reason to mistrust the future."

In the wake of scandals arising from the Coulomb letters and Hodgson investigation, Blavatsky departed India in March 1885. By June, Hodgson issued his initial findings through the Society for Psychical Research. The controversial "Hodgson Report" appeared in December, impugning Blavatsky for mediumistic fraud and writing off Olcott as her dupe. Olcott was devastated to discover that in letters Blavatsky sent an Indian colleague, Hurrychund Chintamon, who violated her trust by sharing them, his old partner called him

* For background, see *The Coulomb Case* by Michael Gomes (*Theosophical History Occasional Papers*, Vol. X, 2005).

a "psychologized baby" and said he was under her hypnotic control. It was almost too much for Henry. "In my whole experience in the movement," he wrote in *Old Diary Leaves* III, "nothing ever affected me so much as this. It made me desperate, and for twenty-four hours almost ready to go down to the beach and drown myself in the sea." (Chintamon's betrayal moved even the generous-spirited Joscelyn Godwin to write, "I have not been able to trace Chintamon's subsequent career, so cannot say whether it ended with a well-deserved knife in the back."*)

Blavatsky once more became a nomad and now a subject of derision. She traveled for two years in Europe, where she began writing *The Secret Doctrine*. In 1887, the occultist settled in the Notting Hill neighborhood of London in the home of an uncle and nephew who belonged to the Theosophical Society. In 1888, Blavatsky published *The Secret Doctrine*, her two-volume work of arcane history and occult cosmology.

After a period of ill-health, Blavatsky died in London on May 8, 1891. She was just fifty-nine, though easily looked ten or more years older. Olcott continued his activities, but in 1894 and 1895 he grew enmeshed in internal Theosophical Society controversies with William Q. Judge, who claimed to receive his own guidance from the masters. Olcott disputed Judge's claims, leading to splits in the society.** Also in 1895, Olcott published the first installment of his surprisingly readable, if not enthrallingly titled, six-volume memoir, *Old Diary Leaves* (issued through 1935, including posthumous volumes). In October 1906, Olcott suffered a severe fall on a passenger ship en route from New York to Italy. He died February 17, 1907, at the Theosophical Society's international headquarters in Adyar on India's southeast coast.

Following the founders' deaths, the society's activities were largely helmed by English Theosophists Annie Besant (1847–1933), a political reformer and protégé to Blavatsky, and Charles Webster Leadbeater (1854–1934), a former Anglican priest with a razor intel-

* "The Hidden Hand, Part III," *Theosophical History*, October 1990.

** The United Lodge of Theosophists, founded in 1909 and active today, views Judge as a legitimate cofounder of Theosophy and encourages return to his and Blavatsky's core teachings.

lect and personality to match. Their tenure was extraordinary in its own way, including development of the 1905 volume *Thought Forms*, a work that weighed enormously on the germination of abstract art.*

To produce the book, Besant and Leadbeater entered trance states in which they "read" the thoughts of one another or a subject. These thoughts appeared to them as visions in the form of geometric, abstract, or aura-like images. They described these images to visual artists who used them to create alluring, haunting, and perhaps unprecedented graphics of shape, wave, color, and symbol. Even a glance through the plates in *Thought Forms* reveals the nascence of psychedelia, spiritual expressionism, and abstract art.** *Thought Forms* was a widely acknowledged influence on pioneering abstractionist Wassily Kandinsky (1866–1944), a Theosophical Society member who owned a copy of the 1908 German edition, which he continued to reference into the 1920s.***

Besant and Leadbeater considered thought an actual presence, a reality in its own realm and dimension, where it takes forms that can be physically represented. Kandinsky wrote as much in his 1911 book, *Concerning the Spiritual in Art*: "Thought is matter, but of a fine and not coarse substance." Thoughts and emotive states, as Besant and Leadbeater saw it, possess discernible properties of representation, such as a glowing aura, spiral image, abstract shape, or shade of color.

One of the mysteries around *Thought Forms* is how the authors so precisely communicated their visions to the artists with whom they worked. The most detailed account appears in a September 1896 article from the Theosophical journal *Lucifer* where Besant described their efforts:

> Two clairvoyant Theosophists [Besant and Leadbeater] observed the forms caused by definite thoughts thrown out by one of them, and also watched the forms projected by other persons under the

---

* Due to a bibliographical error in the first edition, there is persistent confusion over when *Thought Forms* appeared. By accident or mistake, the first edition identifies publication as 1901. But it was 1905—a fact validated by John L. Crow in his article "Thought Forms: Bibliographic Error," *Theosophical History*, July-Oct 2012.

** I co-introduce a reissue of *Thought Forms* published in 2020 by Sacred Bones. It features restored first-edition plates.

*** *Charles Webster Leadbeater 1854–1934: A Biographical Study* by Gregory John Tillett, doctoral thesis, Department of Religious Studies, University of Sidney, 1985.

> influence of various emotions. They described these as fully and accurately as they could to an artist who sat with them, and he made some sketches and mixed colours, till some approximation of the objects was made.

Besant also highlighted three causative factors: "1. Quality of thought determines colour. 2. Nature of thought determines form. 3. Definiteness of thought determines clearness of outline."

Four years after *Thought Forms* in 1909, Leadbeater encountered a poor, undernourished fourteen-year-old boy playing on the beach near Adyar. The boy's aura, marveled Leadbeater, conveyed total selflessness. He and Besant saw the youth as vessel for the incarnation of a messianic "World Teacher," Lord Maitreya.*

This was Jiddu Krishnamurti (1895–1986), who became one of the most unclassifiable and extraordinary spiritual intellects of the new century. Besant and Leadbeater wanted Krishnamurti, as avatar, to helm a new world movement, which would usher in a spiritually evolutionary age. Besant became a maternal figure to the precocious youth. But he began his drive toward independence at least as early as age eighteen, when on October 31, 1912, Krishnamurti wrote Leadbeater:

> I think it is time now that I should take my affairs into my own hands. I feel I could carry out the Master's [Koot Hoomi's] instructions better if they were not forced upon me and made unpleasant as they have been for some years.** If I feel that I am responsible I shall do my best, for being now about 18 years old, I think that with advice I could manage. Of course I shall make mistakes, but I know generally the nature of my duty. I have not been given any opportunity to feel my responsibilities and have been dragged about like a baby. I have not written about this before because I did not wish to worry Mrs. Besant but I think you both know now the whole position.***

---

* Leadbeater's career was pockmarked by charges of pederasty. From 1906 to 1908, the accusations impelled his resignation from the Theosophical Society. Besant claimed him a victim of hearsay. In any case, no violations with Krishnamurti or his brother Nitya are evident.

** Leadbeater and Krishnamurti reportedly visited Koot Hoomi each night in astral form for the adolescent's instruction.

*** *Krishnamurti: The Years of Awakening* by Mary Lutyens (Farrar, Straus and Giroux, 1975).

Relations and plans remained intact but were tempered by Krishnamurti's newfound self-assertion, which stemmed, in part, from financial support he began receiving from wealthy American Theosophist Mary Hoadley Dodge.

The 1925 death of Krishnamurti's beloved younger brother, Nitya, proved shattering. Dogged by lifelong ill health and tuberculosis, Nitya died at twenty-seven. The tragedy "changed [Krishnamurti's] entire philosophy of life, and destroyed his implicit faith in the plans outlined by Leadbeater and Mrs. Besant," wrote historian Gregory John Tillett in his doctoral thesis on Leadbeater.

In August 1929, the projected "World Teacher" famously announced a break in plans to a conference of Theosophists in the Netherlands:

> I maintain that truth is a pathless land, and you cannot approach it by any path whatsoever, by any religion, by any sect. That is my point of view, and I adhere to that absolutely and unconditionally. Truth, being limitless, unconditioned, unapproachable by any path whatsoever, cannot be organized; nor should any organization be formed to lead or coerce people along a particular path . . . This is no magnificent deed, because I do not want followers, and I mean this. The moment you follow someone you cease to follow Truth. I am not concerned whether you pay attention to what I say or not. I want to do a certain thing in the world and I am going to do it with unwavering concentration. I am concerning myself with only one essential thing: to set man free. I desire to free him from all cages, from all fears, and not to found religions, new sects, nor to establish new theories and new philosophies . . . You can form other organizations and expect someone else. With that I am not concerned, nor with creating new cages, new decorations for those cages. My only concern is to set man absolutely, unconditionally free.

Krishnamurti disbanded the organization that Besant had erected around him, Order of the Star (previously Order of the Star in the East). Although he returned to Adyar with Besant and spoke over the coming year at Theosophical conferences, Krishnamurti resigned from the society in 1930.

One of the myths of recent spiritual history is that the teacher fully and decisively separated from Theosophy. That is not exactly the case.* The teacher did, in fact, reject any hierarchical order, including the Theosophical Society. This was an obvious source of pain to Besant who parentally doted on him. But he remained in contact with her almost until her death. Indeed, shortly before Krishnamurti's passing in 1986, the former protégé also spoke at different Theosophical centers.

In May 1933, about four months before Besant's death, Krishnamurti visited his former guardian at Adyar. It would not be long until a vigil formed around her bed. They spent a little time together in Besant's room but she soon sent him away, concerned about the effects of her declining energies on his psyche. Krishnamurti's one-time mentor told him, he recalled, "I must not stay long with her as it was bad for me to be in an invalid's room."**

Whatever one makes of Besant's estimation, consider the personal sacrifice in it. She loved Krishnamurti as a son. In physical decline, rather than drinking in her time with him, she, not he, abruptly ended the visit. Besant took a similar approach to esoteric scholar Manly P. Hall, whom we soon meet, when the budding eminence asked her in Southern California whether to join the Theosophical Society or venture out on his own. She encouraged the latter.***

---

* As with members of the Beatles and Maharishi, relationships prove subtler than headlines. Rumor and tabloid journalism assert that the Beatles resolutely split from the guru. In fact, George Harrison maintained contact with Maharishi. After Linda McCartney's death in 1998, Paul and daughter Stella visited Maharishi in the Netherlands. In 2009, surviving Beatles Paul and Ringo Starr played a benefit concert for the David Lynch Foundation, which teaches Transcendental Meditation. Yoko Ono, who is nothing if not protective of husband John Lennon's memory and wishes, sat in the front row. Harrison's widow, Olivia, was also in attendance. I note this because stories of splits are often more lurid than actual.

** *Annie Besant* by Anne Taylor (Oxford University Press, 1992). Taylor not only admirably traces Besant's life but captures the pathos of her relationships.

*** See "Remembering an American Sage" by Stephan A. Hoeller in *Quest* magazine, Summer 2022, and Hoeller's interview in the documentary *Holywood* directed by Courtney Sell.

CHAPTER SEVEN

You Are As Your Mind Is

In 2017, I was privileged to publish historian Kevin Dann's biography of Henry David Thoreau, *Expect Great Things*. The book focused on the Transcendentalist's spiritual and ethical search. Its infectious title came from a letter Thoreau wrote a neighbor; his note ostensibly relates to botany—yet says more:

> Concord [MA] May 19th 1859
>
> Miss Mary H. Brown,
>
> Excuse me for not acknowledging before the receipt of your beautiful gift of may-flowers. The delay may prove that I did not fear I should forget it, though very busily engaged in surveying. The flowers were somewhat detained on the road, but they were not the less fragrant, and were very superior to any that we can show.
>
> It chanced that on the very day they arrived, while surveying in the next town, I found more of these flowers than I have ever seen hereabouts, and I have accordingly named a certain path "May-flower Path" on my plan. But a botanist's experience is full of coincidences. If you think much about some flower which you never

> saw, you will be pretty sure to find it some day actually growing near by you. In the long run, we find what we expect. We shall be fortunate then if we expect great things.
>
> Please remember me to your Father & Mother
>
> Yours truly
>
> Henry D. Thoreau

Expect great things. The outlook is heavily rooted in the Transcendentalist and self-improvement mindset. This perspective also shaped the nature of New Thought or positive-mind metaphysics. New Thought, in method if not name, resounds through concepts like "power of positive thinking," "Law of Attraction," and "manifesting." It is the most popular form of metaphysics in modern life. The gambits and ideals of positive-mind spirituality emerged directly from the esoteric and occult subcultures we have been considering.

Seen from a certain perspective, every idea that's ever been thought has always been with us. Indeed, the general concept of mind as an *influencing agency,* whether psychological or metaphysical, possesses ancient roots. The determining property of thought is referenced with varying degrees in classical spiritual and ethical literature, including the Vedas, the *Dhammapada*, the *Bhagavad Gita*, and, of course, the Hermetica.

But to locate more immediate antecedents to mind metaphysics requires probing modern influences. In the early eighteenth century, Irish bishop George Berkeley sounded a transformative note in Western philosophy when he argued that material reality has no existence beyond one's mental-sensory perceptions. What appears in our world is a result of observation, Berkeley reasoned. Without a sensate observer, phenomena have nothing in which to be grounded. Berkeley's insight gave rise to the thought school called Idealism. Yet the Anglo-Irish philosopher stopped short of anointing the individual as inventor of reality: there also exists, he insisted, a *rerum natura,* or fixed nature of things.

The next generation of Idealist philosophers, most significantly Immanuel Kant and G.W.F. Hegel, also saw reality as the product of perception—but our senses, they argued, are limited in their ability to perceive true nature. *The mind is finally experiencing itself* rather than ultimate truth. Like Berkeley, Kant and Hegel also believed, more or less, in fixed universal laws, within which an awakened person could serve as a dynamic actor but not an agent of creation.

Some mid-to-late nineteenth century modernists including Arthur Schopenhauer and Friedrich Nietzsche extolled the abilities of human will and spoke of an inner-self that forms an invisible seat of power. (Again, Schopenhauer: "Man had not learnt to direct the light of speculative thought towards the mysterious depths of his own inner self.") But, still, such views did not elevate the mind to author of reality. Indeed, all of the major Idealist philosophers and their offspring, from Immanuel Kant to Ralph Waldo Emerson, held that natural man could *ally* himself with universal forces, and thus attain a kind of greatness or at least integral means of living, but none broke with Berkeley's assertion in his 1710 *Principles of Human Knowledge* that shapes and shades of reality "are not creatures of my will."

A countercurrent of sorts emerged in the eighteenth century writings of Swedish scientist and mystic Emanuel Swedenborg. As was seen, Swedenborg's vast and challenging cosmic philosophy included a "Divine influx"—an animating body of energies and ideas that permeated all of nature, including the mind. Swedenborg's "Divine influx" paralleled aspects of ancient Hermetic thought. American philosopher and essayist Ralph Waldo Emerson took partial influence from Swedenborg's ideas. In a far more readerly manner, Emerson depicted the mind as a *capillary of divine influence*; he described human thought as a kind of concentrically expanding awareness, ultimately capable of godlike perception. Emerson extolled the power of ideas to shape a person's life, noting in his 1841 essay "Spiritual Laws" that "the ancestor of every action is a thought."

All of these ideas presented tantalizing possibilities. Yet even by the mid-nineteenth century, the notion of an empirically empowering mysticism, one that could create and shape circumstance, was unheard of within either reformist or mainstream congregations. The modern West possessed no concept that our thoughts, much less a healthful sense of self-worth, could mold or select outer events. It was only deep within subcultures of religious experimentation that the mind-power ideal began taking shape—and in settings far removed from universities, seminaries, and philosophical societies.

Until the end of his life in 1815, occult healer Franz Anton Mesmer held to his theories of a mysterious life force called *animal magnetism*. Yet the healer's protégés edged away from notions of etheric energies. They adopted a more proto-psychological language. One of the most gifted of them, the Marquis de Puységur, undertook experiments in France in late 1784 and early 1785 that persuaded him that the suggestive powers of the Mesmerist, and his "rapport" with the patient, were the forces at work.

"Animal magnetism," Puységur wrote, "lies not in the action of one body upon another, but in the action of thought upon the vital principle of the body."* In terms Mesmer would not use, the student made the connection between mind and body, if still leaving open the question of what the body's "vital principle" may be. Puységur fashioned a terminology remarkably anticipatory of modern self-development. When Puységur got dispatched to command a French artillery regiment in Strasbourg in August 1785, he began teaching classes in Mesmerism at a local Freemasonic lodge. At the end of the course, the Mesmerist gave his students an affirmation that extolled the forces of thought and will:

> I believe in the existence within myself of a power.
> From this belief derives my will to exert it.
> The entire doctrine of Animal Magnetism is contained in two words: *Believe and want.*
> I *believe* that I have the power to set into action the vital principle of my fellowmen; I *want* to make use of it; this is all my science and all my means.
> *Believe* and *want*, Sirs, and you will do as much as I.**

For all the enthusiasm of Mesmer's followers, the practice of Mesmerism faded in France. The 1789 revolution sent some of Mesmer's aristocratic students fleeing, and others to the guillotine (a fate met, too, by some of the members of the Franklin commission). Puységur spent two years in prison. Séances and magnetic trances were supplanted by political tracts and revolutionary intrigues.

---

* *Psychical Research* by W.F. Barrett (Henry Holt, 1911).

** *The Discovery of the Unconscious* by Henri F. Ellenberger (Basic Books, 1970).

While the influence of Mesmerism dimmed in Europe, the healer's philosophy—or rather a variant reinterpreted by followers—crossed the Atlantic. In America, a new generation of Mesmerists migrating from France and England discovered a public hungry for innovation. And here we reencounter the Poughkeepsie Seer, Andrew Jackson Davis. Davis united the threads of mediumship, Spiritualism, and social progress in a manner that converged with mental-healing experiments and gave rise to the modern belief in practical potentials of the positive mind.

Starting as a teen, Davis said that from a magnetized state he could journey in his astral body to unseen dimensions; he said he could read books without opening the cover; and, like other American and French mediums, he reported the ability to gaze into the bodies of the sick, diagnosing diseases and ailments. Davis also described out-of-body travels to other planets and heavenly realms—accounts that echoed Swedenborg.

After a particularly deep trance-session on a winter evening in 1844, Davis had difficulty returning to ordinary consciousness. His mind illumined and his body light, he said he embarked on a psychical "flight through space," which took him across the frozen landscape of New York's Catskill Mountains. Whether his journey was astral or physical was not altogether clear, although it may have been both as he vanished until the following day.*

His journey culminated inside the stone walls of a small country graveyard deep in the woods. There he said he met the spirit of Swedenborg himself. The Swedish healer told the boy, "By thee a new light will appear." Davis also received a "Magic Staff," which at first seemed physical but he later deemed mental in nature. Afterwards, an astral message revealed to him the true meaning of its magic: "Behold! Here is Thy Magic Staff: UNDER ALL CIRCUMSTANCES KEEP AN EVEN MIND. Take it, Try it, Walk with it. Believe on it. FOR EVER." The staff was not an object but a principle. Davis later called his autobiography *The Magic Staff.*

The next day, Davis reappeared at the home of a Mesmerist friend where he was staying and told of "new directions" their work must

* *The Magic Staff: An Autobiography of Andrew Jackson Davis*, 1857.

take. The youth insisted he would no longer perform clairvoyant feats for local "wonder-seekers." In months ahead, Davis spoke of a "new mountain . . . looming in the distance," summoning him to his true mission. The seer began delivering metaphysical lectures from a trance state. Davis assumed the form of a backwoods Swedenborg, using "mental illumination" to explore cosmic truths and mechanics of creation.

By fall 1845, Davis departed Poughkeepsie for Manhattan and began working with a new pair of helpers. S.S. Lyon, a doctor of herbal remedies became Davis's new Mesmerist control. William Fishbough, a Universalist minister, became his "honored scribe," recording the seer's dispatches from the spirit world. Together, the three began a series of daily sittings. They had little money and bounced among a string of furnished rooms but a remarkable energy animated their readings, which could last hours. Herbalist Lyon would place Davis into a trance in his "sleeping chair," while minister Fishbough took dictation. Davis described visits to heaven, to other dimensions and planets, and, finally, to the heart of universal creation itself.

On January 13, 1846, Fishbough published a letter in the *New York Tribune,* outlining Davis's philosophy—in particular, the powers of a universal "Positive Mind":

> At the back of all the visible operations of nature, however, there is a hidden cause, to which all mechanical and organic causes are but secondary and subordinate; and the admission of this undeniable fact should open our minds to conviction of well-attested phenomena, especially as connected with the mysterious economy of mind . . . that matter was originally formed from a spiritual essence, and that in its progress of refinement, from the earth to the plant, from the plant to the animal, from the animal to man, it will finally form spirit individualized—and that this is endlessly progressive in knowledge and refinement, continually approaching nearer and nearer to the great eternal *Positive Mind*—the Foundation and Controller of all existence.

Although Davis's visions were partly drawn from the ideas of Swedenborg (a repeat criticism of his work), the correspondence did sketch out an excitingly fresh mental metaphysics. Davis stopped just short of calling the psyche a channel of the great "Positive Mind," endowing man with the ability to harness this force for creative purposes. It would fall to another generation of seekers to close the circle he began. Nonetheless, the Poughkeepsie Seer, having not yet published his first book, laid the earliest language of the positive-thinking movement.

By 1847, the men assembled Davis's 157 trance lectures into a metaphysical opus, *The Principles of Nature, Her Divine Revelations and a Voice to Mankind.* It was a massive, sprawling work that retold the story of creation: "The ever-controlling influence and active energies of the Divine Positive Mind brought all effects into being, as parts of one vast whole."

While thickly worded and torturously long, *The Principles of Nature* sold a remarkable 900 copies in its first week of release. Davis's references to the "Great Positive Mind," or "Great Positive Power," established the idea, at least for enthusiasts, that all of creation was a mental act, emanating from a higher intelligence and concretizing all forms of reality.

In the mid-nineteenth century, Davis coined a concept that has far outlasted his name. It was the *Law of Attraction.* But he imbued the term with a different meaning than the one later attached to it. Never one for brevity, Davis in 1855 produced a six-volume treatise on metaphysical laws, *The Great Harmonia.* In volume four, he defined the Law of Attraction not as a principle of cause-and-effect thinking, but, rather, as a cosmic law governing the cycles and maintenance of life.

"The atoms in human souls," Davis wrote, "are attracted together from the living elements of soil and atmosphere; and, when these atoms complete the organization or individuality, they then manifest the same law of Attraction in every personal relation, inward and outward, through all the countless avenues of existence!" He called this law "the fundamental principle of all Life, which is Attraction."

In Davis's rendering, the Law of Attraction was a gravitational force of affinities, one ever-present in cosmic and human affairs. The law dictated where a person's soul would dwell in the afterlife based on traits displayed on earth. It explained human attraction (or its absence). The Law of Attraction governed the types of spirits drawn to séances based on the character of people seated around the table.

Davis did allow that the Law of Attraction governed certain material and earthly goals: "A mysterious wand, termed the 'Law of

Attraction,' guides the traveller." He probably would have agreed with Joseph Campbell's maxim "follow your bliss" and seen the mythologist's expression as a sound interpretation of the Law of Attraction. But it was not until positive-thinking impresarios revised Davis's ideas that the Law of Attraction connoted a direct bond between thought and object.

Historical error holds that Madame Blavatsky coined the Law of Attraction. This is due to a passage in her 1877 book, *Isis Unveiled*: "By whatsoever name the physicists may call the energizing principle in matter is of no account; it is a subtile something apart from the matter itself, and, as it escapes their detection, it must be something besides matter. If the law of attraction is admitted as governing the one, why should it be excluded from influencing the other?" Blavatsky was using the Law of Attraction in the sense of Davis's meaning. She and Colonel Olcott knew Davis's work and at another point in her book she calls him "the great American seer."

The remaking of Davis's law began in 1892, in the final of six volumes by journalist and spiritual explorer Prentice Mulford, *Your Forces, And How to Use Them*. Mulford, who died the previous year, had written: "Such a friend will come to you through the inevitable law of attraction if you desire him or her . . ." In 1897, popular inspirational author Ralph Waldo Trine used the term as a mental law in his bestselling *In Tune with the Infinite*, as did Helen Wilmans, a New Thought pioneer who invoked the Law of Attraction in her 1899 book, *The Conquest of Poverty*. In June of that year, New Thought leader Charles Brodie Patterson showcased the phrase in his influential article "The Law of Attraction," published in his journal *Mind*. Patterson celebrated the Law of Attraction as a metaphysical super-law dictating that everything around us is the product of our dominant thoughts.

While Davis reached into the minds of seekers, another innovator reached into the hearts of people desperately in need of healing. This was a clockmaker from Belfast, Maine, Phineas Quimby. In 1833, quietly and with little forethought, Quimby embarked on a psychological experiment that also formed the germination of the positive-mind outlook—and, specifically, how it could impact health.

A man in his early thirties, Quimby was suffering from tuberculosis. Under doctor's orders he had been ingesting calomel, a popular though disastrous therapy in the first half of the nineteenth century. It was a mercury-based toxin that induced massive salivating and foaming of the mouth. Calomel was a common treatment among physicians who practiced "heroic medicine." The theoretical framework was that draining the body of fluids could rid a patient of disease and serve as an overall tonic to health. Along with calomel, physicians prescribed bleeding or bloodletting, including open or "weeping" wounds and—almost unbelievably in the modern era—application of leeches.

By the early 1830s, calomel ingestion was causing Quimby to suffer from mercury poisoning. The side effects were disfiguring. "I had taken so much calomel," he later wrote in his journals, "that my system was said to be poisoned with it; I lost many of my teeth from that effect."* He continued, "In this state I was compelled to abandon my business and, losing all hope, I gave up to die." At this time Quimby and his wife had two sons and an infant daughter. How they managed to support a family during this ordeal goes unmentioned.

With little left to lose, Quimby turned to a therapeutic procedure recommended by a friend: horseback riding. "Having an acquaintance who cured himself by riding horseback," he recalled, "I thought I would try riding in a carriage as I was too weak to ride horseback."** In actuality, Quimby was reprising a treatment known to the ancient Greeks, who used vigorous horseback riding as a tonic.

One day Quimby set off in his carriage outside Belfast, Maine. He had a "contrary" horse, which kept stopping and finally would not budge unless the clockmaker ran beside him. Exhausted from running the horse up a hill, Quimby collapsed into the carriage and sat stranded two miles from home. He managed to shout to a man plow-

---

* Of the many volumes that survey Phineas Quimby's life and writing, a uniquely helpful resource is Ronald A. Hughes's *Phineas Parkhurst Quimby: His Complete Writings and Beyond* (Phineas Parkhurst Quimby Resource Center, 2009); Hughes's collection identifies errors that persisted in earlier volumes. Also valuable is *The Complete Collected Works of Dr. Phineas Parkhurst Quimby* edited by Rev. Lux Newman and the Phineas Parkhurst Quimby Philosophical Society (Seed of Life Publishing, 2008, 2012). Unless otherwise noted, I quote from Hughes.

** Quimby's recovery is drawn from "My Conversion," January 1863, as published in *Phineas Parkhurst Quimby: The Complete Writings*, vol. 3, edited by Ervin Seale (DeVorss, 1988). Further details on Quimby's life appear in a biographical treatment written by his son George and published in the March 1888 *New England Magazine*, as reprinted in the Belfast (ME) *Republican Journal* on January 10, 1889.

ing a nearby field and asked him to come and start the horse. "He did so," Quimby continued,

> and at the time I was so weak I could scarcely lift my whip. But excitement took possession of my senses, and I drove the horse as fast as he could go, up hill and down, till I reached home and, when I got into the stable, I felt as strong as I ever did. From that time I continued to improve, not knowing, however, that the excitement was the cause . . .

Quimby grew intrigued at how the frenetic carriage ride lifted his symptoms. As his spirits rose, he noticed, so did his bodily vigor. The carriage ride formed Quimby's earliest notions that the mind impacted the body. But it would take the experience of Mesmerism, then reaching America from Paris, to deliver Quimby to the full possibilities.

In 1836, Quimby encountered a traveling Mesmerist in Bangor. A French expatriate named Charles Poyen visited the Maine city on a lecture tour. Poyen himself was a product of the marriage between Mesmerism and French social reform. His dedication to Mesmerism was jointly forged in his opposition to slavery—and his experience of a strange medical episode.*

While studying medicine in Paris in 1832, Poyen suffered a digestive disorder and "nervous disease." After eight months of fruitless treatment the medical student sought out a Mesmerist. His guide placed an innovative twist on the practice. He placed an assistant, a "Madame V," into a state of "magnetic sleep" from which the medium astonished Poyen by seeming to clairvoyantly diagnose his illness. Acting on the medium's advice, Poyen sought to rest his nerves with an extended visit to his family's sugarcane plantations in the French West Indies. What he witnessed on the islands of Martinique and Guadeloupe transformed his view of life. Some of the island's slaveholding plantation owners were themselves skilled in

* Sources on Poyen include "Charles Poyen Brings Mesmerism to America" by Eric R. Carlson, *Journal of the History of Medicine and Allied Sciences*, vol. 15, 1960; "How Southern New England Became Magnetic North" by Sheila O'Brien Quinn, *History of Psychology*, August 2007; and *The Heyday of Spiritualism* by Slater Brown (Hawthorn Books, 1970).

Mesmerism, which they demonstrated on field hands. Poyen was deeply moved to discover that African slaves and French slaveholders both entered trance states and experienced the same effects. For Poyen, this suggested the basic sameness of human beings. It moved him to revile slavery.

After Poyen's fourteen-month stay in the islands, however, his digestive condition was no better. He decided to see if the cold winds of New England proved a better tonic. Poyen arrived in Portland, Maine, in late 1834 and in the following year settled in Lowell, Massachusetts. It proved a good match for the young Frenchman. The town was a center of abolitionism. Poyen grew friendly with Lowell's mayor, a Brown-educated physician intrigued by Mesmerism. With the mayor's encouragement, Poyen embarked on lecture tours in 1836.

Public speaking did not come easily to Poyen. With a halting command of English, he struggled before audiences. Poyen contemplated returning to a more "comfortable existence" in the West Indies but found the islands' slave-based society "repugnant to my sympathies."* He also felt that abandoning his speaking tour meant allowing Mesmerism to die in America. Poyen decided to add some drama to his presentations through live demonstrations. This attracted Quimby's attention in Bangor in August 1836.

In a few years the clockmaker encountered a more impressive Mesmerist. In fall 1841, British physician and magnetic healer Robert H. Collyer made his way to Belfast.** A skilled and persuasive speaker, Collyer attracted large audiences. The October 1, 1841, *Republican Journal* of Belfast reported on Collyer's method:

> The Doctor carries a subject with him, a youngster some 18 years old. They both took chairs upon a table, so as to be in full view. The Doctor then took the boy's knees between his, and both the boy's hands. They then commenced looking each other in the eyes; the Doctor making a very slight movement of the head, neck, and stomach. In this way they remained, say ten minutes, when the boy

* Poyen is quoted from his memoir, *Progress of Animal Magnetism in New England* (Weeks, Jordan & Co., 1837).

** On Collyer's career, I benefited from his book *Psychography* (Redding & Co., 1843); his memoir, *Lights and Shadows of American Life* (Brainard & Co., 1838, 1843); *Abnormal Hypnotic Phenomena*, vols. 1–4, edited by Eric J. Dingwall (J. & A. Churchill/ Barnes & Noble, 1968); and *A History of Hypnotism* by Alan Gauld (Cambridge University Press, 1992).

> gradually closed his eyes and fell asleep, leaning very much over on one side . . . He was stiff as though frozen in position.—When one sleeps they are perfectly limber. The boy was stiff.

Collyer used the technique practiced by Mesmer himself. As Quimby witnessed Collyer's ability to affect the bodily state and sensations of his assistant, he grew more interested in what he felt Mesmerism uncovered: a *method* to connect mind and body. The connection confirmed the relief he felt during his carriage ride. If the mind impacted the body, he wondered, what other powers might it contain?

This trait of inquiry, observed French mind theorist Émile Coué (1857–1926)—who coined the famous mantra, *day by day, in every way, I am getting better and better*—characterized the American intellect. "The French mind," Coué wrote in his 1923 book *My Method, including American Impressions*, "prefers first to discuss and argue on the fundamentals of a principle before inquiring into its practical adaptability to everyday life. The American mind, on the contrary, immediately sees the possibilities of it, and seeks . . . to carry the idea further even than the author of it may have conceived."

Quimby was not a philosopher but experimenter. Although he possessed an extraordinarily sharp mind and a keen grasp of mechanical details, he was unable to write much beyond the level of a schoolhouse boy, a fact that embarrassed him.

Quimby did maintain voluminous notebooks, into which he sometimes dictated his ideas with the assistance of others or, more commonly, arranged for friends and helpmates to rewrite his notes. But Quimby's aims laid beyond the printed page. He wished to rework the revelations of Mesmerism, in combination with his own personal experiments, to devise a protocol to heal the sick—or rather, to allow the sick to heal themselves.

Following Collyer's demonstrations, Quimby met a local teen who, similar to the medium visited by Poyen, could diagnose diseases from a trance state. Quimby believed that the boy, Lucius Burkmar, was capable of clairvoyantly peering into the mind and body of subjects. In fall 1843, Quimby and Lucius, then seventeen, traveled as a team throughout Maine and nearby New Brunswick, Canada, treating the sick, often in the presence of a local physician.* Their method was to sit facing each other, knee to knee, while the older man gazed into Lucius's eyes and gently waved his hands around Lucius's face, placing him into a trance. From his magnetized state, Lucius attempted to mentally scan the organs of patients and prescribed folk remedies such as herbal teas. The local physician prepared and administered the tea. Other times, Quimby assisted area surgeons by inducing a patient into a state of "mesmeric anesthesia." Lucius and Quimby's activities attracted a great deal of attention, and many swore that the pair had relieved their ailments, from migraines to tuberculosis.

But, again, Quimby grew dissatisfied. He found that Lucius's "cures" were often no different from those administered previously—and unsuccessfully—by a physician. In the only apparent difference, the patient was roused to an experience of relief by the presumed authority of the medium. Quimby grew convinced it was neither clairvoyance nor herbal remedies that were curing people. Rather, it was *the ability to awaken hope*: "The patient's disease is in his belief," Quimby wrote in his notes.** And "the cure," he later wrote in a February 14, 1862, letter to the *Portland Daily Advertiser*, "is not in the medicine, but in the confidence of the doctor or medium."

Quimby had the same insight as Mesmer's best students, who theorized that the effects of the mind, rather than magnetic fluid, were helping patients. While no communication existed between Quimby and Mesmer's protégés, each ventured similar conclusions.

Armed with this insight, Quimby stopped working with the clairvoyant around 1847.*** He began treating people on his own. Quimby sympathetically sat face-to-face with a patient, never denying that the subject was sick but encouraging him to "understand how disease originates in the mind and [to] fully believe it." If the patient's confidence was complete, Quimby would then urge the patient to ask:

---

* No precise records show when Quimby and Lucius started collaborating but intrepid researchers Ervin Seale and Erroll Stafford Collie, in *Phineas Parkhurst Quimby: The Complete Writings*, vol. 1 (1988), turned up letters of introduction that show the two men traveling together by early November 1843. Horatio Dresser in *The Quimby Manuscripts* (Thomas Y. Crowell, 1921, 2nd edition) reprints an article of April 1843 from the *Bangor Democrat* (ME) showing Quimby and Lucius, age seventeen, delivering a demonstration.

** Dresser (1921).

*** It is not fully clear when Quimby stopped working with Lucius, but Seale's annotations indicate 1847. Lucius's extant journal writings about his experiences with Quimby conclude in 1845.

"Why cannot I cure myself?"* He further ventured that all experience is determined by perception, writing in his notes: "Our happiness and misery are what follow our belief."**

On rare occasions Quimby referred to "an unconscious power that is not admitted," or a "wisdom that is invisible and unconscious," enunciating a remarkably early psychological insight. Quimby could sound like a medieval alchemist in one breath and a modern psychologist in another; in actuality, he bridged the two.

Quimby's following was among farmers, housewives, and ordinary people. But his ideas attracted the attention of formidable religious thinkers. One of the most significant was Warren Felt Evans, a New England Methodist minister who left his pulpit in early 1864 to dedicate himself to the ideas of Emanuel Swedenborg.

The previous summer, while struggling to combine his Methodist beliefs with Swedenborgian mysticism and private experiments in mental healing, Evans had sought out Quimby. Followers of Swedenborg often took naturally to Quimby's methods, which seemed to suggest that the mind could channel and direct the cosmic laws Swedenborg described. Evans went on to write about mental healing in six books and proved an enormous force in shaping the positive-mind culture.

Starting in early 1859, Evans struggled with a painful bowel disorder. "My health so completely failed me last April that I could not preach," he wrote in his journal on September 19, 1859. "I have not preached for more than six months." In what must have been a particular sorrow for the learned minister, "there was," he wrote, "a time when I could not so much as read."***

In the grip of illness, Evans sought answers in both religion and the reaches of his mind. By the following spring he was convalescing and recording some of his earliest connections between disease and

* "True Origin of Christian Science," unsigned article in the *New York Times*, July 10, 1904.

** Dresser (1921).

*** A rare biographical record of Warren Felt Evans appears in an early twentieth century series of articles by William J. Leonard in the journal *Practical Ideals*, starting with "The Pioneer Apostle of Mental Science," July–August 1903, and continuing with "Warren Felt Evans, M.D.," published in three parts: September–October 1905; November 1905; and December 1905. Unless otherwise noted, Evans is quoted from this series.

mental state. Like Quimby, Evans was perched between religion and psychology—imploring God to cure his "mental disease." He began exploring Swedenborg's theology around 1858 and for several years attempted to combine Methodism with Swedenborg's outlook. His efforts broke down in 1862 when he aroused church ire with publication of *The Celestial Dawn*, a short book that explored Swedenborgian mysticism, though without naming the seer. The following year Evans left Methodism to join the Swedenborgian Church of the New Jerusalem.

As Evans charted his independent course, he discovered himself as a sprightly writer. His 1869 book *The Mental Cure*, while little read today, possesses a surprisingly modern tone. Evans demonstrated a knack for perennial phraseology, including the widely used term "thoughts are things," tucked into his 1876 book, *Soul and Body*. He used the phrase in a Swedenborgian manner to describe the spiritual world in which our inner-selves dwell: "In that world thoughts are things, and ideas are the most real entities of the universe." The phrase entered the popular lexicon through frequent use by mystic-journalist Prentice Mulford (1834–1891) who adopted it in 1886 in the first of six volumes of his widely read mail-order book, *Your Forces, and How to Use Them*.

Evans's discovery of Swedenborg not only commenced his departure from Methodism but brought him into a mental-healing theology. He thrilled to statements from Swedenborg, like this one from the seer's final book in 1771: "There is not anything in the mind, to which something in the body does not correspond; and this, which corresponds, may be called the embodying of that."*

Evans, in his own coda, *Esoteric Christianity and Mental Therapeutics* in 1886, used this passage as justification for a widely embraced insight, declaring: "In case of accidents, or chance occurrences, there is always the relation of cause and effect, for it is inconceivable that a thing should occur without a cause, and all causes are mental." This germinated into the widespread spiritual adage, *there are no accidents*.

But here Evans did not capture Swedenborg's statement in context. The Swedish seer's complete sentence was of a different tenor (and more discursive) than what Evans adapted. It went this way:

* *The True Christian Religion*, English translation published by J. B. Lippincott, 1875.

> There is not anything in the mind, to which something in the body does not correspond; and this, which corresponds, may be called the embodying of that; wherefore charity and faith, whilst they are only in the mind, are not incorporated in man, and then they may be likened to an aërial man, who is called a spectre, such as Fame was painted by the ancients, with a laurel around the head, and a cornucopia in the hand.

Swedenborg is saying that ethics without corresponding action render life a charade (a variant on James 2:26, "faith without works is dead.") He never exactly declared what Evans described in which all events, tragic or cheerful, emanate from mind alone. Regardless, energetic metaphysical journalist Prentice Mulford wasted no time seizing upon this idea—and in the same year as Evans's book wrote in his pamphlet *The Law of Success*: "Success in any business or undertaking comes through the working of a law. It never comes by chance: in the operations of nature's laws, there is no such thing as chance or accident."

And there it was: *there is no such thing as chance or accident*. It formed the premise of the Law of Attraction, the term Mulford resurrected a few years later, and the outlook of the new metaphysics. From coffee mugs and refrigerator magnets to at-your-fingertips philosophy, *there are no accidents* emerged from Evans's misinterpretation of Swedenborg with memorable reworking by Mulford.*

In October 1862, Quimby began treating a New Hampshire woman named Mary Glover Patterson. Passage of years and remarriage changed her name to how it appears in religious history: Mary Baker Eddy.

In the 1870s, Eddy founded one of the nation's most significant new religions, Christian Science. Rather than extol the powers of thought, Eddy saw the mind as the seat of all illness, violence, and illusion—conditions overcome by realization of the one true reality: the divine, all-permeating Intelligence of God. The human mind and

---

* I do not want to leave the impression of cheapness in the work of either man, both of whom I consider more fully in my *One Simple Idea*. Evans was an intrepid thinker as was Mulford, who produced some of the finest popularizations of Swedenborg. Their work must be read in fullness.

earthly matter, Eddy reasoned, possess no ultimate reality; rather, all things are grounded in the Mind of God. Where prejudice, sickness, and sorrow appear, they are *false perceptions* of man and the illusory world he dwells in.*

Careful readers may detect in Eddy a thought strand parallel to Gnosticism. I consider this unintentional: during her experimental years, Eddy's rural environs provided little access to Gnostic literature, nor were translations widely available; she made no telltale references in her work. But the parallel is notable.

Christian Science sought to resurrect the healing ministry of Christ through a rediscovery of spiritual laws and a radical metaphysic that rejected existence of earthly matter. It became a movement of tremendous growth and influence in the late nineteenth and early twentieth centuries. When Eddy met Quimby, however, she had not yet embarked on her theology. Whether, and to what extent, she adapted that theology from Quimby became the subject of a fiery and long-standing debate.

Alone, confused, and suffering from a chronic and undiagnosed spinal disorder, Eddy sought out Quimby's "mind-cure" in fall 1862. Under Quimby's care she began to feel her strength return. She visited again in the summer of 1863 and several times after until the spring of 1865. Eddy grew absorbed with Quimby, talking privately with him, taking notes, occasionally writing local articles and delivering talks on his work.

But her time with Quimby was fated to be relatively brief. The man she called her "doctor" died in January 1866, less than four years after they met. Eddy's own father had died three months earlier. Her second husband was largely absent and unfaithful. Further still, soon after Quimby's death, Eddy suffered a fall on an icy sidewalk in Lynn, Massachusetts, in February 1866, which left her bedridden and frayed her nerves.

---

* On the life and career of Mary Baker Eddy, key books include *Mary Baker Eddy* by Gillian Gill (Perseus/Radcliffe Biography Series, 1998); *Each Mind a Kingdom: American Women, Sexual Purity, and the New Thought Movement, 1875–1920* by Beryl Satter (University of California Press, 1999); *The Emergence of Christian Science in American Life* by Stephen Gottschalk (University of California Press, 1973); Robert Peel's three-volume biography, *Mary Baker Eddy*, published by Holt, Rinehart and Winston: *The Years of Discovery* (1966), *The Years of Trial* (1971), and *The Years of Authority* (1977); and Peel's *Christian Science: Its Encounter with American Culture* (Holt, 1958). Although Peel and Gottschalk were affiliated with the Christian Science church, their scholarship has proven impeccable. I class them with the best "believing historians."

It was a time of psychological extremes for Eddy. Yet at such moments she could display steely determination, vowing to walk again and poring over Scripture for succor and insight. She looked back on it as a period of great spiritual discovery. Yet she also, and inevitably, felt the near-simultaneous losses of a father, a spiritual healer, and a husband, all of it compounded by poor health. In distress, Eddy sought a new mentor. She wrote to another of Quimby's former students, Julius Dresser, also a colleague of Warren Felt Evans. Writing on February 15, 1866, Eddy implored Dresser, who was working as a journalist in Yarmouth, Maine, to take the helm of Quimby's work.

"I am constantly wishing that you would step forward," Eddy wrote. ". . . I believe you would do a vast amount of good and are more capable of occupying his place than any other I know." Eddy struck a tone of desperation: "Now can't you help me? . . . Please write at once."*

Dresser took almost three weeks to reply on March 2. It was a busy time for the Dresser family, as Julius's wife gave birth weeks earlier to the couple's first child, Horatio, who arrived the day before Quimby's death. Horatio later gained note as a historian, philosopher, and student of William James. While Julius felt affection for Quimby, and sincerely believed that he and his wife owed Quimby their health, he had no wish to revisit the past. He refused Eddy's plea. "As to turning Dr. myself . . . it is not to be thought of for a minute," Julius replied. "Can an infant do a strong man's work? Nor would I if I could."

Isolated and uncertain, Eddy answered her own call for spiritual guidance. Reflecting on her experiences of Quimby's healing methods, and embarking on her own intrepid reading of Scripture, she laid groundwork for her theology of Christian Science. Eddy's revelation, however, differed in both subtle and significant ways from Quimby's. While the clockmaker saw the human mind as a vessel of divine power, Eddy saw it as an instrument of illusion. The "mortal mind," she reasoned, must be eradicated so that the Mind of God could be revealed as the one absolute reality.

By about 1872, Eddy seems to have left behind any earlier sense of mentorship by Quimby. Although she once eulogized him as a man

---

* The Eddy-Dresser correspondence of 1866 appears in the first volume of Peel's three-volume biography (1966) and Gill (1998). I viewed Eddy's handwritten note in the archives of the Mary Baker Eddy Library in Boston.

"who healed with the truth that Christ taught," she began working on the text of her own testament and vision, the book that would become known as *Science and Health*.* The book laid out Eddy's philosophy that the healings of Christ were not a onetime miracle but an "ever-operative divine Principle" available to modern people. Quimby, to her mind, was, at most, a way station in her journey but not a teacher. In the years ahead, Eddy saw herself—and followers saw her—as an inspired religious leader. As such, she wanted no association with what she saw as the Mesmeric-influenced outlook of "Quimbyism." Nor did she want any part of the "New Age" movement anticipated by Evans, with its affirmations, inducements to right-thinking, and openness to a plethora of spiritual influences.** In a letter to a friend on July 11, 1871, Eddy dismissed Evans, whom she seemed to know only in passing from her Quimby years, as a "half scientist."*** This marked a decisive split between Christian Science and the developing movements of alternative spirituality.

Following the 1875 publication of *Science and Health*, Eddy's ideas quickly gained popularity. Her prayer therapy treatments, which she taught in classes and wrote about in pamphlets and articles, had deep appeal to a nation suffering under the lingering grotesqueries of "heroic medicine." Yet Eddy's success as a new religious voice, and her break with the memory of Quimby, attracted an unwanted figure from the past, a man with an impassioned and newfound sense of ire toward Eddy. In May 1882, former Quimby patient Julius Dresser, who expressed little interest in Quimby's ideas in 1866 and even less in Eddy, reemerged on the Boston scene.

According to Dresser's supporters, Julius arrived to defend Quimby's reputation; he believed that Eddy was passing off the doctor's ideas as her own. Eddy's partisans place Dresser back in the Boston area to grab a seat, financially and otherwise, in the prospering cultures of Christian Science and mind-cure, which had grown in tandem since Eddy's *Science and Health*. Dresser's motives may have been an amalgam of idealism and self-interest. In any case, it was not until Eddy gained national attention that Dresser reawakened to his interest in Quimby. The two fought

---

* Eddy is quoted from the *Lynn Weekly Reporter* (MA), February 14, 1866.

** Evans used the term New Age, in its modern spiritual-therapeutic sense, in his 1864 work *The New Age and Its Messenger*. The "Messenger" was Swedenborg.

*** Peel (1966).

running battles, in public and private, over Quimby's legacy until Julius died in 1893.

Arguments tend to coarsen rather than lighten over time. And the argument that Dresser embarked upon later solidified into a conviction about Eddy, one that got repeated to me this way by a librarian at a metaphysical center: "She stole all her ideas from Quimby!" That, in lesser or greater terms, is the judgment many historical writers settled on in the Eddy-Quimby affair. In the heat of responding to charges, Eddy worsened matters by dismissing Quimby's writing as "scribblings" and calling him "illiterate" in the *Christian Science Journal* in June 1887.

From the early 1880s to the early 1920s, the Quimby-Eddy debate produced hundreds of articles, books, pamphlets, and lectures. It remains a touchstone in the history of mental healing. Yet the closer one gets to its flames, the lesser the differences seem. If either side had moved an inch toward the other—Eddy acknowledging Quimby's role in preparing her for her later discoveries and Dresser conceding the distinctiveness of Eddy's metaphysic—most of the larger points of contention could have been resolved. No really serious observer concluded that Eddy plagiarized Quimby, whose writings were sprawling, vast, and unfocused. Nor could any thoughtful person deny that Quimby was anything less than a profound early influence on the once anxious and sickly young Eddy, who sought him out at a period of broken marriage, parental death, and strained health. As with most arguments, the differences were more emotional than actual.

In 1884, a Manchester, New Hampshire, housewife in her early thirties left behind her husband and young son to move to Boston to devote herself to Mrs. Eddy, as followers called the Christian Science founder. The housewife's motives were at once evident and inscrutable. She heard Eddy speak in October 1883 and was enthralled. The younger woman's religious and intellectual interest intensified later that year when she traveled to Boston to take a class with Eddy. By August 1884, she resolved to leave her husband and nine-year-old son in order to join the Christian Science fold in Boston.

This was Emma Curtis Hopkins (1849–1925). A mystic, suffragist, and student of Christian Science, she seemed fated to become one of Eddy's most trusted companions. Instead, she became a source of

Eddy's ire—and later her competitor and scourge. The split between the Christian Science founder and her onetime student formed the opening of a chrysalis from which emerged a new and greatly popular strain of mind-power philosophy that went under the name New Thought.*

Emma Curtis Hopkins first encountered Mrs. Eddy in the fall of 1883 when the healer was in Manchester staying at the home of one of her local students. Eddy's hostess prevailed upon her to deliver a short discourse on Christian Science to a group of visiting neighbors. Emma was among them. For her, hearing Eddy was like an intellectual parting of the Red Sea.

She was enthralled with Eddy's idea of a Divine Mind infusing all of life. In December, Hopkins wrote Eddy saying that the same neighbor who had hosted her cured Hopkins of "a late serious illness" using Christian Science methods. Hopkins told the Christian Science founder that she wanted to dedicate herself to her efforts. "I lay my whole life and all my talents, little or great, to this work," she wrote Eddy on January 14, 1884.**

Before Hopkins left home to join Eddy in late summer of 1884, Eddy granted the erudite younger woman the visible and valued position of editor of the church's house organ, the *Journal of Christian Science* (later the *Christian Science Journal*). Hopkins was the first person other than Eddy to hold that title. She was also given a place to live in the women's dormitory of Eddy's Massachusetts Metaphysical College in Boston. Hopkins asked only that Eddy not reveal that her job as the *Journal*'s editor paid no salary, so that her family wouldn't have further cause to question her judgment.

She assumed editorship in September 1884, but by October 1885, little more than a year later and with no evident warning, Hopkins found herself dismissed from the *Journal* and expelled from her room at the Metaphysical College's dormitory. The attractive and intelligent Hopkins came to believe that she had crossed Eddy's unwritten rule: never make references to having your own communication with

---

* Sources on Hopkins include J. Gordon Melton's seminal "New Thought's Hidden History: Emma Curtis Hopkins, Forgotten Founder," *Journal for the Society of the Study of Metaphysical Religion*, Spring 1995. Also important are *Women in Early New Thought* by Gary Ward Materra, Department of Religious Studies, UC Santa Barbara, 1997; *Emma Curtis Hopkins: Forgotten Founder of New Thought* by Gail M. Harley (Syracuse University Press, 2002); *Spirits in Rebellion: The Rise and Development of New Thought* by Charles Braden (Southern Methodist University Press, 1963, 1987); and *History and Philosophy of Metaphysical Movements in America* by J. Stillson Judah (Westminster Press, 1967).

** This letter and correspondence from November 4, 1885, are from Peel (1971).

the Divine. This was something that Hopkins had fleetingly done in a September 1885 *Christian Science Journal* editorial, which otherwise defended Eddy from critics. In the offending piece, "Teachers of Metaphysics," Hopkins wrote: "I was made to know Him face to face of whom I had heard by the hearing of the ear as a name only." It was the kind of reference, however oblique, that made Eddy uneasy.

"You remember that it was said the article Teachers of Metaphysics would get me in trouble," Hopkins wrote a friend on November 4, 1885. She went on to describe a chilling atmosphere: "Everything I said and did after that was watched and exaggerated and reported. I really was under heavy fire mentally . . . But they could not understand my complex way of expressing myself, nor know that I was digging for facts."

By "digging for facts," Hopkins was apparently referencing the Eddy-Quimby controversy. And in that matter she came down squarely on Eddy's side. "I saw all the letters said to be written by Mrs. E. to Dresser and Quimby and not one of them could be held as argument against her supreme originality," Hopkins wrote. Yet a subtler conflict simmered below her inquiries.

Hopkins was digging not only for facts but ideas. She was apparently reading broadly in metaphysics, Eastern religions, and the occult. This, possibly more than her editorial, cut against the culture Eddy was establishing within the church. By the 1880s, Christian Science had become a strict church, with a liturgy composed of prayers and readings dedicated to revealing the healing power of Christ. Eddy decreed that the church's core texts and practices would be subject to no adjustments, innovations, or outside influences. In the months following Hopkins's arrival, Eddy made it clear that students were not to go sampling varieties of metaphysical literature abounding on the New England scene, from Theosophy to mind-cure.

Shaped by the brunt of court battles and widespread pilfering of her vocabulary, Eddy eventually copyrighted the term Christian Science and by the mid-1880s effectively expelled any follower who hinted at independent directions or committed the heresy of studying work from figures in the Quimby circle, especially Warren Felt Evans. For violating these parameters, many of her most intrepid students were frozen out.

By the late 1880s, disputes and faction splits cost Eddy an estimated one-third of her movement. It may be difficult for spiritual seekers today, who select freely among a vast array of ideas, to see why dedicated and growing numbers of people flocked to such a conservative, if not stringent, atmosphere. For all Eddy's rigidity, her ideas could also reflect great humanity and compassion. Her bedside prayer treatments were vastly gentler than the often-harmful practices of late-nineteenth century medicine. Christian Science practitioners did something that would remain almost unheard-of in medicine through much of the early twentieth century: When sitting and praying beside patients, they paid attention to the moods, fears, and emotional needs of the individual. For suffering people, it was a radically new experience. In a sense, Eddy's theology formed an unrecognized influence on the growth of humanistic medicine in the late twentieth century.

Moreover, American medicine in the nineteenth century had no standard licensing procedures, and late into the century backwoods physicians persisted in the "heroic" remedies of bloodletting, narcotics, weeping wounds, and mercury ingestion, methods used even on children. The routines of heroic medicine were especially dangerous for women. In Victorian-age America the diagnosis of hysteria, or neurasthenia, was frequently applied to women and implicitly cemented the idea of female health as inherently fragile. Physicians sometimes regarded the uterus as the seat of symptoms of depression or hysteria and subjected female patients to almost inconceivably grim protocols. In such cases, noted historian Gary Ward Materra, "treatments might include leeching, injections, ovariotomies, and/or cauterization of the clitoris. Leeches were placed on the vulva or on the neck of the uterus, and sometimes the leeches progressed into the uterus itself, causing acute pain."

Eddy sought to keep women out of what may have been the least healthy place for them in the Victorian age: the examination room. While Christian Science was never a politicized movement, Eddy presented an impressive, even extraordinary, figure as the first female leader, both intellectually and spiritually, of a major American faith.

The predominance of female Christian Scientists was striking. In 1900, for example, of 2,564 Christian Science practitioners, or trained healers, 79 percent were women; ten years later, of 4,350 practitioners, 89 percent were women.* Often students were deeply

---

* *Rolling Away the Stone: Mary Baker Eddy's Challenge to Materialism* by Stephen Gottschalk (Indiana University Press, 2006, 2011).

intelligent, independent, and driven by the liberating atmosphere of a female-led church. Those who remained within the Eddy fold, either long or short term, not infrequently experienced a sense of personal agency. Anyone who found relief through Christian Science treatments could, in turn, train to become a practitioner. This summoned feelings of equality not only in health but in religious and social matters, as well.

Ironically, when Eddy shunned followers deemed overly ambitious or unorthodox, she created a cohort of ardently curious, dedicated—and churchless—experimenters, many of whom believed that divine laws could be experienced and wielded in modern life. Set loose from a congregational setting—as occult thinkers historically are—this brigade of spiritual troubadours included a large number of women who had once been drawn to Eddy as a model of female leadership.

This was the backdrop for the arrival and sudden departure of Emma Curtis Hopkins. If Hopkins had come and gone quickly, she just as swiftly developed into an independent and popular teacher on her own terms. Indeed, Hopkins's post–Christian Science career formed a wave of influence still felt on the spiritual scene today. Forced onto her own resources in 1885, Hopkins ventured to Chicago, where she established herself as a teacher of metaphysical healing.

Chicago was an exciting and natural destination for maverick seekers in the late nineteenth century. When Hopkins settled there, the midwestern city already hosted large circles devoted to mind-cure and Christian Science, stocked with followers and ex-followers of Eddy's. Chicago also had thriving scenes in Theosophy, occultism, and metaphysical publishing. The Midwestern city offered one more attractive feature—it took Hopkins far from her New England roots, where there would be no explaining to do over departing her family, only to see her relations with Eddy wither.

For the next ten years, the enterprising seeker threw herself into Chicago life. Hopkins built a growing and respected reputation as a teacher. In classes, lectures, and mental-visualization sessions, she instructed seekers, first from the Midwest and soon from many other parts of the nation, on how to use the divine power of thought. Hopkins's theology edged away from Eddy's focus on health and illness, and she began to expound her own variant of "Christian Science"—remaking the philosophy as an overall metaphysical approach to happiness. In a manner inconceivable to Eddy, though foreseen in

Hopkins's earliest articles, the ex-disciple employed ideas from Kabbalah, Buddhism, and Hinduism, as well as occult teachings from Theosophy.

Yet the former student still venerated Eddy and echoed key concepts of her work, such as the illusory nature of evil, illness, and the material world. Hopkins continued to apply the term Christian Science to her classes and publications and for years continued to see Eddy as her inspiration. If Hopkins hoped for reconciliation, it never came. "Oh, if you could only have been mental enough to see what I might be and do," she wrote Eddy, for the last time, on Christmas Day of 1886, "and given me time to work past and out of the era through which I was passing when . . . suddenly ordered . . . to leave."* There was no reply.

Hopkins's departures, meanwhile, grew increasingly radical. She encouraged using affirmations for personal happiness, which had been pioneered by Warren Felt Evans. She gamely expanded upon Evans's idea that the mind is an engine of well-being. "The day is plastic to you," she told students. "Write on its still walls your decree that the good and true are victorious already. Be explicit. Name the special good you would see through to pass. Declare that it is brought to pass already."** Hopkins extolled Evans's concept that within each person dwells an Inner God, an extension of the Divine. In terms that would have repulsed Eddy—and that became familiar lexicon of the New Age in future years—Hopkins spoke of a "God-Self" within.

In further counterpoint to Eddy, Hopkins urged followers to write, teach, and freely spread the word. In this way, her students became the driving figures of mind metaphysics in the next generation. They included Charles and Myrtle Fillmore, founders of Unity, a widespread Kansas City–based healing ministry of magazines, books, and classes; Ernest Holmes, the founder of Science of Mind, an influential twentieth century mind-power philosophy; Malinda Cramer, who spearheaded the Divine Science movement, which gained popularity in San Francisco and Denver; widely read prosperity author and suffragist Helen Wilmans; writer William Walker Atkinson, who built a robust metaphysical publishing business in Chicago; Annie Rix Militz, who founded Homes of Truth spiritual centers throughout the

* Peel (1971).

** *Class Lessons, 1888* by Emma Curtis Hopkins (DeVorss, 1977).

West Coast; Frances Lord, an energetic British student who devised some of the earliest mental wealth-building methods in the late 1880s; Alice Bunker Stockham, one of the nation's first female physicians and a widely read feminist who advocated a new model of sexual parity in Victorian-era marriages; and inspirational poet Ella Wheeler Wilcox, who penned the world-famous lines: "Laugh, and the world laughs with you/ Weep, and you weep alone."

Hopkins's brand of mind metaphysics went under different names. Yet a phrase used by Ralph Waldo Emerson seemed to capture the movement's broadest ideals: *New Thought.* In December 1858, Emerson began delivering a lecture called "Success," which he published as an essay in 1870. In it he wrote: "To redeem defeat by new thought, by firm action, that is not easy, that is the work of divine men." Emerson had loosely used "new thought" earlier. "There are new lands, new men, new thoughts," he wrote in "Nature" in 1836. But it was in the context of "Success," and the broader exposure it received in 1870, that the phrase stuck. *To redeem defeat by new thought*—the precept seemed not only to define the goals of the burgeoning movement but also the path of Hopkins and its progenitors.

By the mid-1880s the term "new thought" began circulating in mental-healing books and journals. A key reference to "new thought" appeared in 1887 in *Condensed Thoughts About Christian Science,* a pamphlet by Chicago homeopathic physician and Swedenborgian William Henry Holcombe: "New thought always excites combat in the mind with old thought, which refuses to retire." In 1892, the reliable Prentice Mulford prominently featured the term in his posthumous essay, "The Accession of New Thought." In 1894, *New Thought* became the title of a Massachusetts mental-science journal. The following year, a prominent group of mental-science thinkers began using the term in their Boston Metaphysical Club. And, finally, in February 1899, the gavel fell on a "New Thought Convention" in Hartford, Connecticut; a larger follow-up was held in October in Boston. The movement found its name.

New Thought's basic language and methods were in place but one familiar emphasis was missing: *money.* The movement's dominant aim was thinking one's way to health and happiness—not riches. Hopkins remained within the gravity of Eddy's teachings about the corruption of the material world. In 1888, she cautioned students against the "vainglory" of "the riches, profits, and advantages of material transactions." It was a perspective from which she never wavered. "Life," Hopkins wrote a friend on November 20, 1919, "is not made up of bric a brac."*

Indeed, money-getting was not a primary theme or even accepted idea among most New Thoughters of the nineteenth century. The movement's preeminent poet Ella Wheeler Wilcox conceded in 1902 in *The Heart of the New Thought* that mind-power methods could be used for wealth. "But woe unto him who cultivates his mental and spiritual powers only for this purpose," she wrote, adding: "The clear thinker and careful observer must realize there is one and only one main object in life—the building of character."

Wilcox and New Thought's leading lights taught in the vein of William Wordsworth's 1806 poem "Character of the Happy Warrior," which depicts the soulful warrior as one who "makes his moral being his prime care." Such a tone prevailed in England, as well, where nineteenth century writers adapted some of the motivational themes heard in America. The prosperity gospel that most people associate with New Thought did not take shape until the 1890s—and even then, it grew slowly and fitfully. Two causes contributed to its growth.

First, Americans in the late nineteenth century experienced a flurry of economic changes, both promising and disconcerting. An unprecedented wave of mass-produced consumer goods, from glassware to furniture, populated store shelves, shop windows, and mail-order catalogues. As these items proliferated, the economy itself was shifting from its agricultural foundation to a more urban-centered, manufacturing base. Money and markets were spreading, as were cravings and anxieties of consumerism.

In light of these changes, most historians and journalists rush to lump New Thought into the "get rich quick" attitude found in popular culture. This is insufficient. For many widely read New Thought authors, including Helen Wilmans and Ella Wheeler Wilcox, the philosophy was a spiritual adjunct to Progressive Era reforms and economic self-sufficiency. A case in point is Social Gospel advocate Wallace D. Wattles (1860–1911), a popular New Thought voice who at the turn of the century was forced out of his Methodist pulpit in northern Indiana after refusing to accept collection-basket offerings from parishioners who ran sweatshops.

---

* Harley (2002).

Wattles advocated for the rights of striking workers and suffragists. He embraced democratic socialism and foresaw a new world where cooperation would replace animal competition, espoused in his 1910 *The Science of Getting Rich*. His publisher Elizabeth Towne was a prominent suffragist elected the first female alderman of Holyoke, Massachusetts, in 1926.

Wattles himself made three bids for public office on the ticket of the Socialist Party of Eugene V. Debs, to whom he pays tribute in his 1911 book *The Science of Being Great*. In Indiana, Wattles first campaigned for Congress in 1908. After distantly trailing, he ran the following year for mayor of his hometown of Elwood, where he ran a surprisingly close second. Finally, in 1910 he ran for Prosecuting Attorney for Madison County, coming in third.

During his 1909 mayoral campaign, the delicate-framed man stood before 1,300 striking workers during a heated showdown at a local tin mill and pledged them his support.* Yet Wattles' reputation as a one-note wealth guru was sealed. He received posthumous fame in the early twenty-first century when his *Science of Getting Rich* was named an inspiration behind *The Secret*. Only a few latter-day readers noticed that the work is subtly suffused with Marxist (or Marxish) language foreseeing decline of business titans and rise of worker cooperatives.

Early Black nationalist Marcus Garvey (1887–1940) espoused a philosophy of faith-in-self and perpetual self-improvement with roots in New Thought. "What was deemed a new racial philosophy," wrote historians Robert A. Hill and Barbara Bair in *Marcus Garvey: Life and Lessons* (University of California Press, 1987), "was in fact Garvey's wholesale application of the dynamics of New Thought to the black condition . . . Metaphysics and politics were explicitly linked in Garvey's mind."

Garvey's newspapers and pamphlets abounded with New Thought phraseology, such as the call for a "universal business consciousness" in *Negro World*; Garvey's Negro Factories Corporation advertised shares of stock by declaring, "Enthusiasm Is One of the Big Keys to Success;" and a front-page headline in Garvey's *Blackman* newspaper announced: *Let us Give Off Success and It Will Come*, adding the indis-

* "Trouble at Elwood," *Fort Wayne Sentinel*, July 12, 1909.

pensable New Thought maxim: *As Man Thinks So Is He.** In one of his most enduring utterances, Garvey told an audience in Nova Scotia in 1937: "We are going to emancipate ourselves from mental slavery because whilst others might free the body, none but ourselves can free the mind." Some might recognize this from the lyrics of Bob Marley's "Redemption Song."

Second to economic and social shifts, the late-nineteenth century saw long-overdue advances in the examination room, easing the desperation of patients and, for the first time, creating reliable medical protocols. "Heroic medicine" vanished and mainstream procedures grew safer and more effective. In response to calls from allopathic physicians, state legislatures began regulating and licensing medical professionals, with an eye toward restricting or eliminating mind-power practitioners and "irregular" healers, such as homeopaths and botanists.

New currents in economics and medicine changed the needs of the public—and the face of New Thought to what it resembled in later years with books like Napoleon Hill's *Think and Grow Rich* in 1937, a work further considered. In a growing practice, self-help writers such as Hill, Dale Carnegie, Norman Vincent Peale, Ralph Waldo Trine, James Allen, and others jettisoned the term New Thought altogether in their highly popular writings. By 1952, Peale's worldwide bestseller *The Power of Positive Thinking* firmly planted the principles, although not the name, of New Thought into the modern psyche.

---

* Historian Hill has meticulously assembled and annotated *The Marcus Garvey and Universal Negro Improvement Association Papers* for the University of California Press. Volumes I (1983) and VII (1990), in particular, explore Garvey and New Thought.

CHAPTER EIGHT

Secret Teachings Old and New

It is a truism that ideas have consequences. Equally true is that they are often unexpected. When Mary Baker Eddy created strict order within Christian Science, expelling independent voices, the religious thinker unknowingly fostered a cohort of seekers whose churchless experiments gave rise to the endlessly porous culture of New Thought.

Likewise, when Madame Blavatsky relocated to India—and grew increasingly steeped in Vedism and Buddhism (in 1880 she and Colonel Olcott became the first Westerners to take formal Buddhist vows)—some followers quietly rebelled. Seekers in the U.S. and Europe who yearned for the occultist's earlier emphasis on Hermeticism and Western esoterica—and who desired training in practical magick—ventured new orders of their own.

It is easy to see why Vedism and Buddhism became appealing points of gravity within Theosophy and some of the later orders that took shape from it. Vedism, Buddhism, and Christianity are living, uninterrupted traditions with finely developed liturgies and literary traditions, whereas Hermeticism and occultism are, by nature of history, schismatic and patchwork.

The renewed quest for a Western magickal tradition, or remade variant of it, altered the face of occultism in the twentieth century. The most influential effort occurred through the Hermetic Order of the Golden Dawn, a British-based initiatory group whose innovation was matched only by factional disputes and frictions among its leaders, which in turn precipitated still newer forms of occultism.

The traceable history of the Golden Dawn begins in fall of 1887, when London coroner and Freemason William Wynn Wescott (1848–1925), came into possession of a folio of alchemical symbols and encrypted ritualist writings in English, French, Latin, and Hebrew. The sixty-leaf folio was accompanied by a sheet with the name and address of a mysterious (and possibly invented) German countess whom the bearer could contact for guidance.

Wescott said that he received these "Cypher Manuscripts" from the Rev. A.F.A. Woodford, a fellow Freemason who died that year. For his part, Woodford is sometimes said to have purchased the manuscripts from an antiquarian bookdealer in 1880; other accounts have him receiving them from Masonic scholar Kenneth R. H. Mackenzie, who died in 1886.

There is controversy over whether Wescott, seeking to endow himself with magickal authority (a common theme in occult history) forged the coversheet and follow up correspondence with the unseen Countess Anna Sprengel, sometimes said to have died in 1890.

In any case, Wescott claimed to have received from the countess news of hidden masters, later called "Secret Chiefs," who maintained a Hermetic-Rosicrucian order into which he was provisionally invited. Wescott brought the material to two friends and colleagues with whom he was already involved in a self-styled Rosicrucian group. They were William Robert Woodman (1828–1891) and S.L. MacGregor Mathers (1854–1918); Mathers seems to have coined the lasting term "Secret Chiefs."

Wescott and his collaborators deciphered the folios, which were based on a code from a 1518 manuscript called *Polygraphia* by Johannes Trithemius, the German Benedictine abbot and occultist who had worked with Cornelius Agrippa. The three men devised the framework of the Golden Dawn as the outer order of the secret lineage from which the manuscripts were said to have originated.

For a time, the Golden Dawn proved an extraordinary womb of activity for a wide range of both male and female artists, intellectuals and seekers hungry to revive the mythical and magickal. Luminaries included poet W.B. Yeats (1865–1939), magician Aleister Crowley (1875–1947), historian Evelyn Underhill (1875–1941), actress Florence Farr (1860–1917), and occultists A.E. Waite (1857–1942), Dion Fortune (1890–1946), and Israel Regardie (1907–1985).

S.L. MacGregor Mathers, in particular, proved tireless in his labors to restore Western magick. In that vein, occult scholar Donald Tyson avers of Mathers in his *Essential Tarot Writings*:

> He was a gifted psychic and spirit medium who, in conjunction with his wife, Moina, who was also a psychic, received from spirits many of the teachings that formed the Golden Dawn system of magic.
>
> This point is often glossed over but needs to be stressed. Mathers did not compose or create the magic of the Golden Dawn; he received it from spiritual beings. He was in regular communication with the spirits who presided over the Golden Dawn current, known as the Secret Chiefs. It is these spiritual beings who are the ultimate architects of Golden Dawn magic which is firmly rooted in the Western esoteric tradition.

In her impeccable and beautifully written 1995 history, *Women of the Golden Dawn*, Mary K. Greer captures the lives of female initiates who comingled in this world. Regarding the order's activities, Greer notes:

> Magic in the Golden Dawn worked via a number of tools and techniques that had to be carefully learned. They included words of power that vibrated on the astral plane; laws of correspondence between symbol and that which it symbolizes; evocation of Spirits or the assumption of god-forms by the magician; knowledge of timing through the moon, planets, stars, and seasons; and the experience of traveling astral pathways between hierarchies of energies and through the planes to effect changes and bring back information.
>
> As shown in the Magician card of the Tarot, magicians draw power from above (aided by angels and forces of a higher spiritual vibration) and channel it through their bodies and into physical

> reality. They use ritual first to contact the spiritual forces and second to ground the forces, to manifest the effects they desire.
>
> Kenneth Mackenzie, who possibly originated the Golden Dawn cipher manuscripts, defined magic as 'a psychological branch of science, dealing with the sympathetic effects of stones, drugs, herbs, and living substances upon the imaginative and reflective faculties.' While some writers have regarded magic as psychotherapeutic work (Francis King and Israel Regardie, for example), others have characterized it as the discovery of unity within all duality, the truth behind all illusions. W.B. Yeats sought knowledge of what he called 'the single energetic Mind,' and its pole, 'the single Memory of nature,' both of which he believed could be evoked by symbols. But I like Florence Farr's definition of magic best: 'Magic is unlimiting experience.' That is, magic consists of removing the limitations from what we *think* are the earthly and spiritual laws that bind or compel us. We can be anything because we are All.

In 1891, S.L. MacGregor Mathers and his wife and intellectual partner Moina, sister to French philosopher Henri Bergson, relocated to Paris; for him the move was ostensibly to be nearer the Secret Chiefs. Moina (née Mina Bergson) was a deeply incisive graphic artist focused on occult themes; friends urged her return to Paris to continue to study painting, an activity that some felt her husband thwarted. In any case, the pair, though struggling for money, formed the magickal power couple of the belle époque.

By the late 1890s, Mathers maintained that the Chiefs—with whom he was then exclusively in touch—appointed him head of the organization. Woodman had died in 1891 and Wescott, probably under pressure from his employers, resigned in 1893, ceding a leadership role to Farr. London-based challenges arose to Mathers' anointment, which the occultist sought to quell through a strong-willed new deputy: Aleister Crowley. Crowley's magical name in the order was *Pedurabo*, the meaning of which appeared in the closing line of his eponymous 1899 poem: "I shall abide."

Crowley and Mathers met in Paris in 1899 and formed an uneasy bond. Both were unhappy, though for different reasons, with the order's direction. The twenty-five-year-old Crowley was an anarchic and imperious intellect who disliked the Golden Dawn's formality.

Mathers possessed a somewhat authoritarian and dandyish streak, though tempered by a gentler character than his fiery (and brief) disciple. He resented key members' independence and, as he saw it, impetuosity. In essence, both men, though temperamentally different, yearned to be in charge.

That year, Perdurabo had a less encouraging encounter in London with Yeats, ten years his elder and a feted literary voice. The senior poet disliked Crowley personally and found his poems unruly and lacking technical mastery. In early 1900 and extending into spring, Crowley clashed with the London lodges, who refused to recognize the advanced degrees that Mathers had bestowed on him and moved to revoke the Paris chief's authority.

In April, Crowley, wearing a mask of Osiris to ward off magical attacks, changed the locks on one of the lodge doors, an act of aggression on Mathers' behalf who suspected a conspiracy to replace him with a restored Wescott. On April 19, Yeats, another lodge member, the landlord, and a constable confronted and expelled Crowley at the lodge doors. Charges, countercharges, and mutual legal actions quickly followed, presaging the end of at least the first phase of the disputatious order.

In years immediately following, Crowley broke with Mathers—the enduring pattern of the younger man's life—while competing orders spun off, lingered, and frayed, each claiming to carry on the real Golden Dawn legacy. This may have been the inevitable outgrowth of claims of clandestine knowledge, including receipt of secret communiques, an issue that also ruptured Theosophy.

Mathers died of flu in Paris in the days immediately preceding the end of World War I, an early victim of the epidemic that swept the globe claiming tens of millions of lives. He was not yet sixty-five; Moina was fifty-three. Spinoff organizations were already functioning, including the *Stella Matutina* or "Morning Star". Members included Waite, Yeats, Fortune and, for a brief time, Crowley's one-time secretary Israel Regardie who attracted the umbrage of surviving initiates when between 1938 and 1940 he published the Golden Dawn rituals. Mathers had unsuccessfully sued Crowley in 1910 for smaller-scale leakages. For her part, Moina Mathers and members loyal to her husband founded the Alpha et Omega lodge (sometimes rendered Rosicrucian Order of Alpha et Omega).

In 1919, British occultist Dion Fortune joined Alpha et Omega but expressed disappointment over the quality of its teachings. Moina resolved Fortune's misgivings by expelling her in 1922 following charges that the initiate had exposed some of the order's secrets. Fortune believed that she was afterward the victim of "astral attack" by Moina who sicced on her a giant feral cat, which might be considered a *tulpa* or animated thought form in Tibetan Buddhism. The struggle resulted in her popular 1930 manual and memoir, *Psychic Self-Defence* in which she recounted the episode:

> Coming upstairs after breakfast one morning, I suddenly saw, coming down the stairs towards me, a gigantic tabby cat, twice the size of a tiger. It appeared absolutely solid and tangible. I stared at it petrified for a second, and then it vanished. I instantly realised it was a simulacrum or thought form that was being projected by someone with occult powers. I rose up, gathered together my paraphernalia, and did an exorcism then and there.

After ensuing struggles on the astral plane with an "enemy" draped in "full robes of her grade, which were very magnificent," Dion prevailed in a "battle of wills." But a shock arrived: "when I took off my clothes in order to go to bed I found that from neck to waist I was scored with scratches as if I had been clawed by a gigantic cat." Although never explicitly stated, Moina is implicated as the robed female figure, presumed source of the attack. Greer deems it "highly questionable" that the artist-magician played any part in the episodes.

Around that time, Moina clashed with another initiate, an enterprising New Yorker, Paul Foster Case (1884–1954). She accused Case, who had risen quickly through the initiatory ranks, of including sex magick in his teachings, which was considered verboten. The two exchanged accusatory letters, leading to Case's simultaneous expulsion and resignation.

Case went on to organize the extant Builders of the Adytum (Greek for "inner temple") widely known by its acronym B.O.T.A. In Case's hands, B.O.T.A. became one of America's first mail-order occult houses, providing students with weekly mailers in Tarot, symbolism, and occult study. In 1947, Case capped his career with publication of his still-popular book *The Tarot.* It functions as a readable encapsulation of key aspects of Golden Dawn symbolic philosophy. With his mail-order courses, Case signaled the democratizing impulse of American occultism.

Crowley, meanwhile, moved rapidly into new adventures, founding the mysteriously named A∴A∴, an organization whose secrecy extended even to its name. Many reckon it stands for *Argenteum Astrum* (Latin for "Silver Star") but this is disputed. In an inspired leap, trickster philosopher Robert Anton Wilson (1932–2007) suggested that the organization's name A∴A∴ is complete in itself, designed to expose pretenders who endeavor to unknowingly disclose what its initials signify.

The Golden Dawn's influence extends to history's most popular work of Tarot, the Waite-Smith deck. Issued in 1909 by publisher William Rider & Son, it was known for decades as the Rider-Waite deck, a title that omitted one of its creators.

The images were drawn by artist and occult initiate Pamela Colman Smith, known as "Pixie." In 1893 at just fifteen, the London-born prodigy studied art at Brooklyn's Pratt Institute. Following the death of her mother three years later, however, Smith left in 1897 without her degree. Yeats introduced the artist to the Golden Dawn into which she was initiated in 1901. Under commission from fellow initiate Arthur Edward Waite, Smith in just six months produced the first deck with fully illustrated minor suits, a practice widely adopted since. Prior to Smith, only the fifteenth century Sola Busca deck featured spare imagery on selected minor suits.

Smith's work is effectively the urtext of contemporary Tarot as most decks that followed adapted if not directly echoed Smith's designs and illustrative keys. In addition to instructions received from Waite, there is speculation that Smith collaborated on her images with Golden Dawn colleagues Yeats and Florence Farr, who was a friend. In any case, the deck's expressive and shrewdly dramatized figures bear the markings of her distinctive vision.

Smith's illustrations were originally black-and-white line drawings with color later added during the printing process. Her originals are missing and the printing plates were destroyed, Greer reports, when Nazi bombs demolished the London printshop housing them.

Even those who never heard of the Golden Dawn today recognize Smith's images. More than 100 million copies of the Waite-Smith deck have appeared in over twenty nations,* and its illustrations appear on t-shirts, magnets, jewelry, candles, and virtually every form of accoutrement. The artist's only known comment on the deck appeared in a 1909 letter she wrote to photographer and mentor Alfred Stieglitz: "I just finished a very big job for very little cash!"** When Smith died in Cornwall in 1951, her estate was so barren that its contents were sold to settle debts.

Absence of the Golden Dawn in magickal tradition would be akin to absence of Adam Smith in economics. For all that, I harbor mixed feelings about the Golden Dawn's legacy.

I admire the efforts, if not always the discernment, of its founders—not to mention their intrepidness. The organization provided an aesthetic to the modern occult; a hope that magickal practice and initiation could be revived in the modern world; a womb of gestation for artists of radically differing temperaments; and, most importantly, a framework of ceremonial magick for twentieth century seekers. An atmosphere of relative parity prevailed between the sexes; within three years of the Golden Dawn's founding, 48 of 126 initiates were women.***

At the same time, the order commenced and continued with an archly defined hierarchy and degree-based initiatory system that, in some regards, replicated the orthodoxy many seekers were fleeing in the traditional faiths. The inflated-sounding nature of its titles and ranks (just one of Crowley's tongue-twisting garlands was "Lord of the Paths of the Portal of the Vault of the Adepts"—a Kabbalistic-Rosicrucian reference), colored a good deal of the occult in decades ahead.

The order also created what I consider didactic cleavages between "white" and "black" magick, sometimes brandished with catechistic judgment and certainty. Movements that begin in opposition to doctrine often devolve into mirror reflections of it. In my estimation, the Golden Dawn's penchant for secrecy ultimately served less to shield the sacred from the profane than abet the authority (and sometimes puffery) of its leaders. In later years, secrecy descended into habit,

---

* "Reviving a Forgotten Artist of the Occult" by Sharmistha Ray, Hyperallergic.com, March 23, 2019.

** Greer (1995).

*** *Do What Thou Wilt: A Life of Aleister Crowley* by Lawrence Sutin (St. Martin's Press, 2000).

the offspring of custom, owing less to purpose than emotion. This produced divisions and splits.

Even documenting the Golden Dawn's history has taken on the flavor of its dramas. Well intentioned historians, sometimes through no initial impulse of their own, get caught up in this web so that historicizing the order becomes an intrigue in itself. Prior to this writing, I grew interested in the whereabouts of the original Cypher Manuscripts. Some of the adept letters of Theosophy are, for example, housed in the British Library and others at the group's international headquarters at Adyar. In this case, however, no one seemed to know.

Then I encountered revealing passages, often written with the intentional inscrutability of a historian or journalist honoring conditions set by a source. In Ellic Howe's seminally important 1972 study, *The Magicians of the Golden Dawn,* the historian discovered the original Cypher Manuscripts and contemporaneous documents in a "Private Collection" kept by its owner in a "strongroom." This material and others were revealed to Howe, he explained, "on condition that neither their location nor ownership be disclosed." Several of his statements on the matter are so tortuous—again, I assume as a gesture of goodwill toward his sources—that even Howe's references require parsing.

So much writing has been dedicated to Aleister Crowley that any informed researcher hesitates over what remains to add. Contemporary historians including Tobias Churton, Richard Kaczynski, and Lawrence Sutin have done remarkable work in tracking the Great Beast's virtual every step.

Probably no other occultist, including even Madame H. P. Blavatsky, has received greater scrutiny in both scholarly and general literature. Rather than belaboring the byways of Crowley's storied life, I exit the realm of international intrigue, speculative tales, lurid episodes, and broken relationships to focus on what I consider testament of Crowley's literary genius and his most lasting achievement: the gemlike, three-chapter text called *The Book of the Law.*

Literary critic Irving Howe (1920–1993)—who would've groaned at his name being anywhere near Crowley's—wrote in 1982, "Every writer . . . must be read and remembered for his best work."* This is

* *The Portable Kipling* (Penguin Classics).

my approach to Crowley. Although Crowley produced myriad books, essays, poems, translations, letters, and articles, *The Book of the Law* remains his best-known and finest statement. In many respects, the short work formed the basis for much that followed in his career just as a line of Talmud produces voluminous commentary. The slender document is, in my view, one of the greatest and most enduring works of modern occultism. As a work of collaged references, disjointed impressionism, and perturbing power, it is the occult equivalent, in timing, impact, and originality, of T.S. Eliot's "The Waste Land."

Crowley set down the prophetic missive in Cairo in 1904 during three one-hour periods on consecutive days of April 8 to 10. Biographer Lawrence Sutin notes:

> The most famous sentence in this book, familiar to persons who know nothing else of Crowley, is: "Do what thou wilt shall be the whole of the Law." This dictum evokes immediate unease, even fear. With its insistent staccato monosyllables, it testifies to the visceral impact of *The Book of the Law*. Make of that book what you will, it has had a fitful but persistent life from the time it was first written to the close of the twentieth century. And there is every indication that it will continue to exercise an influence on the century to come.

Crowley's formidable achievement is also his most misunderstood. Rather than a paean to moral whimsy or rampant libertinism—although the scribe displayed such in his life—the text, which Crowley reported receiving from an ethereal intelligence called Aiwass, describes a new epoch of human relations and strivings, spiritual insights and modes of being, in the philosophy called *Thelema*.

The term Thelema, Greek for *will*, is rooted—or, as Crowley saw it, foreordained—in the work of French monk and Renaissance writer François Rabelais (c. 1483–1494–1553) and his ode to the libertine "Abbey of Thélème" in his cycle of novels *The Life of Gargantua and of Pantagruel*. The humanist philosopher Rabelais writes of its residents: "In all their rule and strictest tie of their order there was but this one clause to be observed,/ Do What Thou Wilt."*

* Translation by Sir Thomas Urquhart and Peter Antony Motteux, issued singly by The Moray Press, 1894.

Crowley's iteration both comports and differs. In his 1938 introduction, he makes it clear:

> This Book lays down a simple Code of Conduct.
> "Do what thou wilt shall be the whole of the Law."
> "Love is the law, love under will."
> "There is no law beyond Do what thou wilt."
> This means that each of us stars is to move on our true orbit, as marked out by the nature of our position, the law of our growth, the impulse of our past experiences. All events are equally lawful—and every one necessary, in the long run—for all of us, in theory; but in practice, only one act is lawful for each one of us at any given moment.

He continues, "Each action or motion is an act of love"—a theme to which he returns throughout the transmission. In the dawning "Aeon of Horus," the cultivation of "True Will" or True Self is the law. As such, "thou hast no right but to do thy will." In that vein, self-purpose is holy: "Every man and every woman is a star." That statement, so plain yet poised, speaks to me as the magician's greatest.

Crowley's "do what thou wilt" ranks with Nietzsche's "God is dead" from his 1882 manifesto *The Gay Science* as one of the most widely quoted—and misconstrued—concepts in the catalogue of modern ideas. A contemporary adjunct might be political theorist Francis Fukuyama's "end of history" thesis first articulated in 1989. The danger of aphorisms is ease of misapplication, especially by observers who haven't read, and have no intention of reading, the works in which they nest.

As translated by Walter Kaufmann in 1974, Nietzsche wrote:

> *New struggles*—After Buddha was dead, his shadow was still shown for centuries in a cave—a tremendous, gruesome shadow. God is dead; but given the way of men, there may still be caves for thousands of years in which his shadow will be shown.—And we—we still have to vanquish his shadow, too.

Nietzsche was advocating neither nihilism nor despair; he was signaling the demise of *conceptualized sacredness*. Crowley had related concerns. As did Emerson, articulated in his 1841 essay "Self-Reliance," which has something in common with *The Book of the Law*:

> I remember an answer which when quite young I was prompted to make to a valued adviser, who was wont to importune me with the dear old doctrines of the church. On my saying, What have I to do with the sacredness of traditions, if I live wholly from within? my friend suggested,—"But these impulses may be from below, not from above." I replied, "They do not seem to me to be such; but if I am the Devil's child, I will live then from the Devil." No law can be sacred to me but that of my nature.

As these writers perceived it, form had smothered meaning—but, more so, meaning had been divorced from True Self. This is the basis of Crowley's jeremiad against the spirituality of the old and heralding of the cosmic new.

Crowley believed in progressive historical stages regarding humanity's self-conception and the arrival of a "new Aeon," framed in terms of Horus and the Egyptian pantheon. In his 1936 *The Equinox of the Gods*, he described the process and experience of *The Book of the Law*:

> In this revelation is the basis of the future Æon. Within the memory of man we have had the Pagan period, the worship of Nature, of Isis, of the Mother, of the Past; the Christian period, the worship of Man, of Osiris, of the Present. The first period is simple, quiet, easy, and pleasant; the material ignores the spiritual; the second is of suffering and death: *the spiritual strives to ignore the material.* Christianity and all cognate religions worship death, glorify suffering, deify corpses. *The new Aeon is the worship of the spiritual made one with the material, of Horus, of the Child, of the Future.* Isis was Liberty; Osiris, bondage; but the new Liberty is that of Horus. Osiris conquered her because she did not understand him. Horus avenges both his Father and his Mother. *This child Horus is a twin, two in one. Horus and Harpocrates are one, and they are also one with Set or Apophis, the destroyer of Osiris.* It is by the destruction of the principle of

> death that they are born. The establishment of this new Æon, this new fundamental principle, is the Great Work now to be accomplished in the world. [emphases added]

This was, in a sense, Crowley's response to Christ's existential cry on the cross: "My God, my God, why have you forsaken me?" As he saw it, humanity had passed from subsistence materiality to spiritual awareness—but without uniting and honoring the two. *The Book of the Law* resolves this cleavage: "*The new Aeon is the worship of the spiritual made one with the material.*" I consider this the spiritual keynote of our era and a solution to the dilemma of *striving* coupled with *nonattachment*, which, in my observation, often tears the contemporary seeker in two and places him or her in the impossible position of *arguing* for the primacy of one spiritual system over another, a contradiction in the stance of nonattachment itself.

One may ask whether there is any need for the supernatural backstory and sometimes portentous language Crowley proffers. Carl Jung, who experienced his own psychical transmissions from a being called Philemon, observed in 1962 in *Memories, Dreams, Reflections*: "Archetypes speak the language of high rhetoric, even of bombast. It is a style I find embarrassing . . . But since I did not know what was going on, I had no choice but to write everything down in the style selected by the unconscious self." Philemon, he continued, "was a pagan and brought with him an Egypto-Hellenistic atmosphere with a Gnostic coloration." This approach appears in *The Book of the Law* coupled with concepts and language reminiscent of the Golden Dawn and word forms of the King James Bible, a document that shaped the intellect of every English speaker of the era.

But Crowley was unequivocal: he was in communication with a higher being, guardian angel (of sorts), and extraphysical intelligence. He noted in *Equinox*, "The Voice of Aiwass came apparently from over my left shoulder, from the furthest corner of the room. It seemed to echo itself in my physical heart in a very strange manner, hard to describe. I have noticed a similar phenomenon when I have been waiting for a message fraught with great hope or dread." And further:

> I had a strong impression that the speaker was actually in the corner where he seemed to be, in a body of 'fine matter,' transparent as a veil of gauze, or a cloud of incense-smoke. He seemed to be a

> tall, dark man in his thirties, well-knit, active and strong, with the face of a savage king, and eyes veiled lest their gaze should destroy what they saw. The dress was not Arab; it suggested Assyria or Persia, but very vaguely. I took little note of it, for to me at that time Aiwass was an 'angel' such as I had often seen in visions, a being purely astral.

Crowley also viewed the 1904 experience as his final break with Mathers and the Golden Dawn. In *Equinox* he surmised: "I am to formulate a new link of an Order with the Solar Force." This "new link" required eradicating the old. In Crowley's *Magick, Book 4*, he wrote of the Golden Dawn and its rituals: "G.D. to be destroyed, i.e., publish its history & its papers. Nothing needs buying. I make it an absolute condition that I should attain *samadhi* [higher consciousness], in the god's own interest. My rituals work out well, but I need the transliteration." In other words, Mathers and company had forfeited all natural rights to their material and, in Crowley's eyes, it could now be published with impunity—and without compensation.

He wrote in his 1929 *Confessions of Aleister Crowley*, "Various considerations showed me that the Secret Chiefs . . . had sent a messenger to confer upon me the position which Mathers had forfeited." The messenger was Aiwass. For Mathers, he had no further use: "The Secret Chiefs cast him off; he fell into deplorable abjection; even his scholarship deserted him. He published nothing new and lived in sodden intoxication till death put an end to his long misery. He was a great man in his way. May he have expiated his errors and resumed his labours, with the advantage of experience!"

If it seemed as though Crowley's vision of "The New Aeon" suited his own needs that was only to be expected. Crowley's erstwhile secretary, Israel Regardie—with whom, as with nearly everyone in Crowley's life, the occultist bitterly feuded—issued the just charge that *The Book of the Law* was no magickal transmission but strictly Crowley's projection of self: "Despite Crowley's emphatic statement that 'I am utterly incapable, even when most inspired, of such English as I find in that Book again and again,' there are many points of resemblance to his other inspired writing, and there are many places where Crowley's own hand is to be detected, even though we were to admit he were not conscious of doing so." In short, "Regardless of how he operated consciously, it is evident that the contents of this book were part and parcel of Crowley's unconscious psyche." Regardie continued ruefully:

> Under these circumstances, it would be most surprising if this Book—whether dictated by a praeterhuman intelligence or composed by Crowley himself—did not take an identical stand. The miracle in his life would have been for this Book to have agreed with all that he had been fighting against. But this miracle did not occur. With considerable fervor, the Book echoes Crowley's underlying moral, social, and religious attitudes without equivocation or doubt. Dictated or created, it is his Book.

Regardie's critique marked the former disciple's judiciousness, at least later in life. In his 1970 biography *The Eye in the Triangle*, Regardie noted his onetime teacher's "unbroken record of quarrelling with all his friends and colleagues . . . Sooner or later he fell out with his most devoted friends and disciples on the most trivial of grounds." Crowley, Regardie recounts, responded to an insult by publicizing his secretary's agonizing secrets and needling him with antisemitic slurs, a not uncommon trait in the magician. Even as he condemned his mother as a "brainless bigot,"* Crowley, when crossed or simply when in the mood, resorted to the common prejudices of his English childhood belying his heterodox image.

But in his best moments the man's artistry resounded. In that vein, I add an observation by Pulitzer-winning poet James Merrill (1926–1995), who composed some of his most acclaimed verses through nearly twenty years of nightly sessions with a homemade Ouija board, a case to which we return in the final chapter. "If it's still *yourself* that you're drawing upon," the poet said, "then that self is much stranger and freer and more far-seeking than the one you thought you knew." And at another point: "If the spirits aren't external, how astonishing the mediums become! Victor Hugo said of *his* voices that they were like his own mental powers multiplied by five."**

Regardie, capable of vision unclouded by his previous torments, probably would have agreed—and in *The Eye in the Triangle* effectively did: "the Book contains innumerable passages of superb beauty,

---

* *Confessions* (1929).

** *James Merrill* by Judith Moffett (Columbia University Press, 1984).

nobility, and incomparable power and sublimity. The 'transcendental point of view' is often depicted with clarity and precision."

In what may be considered his final reckoning of the book and the man, Regardie wrote:

> It really makes little difference in the long run whether *The Book of the Law* was dictated to him by a praeterhuman intelligence named Aiwass or whether it stemmed from the creative deeps of Aleister Crowley. The book was written. And he became the mouthpiece for the Zeitgeist, accurately expressing the intrinsic nature of our time as no one else has done to date. So his failures and excesses and stupidities are simply the hall-mark of his humanity. Was he not, by his own admission, the Beast, whose number is 666, which is the number of Man?

Regardie is referencing Revelation 13:18: "Let him that hath understanding count the number of the beast: for it is the number of a man; and his number is Six hundred threescore and six." (KJV)

Never fully shedding the influence of Mathers and the Golden Dawn, much of Crowley's broader written work—while evocative, visually beautiful, and meticulously splendid in internal organization (if not always consistent in outlook and temperament)—is, depending on the attitude of the reader, a wellspring of received and bracingly original occult insight, or turgid and sui generis liturgies and ceremonies. Indeed, it can variously be all those things. Crowley's literary output and legacy have been expertly organized and maintained both by the A∴A∴ and the Ordo Templi Orientis, O.T.O, a quasi-Masonic order that predated Crowley's activity but was largely remade by him until his death in 1947.

The original O.T.O was founded and shaped starting in the late nineteenth and early twentieth centuries (the date of its earliest inception is opaque) by German occultists Carl Kellner (1851–1905) and Theodor Reuss (1855–1923). Under the auspices of Reuss, Crowley joined the initiatic order in 1910 and by 1912 chartered his own branch in England. As was his wont, Crowley began remaking the O.T.O into his own Thelemic order.

"There is reason to believe that even Reuss did not intend his O.T.O to be a vehicle for Thelema," writes Peter-Robert König in "The O.T.O. Phenomenon" in *Theosophical History* of July 1992. "Despite that, Crowley was already writing in his diary on 27 November 1921: 'I have proclaimed myself OHO' (Outer Head of the Order)." Following Crowley's death on December 1, 1947, his German deputy, Karl Germer, who survived the ordeal of Nazi imprisonment, took over certain of the master's O.T.O. activities. Due to disputes involving succession and practices—including the embrace of Thelema itself—some O.T.O. branches carried on estranged from one another.

In a prefatory note to König's article, which is a distinctly useful guide to the order's checkered trajectory, Joscelyn Godwin notes: "The rival claims to 'apostolic' succession, mutual recriminations, and expulsions will have a familiar ring to historians of Theosophy. Two things especially mark the O.T.O. phenomenon. One is the yearning for a quasi-masonic structure of grades, initiations, and secrets, such as was envisaged even in the early years of the T.S. in New York." The other is marker is practice of sex magick.

Speaking of spiritual labors, a teacher once told me, "The greatest barrier to the work is ambition *in* the work." The trappings of title and internal conceptions of authority proved one of the primary stumbling blocks of the occult revival orders.

In areas beyond structured realms, there appeared greater freedom—and posterity. In terms of graphic art, Crowley's collaborative *Thoth* Tarot deck, painted by Lady Frieda Harris (1877–1962) in the last decade of Perdurabo's life, is not only startlingly original and lush in detail but trails only the Waite-Smith deck in popularity and influence.

Indeed, it is nearly impossible to conceive of twentieth century art and culture, from the cover *of Sgt. Pepper's Lonely Hearts Club Band* to the underground films of Kenneth Anger to the stylized appearance of a bevy of heavy metal and hip-hop artists to the music and postures of David Bowie, Jimmy Page, and Jay-Z to embraceable movie villains like Loki, Darth Vader, and Maleficent, without Crowley's aesthetic.

Love or hate him—one can hold to both (of which he would probably approve)—Crowley peers out from nearly every corner of modern culture.

To capture this age of high experiment requires exploring a strange byway both emergent from and splitting with the ever-radiating influence of Madame Blavatsky.

In 1884, a secretive European occult order called the H.B. of L., for Hermetic Brotherhood of Luxor, appeared in England. Even its name is laced with intrigue. Joscelyn Godwin notes: "The order in question has always been known by its initials alone, which leaves it ambiguous whether the L. stands for Luxor or Light (though they may mean the same thing)."*

The H.B. of L. founders claimed belowground existence since the group's covert formation in Egypt in 1870. Although to outer appearances, lesser in scale, ambition, and storied members than the Golden Dawn, the H.B. of L. was probably the first initiatory order to provide instruction in practical magick couched in the Western tradition.

At least one known founder, Kabbalist and occultist Max Théon (c. 1848–1927), thought to be born in Warsaw as Louis-Maximilian Bimstein, had authentic occult pedigree. Around 1905 or 1906 when in Algeria he tutored Parisian seeker Mirra Alfassa (1878–1973) who later closely collaborated with esteemed Vedic teacher Sri Aurobindo (1872–1950). H.B. of L. documents suggest Théon's connection to the original Brotherhood of Luxor, the order referenced in the Mahatma letters of Theosophy. (Alfassa also claimed Théon taught Blavatsky.) A similar statement of connection came from the powerful intellect of Traditionalist philosopher René Guénon. Scholar of esotericism K. Paul Johnson suggests that Théon may have been the figure of Tuitit Bey who signed some of the early Mahatma letters from the Brotherhood of Luxor.** The Brotherhood itself may be an umbrella term for occultists that Madame Blavatsky had known in Egypt.*** But all this remains hypothetical and "whether there was in fact any connection between the two brotherhoods is one of the unsolved questions of esoteric history," note Joscelyn Godwin, Christian Chanel, and John P. Deveney in their invaluable 1995 study, *The Hermetic Brotherhood of Luxor.*

---

* *Theosophical History*, January 1991.

** *The Masters Revealed: Madame Blavatsky and the Myth of the Great White Lodge* (State University of New York Press 1994).

*** *The Theosophical Enlightenment* by Joscelyn Godwin (State University of New York Press, 1994).

The authors also remark that René Guénon "expressed vigorous contempt for every modern occult group except the H. B. of L., and showed a definite respect for [Max] Théon. This was expressed first by not attacking him, as Guénon attacked almost every one of his contemporaries in the occult world; second, by according him the (unearned!) title of Dr.; and third, by avoiding mentioning him at all until forced to do so." It must be added, however, that Théon had little evident involvement with the group beyond its founding.

In the 1880s, the Hermetic Brotherhood of Luxor, with branches in Europe and the U.S., was locked in a kind of rivalry with Theosophy. Like the Golden Dawn, the H.B. of L. founders—which included violin-maker Peter Davidson and Thomas Henry Burgoyne (born Thomas Dalton), who was convicted of petty mail fraud*—believed that Theosophy failed to train its members in "practical occultism," such as the uses of oracles (like magick mirrors) and clairvoyance. The H.B. of L. seized upon this educational mission as its aim.

In addition to Théon, a key source of inspiration arrived through the work of Paschal Beverly Randolph. Before his death in 1875, Randolph, along with his adapters in the H. B. of L., considered magick a necessarily hands-on, visceral affair. As noted, Randolph advocated sex magick—the harnessing of sexual energy as an ethereal force to further one's will, a method also used by Crowley. Randolph's practices included invoking prayer for a specific wish before climaxing. But the H.B. of L. materials insisted, in what must have disappointed some ambitious seekers, that such methods be used only for spiritual advancement and development of impersonal love. For his part, Guénon suggested that the outer order of the H.B. of L. may have been rooted in Randolph's Brotherhood of Eulis.**

An intriguing "secret history" is theorized about the dawn of the modern occult and the H.B. of L.—one that also found its way into the work of Guénon, Christian esotericist and antisemite

* Again Godwin: "Poor Burgoyne's swindle was the most timid and pathetic kind of mail fraud, getting people to send him stamps and then keeping them!"

** *The Spiritist Fallacy* by René Guénon translated by Alvin Moore, Jr. and Rama P. Coomaraswamy (Sophia Perennis, 1923, 2001).

C.J. Harrison, remarkable occult writer Emma Hardinge Britten (1823–1899), and was later skillfully written about by historian Joscelyn Godwin.* Without Godwin's virtuosity, this thread of history—already confounding—would prove vastly more difficult to trace.**

Indeed, the "hidden hand" theory is so serpentine that to read its source material induces a kind of intellectual vertigo. And yet the theory emerges with sufficient subtlety, intelligence, and points of corroboration from among diffuse sources that I would be remiss in bypassing it. A caution to the reader: my variation of the "hidden hand" theory is only that, a variation. I am distilling my account, as best as I am able, from composite records, which intersect on certain points. I am omitting details that travel too far afield from my concerns and space limitations. I provide sufficient references so that the interested reader may make his or her own consideration.

Like Theosophy, the H.B. of L. claimed to receive guidance from secret adepts. This loosely knit cohort of hidden superiors grew concerned in 1840 that the Western world was descending into dogmatic materialism. Dispersed across various nations, the unseen chiefs could be divided into what might be considered Liberal Brothers, who wanted to use occultism for common advancement; Conservative Brothers, who were dedicated to keeping esoteric wisdom covert; and Brothers of the Left-Hand Path, who wished to employ occultism for their own self-interested and sometimes inscrutable ends.

---

* Harrison, a British esotericist, wrote in a footnote to his 1923 *Creed for the Twentieth Century*: "In reply to those who deny the existence of a 'Jewish Peril,' we are willing to concede that the majority of Jews (in this country at least) have no more desire to overthrow a civilisation by which they profit than a farmer to slaughter his best milch cow, and also that it is absurd to suppose that the Jews in high position would knowingly lend themselves to such a conspiracy. On the other hand, we call their attention (i) to the fact that in every country the Jew is an alien, and is keenly conscious of it. However much he may pose as a patriotic Englishman, Frenchman, or American, in his heart he despises the Gentile. And (ii) every Jew, even though he may he an atheist, from the financial magnate in Park Lane to the pedlar of lemons in Whitechapel, expects a Messiah who will establish a worldwide Jewish Empire on the ruins of Gentile civilization." Using Harrison as a source is to my distaste. However, his insights into certain aspects of occult revivalism are scrupulously distilled in Christopher Bamford's 1993 introduction to Harrison's *The Transcendental Universe: Six Lectures on Occult Science, Theosophy, and the Catholic Faith*, a collection of lectures delivered in 1893.

** Key sources on the "hidden hand" theory, in addition to those referenced herein, include Godwin's singularly intrepid four-part series in *Theosophical History* (April, July, October 1990, and January 1991); *The Theosophical Enlightenment* by Joscelyn Godwin (State University of New York Press, 1994); Christopher Bamford's aforementioned introduction to *The Transcendental Universe* by C. G. Harrison (Lindisfarne Press, 1993); *The Hermetic Brotherhood of Luxor* by Joscelyn Godwin, Christian Chanel, and John P. Deveney (Samuel Weiser, 1995); "Early Story of TS" by William Stainton Moses, *Light* (London), July 9, 1892, and July 23, 1892; and *Ghost Land Or Researches into the Mysteries of Occultism* by Emma Hardinge Britten (1876), a critical volume to which we return.

Around this time, the Liberal Brothers persuaded the Conservative Brothers to instigate Spiritualist phenomena in the West, and America in particular, to counter rising materialism. The ensuing raps and spirit phenomena were under the control of these super-initiates rather than the communications of departed and ethereal beings. This was the hidden cause behind the Rochester rappings of 1848.

But, as the theory goes, the wave of Spiritualism soon got out of hand, with mediums proclaiming, to the deep consternation of both Liberal and Conservative Brothers, the existence not only of disembodied personas but also reincarnation, a doctrine they rejected. (René Guénon heartily agreed). The circle of adepts, Godwin wrote in July 1990, harbored "far broader doctrines than those held by most American Spiritualists" including existence of "sub-mundane elementals and super-mundane angels, as well as . . . the 'mundane' spirits of the unprogressed human dead. The common run of Spiritualists, on the other hand, believed all manifestations to be due to the latter alone."

This development reflected a disastrous wrong turn in which the table-rapping spectacles of Spiritualism spiraled into an out-of-control Frankenstein monster proffering false ideas and pseudo-theologies. The Liberal and Conservative Brothers sought to halt the phenomena; but Brothers of the Left-Hand path, for enigmatic reasons of their own, sustained it.

The Liberal and Conservative Brothers required a private agent to dispel the unintended myths of their foiled plan. Enter Madame H. P. Blavatsky. "Astrological observation had led the members to conclude that someone of great occult power had appeared in the world at the time of H.P.B.'s birth," writes K. Paul Johnson in *The Masters Revealed*. The Liberal and Conservative Brothers selected the formidable Russian for this role. But they miscalculated once again, failing to grasp Blavatsky's independence and overestimating their ability to control her.

In the early 1870s, Blavatsky was traveling between Egypt and Russia. Summoned to Paris in June of 1873, she was given her mission—but H.P.B. rebelled by demanding entry to an unnamed initiatory order. She was refused and the next month dispatched to America—on just a day's notice, Henry Olcott added. Blavatsky wrote British medium William Stainton Moses in 1875: "I was sent from

Paris to America on purpose to prove the phenomena and their reality, and show the fallacy of the spiritualistic theory of spirits."*

But once in America, Blavatsky demonstrated her independence. She again demanded entry to an unknown order—and if denied she threatened to shut down the unnamed order's activities in America. The Brothers had enough. In April 1878, they decided, through their American branch, to place the former recruit into a comatose state of "occult imprisonment." But Brothers of the Left-Hand path—again for mysterious reasons of their own—freed Blavatsky. The Left-Hand Brothers—who may have been Hindu nationalists—dispatched her to India where H.P.B. ignited the nascent independence movement. Recall early Theosophist A.O. Hume who reported instigating the Indian National Congress under "advice and guidance of advanced initiates." This is the same Hume memorialized on a 1973 Indian postage stamp.

Hume, it should be noted, had tense relations with Blavatsky. He was critical toward her iteration of the masters and appears to have had contact with his own circle of "advanced initiates." K. Paul Johnson quotes a private letter of Hume's from 1883 calling them "a body of men, mostly of Asiatic origin, who for a variety of causes are deeply and especially interested in the welfare and progress of India, and who possess faculties which no other man or body of living men do." These unknown actors "have seen fit . . . to give me their confidence to a *certain limited extent.*"

In the same letter, the retired colonial secretary recounts being introduced in 1848 to a secret society in Paris called "the Association." He broke from the group but in 1880 was reconciled to it through Blavatsky and Olcott, though the pair had different mentors. Johnson reckons that Hume was in touch with the same unnamed informant referenced by C.J. Harrison in connection with his theories of the "hidden hand"—if not, by slender chance, the unknown source himself.

Regarding Blavatsky's psychic captivity, her younger sister, Vera Petrovna de Zhelihovsky, wrote in the January 15, 1895, issue of *Lucifer*, the journal her sibling founded:

---

* "Early Story of TS" by William Stainton Moses, *Light* (London), July 9, 1892, and July 23, 1892.

> In the spring of 1878 a strange thing happened to Madame Blavatsky. Having got up and set to work one morning as usual, she suddenly lost consciousness, and never regained it again until five days later. So deep was her state of lethargy that she would have been buried had not a telegram [from a "Master" in Bombay] been received by Colonel Olcott and his sister, who were with her at the time, emanating from him she called her Master. The message ran, "Fear nothing, she is neither dead nor ill, but she has need of repose; she has overworked herself. . . . She will recover." As a matter of fact she recovered and found herself so well that she would not believe that she had slept for five days. Soon after this sleep, H. P. Blavatsky formed the project of going to India.

Was such a scheme ever hatched? Where there secret schools of brothers, each with its private plans and purposes?

It should at least be noted that the reported phenomena of Spiritualism did give rise to the field of parapsychology, modernity's most direct, though by no means only, challenge to philosophical materialism. (An exploration of parapsychology appears in chapter ten, "Science of the Supernatural.") What's more, the events of Blavatsky's state of unconsciousness and her turn towards India—persuading a hesitant Henry Olcott to join her—had momentous political results, more fully explored in chapter nine, "Politics and the Occult." Some contemporaries noted that Blavatsky exceeded in her writing, producing her most lasting works, *The Secret Doctrine, The Key to Theosophy,* and *The Voice of Silence,* only *after* being "freed from service to hidden Masters," as Johnson put it.

"After knowing this remarkable lady . . . ," Olcott wrote in his 1875 treatise on Spiritualism, *People from the Other World,* "I am almost tempted to believe that the stories of Eastern fables are but simple narratives of fact; and that this very American outbreak of spiritualistic phenomena is under the control of an Order, which while depending for its results upon unseen agents, has its existence upon Earth among men."

Guénon, in a rare area of agreement with a Theosophical point of view—he reviled the organization as a "pseudo-religion" and modern bastardization of esoteric principles—also considered the Hydesville hauntings the result of a hidden hand. “In fact,,” he wrote in *The Spiritist Fallacy* in 1923, “according to information from the ‘H B of L’, the first ‘spiritist’ phenomena were produced not by ‘spirits’ but by men acting from a distance by means known only to several initiates. And these initiates were, precisely, members of the ‘inner circle’ of the ‘H B of L’.” Guénon considered Emma Hardinge Britten a member of the H.B. of L. around 1870, which would argue for the group’s earlier, if underground, formation.

This returns us to the career of Emma Hardinge Britten and her 1876 account *Ghost Land*, mentioned among my sources. *Ghost Land* was published in two parts: the first serialized in Emma’s magazine *The Western Star* in 1872 and the full book issued four years later.

Emma called the work a memoir of a mysterious European occultist and nobleman whom she identifies only as “Chevalier Louis de B.” As Emma explained, she edited and translated the Chevalier’s true account of his occult life, though identifying him no further.

Emma’s Chevalier Louis represents an early thread of the hidden hand theory. When he was 12 in the 1830s, Louis recounts, he was brought into a circle of Berlin occultists: “the German branch of a very ancient secret society.” The initiates placed the adolescent medium into a Mesmeric trance, aided by nitrous oxide, from which he was induced to produce poltergeist-like activity:

> On one occasion, the society having thrown me into a profound sleep by the aid of vital magnetism, and the vapors of nitrous oxide gas, they directed my “atmospheric spirit” to proceed, in company with two other lucid subjects, to a certain castle in Bohemia, where friends of theirs resided, and then and there to make disturbances by throwing stones, moving ponderable bodies, shrieking, groaning, and tramping heavily, etc., etc. I here state emphatically, and upon the honor of one devoted only to the interests of truth, that these disturbances were made, and made by the spirits of myself and two other yet living beings, a girl and a boy who were subjects of the society; and though we, in our own individualities, remembered nothing whatever of our performance, we were shortly afterwards shown a long and startling newspaper

account of the hauntings in the castle of Baron von L——, of which we were the authors.

To recap, the "Rochester rappings" commenced in late March 1848. According to the hidden hand theory, unknown brothers—who rejected simplistic notions of the soul's immortality—used physical methods on living subjects to produce the phenomena at the Fox cabin and other Spiritualist settings and séances. To clarify the brothers' position on reincarnation and life after death, I think it valid to return to Guénon's *Spiritist Fallacy*: "It is not a matter of a return to the same state of existence . . . but on the contrary, the passage of the being to other states of existence, which are defined . . . by completely different conditions from those to which the human being is subject." We will revisit Guénon's views on reincarnation.

As Jocelyn Godwin explained in part I of his series on the hidden hand, "The mechanism of the [Spiritualist] experiment was apparently as follows: the young mediums were made unconscious through hypnotism and laughing gas, and their 'atmospheric spirits,' elsewhere called 'doubles,' were projected to a distance by the controllers, where they were able to work on the physical plane." This meshes with the Emma/ Louis recollection.

British psychical researcher Eric Dingwall (1890–1986) speculated that Emma's Chevalier Louis was Joseph Henry Louis de Palm (1809–1876), or Baron de Palm, who died the same year of the book's appearance and was the subject of Henry Olcott's inaugural cremation ceremony or "pagan funeral" in New York City, explored in the next chapter.

G.R.S. Mead suggested that Chevalier Louis represented the "inner life" of Edward Bulwer Lytton (1803–1873), author of the novels *Vril* (1871) and the more famous *Zanoni* (1842), an influential, at one time even sensational, occult-themed work that also posited the existence of near-immortal masters.

Medieval philologist Robert Mathiesen argued persuasively that Chevalier Louis was occult writer Ernest de Bunsen (1819–1903), a Prussian nobleman of moderate rank. "If this man is indeed Louis de B—," Mathiesen wrote in *The Unseen Worlds of Emma Hardinge Britten* (*Theosophical History Occasional Papers*, Vol. IX, 2001), "he might reasonably have been given his father's title of 'Chevalier.' Moreover, there was indeed extremely compelling mundane reasons for burying his identity in the deepest secrecy. His father was the late Christian Carl Josias von Bunsen, an eminent scholar of the history of religions, but also one of the most famous diplomats of the nineteenth century, who served as Prussian ambassador to England during the years 1841–1854."

Mathiesen adduced the identities of other characters in the work—including the mysterious mirror-gazer "Mr. H." as influential British scryer and antiquarian Frederick Hockley (1809–1885)—establishing real-life figures who populate its pages.

In terms of modern history, the hidden hand theory is the esoteric of the esoteric. Hence, none of its points of reference precisely match colloquial usage.

To clarify one such reference, the term *lefthand*, as used in this chapter, is rooted in the Vedic Sanskrit *vamachara* ("left-handed attainment"). The phrase entered the Western lexicon through *The Secret Doctrine*. In volume one, Blavatsky depicts a reversed or "horns up" pentagram—among the first times this symbol appeared in the West (it is referenced in 1855 in Eliphas Lévi's *Ritual of High Magic*)—and wrote: "The esoteric symbol of Kali Yuga is the five-pointed star reversed . . . the sign of human sorcery, with its two points (horns) turned heavenward, a position every Occultist will recognise as one of the 'left-hand,' and used in ceremonial magic."

Christian scholar John Smulo—who has been called a "Left-Hand Christian philosopher"—agrees with this historical entry point but intriguingly adds: "another possible origin of the term could be found in Matthew's Gospel, where Jesus speaks of placing the sheep (followers of Christ) at his right hand, and the goats (those who didn't follow Christ) at his left hand (Matthew 25:33)."*

The Left-Hand Path is an ethical and spiritual outlook that might be described as "My Will Be Done." This concept could be seen as a more honest philosophical antonym to The Lord's Prayer invocation "Thy Will Be Done," which is often invoked with the same meaning

* "Reaching Nietzschean Individualists" in *Encountering New Religious Movements* edited by Irving Hexham, Stephen Rost & John W. Moorhead II (Kregel, 2004).

covertly or, just as often, unconsciously. The Left-Hand Path is sometimes conflated with the "dark side" or Satanism—although these comparisons are usually proffered with too little subtlety and understanding to be meaningful. (I consider occultic Satanism in chapter twelve.) While the Left-Hand Path is not necessarily Satanic, it by no means precludes exploration of Satanism on the seeker's own terms. Some contemporary seekers who identify with the Left-Hand Path do not necessarily believe in deity or extra-physicality but rather use ritual and symbol for the focus of will.

To return to the hidden-hand theory—for the last time, some readers may be relieved to know—the Left-Hand Brothers, in my reading, were not necessarily maleficent but promoting of their own designs. They found Blavatsky, as did the other initiates, an important, useful, even foreordained—if unpredictable—agent and so freed her from her comatose or suspended state. The purpose of the Left-Hand Brothers is unclear—although it seemed to involve instigating Indian independence. Blavatsky never spoke about the component parts in these terms. So goes one of the most intriguing and little-understood theoretical puzzles of modern occultism.

The early twentieth century not only saw a flourishing of occult organizations but also the advent of a wave of great teachers of lasting impact. The two most significant were Austrian esotericist Rudolf Steiner (1861–1925) and Greek-Armenian philosopher G.I. Gurdjieff (1866–1949). Although both arose in the wake of post-Blavatsky hunger to explore esoteric currents, each proved unclassifiable, extraordinary intellects. They are "occult" only to the extent that their work grew with the culture that the thought movement fostered.

Steiner proved an epically important figure in modern Western mysticism, comparative religion, architecture, agriculture, and education. He began his scholarly career when, at the notably young age of twenty-one, he became authorized curator and anthologizer of works by Goethe. Steiner attained public notice within Theosophy, as did, of course, many fin de siècle artists, composers, seekers, and philosophers. Steiner began speaking before Theosophical gatherings in 1899 and—although he never formally joined the society—the Austrian prodigy was elevated to head its German section in 1902. Two years later, Annie Besant named Steiner leader of Theosophy's inner esoteric section for Germany and Austria. He was obviously held in esteem and considered a leader in grooming. But Steiner developed serious tensions with Besant and Charles Leadbeater, particularly over the anointing of Jiddu Krishnamurti as "World Teacher." For that matter, Krishnamurti could also be ranked with Steiner and Gurdjieff for depth and impact.

Moreover, the scholar chafed against Theosophy's increasing focus on Vedic spirituality and its relatively muted attitude toward Christian mysticism. In 1901, he reportedly told his intellectual partner and second wife, Marie von Sivers, of his frustrations with Theosophy's dominant Vedic orientation, noting that there exist "more significant spiritual influences than oriental mysticism" and further "it is certainly necessary to call into life a movement for spiritual science, but I will only be part of a movement that connects to and develops Western esotericism, and exclusively to this."* Steiner held no brief against Eastern spirituality; rather he believed that the Western seeker was likelier to progress within the framework in which he or she was culturally steeped.

To pursue his interests more directly, Steiner founded the ongoing Anthroposophical Society in late 1912. The following year, with mutual tensions at a pitch, the teacher broke from Theosophy. Steiner intrepidly explored his own systems and ideas, at once highly original and based in Western spirituality and philosophy, as well as his own independent explorations. He abided aspects of Blavatsky's cosmology with his own leavening, terms, and concepts. Steiner retained Blavatsky's supposition of vastly older cultures (including Atlantis) and deeply ancient and far-extending epochs of spiritual development.

He also taught practical ideas about training in clairvoyance and relationships with unseen entities and dimensions. Notably, Steiner pioneered alternative methods in pedagogy, which form the basis of today's highly popular Waldorf Schools. Steiner also expounded deeply humane theories of housing and educating mentally challenged adults, which developed into the living-learning environments called Camphill Villages, more than one hundred of which function across the world today.

---

* *Rudolf Steiner: A Biography* by Christoph Lindenberg (Verlag Freies Geistesleben 1997, Steiner Books 2012

I had the opportunity to visit one of these residential learning centers in Columbia County, New York, and found the experience deeply moving. Residents, both those with developmental disabilities and not, grow herbs, perform crafts and woodwork, bake, run shops, and so on. Developmentally challenged villagers demonstrate a remarkable degree of self-possession and independence. Their questions are thoughtful and pointed. I consider the Camphill Village movement one of Steiner's greatest legacies.

Steiner also developed biodynamic farming, a practice of full-circuit and, hence, environmentally sensitive agriculture and production, which underscores many of today's developments in organic farming. Because biodynamics uses self-encompassing production chains, its farmers, producers, and consumers grow uniquely aware of environmental interconnectedness and impact.

In architecture, Steiner's methods were highly original, at once art-deco, abstract, and practical; he felt his designs heightened and aided development of the psyche. The scholar's building designs at once meld with their natural landscape but present a symphony of non-angular innovations. Not since the Gothic cathedrals had the Western world witnessed this scale and originality of sacred design.

Along the way there were considerable stumbles. Although Steiner viewed racial categories as outmoded classifications facing irrelevance in the progress of spiritual evolution, he also, like Madame Blavatsky, could offer astonishingly obtuse racialist nostrums typical of the age. These form exceptions across his vast oeuvre. Indeed, Steiner was considered a scourge by the early Nazis who regularly denounced him; the Third Reich banned Anthroposophy in 1935. There exist rumors that proto-Nazis burned down the first incarnation of Steiner's architectural masterpiece, the Goetheanum in northern Switzerland near Basel. The celebrated domed structure, named for Goethe, got demolished in a fire on new year's day of 1923, little more than two years after its completion. For Steiner, the fire caused "pain for which there are no words."* The teacher and his followers completed a second Goetheanum on the same spot in 1928.

During this period, Steiner's heterodoxy and unclaimable philosophy attracted umbrage from all sides. "Practically everybody hated

* An excellent recounting—and a review of the unproven charges of arson—appears in "The First Goetheanum: A Centenary for Organic Architecture" by John Paull, *Journal of Fine Arts*, Volume 3, Issue 2, 2020.

him: Catholics, Protestants, Marxists, and proto-Nazis, not to mention other esotericists," writes historian Gary Lachman. "There were at least two attempts on his life, and the number of attacks fomented by 'black brotherhoods' is unknown . . . Steiner endured vilification in the press and disruption at his lectures with equanimity."*

The greatness of Steiner is that he devised a truly integrative philosophy encompassing science, learning, art, education, design, agriculture, and spirituality. Anthroposophy achieved what many philosophers long for but rarely capture: a total approach to life. Iconic Russian film director Andrei Tarkovsky (1932–1986), among the many artists influenced by Steiner, extrapolated in a 1985 interview:

> Steiner offers us a world view that explains everything—or almost everything—and provides human development with an appropriate place in the spiritual domain . . . Although it may have been possible in the past to seriously take the materialist position to explain the function and meaning of human life and society on a physical material basis, it is no longer possible to do so. Nowadays we need other viewpoints: we must develop our spiritual existence and finally ask ourselves what the meaning of life is. Because if one says that life develops according to material laws, it means that life has no meaning. No one who thinks about it even a little can agree that life is meaningless.
>
> When it is said, for example, "No, your life isn't meaningless when you sacrifice yourself in order that future generations can live better"—that is absurd and insincere because it means that the human beings who sacrifice themselves physically have no right to live for a higher objective. To sacrifice oneself for another is wonderful, but it's not enough; it's more important to develop spiritually than to become fodder for future generations.**

Steiner is among the most remarkable figures who passed through Theosophy before fully developing his own career. That short list includes Russian mathematician and philosopher P.D. Ouspensky

---

* *Revolutionaries of the Soul: Reflections on Magicians, Philosophers, and Occultists* by Gary Lachman (Quest Books, 2014).

** "From an Interview with Andrei Tarkovsky" by Nathan Federovsky, *What Is Happening in the Anthroposophical Society* (newsletter), July/August 1985.

(1878–1947) who later became a profoundly important student to G.I. Gurdjieff and communicator of the philosopher's ideas and methods, as is next seen.

It is one of the great "what ifs?" of occult history to consider the dynamism that would have redounded to Theosophy had Steiner remained within its folds. It seems evident that Besant considered him a future leader. Besant grasped the potential of Krishnamurti, Steiner, and Manly P. Hall—and either could not keep them or willingly let them go.

One of the most seminally important and enigmatic spiritual figures of the twentieth century was Greek-Armenian philosopher G.I. Gurdjieff. His essential teaching is that man exists in a state of sleep—not metaphorically but actually.

Human existence, the teacher observed, is not only passed in sleep but man himself is in pieces, at the passive bidding of his three brains or centers: thinking, emotional, and physical, all of which operate in disunity leaving a "man-machine" incapable of authentic activity. "Man cannot do," Gurdjieff said. He meant this in the fullest sense.

Nearly all of Gurdjieff's statements—including his 1950 literary giant *Beelzebub's Tales to His Grandson*—were intended to disrupt rote thought. He instructed that the magisterial allegory be read three times. Author P.L. Travers, best known for the Mary Poppins books, noted aptly, "In *Beelzebub's Tales*, soaring off into space, like a great, lumbering, flying cathedral, Gurdjieff gathered the fundamentals of his teaching."

There is no neat summarizing the breadth of Gurdjieff's system, which extended to sacred dances, self-observation, rigorous and challenging training and confrontation with obstacles, and what might be considered a cosmological-existential-spiritual psychology, explored by one of his greatest students, the aforementioned P.D. Ouspensky, who produced an invaluable record of his experiences with Gurdjieff, *In Search of the Miraculous*, posthumously published in 1949, two years after Ouspensky's death. A brief, though daunting, analysis also appears in Ouspensky's *The Psychology of Man's Possible Evolution*, published in 1950.

Appearing in Russia shortly before World War I, Gurdjieff assembled a remarkable circle of students, some of whom followed him in a harrowing escape across the continent amid the chaos and danger of war and revolution.

A sense of Gurdjieff's relationship to his students and manner of teaching appears in an episode from Fritz Peters' haunting and powerful 1964 memoir *Boyhood with Gurdjieff*. In Peters' book, the author recounts the commitment Gurdjieff exacted from Fritz at age eleven. The young adolescent met Gurdjieff in June 1924 when he was sent to spend the summer at the teacher's school, the Prieuré, a communal estate in Fontainebleau-Avon outside of Paris.

Speaking to Fritz on a stone patio one day, Gurdjieff banged the table with his fist and asked, "Can you promise to do something for me?" The boy gave a firm, "Yes." The teacher gestured to the estate's vast expanse of lawns. "You see this grass?" he asked. "Yes," Fritz said again. "I give you work. You must cut this grass, with machine, every week."

Fritz agreed—but that wasn't enough. Gurdjieff "struck the table with his fist for the second time. 'You must promise on your God.' His voice was deadly serious. 'You must promise that you will do this thing no matter what happens.'" Fritz replied, "I promise." Again, not enough. "Not just promise," Gurdjieff said. "Must promise you will do no matter what happens, no matter who try stop you. Many things can happen in life."

Fritz vowed again.

Very soon, in the lives of Fritz and his teacher, something seismic and upending did occur. Gurdjieff suffered a severe car accident and for several weeks laid in a near-coma recovering at the Prieuré. Fritz, feeling that the whole thing seemed almost foreordained, honored his commitment to keep mowing the lawns. But he met with stern resistance. Several adults at the school insisted that the noise would disturb Gurdjieff's convalescence and could even result in the master's death. Fritz recalled how unsparingly the promise had been extracted and how fully it had been given. He refused to relent. He kept mowing—no one physically stopped him. One day while Fritz was cutting the lawns, he spied the recovering master smile at him from his bedroom window.

One of the greatest benefits students receive from Gurdjieff's teaching (to which I can personally attest) is how it punctures, immediately and sometimes devastatingly, one's cherished images of self. We in the modern West are suffused with contradictions. People are filled with puffed up views of themselves. They are also filled with the opposite. But take one person and give him or her an unfamiliar task at an inconvenient hour and you will see how powerful or special we are. Not very.

Gurdjieff constantly pushed people to surpass their limits of perceived strength. In his posthumous memoir, *Meetings with Remarkable Men*, the teacher described episodes from when he and a band of students fled civil war-torn Russia. In an epilogue, "The Material Question," he addressed their need for money.

In the summer of 1922, after a dangerous flight across Eastern Europe, Gurdjieff and his students reached Paris with razor-thin resources. Procuring an estate, the Prieuré, to function as living quarters and school, Gurdjieff used every means possible to foster his circle's financial survival. "The work went well," he wrote, "but the excessive pressure of these months, immediately following eight years of uninterrupted labours, fatigued me to such a point that my health was severely shaken, and despite all my desire and effort I could no longer maintain the same intensity."

Seeking to restore his strength through a dramatic change in setting as well as fundraise for the institute, Gurdjieff devised a plan to tour America with forty-six students. The troupe would put on demonstrations of the sacred dances they practiced and present Gurdjieff's lectures and ideas to the public. Although intended to attract donors, the ocean voyage and lodgings entailed significant upfront expenses. Last-minute adjustments and unforeseen costs consumed nearly all the teacher's remaining resources.

"To set out on such a long journey with such a number of people," he wrote, "and not have any reserve cash for an emergency was, of course, unthinkable." The trip itself, so meticulously prepped and planned for, faced collapse. "And then," Gurdjieff wrote, "as has happened to me more than once in critical moments of my life, there occurred an entirely unexpected event." He continued:

> What occurred was one of those interventions that people who are capable of thinking consciously—in our times and particularly in past epochs—have always considered a sign of the just providence of the Higher Powers. As for me, I would say that it was *the law-conformable result of a man's unflinching perseverance in bringing all his manifestations into accordance with the principles he has consciously set himself in life for the attainment of a definite aim.* [emphasis added]

As Gurdjieff sat in his room pondering their troubles, his elderly mother entered. She had reached Paris just a few days earlier. His mother was part of the group fleeing Russia but she and others got stranded in the Caucasus. "It was only recently that I had succeeded," Gurdjieff wrote, "after a great deal of trouble, in getting them to France."

She handed her son a package, which she told him was a burden from which she desperately wished to be relieved. Gurdjieff opened the package to discover a forgotten brooch of significant value that he had given her back in Eastern Europe. He intended it as a barter item used to pass a border or secure food and shelter. He assumed it was long since sold or otherwise traded and never again thought of it. But there it was. At the precipice of ruin, they were saved.

"I almost jumped up and danced for joy," he wrote. This was the *lawful result* of "unflinching perseverance." As with all Gurdjieff wrote and said, there is at the back of his statement a level of gravitas and lived experience that makes this teaching warranting of deep pause. Things that might appear homiletic in the mouth of a lesser figure took on life-and-death seriousness from this teacher.

I close this consideration with a statement of Ouspensky's. It is not, perhaps, considered one of his most remarkable observations, but it is useful and instructive insofar as it demonstrates how his and Gurdjieff's ideas cannot be contextualized within familiar categories. Philosopher Jacob Needleman (1934–2022), a student of the Gurdjieff work, remarked, "It's not *like* anything."

Ouspensky made a valuable observation about the nature of a "positive attitude" in a talk reproduced in the posthumously published book, *A Further Record: Extracts from Meetings 1928–1945*. In its lowest and least useful iteration, Ouspensky told students,

> . . . a positive attitude does not really mean a positive attitude, it simply means liking certain things. A really positive attitude is something quite different. Positive attitude can be defined better than positive emotion, because it refers to thinking. But a real positive attitude includes in itself understanding of the thing itself and understanding of the quality of the thing from the point of view, let us say, of evolution and those things that are obstacles. Things that are against, i.e., if they don't help, they are not considered, they simply don't exist, however big they may be externally. And by not seeing them, i.e., if they disappear, one can get rid of their influence. Only, again it is necessary to understand that not seeing wrong things does not mean indifference; it is something quite different from indifference.

What the teacher is saying, albeit on a great scale, is that the individual must seek to understand forces that develop or erode his or her humanity, itself an immense question. We are unconcerned with coordinates of good or bad, happy or sad, but rather with questions of *developmental forces* and what they mean to us.

In the fresh wave of movements and teachers, there appeared a vast influx of new occult literature. Claims of hidden knowledge or secrets of antiquity were common. Few withstood scrutiny or attained posterity. But one work justly gripped seekers of the new era like no other. It was a massive and extraordinary curation formally titled, *An Encyclopedic Outline of Masonic, Hermetic, Qabbalistic and Rosicrucian Symbolical Philosophy, Being an Interpretation of the Secret Teachings concealed within the Rituals, Allegories and Mysteries of All Ages*—or as better known in shorthand, *The Secret Teachings of All Ages*. Privately published on a subscription basis in 1928 by Canadian-born scholar of esotericism Manly P. Hall (1901–1990)—when he was just twenty-seven years old—the magisterial volume immediately became and remains perhaps the most thorough, learned, and variegated codex to esoteric and symbolist mysteries.

Hall's book appeared in oversized folio format, resembling the illuminated manuscripts of the Middle Ages—with a breadth of material that retains its ability to astound: Pythagorean mathematics, alchemical formulas, Hermetic doctrine, the workings of Kabbalah (or Renaissance iterations of it), geometry of Ancient Egypt, Native American mythology, uses of cryptograms, an analysis of Tarot, symbols of Rosicrucianism, esotericism of the Shakespearean dramas, Atlantean theses, and humanity's symbolic connections to nature were just a few of Hall's topics.

The scale of his bibliography alone was extraordinary. Its nearly 1,000 entries ranged from the core works of Plato, Aristotle, and Augustine, to translations of Gnostic, Nicene, and Hermetic literature, to writings of Paracelsus, Claudius Ptolemy, Francis Bacon, Basil Valentine, and Cornelius Agrippa, to works of every variety on ancient and esoteric philosophies—religious mythic, or metaphysical—that have expressed themselves in symbol or ceremony.

The youth's early life provided few clues to his virtuosity: Hall attended no university and had little schooling; his roots in Canada and the American West in the care of his grandmother were comfortable if ordinary; his youthful letters betrayed no special fluency with the complexities of the ancient world; and one of his first forays into professional life was as a clerk at a Wall Street banking firm. Were the book the work of an aged antiquarian, it would appear the worthy capstone of a lifetime of study. Yet the question reasserts itself on nearly every page: how did this large-framed young man with little formal education produce the last century's most unusual and masterly work on the esoteric wisdom of antiquity?

Hall was born in Peterborough, Ontario on March 18, 1901, to a father, William, who was a dentist and a mother, Louise (née Palmer), who was a chiropractor, a notably progressive profession for a woman then. In photographs, Louise appears with long hair, holding a violin, and wearing a wristwatch—an unusual and impressive figure in a buttoned-up late-Victorian era.

His parents divorced before his birth and Manly was raised by his maternal grandmother, Florence Palmer. In 1985, Hall wrote *Growing Up With Grandmother*, a tribute to the woman he called "Mrs. Arthur Whitney Palmer." The short book is notable, in a sense, for what it reveals about Hall's reticence to broach virtually any personal aspect of his childhood or adolescence.

When the boy was two years old, Florence brought him to Sioux Falls, South Dakota, where they resided several years. It could only have been a lonely existence: A sickly child, Hall saw little formal schooling and spent long hours reading voraciously on his own. His contact with other children was limited. But a spark of some indefinable brilliance shone in the youth, which his grandmother nurtured on trips to museums in Chicago and New York.

For a time, Manly and his grandmother lived in a high-end Chicago hotel, Palmer House, which was owned by relatives. There, Manly was mostly in the company of grown-ups, including a traditionally garbed Hindu maître d'hôtel, who taught him adult etiquette. Later on, the bookish adolescent was enrolled— briefly, to his almost certain relief—in a New York City military school.

Tragedy struck early: Manly's grandmother died when he was sixteen and in New York. He soon traveled to California to be with his mother and came under the influence of a self-styled Rosicrucian community in Oceanside, California. Manly lived at the Rosicrucian Fellowship, where he formed close relationships with founder Max Heindel and his wife—but also grew suspicious of the order's claims to ancient wisdom. Soon he moved on his own to Los Angeles, where he fell in with metaphysical seekers and discussion groups.

In 1920, 19-year-old Hall began a precocious career in public speaking, delivering an address on reincarnation in a small room above a Santa Monica bank. He collected about 35 cents in voluntary offerings, just enough to treat himself and a friend to ice cream sundaes across the street. But word spread of the boy wonder's mastery of arcane and metaphysical subjects. He began addressing a liberal evangelical congregation called Church of the People, and quickly rose to the rank of minister.

In 1923, the *Los Angeles Times* seemed positively smitten with the twenty-two-year-old, covering his lectures and sermons at Church of the People in several articles. "He is tall," the *Times* reported on May 28, "with unusually broad shoulders—football shoulders—but he wears his curly, dark brown hair bobbed like a girl's, and even his face and eyes convey an almost feminine impression." In a practice he maintained for life, the youth spoke from a wooden mission-style chair, enrapturing listeners without physical movement or gesticulation. In most of his addresses, he promoted classical ethics as a balm for the torpor of contemporary existence.

Hall already began attracting benefactors in oil and railroads allowing him to travel abroad in search of lost knowledge. Yet his early letters from Japan, Egypt, China, and India were, in many respects, ordinary. They contained little of the eye-opening detail or wonder of discovery that one finds in the writings of other early twentieth century seekers encountering the East, such as legendary British soldier and writer T. E. Lawrence.

In 1922, however, Hall produced a brief, luminescent work on the mystery schools of antiquity, *Initiates of the Flame*. With ease and gracefulness, Hall wrote across a spectrum of subjects, describing Egyptian rites, Arthurian myths, practices of alchemy, and psychological underpinnings of arcane methods. "Man has been an alchemist from the time when first he raised himself," Hall wrote. ". . . Experiences are the chemicals of life with which the philosopher experiments."

Hall expressed alarm over rising materialism of the day, which he encountered firsthand in his brief career at a Wall Street brokerage firm before the Great Depression. In one preface to the *Secret Teachings*, Hall described the "outstanding event" of his Wall Street career as "witnessing a man depressed over investment losses take his life."

What's more, Hall was working in an age that tended to marginalize indigenous religious traditions. Even great spiritual studies of his day, such as *The Golden Bough*, characterized primeval religions as museum pieces, not living philosophies possessed of universal or even serviceable ideas. "With very few exceptions," Hall wrote, "modern authorities downgraded all systems of idealistic philosophy and the deeper aspects of comparative religion. Translations of classical authors could differ greatly, but in most cases the noblest thoughts were eliminated or denigrated . . . and scholarship was based largely upon the acceptance of a sterile materialism."

By 1928, Hall succeeded in publishing his completed opus in a privately financed first printing of 2,200 copies. The work—called the "Great Book" by admirers—would never be out of print, passing into myriad paperback and deluxe editions in the twenty-first century. Indeed, the *Secret Teachings* can be considered the most popular and alluring "underground" book in American history.

Attracting benefactors in Los Angeles's booming economy of film, railroads, agriculture, shipping, and oil, Hall in 1934 founded the Philosophical Research Society (PRS) in the Griffith Park neighborhood. Designed by English architect Robert Stacy Judd, the campus rose as a jewel-box of Mayan-Egyptian-art deco motifs. PRS provided a cloistered setting where Hall spent the rest of his life teaching, writing, and assembling a remarkable collection of antique texts and devotional objects.

It was there in 1944 that the occult thinker produced a short work, one little known beyond his immediate circle: *The Secret Destiny of America*. It caught the eye of a future president, then a middling Hollywood actor gravitating toward politics: Ronald Reagan.

Hall's concise volume described, in fanciful vein, how America was the product of a "Great Plan" for religious liberty and self-governance launched by a hidden order of ancient philosophers and secret societies.

In one chapter, Hall depicted a mysterious "unknown speaker" delivering a rousing speech before the signing of the Declaration of Independence. The "strange man," wrote Hall, invisibly entered and exited the locked doors of the Philadelphia statehouse on July 4, 1776, presenting an oration that bolstered the wavering spirits of the delegates.

"God has given America to be free!" commanded the mysterious speaker, urging the men to overcome their fears of the noose, axe, or gibbet, and seal destiny by signing the great document. Newly emboldened, the delegates rushed forward to add their names. They looked to thank the stranger only to discover that he had vanished from the locked room. Was this, Hall wondered, "one of the agents of the secret Order, guarding and directing the destiny of America?"

At a 1957 commencement speech at his alma mater Eureka College, Reagan, then a corporate spokesman for GE, sought to inspire students with this leaf from occult history. "This is a land of destiny," Reagan said, "and our forefathers found their way here by some Divine system of selective service gathered here to fulfill a mission to advance man a further step in his climb from the swamps."

Reagan then retold the tale of Hall's unknown speaker, without naming his source. "When they turned to thank the speaker for his timely words," Reagan concluded, "he couldn't be found and to this day no one knows who he was or how he entered or left the guarded room."

Reagan revived the story at various points including in 1981, when *Parade* magazine asked the president for a personal essay on what July 4th meant to him. Presidential aide Michael Deaver delivered the piece with a note saying, "This Fourth of July message is the president's own words and written initially in the president's hand," on a yellow pad at Camp David. Reagan retold the legend of the unknown speaker—this time using language very close to Hall's own: "When they turned to thank him for his timely oratory, he was not to be found, nor could any be found who knew who he was or how had come in or gone out through the locked and guarded doors."

Where did Hall uncover the tale that inspired a president? The episode originated as "The Speech of the Unknown" in a collection of folkloric stories about America's founding, published in 1847 under the title *Washington and his Generals, or Legends of the Revolution by American* social reformer and muckraker George Lippard. Lippard, a friend of Edgar Allan Poe, had a strong taste for the gothic—he cloaked his mystery man in a "dark robe." He also tacitly acknowledged inventing the story: "The name of the Orator . . . is not definitely known. In this speech, it is my wish to compress some portion of the fiery eloquence of the time."

Regardless, the story took on its own life and came to occupy the same shadowland between fact and fiction as the parables of George Washington chopping down a cherry tree, or young Abe Lincoln walking miles to return a bit of change to a country-store customer. As with most myths, the story assumed different attributes over time. By 1911, the speech resurfaced in a collection of American political oratory, with the robed speaker fancifully identified as Patrick Henry.

For his part, Hall seemed to know almost nothing about the story's point of origin. He had been given a copy of the "Speech of the Unknown" by a since-deceased secretary of the Theosophical Society, but with no bibliographical information other than it being from a "rare old volume of early American political speeches." The speech appeared in 1938 in the Society's journal, *The Theosophist*, with the sole note that it was "published in a rare volume of addresses, and known probably to only one in a million, even of American citizens." It is Hall's language that unmistakably marks the Reagan telling.

It would be asking too much of Hall—or any teacher—to suggest that he always found his mark. His literary or religious essays sometimes dwell on narrow points, such as a 1946 consideration of Ralph Waldo Emerson's "Compensation," in which Hall appears to miss the work's full scope as a totalizing philosophy of reciprocity. Nor was Hall always judicious. In the first issue of his quarterly journal *Horizon* in August 1941, he published an astonishingly obtuse and inexplicably timed essay, "The Jew Does Not Fit In," in which he postulated of "the Jew": "He does not view business the way we do; of his Asiatic viewpoint we have no practical appreciation, little grasp." In short, he wrote, Jewish business practices are Oriental in nature and chafe against contemporary Western sensibilities.

Hence, in the figure of Manly P. Hall coexisted remarkable powers of discernment and curation mixed with the profoundest flaws of the most common person.

But still the question lingers: how did a modest, solidly built young man craft what is justly considered a one-of-a-kind codex to the occult and esoteric traditions of the world—all before his 28th birthday? To read Hall's work is to experience a readerly joy rarely associated with ordinary compendiums of wisdom—its depth, breadth, and detail are, simply put, not ordinary, and not easily understood.

To the question of how Hall achieved what he did, some admirers suggest that he was born with knowledge from other lifetimes; others that he had a photographic memory. In the end, perhaps one can only conclude such a question with still more questions. But this much is clear: Readers who discover *The Secret Teachings of All Ages* for the first time encounter a book probably unlike any they have seen before. The accomplishment of the *Secret Teachings* is, in part, that it may be the only serious compendium of the last several hundred years that takes the world of myth and symbol on its own terms. It does so with a span and breadth that no related work has attained or likely will.

In terms of his writing practices, Hall disclosed relatively little. Regarding motive, he said, as noted, he was seeking a practical philosophy to help him navigate life, voicing his fear that materialism was overtaking Western culture and his wish to strike a counter-octave. He did mention that he was able to gain access to certain collections that were opening to the public for the first time at the British Library in London and at the New York Public Library. He noted that the books he requested at the New York Public Library were always available as few others seemed interested in them at the time.

Hall's world travels in the early 1920s gave him some degree of proximity to the monuments and philosophies of antiquity. Through the influence of benefactors—including General Sir Francis Younghusband, who led Britain's invasion of Tibet at the turn of the century—Hall gained access to rare manuscripts at the British Museum. Beyond this, he said little, which fueled speculation over the young scholar's virtuosity.

Hall nurtured few close relationships. A first marriage in 1930 ended with his wife's suicide a little more than a decade later. He was into middle age in 1950 when he remarried a diminutive but strong-willed German American divorcée and mother of two, Marie Bauer.

His second wife harbored a deep interest in the occult and an all-consuming belief that a buried vault in Williamsburg, Virginia, contained the secret mystical manuscripts of her and Hall's hero, philosopher Francis Bacon. Marie and her husband also considered Bacon the hidden genius behind the Shakespearean plays—a theory that Hall took considerable efforts to defend in his "Great Book."

Marie was known for mood swings and a dictatorial manner toward friends and guests who ventured near her husband. Possessed of a mercurial temper, Marie Bauer was, in the eyes of some, a formidable equal to her imposing husband. To others, she raised the question of Hall's choice of companions. Two years after Hall's death, two acolytes of Marie's were convicted of trespassing in Virginia's Bruton Parish churchyard, where they conducted an illegal dig for the mythical Bacon vault.*

Unlike his histrionic wife and the many spiritual teachers who flocked to Hollywood, Hall showed little interest in attracting publicity or hobnobbing with movie stars. Later in Hall's life, his best-known friend was folksinger and balladeer Burl Ives, famous for his rendition of "Frosty the Snowman." Ives was also a fellow Freemason. Although

---

* See *Richmond Times-Dispatch*: "New Age Christian Mystic Sure Group Will Unearth Bacon Chest," August 20, 1992; "Pair Seeking Vault Fined for Trespassing," September 25, 1992; and "Mystics Seek New Dig; Say Church Site Holds Secret Keys to Peace," March 19, 2003.

Hall had written about the order for years, he joined only in 1954. In 1973, he was named an honorary 33-degree Mason in Scottish Rite, its pinnacle rank.

Hall rarely involved himself in the movie business, though in 1938 he did contribute the story to a murder yarn with an astrological theme: *When Were You Born*? In a segment at the film's opening, a young Hall gazes into the camera and explains the meaning of the zodiac signs. In those instances when Hall did succumb to Hollywood glitz, the results were more humorous than glamorous. In 1940, an entertainment columnist reported that Hall—"famous Los Angeles student of occult sciences"—hypnotized actor Bela Lugosi for a death scene in a low-budget Lugosi-Boris Karloff vehicle called *Black Friday*.*

Universal Pictures trumpeted Lugosi's portrayal of a man suffocating to death in a closet as "the first scene ever filmed of a player under the influence of hypnotism." The movie trailer briefly showed an angular, mustached Hall sitting over Lugosi and waving his hands across the actor's face in the style of Mesmeric "passes" as depicted in the books of Andrew Jackson Davis. Entertainment pages reported that Lugosi, hypnotically convinced he was in mortal danger, wrecked the movie set in a desperate fight to escape. The affair gave rise to an urban legend that Hall had hypnotized Lugosi before his legendary performance as Dracula.

Off the movie set, the Hungarian actor and Californian occultist became close friends. The pair bonded over shared love for classical music, which they listened to together on phonograph records. In 1955, the seventy-three-year-old Lugosi wed his fifth bride at Hall's Hollywood home. Newspaper photos showed an ashen-faced Lugosi—the image of Martin Landau's portrayal years later in the movie *Ed Wood*—clinking champagne glasses with his thirty-nine-year-old bride, a cutting-room clerk who met the actor while he was under treatment for drug addiction. In matters of friendship, celebrity glamour was no requisite to entering Hall's world.

Hall's 1990 death was roiled in controversy. In the late 1980s, the teacher turned over all of his household and business affairs, and even his and PRS's financial assets, to a self-

* *The Lima News* (Ohio), June 27, 1940.

described shamanic healer and reincarnate of Atlantis, Daniel Fritz. Hall disregarded—and in one case even fired—longtime employees and associates who questioned the relationship. Even a seasoned superior-court judge found Fritz worthy of disdain. "Did Mr. Fritz effectively steal from Mr. Hall?" said Judge Harvey A. Schneider in August 1993 upon invalidating Hall's belatedly amended will. "I think the answer is clearly yes. The evidence is so overwhelming that Mr. Fritz exerted undue influence over Mr. Hall . . . the whole thing just doesn't pass any reasonable person's sniff test."*

Ill and dangerously overweight in his final years, Hall had apparently bought into Fritz's claims as a mystical healer and promises to spread the aged scholar's work across the world. In an especially troubling move, 89-year-old Hall signed his estate over to Fritz less than a week before he died.

It is tempting to speculate that the aged Hall suffered from senility, yet he delivered a typically well-attended lecture just days before his death. It was a death that Hall's widow Marie stoked intense concerns over, telling the *Los Angeles Times* on December 22, 1994: "I firmly believe it was murder." She privately contracted a second autopsy, which confirmed earlier suspicions that Hall's corpse had been moved from outdoors to inside and that his death went unreported for hours.

Marie was far from isolated in her concerns. Investigators with the Los Angeles Police Department found the circumstances suspicious: Hall was alone with Fritz and Fritz's son when he died; hours passed before the death was reported to authorities; the body, bruised and infested by ants, appeared to have been moved from the outdoors to inside; and there was the strange timing of the new will. Charges were never filed, and, after Fritz's death from a rare form of cancer in 2001 and his son's death two years later from an autoimmune disorder linked to AIDS, the file was closed on Manly P. Hall's demise. The cause was listed as heart failure. But previously, the LA County coroner's office had repeatedly revised its report, a circumstance noted in the 1995 O.J. Simpson trial. Defense attorneys reminded jurors considering the forensics of victims Nicole Brown Simpson and Ronald Goldman of the coroner's previous "mistakes and omissions" involv-

* See "A Materialistic Fate for a Philosophical Legacy" by Bob Pool, *Los Angeles Times*, December 22, 1994, and by the same author, "Search for Peace Leads to Court Brawl," *Los Angeles Times*, April 3, 1993.

ing Hall, notes Louis Sahagun in his valuable 2008 biography *Master of the Mysteries.*

Aged, obese, and suffering from a strained heart, Manly P. Hall was probably not the victim of foul play, but his final days remained puzzling. One longtime friend of Hall's wondered how someone like Fritz could so suddenly grow "unduly influential over a man noted for his independence of thought and action."*

Hall's intimate companions—the shifty Fritz, the erratic Marie, the sometimes-sycophantic staffers—all pointed to someone who proved a poor judge of where to place trust. The wisdom that Hall cultivated his whole life appeared lost on him when its fortification was most needed. As though prophesying his own decline, Hall wrote in the *PRS Journal* in 1986: "Noble thoughts out of context lost most of their protective meanings."

Indeed, for all his emphasis on the practicality of ancient wisdom, Hall's personal life was, in some respects, a case in point of a truth not found in his writings: someone can accumulate "wisdom of the ages"—gleaning knowledge from the greatest books, lectures, and research—with little of it penetrating self. That widespread perplexity of human nature, a puzzle at the heart of all ethical philosophies, seems never to have occurred to him.

I write this not to be unduly critical. Without Hall's work and example, I doubt I would have found my way as a historian of the occult. Numerous figures, including seminal twentieth century scholar of myth Mircea Eliade, credited Hall with first igniting their interest in esoterica. Hall's contribution to the study of arcana is, in many ways, unparalleled. But no credit is done to the memory of eminent figures if they are posthumously elevated above the actualities of their existence. Only by appreciating the odds facing those immersed in esoteric study can we begin to understand those facing ourselves.

Although Hall remained largely unknown within lettered culture and academia during his career (this is now changing), a contemporary who studied occult realms gained vast intellectual currency across his lifetime and beyond: Swiss psychiatrist Carl Jung (1875–1961).

* Letter to the *Los Angeles Times* by Cliff Johnson, January 10, 1995.

As with Steiner and Gurdjieff, Jung's outlook and thought system were too broad to be strictly classified. But his intellect, at once precise and adventurous, lent contemporary validation to what William James called the "*further* side" of existence. Indeed, Jung and James shared a key idea: that a conversion experience or religious awakening, sometimes called an epiphany or moment of clarity, could objectively alter the circumstances of a person's life.

Alcoholics Anonymous cofounder Bill Wilson described such an experience, which led him to devise a faith-based approach to addiction recovery. In a letter of reply to Bill on January 30, 1961—which the 12-stepper was thrilled to receive—Jung, just months before his death, wrote that his method for defeating alcoholism was *spiritus contra spiritum*—the Latin phrase could be translated: *Higher Spirit over lower spirits*, or alcohol. It confirmed what Bill and others had experienced, an outlook at the heart of Alcoholics Anonymous and offshoot programs.

Jung's famous break with Sigmund Freud in 1912–1913 focused, in large measure, on Jung's theory of individuation, in which each person had to resolve internal conflicts, needs, desires, connections to the ultimate, and repressed "shadow" traits in a manner that could—and in some ways must—be ardently self-determined and personal. Jung considered the shadow a repository of unspoken desires, fears, impulses, and yearnings. It may also be a fount of unrealized abilities and personal powers. In his view, traumas and sexual repressions are not, of themselves, the core or common pivots of life.

The Jung-Freud break is colloquially characterized as a matter of Jung's occultism versus Freud's materialism; not only is that inadequate but it overlooks a more esoteric side to Freud, explored in chapter ten, "Science of the Supernatural." Indeed, the two psychologists shared an interest—though more muted in Freud's work—in extrasensory transference, mediumship, and even physical manifestation of poltergeist-like activity. Their line of professional difference was less over occult phenomena than Freud's conviction that his theories created a self-contained elemental table of psychical development.

Indeed, for all Freud's deftness in casting psychoanalysis within the context of modern medicine, the master cannot be wholly separated from the DNA of the occult mage. As Erik Davis notes in his 1998 *TechGnosis*:

> British doctor James Braid came up with the term *hypnotism* to describe such magnetic procedures, and researches into the hypnotic state would eventually lead a young Sigmund Freud to develop his early theories of the unconscious. Though little was left of Mesmer's original tactics at that point, Freud did resemble the old magnetizer in attempting to heal the nervous conditions of his patients by exploring altered states of consciousness in a "scientific" manner, all the while exploiting the almost magical rapport between patient and doctor.

Hence, Jung's break was not over Freud's refusal to consider the esoteric. But rather to insist that his system and its touchstones of trauma and resolution are indelibly settled doctrine. Jung, by contrast, perceived diffuse and unacknowledged meaning in humanity's mythical models and experiences.

"For several years prior to 1913," write scholars of Gnosticism Lance S. Owens and Stephan A. Hoeller, "Jung's interest had focused on the evidence he saw in myths, dreams, fantasies and psychotic delusions of an autonomous myth-making function inherently underlying human consciousness. The psyche—the soul—seemingly expressed itself in an arcane language of myth and symbol."* Both Owens and Hoeller are among today's most remarkable historical, spiritual, and expository interpreters of Jung. The field would be far lesser without their work, written separately and in collaboration. Owens observed in 2013 in his foreword to Alfred Ribi's *C. G. Jung and the Tradition of Gnosis*: "The publication in 1982 of Stephan A. Hoeller's landmark study, *The Gnostic Jung and the Seven Sermons to the Dead*, aroused a wider general awareness and discussion of Jung's allegiance with classical Gnosticism."

Indeed, Jung's development of his theory of a "collective unconscious" encompassed ideas of primeval imagery, symbolism, and archetypes embedded in religious tradition and myth. This extended to cycles of alchemy and astrology, which Jung held in more than metaphorical relation to the psyche. In the eyes of Jung (and also

* *Encyclopedia of Psychology and Religion*, 2nd edition (Springer Reference, 2014).

Henry Miller and D.H. Lawrence), Western astrology provides a tantalizing typology or thumbprint of personality. His astrology involved analyzing *the basics of classical celestial objects at the time of an individual's birth*, which is traditionally pegged to first breath. Jung wouldn't quite describe astrology as a science, so much as an elusive but enduring occult or sympathetically correlative psychology. (In that vein, see my note about the correlative astrological research of Michel Gauquelin in chapter ten, "Science of the Supernatural.")

Jung's theory of synchronicity—first articulated in a 1930 lecture (though developed earlier) and brought to full expression in his eponymous 1952 essay—recognized "acausal" but intimately related phenomena, such as simultaneous thought and occurrence, or uncanny connection between disparate lives. Through observation, Jung validated "meaningful coincidence of two or more events where something other than the probability of chance is involved." Yet he never actually defined the *mechanics* of synchronicity, an issue that also appeared in the rigorous statistical studies of extrasensory perception (ESP) conducted by J.B. Rhine, with whom the psychiatrist corresponded, further considered in the next chapter.

Jung emphasized the role of *enthusiasm* in a thought system. In his study of Rhine's Zener card experiments of the 1930s, the doctor noticed what Rhine himself had: ESP test subjects consistently, and inexplicably, scored higher "hits" on a deck of cards early in sessions when excitement and expectancy ran high. As time passed, accurate hits would taper off, though they could spike again if the subject's interest were newly aroused. Thus, reasoned Jung in *Synchronicity*: "Lack of interest and boredom are negative factors; enthusiasm, positive expectation, hope, and belief in the possibility of ESP make for good results and seem to be the real conditions which determine whether there are going to be any results at all."

Jung and his students also worked with the ancient Chinese pictogrammatic device known as the *I Ching* or *Book of Changes*. "For more than thirty years," Jung wrote in his 1949 introduction to Richard Wilhelm's translation, "I have interested myself in this oracle technique, or method of exploring the unconscious, for it has seemed to me of uncommon significance." The *I Ching* is a primeval symbolic alphabet which for millennia has been used for divinatory purposes. Its earliest iterations may extend to the tenth century B.C. in oral tradition. The first known written edition of the *I Ching* dates to the late-ninth century B.C. Notable English translations include Wilhelm (1950) and John Blofeld (1968).

Each of the sixty-four symbols or hexagrams of the *I Ching* contains six lines. The six lines may be variously broken (*yin*) or unbroken (*yang*), like binary code. The querent, using various methods—usually a toss of coins but sometimes, more traditionally, yarrow stalks—arrives at a hexagram intended to reveal a given situation. Each hexagram has a dramatic meaning—like a Tarot card, hieroglyph, or Hebrew character. Each meaning is also *inherently changing and in motion*; depending on your throw, your hexagram may include one or more "changing" lines.

A given hexagram correlates to an environmental or psychological situation, animal, landscape, or particular kind of individual; hence, you can decipher a story within it. This is something to which Jung dedicated himself for many years; he and his students conducted thousands of readings and came to feel that a certain accuracy prevailed—and that the *I Ching* itself possessed a kind of personality including a wry sense of humor.

Demonstrating the possibilities, consciousness explorer Terrence McKenna (1946–2000) in 1987 mapped the *I Ching* into a calendar called Timewave Zero. Collaborating with programmer Peter J. Meyer, McKenna discovered that the ancient Chinese oracle resulted in a calendar ending in 2012, coinciding with the cyclical end-date of the Mayan Long Count calendar. McKenna's insight, coupled with the contemporaneous work of spiritual theorist José Argüelles (1939–2011), ignited the New Age millennialist movement focused on 2012.

A few of Jung's closest students ventured the theory that a pictorial representation, such as an image, symbolic rendering, or sketch, captures a moment in time—but more than just a linear moment. A pictogrammatic image may, for a fleeting interval, capture a multi-dimensional impression of past, present, and future; hence, a hexagram might function as a kind of layered photograph or cartoon strip conveying all that is occurring at a given moment, unbound by traditional perceptions of time. Jung continued in 1949:

> The ancient Chinese mind contemplates the cosmos in a way comparable to that of the modern physicist, who cannot deny that his

> model of the world is a decidedly psychophysical structure. The microphysical event includes the observer just as much as the reality underlying the *I Ching* comprises subjective, i.e., psychic conditions in the totality of the momentary situation. Just as causality describes the sequence of events, so synchronicity to the Chinese mind deals with the coincidence of events. The causal point of view tells us a dramatic story about how *D* came in existence: it took is origin from *C*, which existed before *D*, and *C* in its turn had a father, *B*, etc. The synchronistic view on the other hand tries to produce an equally meaningful picture of coincidence. How does it happen that *A'*, *B'*, *C'*, *D'*, etc., appear all in the same moment and at the same place? It happens in the first place because the physical events of *A'* and *B'* are of the same quality as the psychic events *C'* and *D'*, and further because all are exponents of one and the same momentary situation. The situation is assumed to represent a legible or understandable picture . . . It is assumed that the fall of the coins or the result of the division of the bundle of yarrow stalks is what it necessarily must be in a given "situation," inasmuch as anything happening in that moment belongs to it as an indispensable part of the picture. If a handful of matches is thrown to the floor, they form the pattern characteristic of that moment. But such an obvious truth as this reveals its meaningful nature only if it is possible to read the pattern and to verify its interpretation, partly by the observer's knowledge of the subjective and objective situation, partly by the character of the subsequent events.

Hence, there exists a necessary interplay of observer, event, image, and interpretation. Jung's observation, while divergent from ancient Chinese philosophy, which posits disincarnate or spiritual agencies, has something in common, if indirectly, with the perceptual basis of quantum theory, in which attention or measurement actualizes local reality, a topic more fully explored in the final chapter.

Might it be that perception itself, through whatever medium, in addition to being psychologically persuasive to the emotionally committed observer, may also concretize experience in a more than suggestive manner? This was the kind of consideration to which Jung, along with the founders of quantum physics themselves, all of whom were philosophical idealists, was not closed off.

"By early December 1913," note Owens and Hoeller, "Jung discovered that his focused imaginative activity could evoke autonomous visionary scenes, personages and dialogic interactions." This harrowing activity and his meeting with the psychopomp Philemon—over which Jung felt conflicted—formed the basis for his justly celebrated *Red Book*.

Jung privately assembled the red leather-bound folio manuscript, which includes exquisite calligraphy and visionary—often breathtaking—paintings, between 1915 and about 1930. The largely German text, punctuated by occasional Latin, served to comment and expand on his encounters with the being called Philemon, which occurred between 1913 and 1916. Although now a core part of Jung's oeuvre, *The Red Book*—he had called it *Liber Novus*, the "New Book"—was not published until 2009. During his life, Jung revealed the work to only a handful of students. Following his death in 1961, his estate refused all related research queries and requests to view it.

This extreme reticence—loosened by thirteen years of intensive editorial work by historian, translator, and editor Sonu Shamdasani—was probably due to fear of Jung being classified as a Gnostic guru or prophet versus a professionally accepted clinician. Jung was encouraged in his journey in 1928, when sinologist Richard Wilhelm sent him his translation of the late-seventeenth century (though orally ancient) Taoist-alchemical text, *The Secret of the Golden Flower*.* The psychologist saw in the work parallels to his own—a signpost of perennialism that validated his efforts.

It is easy at points to understand the reticence of Jung and his estate to share this material. In a journal entry from January 5, 1922, Jung recalled an exchange with his "Soul." He is told:

> ***Soul***: You should listen: to no longer be a Christian is easy. But what next? For more is yet to come. Everything is waiting for you. And you? You remain silent and have nothing to say. But you should speak. Why have you received the revelation? You should not hide

---

* "The Hermeneutics of Vision: C. G. Jung and *Liber Novus*" by Lance S. Owens, *The Gnostic: A Journal of Gnosticism, Western Esotericism and Spirituality*, July 2010.

> it. You concern yourself with the form? Is the form important, when it is a matter of revelation?
>
> ***Jung:*** But you are not thinking that I should publish what I have written [*Liber Novus*]? That would be a misfortune. And who would understand it?
>
> ***Soul:*** No, listen! . . . your calling comes first.
>
> ***Jung:*** But what is my calling?
>
> ***Soul:*** The new religion and its proclamation.

A journey of dreams, visions, disincarnate entities, extraphysical experience, and classical scholarship, *The Red Book* eludes summary—it is a symphonic movement of Gnostic, alchemical, Hermetic, and psychological insight.

"My entire life," Jung wrote in *Memories, Dreams, Reflections*, "consisted in elaborating what had burst forth from the unconscious and flooded me like an enigmatic stream and threatened to break me." It is difficult not to see a certain poignant justice in the posthumous appearance of *The Red Book*—almost a mysteriously timed reintroduction of Jung's work after decades of debate, parsing, commentary, scholarism, and historicism that gives the visionary thinker, in a sense, the coda on the nature and outcome of his efforts.

To give Jung the final word from *Liber Novus*:

> When something long since passed away comes back again in a changed world, it is new. To give birth to the ancient in a new time is creation. This is the creation of the new, and that redeems me. Salvation is the resolution of the task. The task is to give birth to the old in a new time.

To give birth to the ancient in a new time is creation. Jung's statement captures the hopes of occult revivalism itself.

It can seem an injustice or anticlimax to follow on the efforts of Jung. But to encompass occultism in the first part of the twentieth century demands further reckoning with the popular or dramatized literature consumed by many adherents.

One such work is the 1908 occult perennial *The Kybalion* attributed to "Three Initiates." Based on sales and manifold editions, the slender book is easily one of the most widely read occult tracts of the century.

The Kybalion claims to be a commentary on a hidden Hermetic work of the same name whose aphorisms are only quoted. Like many readers, I once considered *The Kybalion* little more than a novelty of early twentieth century occultism. I regarded it as a faux-antique work of mind-power philosophy, costumed in pseudo-Hermetic language and offering a handful of serviceable but not greatly significant ideas of practical spirituality. Years of deeper reading into Hermeticism and a return to the book proved my initial judgment wrong.

The little book has earned its posterity. Although some of *The Kybalion*'s reference points and formulations are plainly modern, the book is justly defensible as an authentic if dramatized retention of certain classical Hermetic themes. Indeed, the book serves as something close to what it claims to be: a "Great Reconciler" of metaphysical, transcendental, and New Thought philosophies, at least as practiced in the twentieth and twenty-first centuries.

Before saying more about the value of *The Kybalion*, let me address the question of its authorship. The identity of the "Three Initiates" has long been a source of speculation; this can serve as a distraction from the book's significance. *The Kybalion* was written and published by New Thought philosopher William Walker Atkinson (1862–1932), a remarkably energetic Chicago publisher, writer, lawyer, and spiritual seeker.

Atkinson was among the most incisive New Thought voices of the twentieth century. He ran an innovative esoteric publishing house called the Yogi Publication Society from Chicago's Masonic Temple Building. His company issued a wide-ranging catalogue of highly recognizable, diminutive blue hardcovers from the publisher's offices in the twenty-one-story skyscraper, which couched Masonic meeting rooms at the top. It was built in 1892 and demolished in 1939.

For years, the internet buzzed with debate over the personas of the Three Initiates. Most documentary and contextual evidence supports that it was Atkinson writing alone. Atkinson acknowledged his sole authorship in an entry in *Who's Who in America* in 1912. American occultist Paul Foster Case is sometimes identified as one of the Three Initiates, and he appears to have told as much to some of his colleagues.* But Case would've been just twenty-four when the book appeared in 1908, also at a time that he had just arrived in Atkinson's hometown of Chicago, so I consider the collaboration unlikely, although it's possible that they corresponded about some of the book's concepts. It should also be noted that in traditional literature, Hermes Trismegistus addresses himself to three disciples: Tat, Ammon, and Asclepius, which may have been a source of inspiration for William Walker Atkinson's byline (or possibly his own use of a tripartite byline).

Atkinson wrote prolifically under many pseudonyms. Three Initiates has proven his most enduringly popular but he also used names including Yogi Ramacharaka, Theron Q. Dumont, and the somewhat strained Magus Incognito. Atkinson was a prodigious writer and aficionado of New Thought and the mind-power metaphysics that were sweeping the Western world and have since become deeply entrenched in American spiritual life.

His writing exposed thousands of early twentieth century readers to esoteric spiritual and psychological ideas, which they might not otherwise have had wide opportunities to encounter. He wrote at least thirteen books under the byline Yogi Ramacharaka alone. Some observers tag the works ersatz Vedism, novelty yoga, and phony Swamism. And there is, of course, truth in that verdict. Yet it is also true that this enterprising man introduced many people to variants of Vedic and yogic ideas, which would not explode across the American scene until the mid-to-late 1960s.

Traditional gurus, such as Swami Vivekananda (1863–1902), had visited America prior to Atkinson's calico adaptations. But his popular work, like Madame Blavatsky's, helped prime Americans for the wave of spiritual teaching from the East that was soon to come, especially with relaxed immigration laws instituted in 1965. When Maharishi Mahesh Yogi (1917–2008), for example, traveled to the U.S. in 1959 to

---

* See *Paul Foster Case: His Life and Works* by Paul A. Clark (OHM, 2013).

teach Transcendental Meditation—an authentic technique from Vedic tradition—large swaths of the public, and certainly those within the metaphysical culture, were able to receive and understand what Maharishi and others who followed were offering. Never underestimate the power of novelty to open doors, whet appetites, and prime interest.

More important than *The Kybalion's* dramatic framing is how the book highlights ideas about mind, matter, and thought creativity, some of which demonstrate resonance with philosophical Hermetica. *The Kybalion* is not merely, or at least not only, modern New Thought clothed in antique garb; rather, the book connects readers, however tenuously, to late-ancient Hermetic themes of correspondence, development of psyche, scale of creation, and an all-creative over-mind. Although Atkinson relied on several sources, including the work of accomplished occult writer Anna Kingsford (1846–1888),* he was probably drawing upon the seminal Hermetic translation, *Thrice-Greatest Hermes* by G.R.S. Mead, which appeared two years before his dramatization.

Mead, as noted earlier, was a scholar of ancient mysticism and one-time secretary to Madame Blavatsky, a figure whom Atkinson revered. (The influence of her 1888 opus *The Secret Doctrine* is evident at several points in Atkinson's work.) Mead's 1906 translation of the Hermetica, while turgidly worded in late-Victorian prose, and sometimes almost purposely written as if to assume an antique affect, was then one of the few sources of Hermetic ideas in English. With a skilled and discerning eye, Atkinson identified and distilled insights that paralleled the sturdiest aspects of New Thought, a field in which the writer-publisher was deeply steeped. Atkinson used his considerable curatorial abilities to produce a marriage of ancient and modern psychological insights.

Atkinson focused primarily on the veritable Hermetic principle that Mind is the Great Creator. According to Hermetic literature, a supreme Mind, or *Nous*, uses as its vehicle a threefold process consisting of: 1) subordinate mind (*demiurgos–nous*), 2) word (*logos*), and

* Credit is due historian Mary K. Greer for this insight. Important documentary forensics have also been contributed by scholars Philip Deslippe (*The Kybalion: The Definitive Edition*, TarcherPerigee, 2011) and Richard Smoley (*The Kybalion: Centenary Edition*, TarcherPerigee, 2018).

3) spirit (*anthropos*), concepts that echo, albeit distantly, in Atkinson's work. *The Kybalion* is structured around "Seven Hermetic Principles," which correspond to the Hermetic concept of "seven rulers" of nature. Man, we are told in book I of the *Corpus Hermeticum* (Copenhaver translation), "had in himself all the energy of the rulers, who marveled at him, and each gave him a share of his own nature."

Atkinson is particularly supple in adapting the Hermetic conception of gender, in which the masculine (conscious mind, in Atkinson's terms, and original man in the Hermetica) impregnates the feminine (subconscious mind to Atkinson, and nature in the Hermetica), to create the physical world. Further still—and this is vital to the book's usefulness—*The Kybalion* ably ventures a theory of mind causality. The book explains why, from its metaphysical premises, our minds appear to possess formative, creative abilities; and yet, even as we evince powers of causation, we are also subject to limits of physicality, mortality, and daily mechanics.

As noted in Atkinson's chapter "'The All' in All," the individual may wield traits of a higher causative Force—but that does not make the individual synonymous with that Force. Man, the book counsels, may accomplish a great deal within given parameters, including transcendence of commonly presumed limitations, influence over the minds of others, and co-creation of certain circumstances; but the book reminds the idealist that we bump against physical parameters even as we are granted the capacity, within proscribed framing, to imitate the Power that set those parameters.

Atkinson also offers compelling philosophical definitions of concepts of rhythm, polarity, paradox, compensation, and aforementioned "Mental Gender," or the notion that nonbinary traits occupy every mind and combine to create. In a sense, the philosophy found in *The Kybalion* is a modern application of Hermeticism, Neo-Platonism, Transcendentalism, and New Thought. The book further attempts, however fitfully, to correspond its ideas to the early twentieth century's nascent insights into quantum mechanics and the "new physics," which gained currency in the decades following its publication. In this sense, the author exaggerates only slightly when he writes: "We do not come expounding a new philosophy, but rather furnishing the outlines of a great world-old teaching which will make clear the teachings of others—which will serve as a Great Reconciler of differing theories, and opposing doctrines."

The overall spirit of *The Kybalion* can be traced to book XI of the *Corpus Hermeticum*, in which Hermes is told by Supreme Mind that through the uses of imagination he can discover the workings of Higher Creation: "If you do not make yourself equal to God you cannot understand Him. Like is understood by like."* Hermes is told to use his mind to travel all places, to unite opposites, to know all things, to transcend time and distance: "Become eternity and thus you will understand God. Suppose nothing to be impossible for yourself."

Hermeticism teaches that we are granted a Divine birthright of boundless creativity and expansion within the imagination. This teaching is central to Hermetic philosophy and its modern adaptation in *The Kybalion*. Brief in length yet exhilarating in ideas, *The Kybalion* should be read repeatedly by anyone with an interest in New Thought or practical metaphysics. For the modern seeker, the book can, as its author promises, serve as a source of coherence among various, and sometimes conflicting, modern mystical approaches.

Although not exactly occult in nature, the enduring work of paranormalist writer Charles Fort (1874–1932) served to poke holes in the straight story of materialist science and provide a framework for documentation of oddities and the unknown.

Fort's four books on anomalous phenomena—starting with *The Book of the Damned* in 1919, followed by *New Lands* (1923), *Lo!* (1931), and *Wild Talents* (1932)—drove readers to ask questions about strange airships (in an age before UFOs or UAPs), mysterious beasts, and unknown powers that might otherwise never have gotten considered.

By "damned" the writer meant facts (or at least reports) that did not fit in: outsider testimonies, observations, theories, and ideas; items considered unfit for consumption, and so were pushed to the margins. Fort assembled news reports of things happening around the world that were not supposed to occur, like objects in the sky before we had the term flying saucers; frogs, stones, and blood falling from the heavens; strange beasts (including wolf children and wild men); lights on the moon; floating islands; spontaneous human combustion; talking dogs; levitation; stigmatic wounds; clairvoyant visions; and

* Here and immediately following I quote from *The Way of Hermes* translated by Clement Salaman, et al. (Inner Traditions, 2000).

teleportation, a term he is thought to have coined—all sorts of supposed occurrences that violated the comforts of accepted facts and our means of gathering them.

Fort himself was a fascinating character. Newspapers called him "the Mad Genius of The Bronx."* Born in Albany, New York, in 1874, Fort lived and worked for much of his life in New York City's northern borough. Like Manly P. Hall, the chronicler did a great deal of his research at the New York Public Library, where his papers are archived. For 26 years—nearly to the point of blinding himself (amid other health problems) as he scribbled notes on small squares of paper—Fort functioned as gatekeeper of the damned, deliberating over anomalies that few others acknowledged. In his lifetime, Fort pored over reports of more than 65,000 paranormal events of which he deemed about 1,200 worthy of documentation in his books.**

Fort knew a great deal of heartache in his efforts. In addition to his nonfiction, he wrote ten novels but published only one, *The Outcast Manufacturers*, in 1909. The tenement drama attained little success. He also produced a fragmentary memoir in 1900.*** But in 1915–1916, Fort made a departure, assembling two books on extra-normal phenomena and theories, X and Y. Although esteemed by novelist Theodore Dreiser—a longtime friend and supporter—the manuscripts, even with Dreiser's endorsement, found no takers among publishers. A distraught Fort burned them.**** Dreiser couldn't believe it: "they are so wonderful to me that it would be like destroying Karnak."*****

Publishers be damned, as Mike Dash wrote in the *Fortean Times*:

> Dreiser was nevertheless utter captivated by X, in which Fort suggested that events on earth were controlled by a higher civilization in space and that the world itself, and everyone on it, was not real but an illusion projected from an unknown location, the X of his title. Dreiser's own reading and his semi-pagan Indiana background had increasingly distanced him from orthodox religion and sci-

---

* From a recollection by journalist H. Allen Smith in his memoir *Low Man on a Totem Pole* (Blakiston, 1941).

** *Mysteries of the Unknown: Time and Space*, Volume 18 (Time-Life Books, 1990).

*** "Charles Fort: His Life and Times" compiled by Bob Rickard, 1979, 1997, Forteana.org.

**** "Charles Fort and a Man Named Dreiser" by Mike Dash, *Fortean Times*, issue 51, 1989.

***** Charles Fort: *The Man Who Invented the Supernatural* by Jim Steinmeyer (Tarcher/Penguin, 2009).

> ence; not yet ready to formulate his own philosophy, he seized on Fort's half-formed, semi-satiric, world-view. "I had not read three paragraphs before I said to myself, this is not only beautiful, it's wonderful," Dreiser wrote in an unpublished memoir of Fort . . . But it had less effect on the publishers Dreiser approached on Fort's behalf . . . all rejected the manuscript as they did Fort's second work of non-fiction *Y* (1916), which argued for the existence of a malignant civilization beyond the North Pole.

Fort discovered a new resolve. He set to work on a third book in his immolated canon. After laboring monastically for months, Fort in July 1918 sent Dreiser a letter of just three lines:

> *Dreiser!*
> *I have discovered Z!*
> *Fort!**

In *Z*, Fort not only found new footing in his writing but grasped a truth lost on many writers: *titles matter*. Rather than the obscure appellation *Z*, Fort opted for a new title that proved an irresistible pull on the reader's curiosity: *The Book of the Damned*. The writer also devised a fresh methodology. Biographer Jim Steinmeyer noted:

> The previous formula for "crank" books had been to doggedly gather observations and assign them to a grand theory: *X* continually postulated a race on Mars; *Y* tied its facts together by speculating on a continent concealed at the North Pole. In contrast, long stretches of *The Book of the Damned* seemed content to be damnable, and nothing but damnable. Instead of assembling his data to support a theory, he treated these oddities like his characters in *The Outcast Manufacturers*—releasing them in front of his audience and then stepping back to watch them perform; whispering suggestions in the reader's ear, playing the master of ceremonies with an occasional wry comment or observation.

This time, Dreiser was out for the kill. He told Fort, "I took it—*The Book of the Damned*—direct to my personal publisher, Horace Liveright, and, laying the book on the table, told him to publish it.

* Steinmeyer (2009) here and below.

And when, after a week or so, he announced, 'But I can't do it. We'll lose money,' I said, 'If you don't publish it, you'll lose me.'" And so, the damned found a home.

With the help of PR maestro Edward Bernays (1891–1995), then a publicist for Boni & Liveright, the damned also found readers. "We were able to stir up national interest," Bernays recalled in his 1965 memoir *Biography of an Idea*, "because it challenged the fetish of the logic of science, strong in 1920. Fort wrote about freaks of nature that defied scientific analysis, such as frogs raining from the clouds." Indeed, to the present, Fort's reports of frog downpours, noted several times in *The Book of the Damned*, is the chief reference point for which he is recalled. The episode was recreated in acclaimed psychological drama *Magnolia* in 1999. "I got it first from Charles Fort, then from the Bible," director and writer Paul Thomas Anderson told *Variety*, which oddly called Fort a "novelist."*

The article further noted: "The young auteur also credits Fort with the story that opens the film, about three men being hanged named Green, Berry and Hill, in a town called Green Berry Hill. 'Yeah,' Anderson said, 'that's from Charles Fort's *Wild Talents*.'" Fort had written: "In the *New York Herald*, Nov. 26, 1911, there is an account of the hanging of three men, for the murder of Sir Edmund Berry Godfrey, on Greenberry Hill, London. The names of the murderers were Green, Berry, and Hill."

Bernays concluded: "I do not know to this day whether Fort took himself seriously or wrote tongue in cheek. Whatever his motive, the book received much publicity, as we tied it in with news coverage of scientific events, such as signals reported to have been sent to the earth from Mars."

Although doggedly unorthodox about the reality of his reported events ("I believe nothing," Fort later wrote in *Lo!*), he was deadly serious about the enduring strangeness of our world. In 1919, Fort's opening salvo announced in his singular and sometimes abstruse style:

> A procession of the damned.
>
> By the damned, I mean the excluded.
>
> We shall have a procession of data that Science has excluded.

---

* "'Magnolia' helmer ribeted by novelist's frogs: Fort, 'Wild Talents' were major influences on Anderson" by Steven Gaydos, *Variety*, February 7, 2000.

> Battalions of the accursed, captained by pallid data that I have exhumed, will march. You'll read them—or they'll march. Some of them livid and some of them fiery and some of them rotten.
>
> Some of them are corpses, skeletons, mummies, twitching, tottering, animated by companions that have been damned alive. There are giants that will walk by, though sound asleep. There are things that are theorems and things that are rags: they'll go by like Euclid arm in arm with the spirit of anarchy. Here and there will flit little harlots. Many are clowns. But many are of the highest respectability. Some are assassins. There are pale stenches and gaunt superstitions and mere shadows and lively malices: whims and amiabilities. The naïve and the pedantic and the bizarre and the grotesque and the sincere and the insincere, the profound and the puerile.
>
> A stab and a laugh and the patiently folded hands of hopeless propriety.
>
> The ultra-respectable, but the condemned, anyway. The aggregate appearance is of dignity and dissoluteness: the aggregate voice is a defiant prayer: but the spirit of the whole is processional.
>
> The power that has said to all these things that they are damned, is Dogmatic Science.
>
> But they'll march.

March they did. Amid Fort's blizzard of reports, a discernible philosophy emerged. Fort sought to upend man's presumed status of dominion and his capacity to know reality through positivistic laws. "I think we're all bugs and mice," Fort wrote, "and are only different expressions of an all-inclusive cheese . . . What is a house? It is not possible to say what anything is, as positively distinguished from anything else, if there are no positive differences." In an observation that would sit well—were only it read—among quantum and psi theorists in the dawning era, Fort ventured: "I conceive of one inter-continuous nexus, which expresses itself in astronomic phenomena, and chemic, biologic, psychic, sociologic: that it is everywhere striving to localize positiveness: that to this attempt in various fields of phenomena—which are only quasi-different—we give different names."

In a supposition that would have made physicist Erwin Schrödinger smile, Fort pondered reality as a cosmic wholeness of potential and infinite events "in which all things are localizations of one attempt to break away and become real things." Schrödinger's dual (or infinite) cat perhaps wishes to be known. Hence,

> We are not realists. We are not idealists. We are intermediatists—that nothing is real, but that nothing is unreal: that all phenomena are approximations one way or the other between realness and unrealness.
>
> So then:
>
> That our whole quasi-existence is an intermediate stage between positiveness and negativeness or realness and unrealness.
>
> Like purgatory, I think.

Some readers considered Fort a heterodox genius and modernity's greatest critic of science; because he understood that science in the early twentieth century had succumbed to its own orthodoxy to the point of excluding things that did not fit, thereby concretizing a blinkered model of humanity's capacity to understand or even consider laws and events beyond its ken. "I think we're property," Fort wrote of vaunted man. "I should say we belong to something."

In 1921, an enthusiastic Dreiser wrote to critic H. L. Mencken, "To me no one in the world has suggested the underlying depths and mysteries and possibilities as has Fort. To me he is simply stupendous."* H. G. Wells, on the other hand, referred to Fort in a 1931 letter to Dreiser, who had pushed his work on the sci-fi pioneer and futurist, as "one of the most damnable bores who ever cut scraps from out-of-the-way newspapers . . . And he writes like a drunkard."** Mencken was equally "puzzled" over Dreiser's enthusiasm. The *New York Times* echoed the men of letters, concluding in its review of February 8, 1920, that "[Any] conclusion . . . is so obscured in the mass of words and quagmire of pseudo-science and queer speculation that the average reader will find himself either buried alive or insane before he reaches the end." The paper's future evaluation proved kinder, if still jaundiced, with the *Times* anointing Fort the "Enfant Terrible of Science" in the headline of its March 1, 1931, review of *Lo!*, sometimes considered Fort's most readable effort.

---

* *Dreiser-Mencken Letters: The Correspondence of Theodore Dreiser & H.L. Mencken, 1907–1945*, Volume 2 edited by Thomas P. Riggio (University of Pennsylvania Press, 1986).

** *Letters of Theodore Dreiser*, Volume 2 edited by Robert H. Elias (University of Pennsylvania Press, 1959).

Whatever critics (or frustrated readers) might say, Fort achieved the rarest of oddities: his name became the lasting descriptor *Fortean*—coined by critic Ben Hecht in 1920—for unexplained anomalies. "Whatever the purpose of Charles Fort," the critic wrote in the *Chicago Daily News* on January 21, 1920, "he has delighted me beyond all men who have written books in this world. Mountebank or Messiah, it matters not. Henceforth I am a Fortean."

A well-produced and literate magazine of the strange, the aforementioned *Fortean Times*, was launched in 1973 and has continued today. Fort's nonfiction works were widely reissued and anthologized (as they continue to be) and rarely fell from print.

Historian Jim Steinmeyer subtitled his 2009 biography of Fort, which I published, "The Man Who Invented the Supernatural." Whether announced or not, Fort's influence framed our modern conceptions of UFOs and cryptozoology—terms that did not yet exist in his era—and heralded an extant age of cataloguing the paranormal. *X* was lost to ashes. But it is unlikely that there would have existed an *X-Files* without it.

In an era of democratized spiritual and paranormal search, there emerged new forms of communication modeled on Blavatsky's vision but also diverging from it. This thought school is sometimes called Neo-Theosophy, a term believed to have been coined around 1912 by Irish Theosophist Ferdinand T. Brooks, who served as tutor to an adolescent Jawaharlal Nehru (1889–1964), India's first prime minister. Nehru is notable for navigating currents of India's diffuse religious constituencies, a fact punctuated by his distinctive traditionalist-modernist garments, which combined elements of the nation's different cultures, highlighted by his collarless Nehru jacket.

The term Neo-Theosophy was, at its inception, used pejoratively but that is not my practice here. The directions, ideas, and vocabulary of Neo-Theosophy left a pronounced mark on the alternative spiritual culture. Most notably, at least in terms of popularity, the latter-day phrase Ascended Masters, now widely heard across the New Age, was coined in the early 1930s by a Chicago couple named Guy and Edna Ballard who maintained a once large (and continuing) ultrapatriotic and nationalistic metaphysical sect called "The Mighty I AM."

Conceptually, references to Ascended Masters appeared in 1924 in Baird T. Spalding's first of six volumes (one posthumous) of *The Life and Teaching of the Masters of the Far East,* although he did not specifically use the term. The Ballards had studied Spalding's work and were evidently influenced by it. They claimed tutelage under figures who wove in and out of Madame Blavatsky's and Annie Besant's work, including the adept called Saint Germain.

As a result of the "masters narrative," hidden teachers became de rigueur on the occult scene. Influential Angelo-American occult teacher Alice Bailey (1880–1949), of whom more is soon heard, wrote of tutorial dialogues with a higher teacher known as the Tibetan. Medical clairvoyant and Christian mystic Edgar Cayce (1877–1945) on four occasions reported visits from a mysterious, turbaned spiritual master from the East. Cayce, too, is soon subject to deeper consideration. Historically, it is important to understand that reports of latter-day communication with masters were not tied to Theosophy and such claims were often in tension with it.

Many people within New Age culture today speak of Ascended Masters, which means different things in different contexts. For her part, Blavatsky said the masters were actual people but they had entered a state of development untethered from the time-distance dimension, granting them powers of clairvoyance, materialization and dematerialization, and production of phenomena, such as precipitating the letters she and Henry Olcott received. In his 1994 historical study *The Masters Revealed,* scholar of esotericism K. Paul Johnson maintained that Blavatsky's teachers were mythical versions of real personas she had encountered.

Some teachers in Blavatsky's wake had their own visible dialogues with Eastern adepts, such as Paul Brunton (1898–1981), an adventurous British spiritual writer and thinker who worked for a time with the Vedic sage Ramana Maharshi (1879–1950). Scholar J. Glenn Friesen captured an evocative exchange from one of their 1931 dialogues, simple in content but richer in meaning:

> ***Brunton***: Many people do meditate in the West but show no signs of progress.
>
> ***Ramana Maharshi***: How do you know that they don't make progress? Spiritual progress is not easily discernible.*

* See paper "Paul Brunton and Ramana Maharshi," 2005.

There also abounded references, especially in psychically received or channeled literature, to "Akashic records," a concept indirectly rooted in Blavatsky's work. The best-known reference emerges from Cayce who began noting in the 1930s that he was reading "Akashic records" in his trance states. Cayce himself originated the spiritual use of the term *channel*. In a talk delivered in Norfolk, Virginia, in February 1933, Cayce said:

> As a matter of fact, there would seem to be not only one, but several sources of information that I tap when in this sleep condition. One source is, apparently, the recording that an individual or entity makes in all its experiences through what we call time. The sum-total of the experiences of that soul is 'written,' so to speak, in the subconscious of that individual as well as in what is known as the Akashic records. Anyone may read these records if he can attune himself properly.

Cayce's notion of the "Akashic records"—now a keynote of New Age spirituality—has its earliest origin in ancient Vedic writings, in which *akasha* is a kind of universal ether. Like much else, this idea of universal records was popularized to Westerners in the late nineteenth century through Blavatsky. A generation before Cayce, Blavatsky told of a cosmic record bank that catalogs all human events. In her 1877 study of occult philosophy, *Isis Unveiled*, she described an all-pervasive magnetic ether that "keeps an unmutilated record of all that was, that is, or ever will be." These astral records, she wrote, preserve "a vivid picture for the eye of the seer and prophet to follow." Blavatsky equated this archival ether with the "Book of Life" from Revelation, a description that coalesced with Cayce's Christian outlook. Returning to the topic in 1888 in *The Secret Doctrine*, Blavatsky depicted these etheric records in more explicitly Vedic terms (having spent several preceding years in India). In the first of her two-volume study, she referenced "Akâsic or astral-photographs," inching closer to the term "Akashic records" as used by Cayce.*

Cayce was the best-known but not the first channeler to credit "Akashic records." In 1908, retired Civil War chaplain and Church of

* Blavatsky's reference—easily overlooked but widely influential—appeared in a footnote: "It is not the physical organisms that remain in *statu quo*, least of all their psychical principles, during the great Cosmic or even Solar pralayas [dissolutions], but only their Akâsic or astral 'photographs.'"

Christ pastor Levi H. Dowling reported that he clairvoyantly channeled an alternative history of Christ in *The Aquarian Gospel of Jesus the Christ*. In Dowling's influential account, Christ travels and studies throughout the religious cultures of the East before dispensing a message of universal faith that encompasses all the world's traditions. Dowling, too, attributed his insights to "Akashic records" accessed while in a trance state in his Los Angeles living room. The book, as with Cayce's visions, captured the hopes of many seekers for a universal world faith.

Indeed, the late nineteenth and early twentieth centuries saw an upcropping of alternate or universalistic scriptures. In 1882, American Spiritualist and dentist John Ballou Newbrough (1828–1891) published *Oahspe: A New Bible*, produced through automatic writing. Although mostly in English, the book seemed to derive original terms or spellings from a combination of Vedic and semitic languages. Referring to believers as "Faithists," *Oahspe*—which means "the sum of corporeal and spiritual knowledge as at present"—extolled nonsectarianism and belief in a male-female Creator: "Nor shall any man say anymore: I worship the Brahmin principle, or the Buddhist principle, or the Ka'yuan [Confucian] principle, or the Kriste'yan [Christian] principle, or the Mohammedan principle. For all of these have proved themselves to result in war and destruction . . . Seek, O man, to believe in the All Person, Who is Ever Present, Whose eye is upon you, Whose ear hears you; for He is the All One, Who is the password to the highest of heavens."

One of the most challenging and influential of alternate scriptures is *The Urantia Book*, a more than 2,000-page work produced in Chicago between 1924 and 1955. The latter is its date of publication. Transcribed voices of the celestial beings collected in *Urantia* are sometimes attributed to trance medium Wilfrid C. Kellogg (1876–1956), a businessman and member of the Kellogg's Cornflakes family who received the material in 1934-35, though this is a matter of dispute.*

Divided into four parts, *Urantia* presents a vast and daunting cosmology, capped with "The Life and Teachings of Jesus," considered its most accessible section. Joscelyn Godwin notes, "Urantia's doctrines are consistent with Adventism, a movement that began in 1844 with

* "Stockhausen's *Donnerstag aus Licht* and Gnosticism" by Joscelyn Godwin, *Gnosis and Hermeticism* edited by Roelf van den Broek and Wouter J. Hanegraaff (State University of New York Press, 1998).

the revelations of Ellen White. But the Kellogg-Sadler revelations go much further, presenting a panorama of cosmic and human history, then a year-by-year account of Jesus' life . . . The equation of Christ with Michael is one of the main doctrines of *Urantia*, as of the original Adventism." Godwin notes the role of William S. Sadler (1875–1969), a psychiatrist and Seventh Day Adventist minister, who is sometimes said to have transcribed and assembled the passages.

In the long catalogue of anomalies he dismissed yet felt compelled to write on, skeptic Martin Gardner (1914–2010) compared *Oahspe* with *The Urantia Book*, pronouncing it, "even crazier than the works of Swedenborg and [Andrew Jackson] Davis."* That notwithstanding, *Urantia* found public-facing readers among an unusual range of modern artists, including electronic classical and operatic composer Karlheinz Stockhausen and musicians Stevie Ray Vaughan, Jerry Garcia, and Jimi Hendrix.

Of all the twentieth century migrants from Theosophy, among the most remarkable is Alice Bailey (1880–1949), an esoteric teacher who began her career in the Theosophical Society and branched off to found her own widely influential school, publisher, and spiritual groups.

Born Alice La Trobe-Bateman, she was product of a wealthy but isolated and deeply unhappy British childhood. Bailey's father, she wrote, was indifferent toward her and her mother died when she was six. She described herself in her unfinished autobiography as "skinny, scared, and startled looking." The future seeker attempted suicide three times before age 15. After her third failed attempt, a turbaned master, later identified as Koot Hoomi, visited the adolescent to speak of her life's mission, giving her a new sense of dispensation and direction.**

As she grew older, Bailey, like Blavatsky in an earlier generation, claimed tutelage to the masters, including a previously unidentified figure called "The Tibetan" or Djwhal Khul. In 1907, Alice met a future Episcopal priest whom she married and accompanied to America for his seminary studies. The abusive marriage ended in 1915, leaving

---

* *Urantia: The Great Cult Mystery* (Prometheus Books, 2008).

** See *The Unfinished Autobiography* by Alice Bailey (Lucis Trust Publishing, 1951) and *The History and Philosophy of the Metaphysical Movements in America* by J. Stillson Judah (The Westminster Press, 1967).

Alice, mother of three daughters, destitute and forced to work at a sardine cannery in Pacific Grove, California.* "I lived once for three weeks on tea (without milk or sugar) and dry bread," she wrote, "so that my three children could have what was essential to eat."

At this time, Alice came into contact with the Theosophical Society. She and her second husband-to-be Foster Bailey proved a dynamic pair eager to restore the core teachings of Blavatsky to the group's central focus. They grew prominent in American Lodges. But tensions flared with Annie Besant (whom, as it happens, Bailey perceived as a figure of Neo-Theosophy), and, more subtly, over Alice's own claimed communiques with the adepts. The Tibetan had begun communicating with her in 1919. Alice and Foster married that year and left the Theosophical Society the following one.** It should be noted that Charles Leadbeater continued to admire Bailey and her work. Remaining aloof from the "official" position, Leadbeater never criticized her, observes biographer Gregory Tillet.

In 1922, Alice and Foster founded their own spiritual, educational, and publishing arms, the Lucis Trust, followed in 1923 by the Arcane School. (The former was originally termed Lucifer, in the "light-bringer" sense.***) Through the Tibetan's telepathic teachings, Alice produced seventeen books along with five of her own focused on the "Ageless Wisdom." She noted in her memoir, "I have been told that [Carl] Jung takes the position that the Tibetan is my personified higher self and Alice A. Bailey is the lower self. Some of these days (if I ever have the pleasure of meeting him) I will ask him how my personified higher self can send me parcels all the way from India, for that is what He has done."

Although her work posits a formal schema of creation—in particular emanations of "Seven Rays" of energy, a concept also appearing in Theosophy, the work of Dion Fortune, and other esoteric systems—her 1932 book *From Intellect to Intuition*, made this observation, rare for the era:

> We must remember that in using all such words as "upwards" and "downwards," "higher" and "lower," we are talking symbolically.

---

* "Alice Ann Bailey" by James A. Santucci, *Dictionary of Gnosis & Western Esotericism* (Brill, 2006).

** These dates are not always clear. For 1919 as year of marriage, I am relying on Santucci (2006); 1921 is sometimes given. For 1920 as year of departure, I am relying on Judah (1967).

*** *Atlantis and the Cycles of Time* by Joscelyn Godwin (Inner Traditions, 2011).

> One of the first things a mystic learns is that dimensions do not exist in consciousness, and that the "within" and "without," the "higher" and the "lower" are only figures of speech, by which certain ideas are conveyed as to realized conditions of awareness.

It seems to me that modern esoteric spirituality is excessively focused on conceptual or hierarchical orders of creation—Alice Bailey's system included—yet this kind of observation is a seedling that prefaces loosened fealty to such models or at least serves as a reminder that ontologies are no more than *concepts* of reality, which easily harden into orthodoxies. In that vein, I sometimes detect a sui generis quality in Bailey's cosmology. Godwin in *Atlantis and the Cycles of Time* noted, "Bailey's hierarchy [of masters and initiations] seems like a parody of corporate bureaucracy."

Bailey was among the early spiritual figures to popularize the term New Age, as in her 1944 book *Discipleship in the New Age, Vol. I.* Widely adopted terms always seem to have many parents. William Blake was perhaps the first modern to use "New Age" in his epic poem "Milton," composed in its earliest stages in 1804. Blake intoned in his preface, "but when the New Age is at leisure to Pronounce, all will be set right . . . Rouze up O Young Men of the New Age!" As noted earlier, minister and New Thought pioneer Warren Felt Evans used the term in his 1864 work *The New Age and Its Messenger,* referencing Swedenborg. One of Gurdjieff's most brilliant students, literary critic and essayist A.R. Orage (1873–1934), founded the British political and cultural journal *The New Age* in 1907.

For all her cosmic vision, Bailey echoed the tone and prejudices of her upper-class English background—not dissimilar to the supposedly heterodox Aleister Crowley—displaying over-interest in conforming discordant Blacks and Jews into her *noblesse* conceptions of harmonious society.

Although Bailey's system of human evolution was, like Blavatsky's, based on spiritual development, Bailey, unlike Blavatsky—and perhaps due the influences of World War II and twentieth century European politics—dwelt excessively on racial and religious issues, readily prescribing as social remedies universal consciousness and intermarriage—but with explicit limits: "I had no anti-Negro feeling," she wrote in her autobiography, "except that I did not believe in marriage between the coloured races and the white for it never seemed to work for happiness on either side."

In a typically telling passage from her autobiography—always with a *some-of-my-best-friends-are* disclaimer—the teacher wrote,

> The Jew never seems assimilable . . . Personally, I have never yet found a Jew who would admit that there might be faults or provocation on their side. They always take the position that they are the abused and that the whole problem could be solved by the Christian taking right action. Lots of us, thousands of us are trying to take right action but we get no cooperation from the Jews.

There were, inevitably, references to "homosexuality, which is one of the greatest menaces confronting the boys and girls today." Further such statements appear in Bailey's posthumous *Esoteric Healing* (1953). If ever one wished for an absence of *engagé* thought in twentieth century occultism, it is in Bailey's work. Politics and the occult are considered in the next chapter.

In 1935, Bailey and collaborators founded the still-active Grand Lodge, Ancient Universal Mysteries (AUM), a coed Freemasonic body that seeks to deepen and decipher Masonry's esoteric mysteries.

The group combines traditional Masonry with teachings from Bailey's work. The lodge room of the Lodge of the Seven Rays in New York City includes above the north officer's chair images of the Buddhist dragon of wisdom along with Masters Morya, Koot Hoomi, and Saint Germain, associated with Prince François Rákóczy II of Transylvania (1676–1935), who died in exile after leading Hungary in an unsuccessful uprising against the Habsburg Empire. The Prince is sometimes theorized to have fathered the Comte de Saint Germain (c. 1691 or 1712–1784), a European composer and alchemist viewed as an immortal master in some modern esoteric traditions.*

---

* For those wishing to dive all the way down the rabbit hole, Manly P. Hall wrote in *The Secret Teachings of All Ages* in 1928, "E. Francis Udny, a Theosophical writer, is of the belief that the Comte de St. Germain was not the son of Prince Rákóczy of Transylvania, but because of his age could have been none other than the prince himself, who was known to be of a deep philo-

One of Bailey's most notable public legacies is the universal prayer called the Great Invocation, which she conveyed in April 1945 toward the end of World War II. In a signature moment, Eleanor Roosevelt recited the Great Invocation from the United Nations over radio in 1952 to mark the passage of the Universal Declaration of Human rights four years earlier.

"It seems to me to express the aspirations held by many people throughout the world," Roosevelt said. Although Roosevelt may not have realized the full nature of the prayer (which "someone sent me the other day"), its lines include, "From the centre where the Will of God is known/ Let purpose guide the little wills of men—/The purpose which the *Masters* know and serve." [emphasis added]

Whether purposely or in error, Roosevelt recited, "The purpose which the *Master* knows and serves."

In an age of bounding occult literature and revelations, many seekers wondered whether there were any further messages from the masters of Theosophical tradition—and, if not, why?

As it happens, the answer lies with Annie Besant's successor as president of the Theosophical Society, George S. Arundale (1878–1945), a British writer, editor, and independence-movement activist who was placed under house-arrest by colonial authorities with Besant in 1917. Arundale organizationally brought a close to the era of communiques from the masters, at least as far as traditional Theosophy was concerned. This was the case even though Mrs. Besant told him that the masters themselves has selected him as her successor.*

Arundale served as president from 1934 to 1945, the year of his death. He avowed the validity of earlier communications from the masters, including those he received, but gradually edged away from the claimed phenomena and probably felt that the topic had become divisive. Arundale instituted a back-to-basics movement in Theosophy, called the "Straight Theosophy" campaign, emphasizing core texts and foundational principles.

---

sophic and mystic nature. The same writer believes the Comte de St.-Germain passed through the 'philosophic death' as Francis Bacon in 1626, as François Rákóczy in 1735, and as Comte de St.-Germain in 1784." In Bailey's system, Germain/Rákóczy is considered Master of the Seventh Ray, that of ceremonial organization and ritual.

* Tillet (1985).

In his 1937 presidential address at Adyar, Arundale signaled the close of what might be called the "Masters Era." Referencing the adepts, he said,

> Yet so sacred are They, and so intent upon slowly but surely lifting life everywhere to Their stature, that They ask for no recognition, not even as plausible hypotheses, nor do They permit either the experience or the authority of Their Truth to influence in any way our own individual search for Truth. Freedom has made Them Masters. Freedom alone can make us Masters too.

Arundale's tribute marked a subtle adieu to the mysterious communiques. Arundale may have been motivated, in part, by the organization's drop in prestige, morale, and membership following Krishnamurti's departure. Perhaps enough had been made of messianism. Privileging Arundale's remarks, it seems to me that ours is not an age of "Masters of Wisdom," unseen adepts, hidden transmissions, or even iconic teachers, certainly not on the scale of Gurdjieff, Jung, Blavatsky, or Steiner.

Indeed, at one point in my search I wondered, where are the great teachers? About twenty years before this writing, I put that question to philosopher Jacob Needleman. He replied, "Today we have the group." I honor that. Yet since then, I have come to feel that we have reached another change in landscape. I believe that ours is an age of *experiment*. Although there may occasionally appear notable individuals, I favor—and detect timely primacy of—the approach signaled by Arundale, one of the "individual search for Truth."

CHAPTER NINE

Politics and the Occult

It is inherently controversial to write about the occult and politics. I am going to start with the key controversy because I consider it important historically, culturally, and ethically, to confront this question as we enter the era of World War II and beyond.

In late 2020, I was invited to sit in on a Zoom call of scholars, curators, and historians who were planning a Holocaust memorial monument in Ukraine. The session occurred just over a year before Putin's invasion; in the time since, I've often wondered about the fate of some of those on the call that day.

I was invited by a friend, a distinguished curator, who was delivering a presentation to the committee. He spoke on ancient funerary traditions to examine how the ancients abided death, memory, and interment rites and whether such practices held ideas for the nature and design of the planned memorial. He discussed burial mounds, markers, and pyres, as well as numeric, calendric, and astronomical formulas used to calculate their direction and placement. The presentation was, in my estimation, thorough and brilliant.

When the floor opened, I remarked that Henry Steel Olcott, co-founder of the Theosophical Society, hosted what the press called a "pagan funeral" in New York City in 1876. Henry publicly reintroduced the practice of cremation, which today accounts for more than half of interments in the United States. At the time, however, the practice was scandalous. Most Westerners considered cremation, if they had even heard of it, an exotic curiosity of the East or an oddity tucked into the mists of pagan antiquity, fit for Ripley's-Believe-It-Or-Not cartoons. For all its popularity today, cremation was considered improper to Western nations.

But Henry, eagerly flying into the storm, contended that cremation is more hygienic, economical, and environmentally sound than burial. And there was, in his eyes, another benefit: deterrence of vampirism. "If any [further reason] were needed by thoughtful persons," he later wrote in *The Theosophist* in 1891, ". . . there are no vampires save countries where the dead are buried." In Olcott's eyes, the practice evinced such benefits in India, where "we do not hear of Hindu vampires."

In more mundane terms, his funerary subject, an impoverished Bavarian nobleman living in New York, Baron de Palm—speculated as the identity of Chevalier Louis de B. of the "hidden hand" theory—was not actually cremated until six months later (the body packed in potter's clay for preservation) when Henry finally located a private crematorium outside Pittsburgh, Pennsylvania.

His public service, which effectively doubled as a coming out ceremony for the nascent Theosophical Society, caused a near-riot at Masonic Hall on West 23rd Street in Manhattan. Few recall Henry as the forefather of modern cremation in America, but there it was—another instance of Theosophy's fingerprints, this time reintroducing a practice, once obscure or verboten among moderns and now widely popular.

During the exchange on the call, an eminent professor, from whom others seemed to be waiting to hear, spoke up in a rather dramatic way. "It is particularly ironic that you're giving this presentation," he told my friend, "because the Nazis were an occult and green movement. In fact, if Heinrich Himmler himself had been on this call he would have liked your presentation very much."

Personally, I detected both extravagance and reductionism in his remarks. As a guest on the call, I didn't feel it my place to enter a debate. My friend took the comments in great spirits. The following day he asked me, "Now that I've been named Heinrich Himmler's favorite intellectual, what did you think of the talk?"

I thought highly of it, I said. But, I added, there exists today, in both academia and on social media, willful overestimation of the extent to which occult themes were present or doted upon within Nazi circles. In general, I believe we overdetermine the sources of Nazism. There existed little constancy, aside from nationalism and race hatred, within Nazi ideology; wide-ranging symbolic and historical material was embraced, copied, discarded, and contradicted.

Over-reading occult themes into Nazism is an easy trap to fall into because the Nazis, as with nearly all fascist and absolutist movements, made broad use of heraldry, symbolism, and pageantry, often of a primeval and archetypal nature. Occultism itself is a revivalist movement of ancient and readapted religious forms, as seen in Henry Olcott's cremation service. Hence, when political movements harken backwards for heraldry and symbol, whether the eye-and-pyramid, obelisk, or grimmer repurposings, they look familiarly "occult." These judgments, in my experience, are heightened by the general distaste many intellectuals feel toward occultism and metaphysics, which chafe against modern values of physicalism, replication, and classification.

Europe was suffused with competing ideologies in the early twentieth century and the impact of an occult revival appeared almost everywhere, including, as explored, in the germination of abstract art. Occult ideas sometimes spilled into social movements, both authoritarian-fascistic and democratic, with no definitive plurality in either.

But the Nazi-occult connection, not only for the reasons noted but due to general (and I aver prurient) fascination with the regime, sustains a popular thought current, appearing in scholarly works, like Eric Kurlander's celebrated *Hitler's Monsters* (Yale University Press, 2017), and popular media, such as podcasts, YouTube videos, and below-the-radar bestsellers.

An example recent to this writing appears in the widely read article, "Nazi Hippies: When the New Age and Far Right Overlap" by Jules Evans (Medium, September 4, 2020). Among its claims: "The Nazis were also huge fans of organic farming and of Rudolf Steiner's biodynamic agriculture which sees farming as a mystical communion with the land and its spirits/energies." Heinrich Himmler and Rudolf Hess were interested in organic farming—including Steiner's methods—

but, as we've seen, Steiner's movement of Anthroposophy was attacked and then banned in 1935 for its universalistic humanism. Again: "The first ever institute devoted to parapsychology research—the Paracelsus Institute—was set up under the Nazis, at the Nazi-founded Reich University of Strasbourg." Both Kurlander's book and Anne Harrington's *Reenchanted Science* (Princeton University Press, 1996) briefly reference "the Paracelsus Institute," an idea hatched in 1942. J.B. Rhine's Parapsychology Laboratory at Duke University in Durham, North Carolina, was founded twelve years earlier, a historical episode explored in chapter ten. The "green" charge is increasingly heard, which localizes to Nazism a sprawling fin de siècle movement ranging from back-to-nature and natural health to arts-and-crafts and physical culture. For fuller context, I recommend *Eco-Alchemy: Anthroposophy and the History and Future of Environmentalism* by Dan McKanan (University of California Press, 2017) who achieves an admirable blend of historical sensitivity and sharp critique.

That much said, the sympathetic critic—me included—must never propagate a defense of occultism, or any other philosophy, for the sake of perfumery; the full spectrum must be considered. Hence, in this chapter we encounter occultist William Dudley Pelley's "Silver Shirts"—America's first neo-Nazi order—and other nativist-esoteric movements. Indeed, several early twentieth century proto-fascist movements seized upon esoteric ideas and symbols, including the Vedic swastika, from Madame Blavatsky's 1888 opus *The Secret Doctrine*, also considered.

Movements that foster spiritually emancipatory attitudes often produce socially liberatory counterparts, some of which we've seen: Spiritualism and suffragism, New Thought and democratic socialism, Freemasonry and abolitionism, Romantic-era Satanism and feminism, and Theosophy and the Indian independence movement. At the same time, movements that idealize "lost" or "hidden" traditions—which also include some I've just mentioned—can subtly degrade precious modern values, including democratic liberalism.

To meaningfully address occultism and politics, including extremist variants, requires definitions. The term "fascism" is commonly used and misused. Historically, I find three defining traits of fascism-authoritarianism, which extend to Nazism as well as other totalitarian movements, including Soviet-style Communism: 1) A compact of government, judicial, military, and economic power. 2) Some degree of national, racial, or class-based exclusivity, or a combination. 3) *Pageantry*: the mass rally, ceremony, badge, banner, flag, and national symbol. Usually, these symbols are intended to reinvigorate a sense of lost pride or grievance, either real or imagined, ethnic or economic. Indeed, a key feature of fascistic or undemocratic movements is conviction among those who hold power, such as national majorities, that they hold *no power*. Tapping this grievance, political actors offer programs, emblems, and slogans of national rebirth.

The Nazis exemplified this to the furthest extent. The most obvious representation of Nazism was the swastika, an ancient Vedic symbol of eternal recurrence with no relation to nationalism or exclusivity. In Vedic literature, the swastika is a symbol of the individual's continuity with the cosmos and all of life. At the same time, it must be stated plainly that racialist demagogues who formulated what became Nazi ideology almost certainly discovered this Vedic symbol in Madame Blavatsky's *The Secret Doctrine* or direct offshoots of it.

As early as 1875, the Theosophical Society combined the symbol with other religious images—including the Egyptian ankh, star of David, and ouroboros (serpent swallowing its tail)—to fashion its organizational insignia. For Theosophy, the swastika represented karma and recurrence. Around its emblem revolved a Vedic maxim, added in 1880: *There Is No Religion Higher than Truth*. Yet a handful of racial mystagogues—including pan-German theorist Guido von List (1848–1919)—falsely conflated the swastika with images found in Germanic runes, which had been experiencing an early twentieth century revival. The symbol began appearing in Austrian occult journals as early as 1903.

List was a nationalist-racialist mystagogue who yearned to revive worship of Wotan, or Odin, and instigate resurgence of Nordic religion. In that vein, he can justly be called occult. Some of his followers coalesced around the Thule Society, which was connected to the early German Workers Party, the vehicle that eventually provided machinery for Hitler's National Socialist movement. In this connection appears organizational lineage between an occultic and *völkisch* religious movement and Hitler's early apparatus.

List was loosely part of a trend during the late-industrial age that favored getting "back to nature," engaging in arts and crafts versus factory-made goods, and resuming the supposed idyls of rural versus urban life. This movement ventured both benign and corrupt expressions, as it was given to nostalgizing the distant past in opposition to consumerism and automation. With his eye for runes and symbols, it was probably List who laid hands on Madame Blavatsky's introduction of the swastika to Western readers and who made its first decontextualization as an insignia for German rebirth.

Likewise, in the years preceding World War I, a handful of German pamphleteers and racial-mystical demagogues—List chief among them—seized upon the concept of the "Aryan" race, probably from *The Secret Doctrine* again. The term Aryan, as used by Blavatsky, also derived from Vedic literature, where it described some of the earliest Indian peoples. Competing notions of "Aryanism" began to appear in the late eighteenth century, but Blavatsky's was among those that German occultists would most likely have heard of in the early twentieth century.

Blavatsky adapted the term Aryan to include the present epoch of human beings, which she classified as the fifth of seven root races. These races, as was seen, stretch from the ancient past into the faraway future, eventually birthing a new branch of humanity, possibly exhibiting greater psychical or extraphysical development. Blavatsky was writing expressly in terms of spiritual evolution; at times, however, the smasher of convention lapsed into language that smacked of bastardized Darwinism or racial conventions of the day.*

For German racialists, the notion of a primordial race emergent from Asia had long been appealing: "If the Germans could link their origins to India," wrote Joscelyn Godwin in his 1993 *Arktos: The Polar Myth in Science, Symbolism, and Nazi Survival*, "then they would be forever free from their Semitic and Mediterranean bondage"—that is, from Abrahamic lineage. How exactly Germany's racial theorists came to conflate these patently Asian "Aryans" with their blond, blue-eyed ideal is the essence of muddled thinking. Especially since Blavatsky wrote that the Aryan race would reach its zenith in centuries ahead in America—a nation whose good character she unambiguously, if oddly, praised as, "owing to a strong admixture of various nationalities and inter-marriage."

---

* For a well-contextualized critique of this issue, see "Mythological and Real Race Issues in Theosophy" by Isaac Lubelsky, *Handbook of the Theosophical Current* edited by Olav Hammer and Mikael Rothstein (Brill, 2013).

With these facts stated, the following cannot be made clear enough: Hitler was not a philo-occultist. He contemptuously dismissed the work of fascist theorists who dwelled upon mythology and mystico-racial theories. In *Mein Kampf*, he specifically condemned "völkisch wandering scholars"—that is, second tier mythically and mystically inclined intellects who might have belonged to occult-nationalist groups, such as the Thule Society, with which the Nazis shared symbols.

From the earliest stirrings of Hitler's career in the German Workers' Party and its street-rabble rallies, he was consumed with brutal political and military organization, not theology or myth. He employed a symbol as a party vehicle when necessary and immediately discarded the flotsam around it, whether people or ideas. He castigated those members of his inner circle who showed excessive devotion to Nordic mythology, dismissing the theology of Nazi theorist Alfred Rosenberg as "stuff that nobody can understand" and a "relapse into medieval notions!"*

Historian Nicholas Goodrick-Clarke (1953–2012), who I believe has done more than any other scholar to clarify these issues, noted:

> Hitler was certainly interested in Germanic legends and mythology, but he never wished to pursue their survival in folklore, customs, or place-names. He was interested in neither heraldry nor genealogy. Hitler's interest in mythology was related primarily to the ideals and deeds of heroes and their musical interpretation in the operas of Richard Wagner. Before 1913 Hitler's utopia was mother Germany across the border rather than a prehistoric golden age indicated by the occult interpretation of myths and traditions in Austria.**

Under the Nazi regime, Theosophical chapters, Masonic lodges, and even sects that had produced some of the occult pamphlets a young Hitler may have encountered as a Vienna knockabout were shunted or savagely oppressed, their members murdered or harassed.

---

* *Inside the Third Reich* by Albert Speer (Macmillan, 1970).

** This passage is from Goodrick-Clarke's now-classic *The Occult Roots of Nazism* (New York University Press, 1992). Goodrick-Clarke's title is odd, and prone to misunderstanding, insofar as his vital study rebuts willful or excessive interpretations of occult influences behind Nazism.

Despite astrology's well-publicized appeal to a few of Hitler's cadre, the ancient practice was effectively outlawed under Nazism, and many of its practitioners were jailed or killed.

The man sometimes mislabeled "Hitler's astrologer," Karl Ernst Krafft, had no contact with Hitler but briefly reached the attention of mid-level Reich officials for predicting the 1939 assassination attempt on him. Krafft later died en route to Buchenwald. Nazi authorities sentenced Karl Germer (1885–1962), the German protégé of British occultist Aleister Crowley, to a concentration camp on charges of recruiting students for Crowley, whom they branded a "high-grade Freemason."* History has recorded a few self-styled magi or occult impresarios, like Savitri Devi, who, often from the safety of distant borders, venerated Hitler as a dark knight of myth. Those same figures would have suffered the fate of Krafft and Germer had they lived within the Reich's reach.

What of the aforementioned Heinrich Himmler, Hitler's deputy and an architect of the Holocaust? The Nazi officer was dedicated to reviving or reimagining certain Nordic or pagan ceremonies, which he saw as a replacement for Christianity.

Indeed, he was impassioned to create initiatic orders, including the SS, and ceremonial liturgies that would replace Catholicism and Protestantism because, given the nature of fascism as I've described it, there could exist no alternate center of cultural or religious power. Hence, in Himmler's machinations, a novelized and reconstructed Nordic spirituality—intimately wed to Nazism, extermination, antisemitism, racial exclusivity, and Germanic expansion—was envisioned to usurp extant churches and congregations.

As noted, some Nazi theorists, Himmler included, wanted to free the movement from perceived associations with Abrahamic religions. In that vein, starting in 1936 he sponsored the work of speculative archeologist Otto Rahn (1904–1939), whom he sent on excursions to Southern France and Iceland searching for the Holy Grail and links to a mythologized pagan past. Rahn was openly gay and ran afoul of SS brass who decided to add fiber to his spine by drafting him into guard duty at Dachau in 1937. Rahn was horrified, writing a friend, "I have

* E.g., see *Aleister Crowley: The Beast in Berlin* by Tobias Churton (Inner Traditions, 2014).

much sorrow in my country . . . impossible for a tolerant, liberal man like me to live in a nation that my native country has become."*

He quit the SS in early 1939, submitting his resignation to Himmler himself. Two weeks later, the bookish thirty-four-year-old was found frozen to death on a mountainside in Austria, whether by suicide or murder is unknown. Around that time, Himmler endorsed a new SS-led excursion into Tibet with the aim of unearthing mythical threads of Aryanism. Himmler also sponsored a pet project of leasing Renaissance-era Wewelsburg castle in the Northern Rhine region to serve as headquarters for an initiatory order within the SS, a fascistic revival of King Arthur's Knights of the Roundtable. It was never acted on in a more than spotty way, according to most records, although esotericist and neofascist Julius Evola, who is soon met, apparently lectured initiates.**

Personally speaking, I grew up during a period when these topics were of great interest on cable documentaries and in speculative books. But often whole garments were woven out of spare threads. The urtext of this way of thought is an intriguing historical work, *The Morning of the Magicians* by Louis Pauwels and Jacques Bergier published in French in 1960 and translated into English in 1963.

With a degree of artfulness, the authors introduce a wide variety of esoteric themes, including the Nazi-occult connection, which tapped the imagination of later writers. On this topic, Pauwels and Bergier were highly speculative, sometimes intentionally provocative, and inspired a wave of future literature and documentaries. Most of it descended in scale from their work, such as Trevor Ravenscroft's widely read 1972 book *The Spear of Destiny*, an almost wholly imagined account of Hitler's pursuit of the lance said to have pierced the side of Christ on the cross.

The case of Ravenscroft's bestseller is ably settled by historian Stephen E. Flowers, Ph.D., who writes in *The Occult in National Socialism* (Inner Traditions, 2022):

* "The original Indiana Jones: Otto Rahn and the temple of of doom" by John Preston, *The Telegraph*, May 22, 2008.

** *Dark Star Rising: Magick and Power in the Age of Trump* by Gary Lachman (TarcherPerigee, 2018).

> the largely fictional character of the story told in *The Spear of Destiny* came out in a court case in 1980, when Ravenscroft sued novelist James Herbert for copyright infringement in the latter's novel titled *The Spear* (1978). Ravenscroft asserted that the contents of his own book were fictional creations, and not historical material. Herbert had wrongly assumed that the material was actually a matter of history, and so not subject to copyright. The court ruled in Ravenscroft's favor: the contents of *The Spear of Destiny* are indeed *fictional.* Evidence shows that Ravenscroft originally offered the book as a work of fiction, but the initial publisher preferred that it be cast as a historical reality.

It is important to note that the Nazi-occult theme began, and has continued, as a literary genre—heavily amped up following Pauwels and Bergier—which has left much of the public with the impression of settled history; this genre uses historicism as a device to support a foreordained thesis. This approach appears even in scholarly works like Kurlander's *Hitler's Monsters,* which relies on the *apriorism* of there *being* a Nazi-occult connection, thereafter filled in with historical episodes and stories, rather than foundationally arguing for one.

This tendency is again illuminated by Flowers, whose 2022 volume provides a valuable "Chronological Annotated Bibliography" of Nazi-occult literature from 1940 to 2017. Careful readers will note a paucity of scholarly or journalistic books on the topic, which, excluding fiction, is dominated by works of sensationalism.

Unlike Nazi racial theorists, controversial and fascist-adjacent Italian philosopher of esotericism Julius Evola (1898–1974) regarded "Indo-Aryan civilization" primarily from the perspective of its spiritual organizing principles or his extrapolative interpretation of them, seen in his 1934 book *Revolt Against the Modern World.*

From a certain perspective, Evola's philosophy sought to recreate in earthly existence the dimensions of spiritual battle emanant from myth, oral tradition, and religious scripture. It is precisely the dangers of this approach, inherent if not pronounced, that have resurrected Evola's reputation on both the intellectual far-right and the anti-fascist left—the former hallows his writing as a modern manifesto and the latter as the incantation of an evil "wizard behind the curtain."

These passions, rather than critical reading of Evola (which is not always absent), render him a source of fascination. Indeed, mere mention of his name summons charges and countercharges, usually falling into two categories: those who embrace his work resist nearly any effort at classification and those who presume to oppose it rush toward classification. Neither, in my view, suffices. Both approaches beckon the surface politics that Evola claimed, not always convincingly, to oppose. I know of few twentieth century philosophers—classical conservative Leo Strauss is one—who have done a fuller job of ensuring their posterity of mystique.

The earliest English translation of Evola, who wrote in Italian, was *The Doctrine of Awakening* with British publisher Luzac & Co. in 1951. A more popular work, *The Metaphysics of Sex*, did not follow until 1983 from Inner Traditions, with future translations of his books arriving from that press in the 1990s and early 2000s. Except for readers versed in Italian, the esotericist was not much read until the present generation. Today, Evola's is a rare headline-making name among esoteric philosophers because of references to him by American rightwing activist Stephen K. Bannon and Russian nationalist Alexander Dugin.

As of this writing, Russian politico-mystic Dugin dotes on a mélange of nationalist, occult, and Traditionalist ideas like Evola's and those of French intellectual René Guénon (1886–1951).

Guénon, from whom we've heard, was a powerful and formative force in the movement called Traditionalism (he used the term "Primordial Tradition"), which seeks esoteric wisdom within the historic faiths and disdains perceived bastardizations of ancient religious ideals within modern occult and alternative spiritual movements.

Guénon's anti-modernist approach is a vivifying tonic against careless or burlesque adaptations of ancient religious forms. At the same time, the philosopher sometimes issued erroneous polemics of his own, although often couched in brilliant reasoning. If an insight can be accidental, so can an error be brilliant.

In his 1923 book *The Spiritist Fallacy*—adroitly issued and translated along with most of his oeuvre by Sophia Perennis press—Guénon insisted that among "all traditional doctrines . . . there is not a single one that has ever taught anything remotely resembling reincarnation." Guénon argued with typical elegance and rigor that our understandings of reincarnation from antiquity are *misinterpretations* of symbolic language and that the concept is nothing more than a Spiritualist-age fancy.

He noted the impossibility of reincarnation based on the infinite, and unrepeatable, elements of being and on the fact that human life is a compound unity, encompassing diffuse qualities of existence.* The Traditionalist allowed that certain psychic residues may linger, affording the appearance of reincarnated traits along with frivolous communications at the séance table, a perspective close to Madame Blavatsky's, whom Guénon nevertheless despised as a modern vulgarian.

It should be noted, however, that Guénon also believed in *cycles*, such as the Vedic yugas, in other facets of life. And there are, of course, widely diffuse interpretations of recurrence or reincarnation, as with karma, in Vedic tradition, sometimes involving the question of whether personality transmigrates or the essence of the individual rejoins the whole. The latter view was favored by Blavatsky. She also alluded to how only spiritually developed personas undergo a karmic process of recurrence; this comports on certain lines with the teaching of G.I. Gurdjieff that man is not "born" with a soul—it must be developed. "In fact," Jacob Needleman told *Gnosis* magazine in summer 1991, "you can find that teaching in other traditions. In the *Guide to the Perplexed* [by Maimonides] you'll find this thing stated, almost exactly, and you can find it, for example, in second-century Christianity in the writings of Irenaeus."

Wouter J. Hanegraaff notes in *New Age Religion and Western Culture* that Hermetic tradition is suggestive of reincarnation for a related reason: "*Corpus Hermeticum* XI . . . states that an understanding of God can only be attained by those who have experienced to the fullest all aspects of the universe; and under the impact of the 'temporalization of the Great Chain of Being', the conclusion was drawn that such understanding would require many lifetimes."

* An excellent exploration of Guénon's analysis appears in "The Case Against Reincarnation" by Joscelyn Godwin, *Gnosis* magazine, Winter 1997.

For final clarity, I turn to Richard Smoley's article "Against Blavatsky: René Guénon's Critique of Theosophy" from the winter 2010 *Quest* magazine:

> Guénon insists that the Theosophical view [of reincarnation] is a pure fabrication and has nothing to do with genuine Eastern teaching: 'The idea of reincarnation . . . , like that of evolution, is a very modern idea; it appears to have materialized around 1830 or 1848 in certain French socialist circles' (Guénon, *Theosophy*, 104).* This may be true of the term 'reincarnation' per se, but the teaching can be found in the West as far back as Pythagoras, and is discussed at length in Plato's *Republic* and *Phaedo*, not to mention its long heritage in Hinduism and Buddhism.

Gnostic texts likewise reference reincarnation or recurrence.

That said, there can be no dismissing the intellectual power of Guénon and many of the Traditionalist writers, a fact lost on most journalists encountering their ideas randomly when analyzing Traditionalist influence on the intellectual right in Europe or America.

The chief critique of Guénon from an informed liberal perspective arrived in 1974 from philosopher Jacob Needleman in his pioneering anthology of Traditionalist writings, *The Sword of Gnosis* (Penguin). In his introduction, Needleman scrutinized Guénon as a critic who *read* rather than read *about* the French philosopher, concluding: "He seems never to have considered the possibility of a Way that does not demand the immediate alteration of the conditions of twentieth-century life, but that nevertheless emanates from the same source as the recognized traditions."

Ripples from tossed stones are not always predictable: one of Guénon's admirers was radically ecumenical scholar of religion Huston Smith (1919–2016) whose widely read textbook *The World's Religions* argued for a common core to the historic faiths and posited a universalistic spirituality—themes Guénon opposed.

On a dimmer note, we return to Dugin, a vocal supporter of Putin's 2022 invasion of Ukraine. The nationalist philosopher selected for the symbol of his Eurasia Party the eight-pointed "chaos star" of the Illuminates of Thanateros, an international order of

---

* Smoley references Guénon's 1921 book *Theosophy: History of a Pseudo-Religion*.

chaos magickians, many of whom want no association with him. Chaos magick is explored in chapter eleven. Rightwing American political operative Steve Bannon, who reached out to me shortly after the publication of my first book and was a source of encouragement in the writing of my second—since Bannon's destructive election denialism our communication has ceased—has cited Julius Evola and evinced interest in a wide range of esoteric ideas, including the metaphysics of mind power.

Historian Gary Lachman notes in *Dark Star Rising*:

> As a wide-ranging esoteric scholar and practitioner, in the 1920s Evola edited an occult journal called *UR*, which focused on a number of magical themes. Evola contributed many articles to *UR*, under several pseudonyms, and one of the themes he came back to regularly was the magician's ability to *alter reality* through the power of the mind alone, something, we've seen, that both New Thought and chaos magick are interested in. For Evola, the aim of the magician is to develop his own personal power, his *will*, which is a kind of force that he can exert in order to refashion the world as he would like it.

In our hyper-politicized era, many commentators find it enticingly easy to view the Traditionalists as simply a reactive political force. That is inadequate. As a thought movement, Traditionalism is not monochromatic. Its ranks, broadly speaking, include Kabbalist Leo Shaya, Vedic philosopher Ananda K. Coomaraswamy, classicist Philip Sherrard, Islamic scholars Martin Lings, Frithjof Schuon, and Seyyed Hossein Nasr, symbolist Titus Burckhardt, Catholic theologian Valentin Tomberg, and—arguably—Cardinal Hans Urs von Balthasar and esoteric Egyptologist R. A. Schwaller de Lubicz, all widely read scholars of belief, some possessed of controversy but none whose work is limited to subculture or occultism.

"On close reading," Needleman wrote in 1974 of the Traditionalists, "I felt an extraordinary intellectual force radiating through their intricate prose. These men were out for the kill . . . They were clearly men 'under authority'—but under what authority, and from where did they receive the energy to speak from an idea without veering off into apologetics and argumentation?"

In a 2020 assessment almost laughable in intellectual conceit and unrecognizable in strawman examples, Fulbright scholar Nick Burns (whose accompanying biographical note stated he is "studying intellectual history") wrote of Traditionalism in political journal *The American Interest*:

> As a philosophy it is entirely worthless, a confection of middle-school-level readings of Hegel, Marx, and Spengler attached to a wild caricature of ancient Persian or Indian civilization . . . The role of shadowy, esoteric, occultist ideologies has turned out to be, if initially broader than anyone would have guessed, still in the end more or less as self-limiting as could be expected. Now, imaginably, these fanatics can get back to reading their tarot cards and going to black metal shows, or whatever it is they do.*

Ironically—and with notable exceptions—some of the chief mangling of esoteric history and ideas emerges from mainstream letters due to under-research, apathy, and cultural disdain. Many journalists and bloggers (never mind downstream on social media) paint with a broom when a liner brush is required. As essayist Michel de Montaigne (1533–1592) wrote in another context, "nothing is so firmly believed, as what we least know."

Something in human nature, probably fear of disorder and accident, overdetermines patterns after the fact—a particular pitfall to those of us who experiment with metaphysics. This tendency also informs conspiracist reaction to secret societies. Regarding political dimensions of the occult, historical observers often overlook or misunderstand that Europe in the early twentieth century was a hothouse of ideas—political, scientific, cultural, and occult—all of which crisscrossed through every movement, whether democratic, fascistic, liberal, anarchistic, conservative, including those that ostensibly *rejected* religious underpinnings, such as communism and socialism.

The metaphor of Lucifer or Satan was, for example, embraced in the late nineteenth century by some social democrats, socialists,

* "The Occultists Who Almost Ran Your Country," May 9, 2020.

anarchists and feminists because it was seen as the post-Romance image of the rebel and purposeful malcontent.* In 1894, Sweden's Social Democrats issued *Lucifer*, a "worker's calendar." Never one to go gently, Blavatsky herself inaugurated a journal called *Lucifer* in 1887; it ran for a decade after which it got redubbed with the less-than-thunderous title, *The Theosophical Review*.

Bolshevik movements seized upon the mass rally, imposing banner, heroic statue, and badge, even as such things had their earliest forms in Hellenic and Baltic pagan antiquity, because they celebrated the human form and, hence, idealized the image of the worker. The hammer-and-sickle itself was designed in its official form in 1918 by artist Yevgeny Kamzolkin, who was not a communist but a member of the mystical artists' circle, Society of Leonardo da Vinci. In occult revivalist vein, the artist used the hammer of the Slavic thunder god Svarog and the sickle of the earth goddess Mara.**

As noted, archetypal symbols are part of any on-the-march political movement. This returns us to psychologist Carl Jung, sometimes accused of a too-accommodating stance toward early Nazism. This indictment hinges partly on Jung's political maneuverings to balance between Nazi blacklists and continued international membership of Jews in psychological organizations within which he was active from Zurich. Jung, operating as Agent 488, also created a personality profile of Hitler for Allen Dulles at the Office of Strategic Services (OSS), precursor to the CIA.

"Shortly after the war," wrote venerable journalist Christopher Dickey in 2018, "Allen Dulles told one of Agent 488's longtime disciples, 'Nobody will probably ever know how much Professor Jung contributed to the Allied Cause during the war, by seeing people who were connected somehow with the other side.' But Dulles said there was no way to reveal them: Jung's services were 'highly classified,' they 'would have to remain undocumented,' and so they are."***

In a 1938 interview, published in the February 1942 issue of *Omnibook Magazine*, the scholar of archetype and myth remarked,

---

* See Per Flaxneld's masterful study *Satanic Feminism: Lucifer as the Liberator of Women in Nineteenth-Century Culture* (Oxford University Press, 2017).

** *The Occult Roots of Bolshevism: From Cosmist Philosophy to Magical Marxism* by Stephen E. Flowers (Lodestar, 2022).

*** "The Shrink as Secret Agent: Jung, Hitler, and the OSS," *The Daily Beast*, October 22, 2018.

> Hitler's power is not political; it is *magic.* To understand magic you must understand what the unconscious is. It is that part of our mental constitution over which we have little control and which is stored with all sorts of impressions and sensations; which contains thoughts and even conclusions of which we are not aware . . . Now the secret of Hitler's power is not that Hitler has an unconscious more plentifully stored than yours or mine. Hitler's secret is twofold; first, that his unconscious has exceptional access to his consciousness, and second, that he allows himself to be moved by it. He is like a man who listens intently to a stream of suggestions in a whispered voice from a mysterious source, and then *acts upon them.*

That this "stream of suggestions" included mythical symbols and concepts is not surprising; only their absence would be.

For clarity, I must add a word about magician Aleister Crowley's controversial activities during wartime; which, with respect to controversy, differed little from other periods in the occultist's life. Several biographers have wrestled with whether Crowley functioned as a spy for one side or another. The answer is elusive.

During World War I, Crowley lived in New York City with few sources of income. Proclaiming himself an Irish nationalist, he wrote bombastic, pro-German articles for a weekly called *The Fatherland.* Some British commentators denounced him as a traitor to the Allied cause. But several biographers, including Richard B. Spence, Tobias Churton, and Lawrence Sutin, have presented evidence from intelligence files and correspondence suggesting that Crowley was actually employed by British intelligence to write *purposefully absurd* pieces in order to sully the pro-German position. Crowley later claimed as much himself.

Twentieth century intelligence authorities from time to time showed interest in occultists either for propaganda purposes or in hopes they could penetrate certain innards of enemy or foreign thought, since occult groups were frequently international in activity. That Crowley was in dire need of funds suggests a motive for his activities.

Crowley generally stood aloof from overt politics although there exist inconclusive letters and claims that during Hitler's rise he sought to place a copy of *The Book of the Law* in front of the future führer as a potential exemplar of Thelema, which Crowley insisted was free from racial animus. Following Karl Germer's arrest in 1935, any such chimeras burst on the rocks of reality. Crowley then tried to tailor Thelema's appeal to British war needs, with little official interest.

In 1941, the magician wrote a pamphlet of poems for Allied victory titled, "Thumbs Up!" It was a natural extension of wartime patriotism and self-interest. He privately printed 100 copies; a signed edition appears in the special collections of the New York Public Library. Crowley apparently offered his services to British Intelligence during World War II but no need for them was found, especially with the capture of Rudolf Hess after his misbegotten flight to Scotland in 1941, when the Allies held a prisoner who could provide whatever information was significant about occult groups around the Nazis.

I now want to elucidate a different facet of history, which is not heard enough. The story of the modern encounter between politics and the occult, if whole, must be complicated and consider diffuse personalities and relationships, only a fraction of which we are able to explore in this space. This one is of unique importance.

Growing up in Western India under English rule, the sensitive young Mohandas K. Gandhi (1869–1948) had little interest in religion. His ambitions were to be a lawyer—and to leave behind the esoteric Hindu philosophies and practices of his parents' generation.

When Gandhi turned nineteen in 1888, he ventured to London to study law. He was overjoyed to be in the grimy, bustling metropolis, the world's largest city and the beating heart of the British Empire. Gandhi tried to fit the very picture of an English barrister, with neatly parted hair and crisply starched collars. But something got in the way of his mind's eye image of where he was headed.

In 1889, following a difficult school year in which Gandhi struggled with his studies at London University (he later failed matriculation exams), he met two friendly Englishmen calling themselves Theosophists. The law student recognized Theosophy as the pro-Hindu, anticolonial movement that had spread around his homeland through American Colonel Henry Steel Olcott and his mysterious partner, Madame Blavatsky. The two Theosophical "brothers" asked the young Indian if he could help them read the original Sanskrit of the central holy text of Hinduism, the *Bhagavad Gita* ("Song of God"). "I felt ashamed," Gandhi wrote in his memoirs, "as I had read the divine poem neither in Sanskrit nor in Gujarati. I was constrained to tell them that I had not read the Gita, but that I would gladly read it with them."*

The three began meeting together, and Gandhi became unexpectedly enchanted: "The Gita became an infallible guide of conduct. It became my dictionary of daily reference." As for his new friends, they were not just any Theosophists but a wealthy nephew and uncle who had recently opened their Notting Hill home to Blavatsky, who was fleeing charges of fraud and scandals in India. They made Gandhi an offer that filled him with intrigue and dread: Would he like to personally meet the high priestess of the occult—along with her most recent "convert," the esteemed British orator and social reformer Annie Besant? "I was a mere Bombay matriculate," he recalled. "I could not understand the British accent. I felt quite unworthy of going to Mrs. Besant."

But Gandhi did go. And while no records survive of the meeting between Blavatsky, Besant, and Gandhi, he later credited Theosophy for instilling in him the principle of equality among the world's religions, a revolutionary idea to a student from a caste-based society. In this sense, he explained in 1946 to biographer Louis Fischer, "Theosophy . . . is Hinduism at its best. Theosophy is the brotherhood of man." The organization's motto—*No Religion Higher Than Truth*—appeared to move Gandhi toward one of his central principles: that "all religions are true," to which he carefully added, "all have some error in them."** A generation later, Gandhi's ideal of universal brotherhood and his ethic of nonviolence touched the heart of American social reformer and divinity school student Martin Luther King, Jr.

Gandhi partnered with the Theosophical Society during India's independence movement, crediting it with easing relations between Hindu and Muslim delegates to the Indian National Congress, the

* *Autobiography: The Story of My Experiments with Truth* (Public Affairs Press, 1948). For accounts of Gandhi in London and his encounters with Theosophy there and in India, also see his Collected Works, Vols. 36, 41, and 44; *Gandhi in London* by James D. Hunt (Nataraj Books, 1993); and *The Life of Mahatma Gandhi* by Louis Fischer (Harper & Brothers, 1950). Gandhi's relations with Annie Besant are explored in *Annie Besant: A Biography by Anne Taylor* (Oxford, 1992) and *Gandhi: A Life* by Yogesh Chadha (John Wiley & Sons, 1997).

** *Young India* (newspaper), March 22, 1928.

movement's policy-making body. As previously noted, so prominent was Theosophy in India's political life that even the Congress's founding in 1885 had been instigated by an early Theosophist, A.O. Hume, a retired Anglo-Indian government secretary who said that he was acting under "advice and guidance of advanced initiates." In 1917, Blavatsky's successor, Annie Besant, was elected president of the Congress, making the Theosophist the first woman and last European to hold the position. Besant herself arguably bestowed upon Gandhi the title by which he became world famous: *Mahatma*, a Hindu term for Great Soul and the same name by which Theosophy called its own masters.*

For all that Gandhi discovered within Theosophy, however, he was suspicious of the organization's secrecy, including its communiqués from hidden masters. He declined to become a member. (Lodge records from London show that he did briefly join in 1891, his last year there.) In a letter he published in the newspaper *Young India* on September 16, 1926, Gandhi drew a line that forever divided his fealty to Theosophy's ideals from Theosophy as an organization. "Whatever critics may say against Madame Blavatsky or Col. Olcott or Dr. Besant," Gandhi wrote, "their contribution to humanity will always rank high. What has been a bar to my joining the society . . . is its secret side—its occultism. It has never appealed to me. I long to belong to the masses. Any secrecy hinders the real spirit of democracy."

Gandhi demonstrated a degree of deftness in stepping around his occult contacts that might have proven instructive to an American contemporary—an earnest and open seeker in arcane realms: Henry A. Wallace (1888–1965), the second vice president to Franklin Roosevelt and probably the most effective secretary of agriculture the nation has ever known. His efforts saved thousands of family farms during the Great Depression.

Wallace freely called himself a "practical mystic." His interest in esoteric philosophy resulted from a long and considered journey. He often seemed baffled that others could not understand much less

* There are competing claims around this, with credit sometimes going to poet Rabindranath Tagore. I am relying on scholar of religion Arthur H. Nethercot's biography, *The Last Four Lives of Annie Besant* (University of Chicago Press, 1963).

respect the seriousness of his search, which resulted in considerable political damage.*

As a young man growing up in Des Moines, Iowa, Wallace left the Presbyterianism of his youth to journey through various occult and metaphysical systems, from Theosophy to Native American shamanism. In high school in the early 1900s, he hungrily took in William James's 1902 classic of comparative religion, *The Varieties of Religious Experience*—a volume marked by the philosopher's deep interest in New Thought. Wallace read Ralph Waldo Emerson and took a particular interest in the work of the twentieth century metaphysician named for him: Ralph Waldo Trine, author of the 1897 inspirational bestseller *In Tune with the Infinite.* Trine's idea of the mind as a material, creative force touched the young Wallace. But it was Theosophy that placed the deepest mark on his expanding worldview.

Around 1919, as Wallace entered his thirties, he attended a meeting of the Des Moines Theosophical lodge. And by 1925 he became active in the Liberal Catholic Church, a movement closely linked with Theosophy and founded by one of its most colorful and controversial leaders, the English author Charles Webster Leadbeater, met earlier. The Liberal Catholic Church was designed as an alternative to the Anglican and Catholic churches: It practiced traditional Christian liturgy and the mass but permitted worshippers the freedom—very much in the vein of Theosophy—to acknowledge and pursue truths in all the world's religions.

The church's doctrine noted: "There is a 'communion of Saints' or Holy Ones, who help mankind, also a ministry of Angels." This cracked open the door for belief in the hidden masters of Theosophical tradition. For several years, the Liberal Catholic Church was Wallace's spiritual home—he performed elements of the service, wore vestments, and helped organize its Des Moines branch. He left by 1930, after the reemergence of one of many scandals over Leadbeater's suspected intimacies with underage boys.

Following in the footsteps of his father, who had been secretary of agriculture to Warren G. Harding, Wallace also joined Freema-

---

* Sources on the career of Henry A. Wallace include the seminal *American Dreamer* by John C. Culver and John Hyde (Norton, 2001); *Henry A. Wallace: His Search for a New World Order* by Graham J. White and John R. Maze (University of North Carolina Press, 1995); *Tournament of Shadows: The Great Game and the Race for Empire in Central Asia* by Karl Ernest Meyer and Shareen Blair Brysac (Basic Books, 2006); and "Who Was Henry A. Wallace?" by Arthur Schlesinger, Jr., *Los Angeles Times*, March 12, 2000.

sonry, in which he attained all but the order's highest rank. In the early 1930s, he entered a serious study of astrology, trying to determine if heavenly phenomena could predict the weather for farmers. In a way, his inquiry wasn't terribly foreign to the world of farmer's almanacs in which he was raised. Indeed, he became the third-generation editor of his family's magazine, *Wallaces' Farmer.* Many planting almanacs in the nineteenth and early twentieth centuries featured lore on how the moon and planets affect weather patterns and included zodiacal information on the earth's position amid the constellations.

Indeed, the earliest references to Mercury Retrograde as an astrological phenomenon—when communications and commerce are said to be upended due to the appearance of the planet moving backwards from earth's vantage point—began in the mid-1700s in British agricultural almanacs read by farmers who believed that the motions of astral bodies impacted planting seasons. "Mercury is turn'd retrograde in Sagittarius, which brings him back to meet the Sun in Conjunction," went a reading for December 9, 1754, in *Vox Stellarum: Or, a Loyal Alamack.*

In some respects, Wallace's inquiry into the occult—as into new farming methods—represented a deepened study of the agricultural culture from which he emerged.

Native American rituals were another subject of fascination. In 1931, Wallace grew close with a "medicine man"—a white Minnesotan poet and composer named Charles Roos. Roos studied Indian mysticism, of which he considered himself a master. Through Roos, Wallace began to believe that he might have had a past life as an Indian brave, a theory he determined to explore.

In 1932, Franklin Roosevelt, then governor of New York, invited the respected agriculturalist to his Hyde Park home for a getting-to-know-you session. Wallace was thrilled to accept. "There was, however, another reason the invitation delighted him," wrote Wallace biographers John C. Culver and John Hyde in their enthralling 2000 biography, *American Dreamer,* "and Roosevelt would have been flabbergasted by it. He saw the trip as an opportunity to explore American Indian religion and search for a past life in which he and Charles Roos roamed together as warriors." And, indeed, Wallace did spend some time with elders of the Onondaga tribe in the environs of New York's Burned-Over District, northwest of Hyde Park. Tribal elders apparently confirmed his past-life recollections and initiated him into their mysteries, including in the use of "true Indian tobacco," wrote Culver and Hyde.

But all of this was prelude to Wallace's brief, though intense, involvement with the Russian émigré, artist, and mystical philosopher Nicholas Roerich (1874–1947). It began in full in 1933, the year that marked Wallace's ascendancy to Roosevelt's cabinet as secretary of agriculture. It was a relationship that produced bracingly original political ideas—and that would later haunt and damage Wallace's political career beyond recovery.

Roerich was many things: a spiritual writer and philosopher, a Theosophist, a distinguished set designer who collaborated with composer Igor Stravinsky, and a modernist painter whose work captured Russian churches and Buddhist monasteries in a way that revealed stark similarities between the composition of Western and Eastern holy sites. He was also a self-styled cultural ambassador who appeared on the New York scene in the 1920s, where he attracted a great deal of attention and patronage, including from Governor Franklin D. Roosevelt, who met with him in 1929.

At that time, Roerich left a unique mark on the New York City skyline, "The Master Building" (today The Master Apartments) a stunning 1928 art-deco skyscraper residence on Manhattan's Upper Westside. As originally planned, the twenty-seven-story dwelling was intended by Roerich and his wife and collaborator Helena to house artistic studios, conference rooms, classrooms, auditoriums, a museum, and apartments—a combination urban ashram and cultural center.

The building's steeped uppermost chamber, resembling a Buddhist stupa, was set aside by the Roeriches for a special purpose hinted at in the structure's name: it was to summon the return of Master Morya, the being who visited Henry Olcott, ushering in a new era of spiritual understanding. The chamber was to function as the Mahatma's quarters. But financial disputes between the Roeriches and developer Louis Horch, who with his wife Nettie had been their dedicated disciples, wrestled The Master Building away from the couple and ended their plans. Recent to this writing, friends of mine surreptitiously entered Morya's once-designated chamber only to find an empty, half-finished space strewn with building and construction materials.

Roerich also had an intriguing idea for establishing a worldwide treaty to protect cultural sites and artifacts during wartime. He designed a three-ringed flag intended to fly above great monuments to signal their being off-limits to bombers and invaders, in the fashion of the Red Cross insignia.

Most historians and journalists scornfully recall Roerich as a makeshift mystic and con artist who managed to get Roosevelt, Wallace, and others to bankroll his schemes. But the Banner of Peace flags and the Roerich Pact, as the proposed treaty was known, attracted widespread attention and represented a prescient, even pioneering, effort at international law. For Wallace, the treaty took a mystical principle—unity among the world's religions and artistic expressions—and sought to apply it on the political stage. At the high-water mark of Roerich's influence, FDR commissioned Wallace to sign the Roerich Pact on behalf of the United States, which Wallace proudly did at a White House ceremony on April 15, 1935, with FDR and signatories from several Latin American nations looking on. While other nations followed suit, the treaty was acted on only spottily.

Wallace's relationship with Roerich brought out a less attractive side of the agriculturalist, however. As though in rebellion against his straightforward Midwest persona, Wallace displayed a weakness for the kinds of secrecy and spiritual theatrics sometimes found within the European occult—traits in which Roerich reveled. The pale Russian often scowled before cameras in Oriental robes and a Fu Manchu–style beard, resembling the Hollywood image of a mystic. In fact, Roerich's tales of his faraway Asian travels are often rumored to have influenced the popular novel and Frank Capra film *Lost Horizon*, which depicted a mythical land of Shangri-La deep in the Himalayas. In the early 1930s, Roerich bestowed on his friend Wallace an initiate name, "Galahad"—after the Arthurian knight—and Wallace then used his *nom de mystique* to sign dramatic, imagery-laden letters to Roerich.

"Dear Guru," began one of the most oft-quoted and enigmatic, in 1933, "I have been thinking of you holding the casket—the sacred most precious casket. And I have thought of the New Country going forth to meet the seven stars under the sign of the three stars. And I have thought of the admonition 'Await the Stone.'" Imbued with the insider jargon of the Roerich circle, Wallace's letters could sound like scenarios from a fantasy role-playing game. Wallace's love for mythical terms and code words spilled over into White House correspondence to FDR. This 1935 note from Wallace to Roosevelt probably ranks as one of the oddest interoffice memos in White House history:

> I feel for a short time yet that we must deal with the "strong ones," the "turbulent ones," the "fervent ones," and perhaps even with a temporary resurgence, with the "flameless ones," who with the last dying gasp will strive to reanimate their dying giant "Capitalism." Mr. President, you can be the "flaming one," the one with an ever-upsurging spirit to lead into the time when the children of men can sing again.

On one such occasion, FDR was reported to remark, "By God! What's the matter with Wallace?"* An undersecretary joked, "I don't dare let a Theosophist in to see Henry—he'd give him a job right away. I have to be careful, or the place will be overrun with them."** Wallace cooled suspicions by breaking with Roerich in the fall of 1935, just months after the signing of the Roerich Pact. The mystic and his son had turned a White House-funded agricultural expedition to Mongolia into an international charade in which Roerich proved more interested in political skullduggery than gathering strains of drought-resistant grass. For inscrutable reasons of his own, Roerich managed to pick up an armed band of White Russian Cossacks on the Mongolian frontier, whom he led on a traverse of Russo-Asian borderlands, alarming Soviet, Chinese, and Japanese authorities. The ill-defined detour got Roerich branded as everything from a White Russian spy to a general pest meddling in Eurasian hot spots. White House colleagues were relieved when Wallace finally ordered the mission to an end and cut all ties with Roerich.

The last thing Wallace wanted was for his spiritual interests to cast a shadow over his cabinet duties. But slowly that shadow began to fall, even while his political influence continued to rise.

---

* From "The Morgenthau Diaries" by Henry M. Morgenthau, Jr., part V, in *Collier's* magazine, October 25, 1947.

** *Henry Wallace: The Man and the Myth* by Dwight Macdonald (The Vanguard Press, 1948).

In oral histories of his White House years, Wallace proudly took credit for calling to Roosevelt's attention the little-known image of the eye-and-pyramid on the back of the Great Seal of the United States and suggesting that it be used on currency. From America's founding up through the New Deal era, the Great Seal had been used mostly for treaties and other official government business. It was an unfamiliar ceremonial insignia when it first caught Wallace's attention in 1934. He considered its Latin maxim, *Novus Ordo Seclorum*—New Order of the Ages—as translatable to *New Deal of the Ages*. At the signing of the Roerich Pact, Wallace spoke of the need for a "spiritual New Deal," one that "places that which is fine in humanity above that which is low and sordid and mean and hateful and grabbing." Roosevelt, himself a Freemason, was not uncomfortable with portentous symbols and grand imagery. Wallace recalled that when he raised the issue of using the image,

> Roosevelt was first struck with the representation of the "All-Seeing Eye," a Masonic representation of The Great Architect of the Universe. Next he was impressed with the idea that the foundation for the new order of the ages had been laid in 1776 but that it would be completed only under the eye of the Great Architect.

According to surviving Treasury Department records, FDR personally supervised the placement of the heraldic imagery on the back of the dollar bill in 1935, handwriting instructions to reposition the "pyramid" side (the seal's reverse) in front of the "eagle" side (the seal's obverse) so that the eye-and-pyramid would appear first when reading the bill from left to right. Hence, most Americans, intentionally or not, were left with the impression that the mysterious pyramid and its heralding of a "new order" were the foremost symbols of the American republic, rather than the more ordinary eagle and shield.

As it happens, the infamous phrase "new world order" gained new currency through President George H.W. Bush (1924–2018). In two addresses to joint sessions of Congress, on September 11, 1990, at the start of the first Iraq War, and on March 6, 1991, at the war's end, the elder Bush described the emergence of a "new world order." His use of this phrase at the dawning of the digital era caught fire as code for world domination by hidden global elites. If you read the speeches themselves, Bush, validly or not, was referencing the possibility that, with the conclusion of the first Iraq War, there could emerge a new era of commerce, peace treaties, cultural exchange, and so on; it was a bit of fanciful idealism. He drew the phrasing from *New Order of the Ages* from the Great Seal

In any case, Roosevelt's Treasury Secretary Henry M. Morgenthau was displeased with the whole affair. He suspected Wallace's "strange mystical drives," as he recalled in his memoirs, and questioned his motives. "It was not till later," an unhappy Morgenthau recalled in *Collier's* magazine in 1947, "that I learned that the pyramid . . . had some cabalistic significance for members of a small religious sect," by which he meant the Roerich circle. Morgenthau was actually mistaken in connecting the eye-and-pyramid to Roerich. But it was the kind of judgment that was taking hold and falsely cementing the belief that Wallace was a propagandist for esoteric causes.

After Wallace's nomination for the vice presidency in 1940—he remained a liberal hero to New Deal voters—rumors arose about the "Dear Guru" letters to Roerich. Jilted members of Roerich circle's may have leaked several to the press. But the White House managed to keep the matter quiet, suggesting behind the scenes that no such correspondence was trustworthy—especially coming from Roerich, who at that point was under investigation by the Internal Revenue Service. The matter died and Wallace avoided embarrassment.

He proved a popular vice president, but by 1943 he began to face political losses. As head of the Board of Economic Warfare, Wallace wanted guarantees of fair wages and working conditions for foreign workers producing the raw materials for America's munitions industry. It was another early attempt at international lawmaking, this time pertaining to global labor standards. But foes in the administration and Congress fought the measures, and Wallace's initiative floundered when Roosevelt failed to back him.

Sensing a more conservative national mood in 1944, Roosevelt was willing to let his vice president twist in the wind. Centrists and political bosses wanted Wallace off the next presidential ticket, and Roosevelt issued only the most tepid of defenses. While Wallace was greeted with thunderous cheers at the 1944 nominating convention in Chicago, political insiders maneuvered against him. Missourian

Harry Truman was nominated in Wallace's place. When a somewhat bewildered Truman approached Wallace to ask whether the two men could still be considered friends, Wallace smiled and replied, "Harry, we are both Masons."

The years that followed were punishing for Wallace. Although he was awarded the enticing consolation of becoming secretary of commerce in the final Roosevelt administration, Wallace first saw the job's power reduced and then he lost it after FDR's death, when Truman removed him. Embittered and alarmed at the decline of New Deal influence in the White House, Wallace mounted a progressive challenge to Truman's reelection. In 1948, he ran for president on the ticket of the Progressive Party. Democrats feared Wallace could rally the New Deal faithful and steer the election away from Truman, perhaps introducing a real third-party force into national politics. But for Wallace the whole episode amounted to one last political loss when his "Dear Guru" letters finally came to light.

Jaunty right-wing columnist Westbrook Pegler—widely read in newspapers through the Hearst syndicate—had managed to obtain a cache of Wallace's letters, probably from the hands of Roerich's followers. Pegler used them over a period of months in 1947 and 1948 to steadily bury the liberal icon, routinely goading the former vice president with names like "Old Bubblehead" and "drooling mystic."* Wallace unintentionally assisted Pegler's efforts by refusing to confirm whether he had penned the letters to Roerich, which served only to deepen suspicions that Wallace had something to hide. Despite a promising beginning, his upstart candidacy fizzled.

Afterward, Wallace mostly he retired from public life at his experimental farm, called Farvue, in Westchester County, New York. Some may have imagined it to be the place where Wallace was most comfortable, amid his plants and books. For Wallace, though, esoteric philosophy and intellectual searching were never retreats from life but ways to see justice carried into the world. Looking back on his spiritual explorations, he said in his oral history, "Karma means that while things may not balance out in a given lifetime, they balance out in the long run in terms of justice between individuals, between man and the whole. It seems to me one of the most profound of all

---

* Pegler's writing on Wallace includes syndicated columns of May 18, 1947; August 27, 1947; March 11, 1948; and July 26, 1948.

religious concepts. To that extent, I'm everlastingly grateful to the Theosophists."

One of the questions facing occultism—and all religious strains—is how its influence can, as in the case of Henry Wallace, abet meaningful and ethical development, and in other cases produce disordered thinking and hate. Such is the case of an occultist who died the same year as Wallace in 1965 and who founded America's first neo-Nazi order, the Silver Shirts: William Dudley Pelley (1890–1965).

Pelley was among the nation's most notorious hate leaders: a fervent admirer of Hitler, organizer of America's prototype neo-Nazi order, literary influence on the anti-Semitism of poet Ezra Pound, and a popular writer who reported receiving "hyper-dimensional instruction" from "Spiritual Mentors." He met them during an out-of-body experience in 1928, which he wrote about for a large and enthusiastic audience.

Before his turn to fringe politics in the 1930s, Pelley was a journalist and successful short-story writer. First in 1920 and again in 1930, he won the O. Henry Award for short fiction. For this largely self-taught son of a minister, sent early to work during a poor childhood in Lynn, Massachusetts, it was a remarkable achievement. He also spent the 1920s as a successful Hollywood screenwriter; two of his films featured horror pioneer Lon Chaney.

Pelley's public profile took an immense leap in March 1929 with the publication of a popular article on the cover of *The American Magazine*: "Seven Minutes in Eternity." Pelley depicted a quiet spring night in 1928 in which a near-death experience transported him to the regions of the spirit world. This marked Pelley's first encounter with the "Spiritual Mentors" who tutored him, as they would many times in the years ahead, on karma, reincarnation, and the afterlife. Only later would their ideas turn political. If not quite the first, "Seven Minutes in Eternity" was certainly the nation's most influential tale of near-death experience.

Somewhere between Pelley's out-of-body journey and the triumph of the fascist ideologies of the 1930s, something in the writer's outlook grew twisted. His gifts for crafting a memorable phrase were abruptly refocused on producing some of the darkest antisemitic tracts in

American history. By 1933, acting under "clairaudient" instructions from his cosmic Mentors, Pelley started the Silver Legion of America, or Silver Shirts, a paramilitary order that would weigh in on "the ultimate contest between Aryan mankind and Jewry."

Within a few years Pelley appeared transformed: Photographs showed his goateed face squinting and scowling and his diminutive five-foot-seven-inch frame decked out in a paramilitary uniform of pantaloons, a silver shirt, and a leather band strapped across his chest. By 1939, his icy visage appeared on a sheriff's WANTED poster in North Carolina, where he was convicted of securities fraud.

The Silver Shirts' popularity centered mainly on the West Coast. The group engaged only sporadically in armed training—though notably so in its San Diego chapter. More typically, the Silver Shirts served as a vehicle for pro-Hitler rallies and Pelley's campaign for the White House. The group also developed into a clearinghouse for Pelley's string of propaganda publications— professionally produced hate sheets that blamed all the world's ills, from the Lincoln assassination to Pearl Harbor, on international Jewry.

In 1934, Pelley's magazine *Liberation* attracted its most famous subscriber: the modernist poet Ezra Pound. The long, tortuous path of Pound's own antisemitism and his support of fascist ideology appear to have taken a leaf directly from Pelley. Apparently in an effort to dissuade Pound from his growing attachment to racialist conspiracies, one of his literary friends and interlocutors, the Jewish modernist poet Louis Zukofsky, sent him a Pelley article alleging that a cabal of Jewish bankers had instigated the American Civil War. The effect, however, was the opposite of what Zukofsky intended.

Instead of seeing the absurdity of it, Pound delighted in the article, praising Pelley in letters back to Zukofsky as a "stout felly" and rhetorically asking if "all bankers is jooz?" For Pound, it was a turning point: "With two exceptions," wrote historian Leon Surette in his 1999 study *Pound in Purgatory*, "this is the earliest occurrence of overtly anti-Semitic remarks I have found in Pound's correspondence or publications." A further reference to Pelley's Civil War theory emerged in one of Pound's famed *Cantos*. "It seems reasonable to conclude," Surette wrote, "that Zukofsky unwittingly set Pound on the course of anti-Semitism and conspiracy theory by sending him *Liberation* in early 1934."

By the mid-1930s, the Silver Shirts reached a peak membership of about 15,000. Pelley had become sufficiently infamous to serve as the model for novelist Sinclair Lewis's American dictator, Buzz Windrip, in his 1935 *It Can't Happen Here*. In the pages of *Liberation*—whose subscriber list may have run as high as 50,000—Pelley repeatedly hammered the Roosevelt administration for its support of England, declaring that the president was a puppet of the "house of Judah" and calling him a scheming, Dutch-descended Jew. Pelley finally pushed a button that Roosevelt would not ignore. In a 1939 pamphlet, "Cripple's Money," Pelley wrote that the polio-stricken president was personally pocketing money raised through his Warm Springs Foundation for Crippled Children (and, of course, sharing it with his Jewish puppeteers). Roosevelt asked Attorney General Frank Murphy and FBI Director J. Edgar Hoover about prosecuting Pelley for libel. But the plans were dropped for fear that Roosevelt would be subpoenaed to testify.

At the dawn of World War II, however, with the nation reeling from Pearl Harbor and Pelley praising Hitler as "the outstanding statesman-leader of the world," the federal government was ready to strike. "Now that we are in a war," Roosevelt wrote Hoover in January of 1942, "it looks like a good chance to clean up a number of these vile publications." In April, the FBI raided Pelley's offices, and by August a circuit court in Indianapolis sentenced him to fifteen years in federal prison on 11 counts of sedition.

Authorities feared that ultra-right-wing groups could serve as a fifth column in the event of an Axis invasion of the West Coast. The government made Pelley an example in a general mop-up of racist cults and paramilitary movements at the start of the war. He was likely seen as an easier target than better-known Axis sympathizers such as the "radio priest" Father Charles Coughlin, who had far more followers and political connections. The Pelley prosecution was a warning shot—and it seemed to work. Coughlin was soon silenced, the Ku Klux Klan continued a precipitous decline, and several other religio-political organizations, such as Arthur Bell's conspiracy cult Mankind United, faced federal prosecution or fell under intense scrutiny.

As the war wound down and America faced a new foe in Communism, the controversy around Pelley ebbed. In early 1950, friends and supporters—recasting their jailed chief as a pioneering foe of Bolshevism—secured his release on parole. Legally barred from political activity, Pelley spent the rest of the decade creating a massive output of channeled writings from his higher messengers, which he called the Soulcraft teachings. Moving with the times, Pelley saw the burgeoning phenomenon of UFOs as evidence of divine intelligences—or "Star Guests." For the remaining years of his life, the "beloved Chief" crafted an astral–Spiritualist religion based on cosmic messages from interstellar guides.

In 1965, at seventy-five, Pelley died quietly of heart failure in Noblesville, Indiana. His passing was marked by an anonymous cross-burning on the lawn of the funeral home where he lay. It would appear that the prophet of hate went to his grave a largely forgotten man.

But Pelley's brand of pseudo-patriotism touched the imaginations of other mystical sects that also attempted to "save" America under the guidance of hidden powers. The largest was the Chicago-based "Mighty I AM" movement, referenced earlier, which offered a mélange of teachings from "Ascended Masters" who extolled prosperity, ultra-patriotism, and mystical awakening. The group gained and quickly lost wide popularity during the 1930s under the leadership of a husband–wife team, Guy and Edna Ballard. The Ballards' efforts, in turn, served to influence the Church Universal and Triumphant (CUT). Under its guru, Elizabeth Clare Prophet (1939–2009), CUT gained notoriety in the late 1980s, when church members dug an elaborate network of underground chambers near Yellowstone National Park, stockpiled weapons and provisions, and awaited American–Soviet nuclear Armageddon.

By far the grimmest legacy of William Dudley Pelley was the influence he left among America's emerging hate groups. The Silver Shirts were an identifiable starting point for the careers of at least two figures whose names became synonymous with violence and bigotry later in the twentieth century. Henry L. Beach, a former Silver Shirt chapter leader, cofounded the white hate group Posse Comitatus, known for a series of 1983 shootouts that killed two federal marshals in North Dakota and a sheriff in Arkansas. Another ex–Silver Shirt, Richard Butler, founded the violent Aryan Nations, which he directed from Idaho until his death in 2004, going to his grave as the most visible leader of white hate. Pelley's writings and theories, and the Silver Shirts' uniforms and paramilitary posturing, gave post-Klan hate groups a style, a language, and an aesthetic.

Aside from what I've observed about Steve Bannon, I sense virtually no major connections between esotericism and current politics, at least in the U.S. But I close on a more benign story that may prove elucidating.

It is not widely remembered, but during Bill Clinton's first term, Hillary Clinton was actually considered a somewhat New Agey figure in the media. This got cemented by a *New York Times Magazine* cover story headlined "Saint Hillary" by Michael Kelly on May 23, 1993. At the time, she was talking with a leftwing rabbi and activist, Michael Lerner, for whom I worked after college. Michael coined the term "politics of meaning," which Clinton used in at least one of her speeches. Michael was interested in investing politics with questions of self-worth and the search for higher aims. The media called him "Hillary's Guru" or "Hillary's Rasputin," perceptions he never cultivated.

A greater sensation arose around Clinton's White House meetings with mythologist and spiritual writer Jean Houston, who I once published. They met together while Clinton was writing her 1996 book *It Takes a Village*. They held creativity sessions where Jean asked Clinton to conduct an imaginary conversation with Eleanor Roosevelt, one of the first lady's heroes. Based on reportage by the *Washington Post*'s Bob Woodward, newspapers announced that Clinton was hosting "séances" in the White House. This kind of shorthand is ridiculous and typifies most of the mainstream media's inability or unwillingness to contextualize alternative therapies or spirituality.

Jean did tell me personally that one time that Bill Clinton dropped in on one of their sessions and sat down. Jean told the president, "You are an undeveloped shaman." At that, he got up and walked out. I share that story just by way of saying that esoteric or New Age movements tend to attract the same demographics and respective interests of people in power as they do everyday people, who may embrace, experiment with, or reject them.

CHAPTER TEN

Science of the Supernatural

Let me depart momentarily from my timeline to pay tribute to a brilliant twentieth century sociologist Marcello Truzzi (1935–2003) who called himself a "constructive skeptic" of paranormal phenomena. In 1975 and again in 1978, Truzzi, a man of even temperament, refined ethics, and dedicated but authentically questioning skepticism, stated a principle—not wholly original to him—that was later popularized by astronomer Carl Sagan. Truzzi's maxim was: "An extraordinary claim requires extraordinary proof."* This widely quoted precept, redubbed the "Sagan standard," was repeated by the televised astronomer in 1980 as: "Extraordinary claims require extraordinary evidence."

Truzzi resigned from the professional skeptics' organization he cofounded, Committee for the Scientific Investigation of Claims of the Paranormal (CSICOP), now the Committee for Skeptical Inquiry (CSI), about a year after its 1976 launch. Truzzi protested the group's dominance by "pseudo-skeptics" more interested in injurious behavior toward claimants of the supernatural versus actual skeptical inquiry.**

---

* *Zetetic Scholar*, Volume 1, Number 1, 1978, a journal Truzzi founded.

** "Marcello Truzzi, 67; Sociologist Who Studied the Supernatural" by Douglas Martin, *New York Times*, February. 9, 2003.

"I found myself attacked by the Committee members and board, who considered me to be too soft on the paranormalists," he later wrote. "My position was not to treat protoscientists as adversaries, but to look to the best of them and ask them for their best scientific evidence. I found that the Committee was much more interested in attacking the most publicly visible claimants . . . The major interest of the Committee was not inquiry but to serve as an advocacy body, a public relations group for scientific orthodoxy."*

I hope this chapter proves not only historically elucidating but also honors the level of query and discourse Truzzi endorsed. One of the flowerings that I believe emerged from the occult revival of the late nineteenth and early twentieth centuries, is yearning for *higher standards of scientific and historical evidence* for claims of the extraordinary.

Beginning in 1870, physicist Sir William Crookes, a pioneer in microphysics and cathode ray studies, used the pages of the *Quarterly Journal of Science* to endeavor a study of psychical phenomena and Spiritualist claims using at least the coordinates and basic methods of scientific study.

"No observations are of much use to the student of science unless they are truthful and made under test conditions," he wrote, "and here I find the great mass of Spiritualistic evidence to fail."**

In particular, Crookes studied the physical mediumship claims of Daniel Dunglas Home (pronounced "Hume") and conducted sittings with Kate Fox of the Rochester Rappings. In Crookes' experiments with Home, the physicist thought he detected some kind of "Psychic Force." In 1871, the Royal Society, Britain's premier academy of sciences, rejected two of his reports on Home. One scientist working alone, and sometimes with ad hoc colleagues, could not get very far. But what if there existed a more concerted and organized effort? These were the lines along which some of Crookes' contemporaries were thinking.

---

* "Reflections on the Reception of Unconventional Claims in Science," colloquium presented by Marcello Truzzi, Ph.D., Professor of Sociology at Eastern Michigan University at Ypsilanti, Michigan, and Director, Center for Scientific Anomalies Research, Ann Arbor, MI, November 29, 1989.

** "Spiritualism Viewed in the Light of Modern Science," *Quarterly Journal of Science*, July 1870.

"Organized psychical research can be dated, symbolically, from a conversation between Henry Sidgwick and his student F.W.H. Myers, one moonlit night in Cambridge about 1870, over the need to validate religious belief through the methods of empirical science," wrote historians Seymour H. Mauskopf and Michael R. McVaugh in their valuable study of psi research, *The Elusive Science.* It would not be until 1882, however, that formal scientific scrutiny of anomalous phenomena marked its official starting point with the founding in London of the Society for Psychical Research (SPR) by scientists including Myers (who coined the term telepathy for mind-to-mind communication) and pioneering psychologist and philosopher William James—and included a remarkable array of clinical luminaries, such as physicist Oliver Lodge, Sigmund Freud (a member of both the British and American chapters), economist and ethical philosopher Henry Sidgwick, and Arthur Balfour, Britain's prime minister from 1902 to 1905. Crookes in the late 1890s served as its president.

German philosopher and psychologist Max Dessoir (1867–1947) coined the term *parapsychologie* in 1889 to describe empirical study of extraphysical phenomena, including clairvoyance, mediumship, precognition, and after-death survival.* At its inception, parapsychology—scientific study of paranormal phenomena—sought to test mediumistic claims under controlled conditions. The early SPR worked with rigor to hold spirit mediums to proof. Researchers such as the strong-willed Richard Hodgson (1855–1905) and James himself ventured to the séance table intent on safeguarding against fraud and documenting claimed phenomena, including physical mediumship, after-death communication, and clairvoyance or what is today called channeling. (The twentieth century medical psychic Edgar Cayce, who is later encountered, first used the term "channel" in a metaphysical sense.) They probed unexplained cases, exposed frauds, and created historical controversies that have lingered until today. In 1886, William James issued a confirmatory initial report on American medium Leonora Piper (1859–1950), followed by continued SPR investigations by Hodgson. In James's 1896 Presidential Address to the SPR, he famously remarked:

---

* Dessoir later became a skeptic, a topic well considered in "Max Dessoir" by Andreas Sommer, *Psi Encyclopedia*, London: The Society for Psychical Research, 2021.

> If I may employ the language of the professional logic-shop, a universal proposition can be made untrue by a particular instance. If you wish to upset the law that all crows are black, you must not seek to show that no crows are; it is enough if you prove one single crow to be white. My own white crow is Mrs. Piper. In the trances of this medium, I cannot resist the conviction that knowledge appears which she has never gained by the ordinary waking use of her eyes and ears and wits. What the source of this knowledge may be I know not, and have not the glimmer of an explanatory suggestion to make; but from admitting the fact of such knowledge I can see no escape. So when I turn to the rest of the evidence, ghosts and all, I cannot carry with me the irreversibly negative bias of the 'rigorously scientific' mind, with its presumption as to what the true order of nature ought to be.

1886 marked the publication of the two-volume *Phantasms of the Living* by Edmund Gurney, F.W.H. Myers, and Frank Podmore, which explored 702 cases of spontaneous and crisis apparitions. But SPR researchers were functioning largely on testimony and within the lace-curtained settings of Victorian parlors. On the whole, the investigators were not operating in clinical environments, so-called white coat lab settings where an atmosphere of experimenter control abetted seeking evidence for extraphysical phenomena, whether in statistical patterns or documentation of observed events. The American chapter of the SPR, meanwhile, grew stymied by factional disputes between members primarily interested in the after-death survival thesis versus those committed to the more conservative direction of documenting mental phenomena.

I do not intend to leave the impression that lab-based study of psychical phenomena was absent. In the 1880s, Nobel laureate and SPR president Charles Richet, one of France's most highly regarded biologists, studied telepathy with subjects under hypnosis. Richet also introduced the use of statistical analysis in ESP (extrasensory perception) card tests, presaging today's near-universal use of statistics throughout the psychological and social sciences.* In the early 1920s,

* See "Telepathy: Origins of Randomization in Experimental Design" by Ian Hacking, *Isis*, Sept 1988, Vol. 79, No. 3; "J. B. Rhine's Extra-Sensory Perception and Its Background in Psychical Research" by Michael McVaugh and Seymour H. Mauskopf, *Isis*, June 1976, Vol. 67, No. 2; and "Charles Richet" by Carlos S. Alvarado, *Psi Encyclopedia*, London: The Society for Psychical Research, 2015.

French engineer René Warcollier conducted a series of experiments on long-distance telepathy.

Freud himself, often seen as a materialist counterpart to his more occult-leaning former disciple Carl Jung, publicly and privately pondered the possibilities of telepathy, sometimes delaying publication of key statements posthumously to avoid professional fallout. This was the case with Freud's "Psychoanalysis and Telepathy," his earliest paper on the topic written in 1921—but withheld from publication until 1941, two years after his death. (This was likely at the urging of his English biographer Ernest Jones, who found the topic professionally compromising.) Freud's posthumous essay contains the interesting passage, "It does not follow as a matter of course that an intensified interest in occultism must involve a danger to psychoanalysis. We should, on the contrary, be prepared to find reciprocal sympathy between them. They have both experienced the same contemptuous and arrogant treatment by official science." But Freud dismissed the prospect of an alliance between the embattled camps: "Analysts are at bottom incorrigible mechanists and materialists," adding, "even though they seek to avoid robbing the mind and spirit of their still unrecognized characteristics."

The analyst's first published statement on ESP appeared in what biographer Jones called the "more cautiously worded" paper "Dreams and Telepathy" in 1922, where he observed: "Psychoanalysis may do something to advance the study of telepathy, in so far as, by the help of its interpretations, many of the puzzling characteristics of telepathic phenomena may be rendered more intelligible to use; or other, still doubtful phenomena be for the first time definitely ascertained to be of a telepathic nature."

In a 1925 exchange with Freud, Jones protested that acknowledging telepathy "would mean admitting the essential claim of the occultists that mental processes can be independent of the human body."* Again, Freud himself appeared more sanguine on the matter, responding: "*Dans ces cas pareils, ce n'est que le premier pas qui coute. Das weistere findet sich*"—"It is only the first step that counts. The rest follows." I take Freud to be saying: we must acknowledge facts without extrapolating implications—never permit implication to stymie reportage.

---

* For a revealing and sometimes-humorous exchange of their letters on the topic, see volume III of Jones's *The Life and Work of Sigmund Freud* (Basic Books, 1957) and *The Future of the Body* by Michael Murphy (Jeremy P. Tarcher, 1992).

On July 24, 1921, Freud had written even more bluntly to British-American psychical researcher, Hereward Carrington: "I do not belong with those who reject in advance the study of so-called occult phenomena as being unscientific, or unworthy, or harmful. If I were at the beginning of my scientific career, instead of at the end of it as I am now, might perhaps choose no other field of study—in spite of all its difficulties."*

Based on these statements, it is tempting to ponder the existence of an "occult Freud" outside mainstream perception. There is validity that interpretation—but it must be approached carefully. Some historical writers, often with scant referencing, argue for Kabbalistic influences on Freud. I question this. Born into a then-secular Jewish family in Austria in 1856, Freud's milieu was unlikely to include exposure to Kabbalah, which was neglected even among dedicated Jewish scholars in modernity. This began to reverse with the 1946 publication of *Major Trends In Jewish Mysticism* by Gershom Scholem (who, as previously noted, grudgingly acknowledged Eliphas Lévi for at least keeping an ersatz version of the tradition in front of Western eyes). While confluences are intriguing, and certainly Freud's Jewish background influenced his work, I find purported Kabbalistic connections indirect, at most. Indeed, Freud, as I hope these and other brief passages demonstrate, was not averse to publicly naming sources and interests that departed from his proper "Herr Doktor" reputation.

Parapsychology finally burgeoned into an acknowledged, if hotly debated, academic field thanks largely to ESP researcher J.B. Rhine (1895–1980) and his wife and intellectual partner Louisa Rhine (1891–1983). In the late 1920s and early '30s, the Rhines established the research program that became the Parapsychology Laboratory at Duke University in Durham, North Carolina, which made paradigmatic advances in the scientific study of ESP.

The Rhines trained as statisticians and botanists in the early 1920s at the University of Chicago where both received doctorates, a considerable rarity for a woman then. In the 1920s, botanists were

* For this reference, I am indebted to Raymond Van Over, "Freud and Occultism," letter, *New York Times*, May 19, 1974. In volume III of *Life and Work*, Jones reports Freud replying to Carrington, "If I had my life to live over again I should devote myself to psychical research rather than to psychoanalysis."

considered at the forefront of statistical theory. In Chicago in 1922, they were inspired by a talk on Spiritualism by English author Arthur Conan Doyle. Doyle, the creator of Sherlock Holmes, was a committed though sometimes less-than-meticulous advocate of Spiritualism. That year marked the appearance of his book, *The Coming of the Fairies*. After World War I, the storyteller grew enthralled with a series of photographic plates taken by two English schoolgirls that showed winged fairies frolicking in the Yorkshire countryside. Seen through contemporary eyes, the black-and-white prints hauntingly mirror the hopes of Doyle, and others of the World War I generation for a mythical, childlike world where hidden beings abound and the dead are never really gone. But the images were also appallingly fake: Some of the angelic fairies sported stylish Parisian hairdos (they were cutouts from fashion magazines) and, on close scrutiny, one figure could be seen with a hat pin protruding from its middle. Unsurprisingly, Doyle later feuded with the more stringent Rhine. (I must add in Doyle's defense that at times in the book he writes with a light touch even bordering on tongue-in-cheek.)

With his eyes on greater horizons, J.B. soon grew restless in his chosen career. "It would be unpardonable for the scientific world today to overlook evidences of the supernormal in our world," he told what must have been a mildly surprised audience of scientific agriculturalists in 1926 at the University of West Virginia, where he held a teaching position.*

The Rhines began casting around, venturing to Columbia University and Harvard seeking opportunities to combine their scientific training with their metaphysical interests. Initial progress proved fitful. As often occurs in life, just before they gave up their immense efforts, an extraordinary opportunity appeared. In 1930, the new chairman of Duke's psychology department, William McDougall, made J.B. Rhine a formal part of the campus.

Although the founding of Duke's Parapsychology Laboratory is often dated to that year, the program was not christened the Parapsychology Laboratory until 1935 (in 1929 J.B. called his prototype the "Institute for Experimental Religion"), where it remained until 1965. Today the Rhine Research Center continues as an independent lab off

* *The Elusive Science: Origins of Experimental Psychical Research* by Seymour H. Mauskopf and Michael R. McVaugh with an afterword by J.B. and L.E. Rhine (The Johns Hopkins University Press, 1980).

campus. It proved a watershed episode in which parapsychology was formally folded into an academic structure.

At Duke, J.B. did not quite originate but popularized the term *extrasensory perception*, or ESP, initials that quickly became a household word. The work begun at Duke's Parapsychology Lab in the early 1930s has continued among different researchers, labs, and universities to the present day. The effort is to provide clinically documented evidence that human beings participate in some form of existence that exceeds cognition, motor skill, and commonly observed biological functions—that we participate in trackable, replicable patterns of extra-physicality that permit us, at least sometimes, to communicate and receive information in a manner that surpasses generally acknowledged sensory experience and means of data conveyance. This field of exchange occurs independently of time, space, and mass.

Researchers have also accumulated a body of statistical evidence for psychokinesis (i.e., mind over matter) and precognition or what is sometimes called retrocausality, in which events in the future affect the present. For several years, Dean Radin, chief scientist at the Institute of Noetic Sciences (IONS) in Northern California, has performed and replicated experiments in precognition in which subjects display bodily stressors, such as pupil dilation or increased heart rate, seconds *before* being shown distressing or emotionally triggering imagery.*

These are fleeting references to a handful of recent findings from modern parapsychology. As a self-acknowledged believing historian, I take it as my privilege to state a position and then argue for it: *we possess heavily scrutinized, replicable statistical evidence for an extraphysical component of the human psyche.* For decades, this evidence has appeared in—and been reproduced for—traditional, academically based journals, often juried by scientists without

* See: "Time-reversed human experience: Experimental evidence and implications" by Dean Radin, Esalen Draft, 7/31/00, https://www.researchgate. net/publication/239611072_Time -reversed_human_experience_Experimen-tal_evidence_and_implications and "Intuition Through Time: What Does the Seer See?" by Dean Radin, Ph.D., and Ana Borges, J.D., *Explore*, 2009; Vol 5, No. 4. For a meta-analysis of recent precognition experiments see "Precognition as a form of prospection: A review of the evidence" by Julia A. Mossbridge and Dean Radin, *Psychology of Consciousness: Theory, Research, and Practice*, March 2018, Vol 5, No. 1.

sympathy for its findings.* This evidence has been procured and replicated under rigorous clinical conditions. It demonstrates that the individual possesses or participates in a facet of existence that surpasses what is known to us biologically, psychologically, sensorily, and technologically.

The search for greater dimensions of life is as old as humanity itself. But what is new and revolutionary is *the advent of science as a method of protocols to identify processes that affirm primordial humanity's basic instinct for the extraphysical.* This places our generation before a remarkable precipice. It is one that we have not yet been able to cross.

The precipice is the philosophy called materialism, by which Western life has organized itself for nearly 300 years. Philosophical materialism holds that matter creates itself, and that your mind is strictly an epiphenomenon of your brain. Furthermore, thoughts are a localized function of gray matter which, like bubbles in a glass of carbonated water, are gone once the water is gone. And that is the extent of the psyche.

As I write these words in the early decades of the twenty-first century, that philosophy is obsolete. Firstly, an enormous amount of data has been amassed verifying both the perceptual basis of reality and the extraphysical—gathered through the same methodology that materialism purports to defend. Secondly, we face the progressing realization that materialism is simply a position, a theory, an ideology, of which science is independent.

This does not mean that materialism will fade gently. Its outlook—that matter evinces no calculable reality beyond classical mechanics and that all contrary evidence or implications are false because they contradict its founding premise—will retain influence for decades. The materialist perspective is concretized within key parts of our culture and media. Many opinion-shaping personalities hold to it with conviction.

In his famous 1974 commencement address at Caltech, physicist Richard Feynman (1918–1988) eviscerated believers in "cargo cult science," including those, like me, who are interested in ESP, UFOs, and astrology.** The problem, Feynman said, is embracing confirma-

* E.g., a meta-analysis of psychical research data appeared in the flagship journal of the American Psychological Association: "The Experimental Evidence for Parapsychological Phenomena: A Review" by Etzel Cardeña, *American Psychologist*, 2018, Vol. 73, No. 5.

** See "Cargo Cult Science" by Richard Feynman at Caltech.edu.

tion or correlation versus laboring to disprove a hypothesis. This is, ironically, the same pattern into which most professional skeptics fall today. Spiritual philosopher G.I. Gurdjieff observed "how the line of the development of forces deviates from its original direction and goes, after a certain time, in a diametrically opposite direction, still preserving its former name."* In light of Feynman and Gurdjieff, consider this 1977 statement from CSICOP's executive director, Lee Nisbet, in *Science* magazine: "We feel it is the duty of the scientific community to show that these beliefs are utterly screwball."

Until now, my observations have been largely historical. What replicable evidence exists for my chin-out claims of science affirming the infinite? Here I return to Duke's Parapsychology Laboratory in the early 1930s. Rhine's innovation as a researcher was developing clear, repeatable, and unimpeachable methods, with rigor and without drama or speculation, for testing and statistically mapping evidence for anomalous communication and conveyance. To attempt this, Rhine initially created a series of card-guessing tests that involved a deck called Zener cards designed by psychologist Karl E. Zener (1903–1964). Zener cards are a five-suit deck, generally with twenty-five cards in a pack, with symbols that are easily and immediately recognizable: circle, square, cross, wavy lines, and five-pointed star. After a deck is shuffled, subjects are asked to attempt blind hits on what symbol will turn up.

Probability dictates that if you are operating from random chance over large spreads, you are going to hit 20 percent, or one out of five. But Rhine discovered, across tens and eventually hundreds of thousands of rigorously safeguarded trials (by 1940, the database included nearly a million trials) that certain individuals, rather than scoring 20 percent, would score 25 percent, 26 percent, 27 percent, sometimes 28 percent (and in select cases a great deal higher).**

At the time, social scientists commonly withheld negative sets on the questionable grounds that something was flawed with the methodology. Rhine reversed this practice early on at his lab and helped lead

---

* *In Search of the Miraculous: Fragments of an Unknown Teaching* by P. D. Ouspensky (Harcourt Brace, 1949).

** E.g., see *Extra-Sensory Perception* by J.B. Rhine (1934, Boston Society for Psychic Research).

the overall social sciences to do so. All of the data were reported. Nothing was withheld in the file drawer. No negative sets were excluded.*

In Rhine's work, every precaution was taken against corruption, withholding, or pollution of data, which was also opened to other researchers (and non-research-based critics) for replication, vetting, and review. In a letter of March 15, 1960, to mathematician and foundation executive Warren Weaver, Rhine spoke of the extra lengths to which the parapsychologist ought to go: "Even though the methodology and standards of evidence may compare favorably with other advances of natural science, they have to be superior in parapsychology because of its novelty; and conceivably, too, by making them still better, everything may be gained in overcoming the natural resistance involved."**

The "natural resistance" or partisanship around such findings can be so intense—and sometimes purposefully obfuscating—that lay seekers may come away with the mistaken impression that Rhine's work, or that of more recent parapsychologists, has proven unrepeatable or compromised.

Parapsychologist Charles Honorton (1946–1992) sought to analyze critical challenges to Rhine's figures in the years following their publication. In 1975, he found that "61 percent of the independent replications of the Duke work were statistically significant. This is 60 times the proportion of significant studies we would expect if the significant results were due to chance or error."***

Rhine's experiments have proven so bulletproof that even close to 50 years later, his most resistant critics were still attempting to explain them by fantastical (and often feckless) fraud theories, including a prominent English skeptic's nearly vaudevillian supposition that one of the test subjects repeatedly crawled through a ceiling space to peek at cards through a trapdoor over the lab.**** At such excesses,

---

* E.g., see "Editorial" by Gardner Murphy and Bernard F. Riess, *The Journal of Parapsychology*, June 1939, Vol 3, No. 1, in which the authors review Rhine's protocols.

** Rhine's letter is from the Parapsychology Laboratory Records, 1893–1984, Rare Book, Manuscript, and Special Collections Library, Duke University, Durham, NC.

*** "Has Science Developed the Competence to Confront the Paranormal?" by Charles Honorton, *Extrasensory Perception*, Vol. 2, edited by Edwin C. May and Sonali Bhatt Marwaha (Praeger, 2015).

**** See *ESP and Parapsychology: A Critical Re-Evaluation* by C.E.M Hansel (Prometheus Books, 1980); "Rhetoric over substance: the impoverished state of skepticism" by Charles Honorton, *Journal of Parapsychology*, June 1993; and Stacy Horn's invaluable study of the Rhine labs, *Unbelievable* (HarperCollins/ Ecco, 2009).

rationalists fail the test that Enlightenment philosopher David Hume (1711–1772) set for validation of miracles: counterclaims must be less likely than reported phenomena. In any case, Rhine's methods and results have never been upended.

For all that, Rhine may have proved too idealistic regarding what it took to overcome "natural resistance." Mainstream media sources engage in pushback and even disingenuousness against data from parapsychology. A prime example appears in how polemical skeptics today ride herd over articles on parapsychology on the most-read reference source in history, Wikipedia. As of this writing, Wikipedia's article on Zener cards states in its opening, "The original series of experiments have been discredited and replication has proven elusive." This statement is unsourced, something that would get red-flagged on most of the encyclopedia's articles.

How does this occur on the world's go-to reference source? Dean Radin of IONS, described to me the problem of an ad hoc group calling itself "Guerrilla Skeptics" policing Wiki entries on parapsychology: "While there are lots of anonymous trolls that have worked hard to trash any Wikipedia pages related to psi, including bios of parapsychologists, this group of extreme skeptics is proudly open that they are rewriting history . . . any attempt to edit those pages, even fixing individual words, is blocked or reverted almost instantly."*

Even if parapsychology as a field had ended with Rhine's initial Duke trials, we would possess evidence of paranormal mechanics in human existence. Those basic (though painstakingly structured) card experiments, those few percentage points of deviation tracked across tens of thousands of trials (90,000 in the database by the 1934 publication of *Extra-Sensory Perception*), demonstrate an anomalous transfer of information in a laboratory setting and an extraphysical (call it metaphysical), non-Newtonian exchange of information.

But things did not end there. In the decades ahead, extraordinary waves of diversified experiments occurred in the U.S. and other nations growing from the efforts of the scientists at Duke's Parapsychology Laboratory. These efforts demonstrated, again and again, anomalous mental phenomena, including precognition, retrocausal-

* See my articles "The Man Who Destroyed Skepticism," Boing Boing, October 26, 2020, and "The Crisis of Professional Skepticism, Medium, February 27, 2023.

ity, telepathy, and psychokinesis (PK). Rhine's lab began studying PK in 1934, an effort that continued until 1941, after which many lab members were summoned to the war effort. During their nine years of investigation, researchers conducted tens of thousands of runs in which individuals would attempt to affect throws of random sets of dice. Devices were soon employed to toss the dice in such a way that ensured randomness, which ought to demonstrate no pattern whatsoever. Again, similar statistical results to the Zener card experiments appeared: among certain individuals, across hundreds of thousands of throws, with every conceivable safeguard, peer review, methodological transparency, and reportage of every set, there appeared a deviation of several percentage points, suggesting a physical effect arising from mental intention.*

We have now logged generations of experiments designed to test the effects to which I am referring. Today's parapsychologists believe, I think with justification, that the basic, foundational science for psychical ability has already been laid. Although parapsychology remains controversial, the field has already moved on from basic testing for ESP, a matter that was more or less settled in the 1940s.

Recent researchers are concerned with questions including telepathy (mind to mind communication); precognition (the ability to foresee or be affected by things that, within our model of the mind, have not yet occurred); retrocausality (the effect of future events on current perceptions or abilities); a biological basis for psi (including biologist Rupert Sheldrake's morphic field theories); spontaneous psi events, such as premonitions or crisis apparitions; dream telepathy; a "global consciousness" effect during periods of mass emotional reaction; and the practice of remote viewing or clairvoyance. The field also investigates other important areas, including out-of-body experiences, near-death experiences, deathbed visions, after-death survival, and reincarnation.

The scientific study of reincarnation was pioneered as an academic field by the remarkable research psychiatrist Ian Stevenson

---

* See "Chapter 6: Psychokinesis," *An Introduction to Parapsychology*, fifth edition, by Harvey J. Irwin and Caroline A. Watt (McFarland, 2007). Also see www.williamjames.com/Science/PK.htm: "By the end of 1941, a total of 651,216 experimental die throws had been conducted. The combined results of these experiments pointed to a phenomenon with 10,115 to 1 odds against chance occurrence." The Rhines published their initial results in 1943: "The psychokinetic effect: I. The first experiment" by J.B. Rhine and Louisa Rhine, *Journal of Parapsychology* 7.

(1918–2007), who in 1967 founded the Division of Perceptual Studies at the University of Virginia School of Medicine. For five decades, this conservative researcher "traveled six continents, accumulating more than 2,500 cases of young children who recounted details of previous lives, which he meticulously verified with witnesses, hospital records, autopsy reports, death certificates, and photographs," eulogized the *Journal of Near-Death Studies* in Spring 2007.

The research group Stevenson founded remains active at UVA. It is a clinical psychology lab that studies potential cases of reincarnation and after-death survival based on physical evidence, forensic records, on-site visits, historical data, and psychological exams. As noted, Stevenson reviewed thousands of cases where people claimed past-life memories; he documented episodes in countries and households around the world where children described past-life experiences, sometimes through dreams or overt memories, and in some cases the subjects bore birthmarks, blemishes, or birth defects that correlated to the circumstances of someone who had died, at times nearby, prior to the birth of the child and who was unknown to the child and family.

For example, this may have included someone dying of a bullet wound to the abdomen and a child reporting past-life memories has a correlating abdominal birthmark or deformity. A plurality of Stevenson's suggestive cases, between 30 and 80 percent depending on nation, featured a violent death. He also found a notable number of cases where people who identified as a different gender than that assigned at birth suggested a gender difference in a past-life context.

Like Rhine, Stevenson proved rigorous at establishing protocols. In 2013, a skeptic writing of Stevenson's body of data in *Scientific American* noted:

> I'd be happy to say it's all complete and utter nonsense—a moldering cesspool of irredeemable, anti-scientific drivel. The trouble is, it's not entirely apparent to me that it is . . . I'm not *quite* ready to say that I've changed my mind about the afterlife. But I can say that a fair assessment and a careful reading of Stevenson's work has, rather miraculously, managed to pry it open. Well, a *tad*, anyway.*

* "Ian Stevenson's Case for the Afterlife: Are We 'Skeptics' Really Just Cynics?" by Jesse Bering, *Scientific American*, November 2, 2013.

In September 1977, *The Journal of Nervous and Mental Disease*—a peer-reviewed, mainstream medical journal—dedicated a full issue to Stevenson's work, as did the *Journal of Scientific Exploration* in 2008 (volume 22, number 1). Motivated readers can explore Stevenson's magnum opus, *Reincarnation and Biology: A Contribution to the Etiology of Birthmarks and Birth Defects* (Praeger, 1997), a work of 2,268 pages. I also recommend Stevenson's first book on the topic from 1966, *Twenty Cases Suggestive of Reincarnation* (University Press of Virginia) and the ongoing efforts of his colleague Jim B. Tucker, M.D. at UVA's medical school.

One of the most important figures in psychical research died of heart failure in 1992 at the tragically young age of forty-six. I mentioned him earlier: Charles Honorton. Honorton's passing was a tremendous loss for the field, nearly equivalent to losing Einstein at the dawn of his relativity theories.

It is critical to understand what Honorton accomplished. In the late 1960s and '70s, he engaged in research into dreams and ESP at the innovative Division of Parapsychology and Psychophysics at Maimonides Medical Center in Brooklyn. Honorton proceeded to assemble possibly the most significant body of data we possess in the parapsychology field. It was through a long-running series of experiments designed with colleagues in the 1970s and '80s known as *ganzfeld experiments*. *Ganzfeld* is German for *whole* or *open field*. Honorton had an instinct for the conditions under which ESP or telepathy—mind-to-mind communication—might be heightened, which formed the basis of his studies.

Honorton noted that the classic Rhine experiments were largely focused on subjects believed to have a predilection for ESP. Rhine thought that ESP may be detectable throughout the human population but was readily testable through figures who possess innate abilities. He did not consider ESP something for which you could train or that was necessarily intrinsic to everyone. Rather, he focused on what he considered naturally gifted individuals, who made prime subjects.

Honorton took a different tack. He wondered whether psychical abilities are, in fact, general throughout the population—but perhaps the psychical signal, so to speak, gets jammed or the psyche's circuitry gets overloaded due to excessive stimuli in daily life.

Honorton pondered what it might reveal to test for ESP among subjects who are placed into conditions of relaxed, comfortable sensory deprivation. He ventured that you may be able to spike the ESP effect if you place a subject into sensory-deprived conditions without noise or bright light—for example, seating the person in a comfortable recliner in a noise-proof, dimly lit room or chamber, fitted with eyeshades, and wearing headphones that emit white noise. These conditions induce the state called *hypnagogia*, a kind of waking hypnosis.

In fact, you enter into the hypnagogic state twice daily: just before you drift to sleep at night and just as you are coming to in the morning. It is a deeply relaxed, motionless state in which you might experience hallucinatory or morphing images, aural hallucinations, tactile sensations of weightlessness, or even bodily paralysis. Yet you remain functionally awake: you are self-aware and able to direct cognition. The morning state is sometimes called *hypnopompia* (another term coined by psi research pioneer F.W.H. Myers). Hypnagogia and hypnopompia are similar with some differences; for example, hallucinations occur somewhat more commonly during the nighttime state.*

Since this state is an apparently inviting period for self-suggestion—the mind is supple, the body relaxed, and the psyche unclouded by stimuli—Honorton pondered whether these conditions might facilitate heightened psychical activity. To test for telepathy, he placed one subject—called the receiver—into the relaxed conditions of sensory deprivation I have described, while a second subject—called the sender—is seated outside the sensory deprivation tank or in another space. In the classical ganzfeld experiments, the sender attempts to "transmit" a preselected image to the receiver. After the sending period ends, the receiver then chooses among four different images (one target image and three decoys) to identify what was sent.

Like the Zener cards, there is a randomly selected target on each successive trial and, in this case, a one in four or 25 percent chance of guessing right. In meta-analyzed data, subjects on average surpassed the 25 percent guess rate. Depending on the analytic model, the most

---

* French dream researcher and physician Alfred Maury (1817–1892) originated the term hypnagogia, which was popularized by psychologist Andreas Mavromatis in his 1987 monograph, *Hypnagogia: The Unique State of Consciousness Between Wakefulness and Sleep* (Routledge).

stringently produced experiments demonstrated an overall hit rate of between 32 percent and 35 percent.* Since the mid-1970s, this data has, in varying forms, been replicated by dozens of scientists across different labs in different nations, often under increasingly refined conditions. The ganzfeld experiments not only documented a significant psi effect but also suggested that a detectable ESP or telepathic effect may be more generally distributed among the population. The protocols themselves suggested conditions under which psi phenomena are most likely to appear.

Given its significance, the ganzfeld database attracted intense scrutiny. In a historic first, which has never really been repeated, Honorton in 1986 collaborated on a paper with a prominent psi skeptic, Ray Hyman, a professor of psychology at the University of Oregon. After trading written disputes over the validity of parapsychological experiments, the interlocutors decided to collaborate on a joint study for the *Journal of Parapsychology*, analyzing the data, highlighting areas of agreement and dispute, and recommending protocols for future experiments. In an arena where arguments often devolve into rhetoric, it proved a signature moment.

"Instead of continuing with another round of our debate on the psi ganzfeld experiments," they wrote, "we decided to collaborate on a joint communiqué. The Honorton-Hyman debate emphasized the differences in our positions, many of these being technical in nature. But during a recent discussion, we realized that we possessed similar viewpoints on many issues concerning parapsychological research. This communiqué, then, emphasizes these points of agreement."**

Importantly—and in a statement that ought to serve as a general guardrail in our era of digital attack speech—Honorton and Hyman wrote: "Both critics and parapsychologists want parapsychological research to be conducted according to the best possible standards. The critic can contribute to this need only if his criticisms are informed, relevant, and responsible."

---

* "Does Psi Exist? Replicable Evidence for an Anomalous Process of Information Transfer" by Daryl J. Bem and Charles Honorton, *Psychological Bulletin*, 1994, Vol. 115, No. 1. Also see "Chapter 4: Experimental Research on Extrasensory Perception," *An Introduction to Parapsychology*, fifth edition by Irwin and Watt (McFarland, 2007): "In an assessment of the literature by Honorton (1978), 23 of 42 experiments conducted in ten different laboratories had yielded significant ESP performance under ganzfeld conditions; this success rate of 55% was far beyond that expected by chance."

** "A Joint Communiqué: The Psi Ganzfeld Controversy" by Ray Hyman and Charles Honorton, *Journal of Parapsychology*, vol. 50, December 1986.

Beyond laying down general principles and research protocols, the collaborators conducted a joint meta-analysis of key ganzfeld experiments up to that moment. “The data base analyzed by Hyman and Honorton,” wrote UC Irvine statistician Jessica Utts in 1991, “consisted of results taken from thirty-four reports written by a total of forty-seven authors. Honorton counted forty-two separate experiments described in the reports, of which twenty-eight reported enough information to determine the number of direct hits achieved. Twenty-three of the studies (55%) were classified by Honorton as having achieved statistical significance.”* The success rate was similar to Honorton’s findings in his own 1978 meta-analysis.

Notably, the psychical researcher and the skeptic wrote in their abstract: “We agree that there is an overall significant effect in this data base that cannot be reasonably explained by selective reporting or multiple analysis.” And further: “Although we probably still differ on the magnitude of the biases contributed by multiple testing, retrospective experiments, and the file-drawer problem, we agree that the overall significance observed in these studies cannot reasonably be explained by these selective factors. Something beyond selective reporting or inflated significance levels seems to be producing the nonchance outcomes. Moreover, we agree that the significant outcomes have been produced by a number of different investigators.”

In sum, here was a key psychical researcher and a leading skeptic (Hyman was among the few skeptics who conducted his own research) disagreeing over the general nature of the ESP thesis—a reasonable disagreement—but affirming that the most important psychical data of the period proved unpolluted and that the methodology of the studies in their sample reflected significant improvement from the dawn of the experiments in the early to mid-1970s. The key data, they wrote, was free from substantial error, corruption, or selective reporting. Hyman agreed that a statistically significant effect appears in the data and justifies further research. That’s all. No concession of belief in ESP. Nor was any needed. Just an informed critique by a parapsychologist and a career-long skeptic, both with significant credentials, concluding that the data and practices are normative and a statistically significant anomaly appears.

---

* “Replication and Meta-Analysis in Parapsychology” by Jessica Utts, *Statistical Science*, Vol. 6, No. 4, 1991.

It is tragic, both in terms of human pathos and intellectual advancement, that Honorton died six years after that paper was published. He was one of the only parapsychologists able to reach across the nearly unbridgeable partisan divide to a professional skeptic and create progress in dialogue and research. That process has never been repeated. Indeed, as of this writing, Wikipedia's article on the ganzfeld experiments introduces them as a "pseudoscientific technique," without sourcing.

It is worth asking why this chasm has remained so wide. Wonderful strides have occurred in parapsychology, but the advances are not what they could be. Statistician Jessica Utts has noted that during the more than 110 years since the founding of the Society for Psychical Research, "the total human and financial resources devoted to parapsychology since 1882 is at best equivalent to the expenditures devoted to fewer than two months of research in conventional psychology in the United States."* For comparison, the American Psychological Association reports that in 2017, $2 billion of the United States' $66.5 billion in federal research funding went to psychological research.**

Consider: the field of parapsychology has, since its inception worldwide, been funded in adjusted dollars at a rate of less than two months of traditional psychological experiments in the U.S. (experiments which, like much of the work in the social sciences, are routinely overturned to reflect changes or corrections in methodology). That is less than $333,500,000, or a little more than the cost of four fighter jets. This figure compares with trillions that have been spent worldwide during the same period on physics or medical research. This funding situation reflects, in part, the success of the most vociferous skeptics in disabling the legitimacy of parapsychological data. Most academic researchers steer clear, fearing damage to their reputation and ability to get other projects funded.

Even in this atmosphere, however, some scientists prevail against the tide. A historic episode occurred in 2011, which marked the publication of a paper called "Feeling the Future" by well-known research

---

* "Response to Ray Hyman's Report of September 11, 1995" by Jessica Utts, which appears in in both *Journal of Parapsychology*, 1995, Vol. 59, No. 4 and *Journal of Scientific Exploration*, 1996, Vol. 10, No. 1.

** "Federal research funding for psychology has not kept up with inflation" by Luona Lin, MPP, Peggy Christidis, PhD, and Jessica Conroy, BA, apa.org.

psychologist Daryl J. Bem of Cornell University.* For about ten years, Bem conducted a series of nine experiments involving more than 1,000 participants into precognition or "time reversing" of widely established cognitive or psychological effects, such as memorization of a list or responding to negative or erotic stimuli flashed as images on a screen. Bem's discoveries demonstrated the capacity of cognition across boundaries of linear time.

Bem, like other researchers including Dean Radin, identified factors that seem to correlate with precognition, such as the body's response to arousing or disturbing imagery. As Bem wrote of previous experiments: "Most of the pictures were emotionally neutral, but a highly arousing negative or erotic image was displayed on randomly selected trials. As expected, strong emotional arousal occurred when these images appeared on the screen, but the remarkable finding is that the increased arousal was observed to occur a few seconds before the picture appeared, before the computer had even selected the picture to be displayed."

In one of Bem's trials, subjects were asked to "guess" at erotic images alternated with benign images. "Across all 100 sessions," he wrote, "participants correctly identified the future position of the erotic pictures significantly more frequently than the 50% hit rate expected by chance: 53.1% . . . In contrast, their hit rate on the nonerotic pictures did not differ significantly from chance: 49.8% . . . This was true across all types of nonerotic pictures: neutral pictures, 49.6%; negative pictures, 51.3%; positive pictures, 49.4%; and romantic but nonerotic pictures, 50.2%."

The response to either arousing or disturbing imagery is suggestive of the *emotional stakes* required for the presence of a psi effect. Stakes must exist and strong emotions must be in play. Passion is critical. In his 1937 book, *New Frontiers of the Mind*, Rhine emphasized the role of spontaneity, confidence, comity, novelty, curiosity, and lack of fatigue. (And, as it happens, caffeine.)

But Bem's horizons extended further. In the most innovative element of his nine-part study, he set out to discover whether subjects displayed *improved recall* of lists of words that were to be practice-memorized *in the future*. In Bem's words, he probed "whether

* "Feeling the Future: Experimental Evidence for Anomalous Retroactive Influences on Cognition and Affect" by Daryl J. Bem, *Journal of Personality and Social Psychology*, 2011, Vol. 100, No. 3.

rehearsing a set of words makes them easier to recall—even if the rehearsal takes place after the recall test is given."

In experiment eight, participants were first shown a set of words and given a free recall test of those words. They were then given a set of practice exercises on a randomly selected subset of those words. The psi hypothesis was that the practice exercises would retroactively facilitate the recall of those words, and, hence, participants would recall more of the to-be-practiced words than the unpracticed words. Bem found a statistically significant improvement of recall on the lists of words studied in the near future: "The results show that practicing a set of words after the recall test does, in fact, reach back in time to facilitate the recall of those words." In short, future memorization heightened current recall.

In experiment nine, this retroactive effect was heightened when researchers added a refined practice exercise. ("A new practice exercise was introduced immediately following the recall test in an attempt to further enhance the recall of the practice words. This exercise duplicated the original presentation of each word that participants saw prior to the recall test, but only the practice words were presented.") The results improved: "This modified replication yielded an even stronger psi effect than that in the original experiment."

Unsurprisingly, Bem's 2011 paper met with tremendous controversy. Within a year of Bem's publication, a trio of professional skeptics published a rejoinder. Playing off of Bem's "Feeling the Future," their paper sported the media-friendly title, "Failing the Future."* The experimenters reran Bem's ninth experiment. They concluded, "All three replication attempts failed to produce significant effects . . . and thus do not support the existence of psychic ability."

But the authors omitted a critical detail from their own database. By deadline, they possessed two independent studies that validated Bem's results. They made no mention of these studies, despite their own ground rules for doing so. Bem wrote in his response: "By the deadline, six studies attempting to replicate the Retroactive Recall effect had been completed, including the three failed replications reported by [coauthor Stuart J.] Ritchie et al. and two other replications, *both of which successfully reproduced my original findings at*

* "Failing the Future: Three Unsuccessful Attempts to Replicate Bem's 'Retroactive Facilitation of Recall' Effect" by Stuart J. Ritchie, Richard Wiseman, Christopher C. French, *PLoS ONE*, March 2012, Volume 7, Issue 3.

statistically significant levels [emphasis added] . . . Even though both successful studies were pre-registered on [coauthor Richard] Wiseman's registry and their results presumably known to Ritchie et al., they fail to mention them in this article."

This kind of selectivity has characterized other formal skeptical efforts at debunking. In 1980, members of the Committee for the Investigation of Scientific Claims of the Paranormal (CSICOP) sought to rerun a section of research by French psychologist Michel Gauquelin (1928–1991) that correlated the planet Mars in astrological charts with champion athletic performance, a phenomena dubbed "The Mars Effect." In short, the skeptics replicated Gauquelin's study, found its data confirmatory, but obfuscated the results, leading to controversies and resignations within the organization. This is explored in detail in a journal edited by Marcello Truzzi, *Zetetic Scholar*, issues No. 9 (1982), No. 10 (1982), and No. 11 (1983).* Soon after, Truzzi's critical organ of constructive skepticism, which featured articles by skeptics and parapsychologists alike, ceased publication.

In a coda to Bem's work, as of July 2020, his experiments (including the original trials) proved confirmatory in a meta-analysis encompassing ninety experiments in thirty-three laboratories in fourteen countries, "greatly exceeding" the standard for "'decisive evidence' in support of the experimental hypothesis," as Bem and his coauthors wrote in the abstract of their follow-up paper.**

I believe that I am highlighting only the glacial tip of how parapsychological data is misreported within much of mainstream news media and large swaths of academia. The question returns: *why?* I have difficulty understanding human nature, which is, finally, the crux of the matter. Harvard psychiatrist John Mack (1929–2004), who studied testimony of alien abduction experiences, observed in an undated interview with consciousness theorist Terrence McKenna:

* As of this writing, parapsychologist George P. Hansen, has posted an invaluable PDF archive of its issues at: tricksterbook.com/Truzzi/ZeteticScholars.

** "REVISED: Feeling the future: A meta-analysis of 90 experiments on the anomalous anticipation of random future events" [version 2; peer review: 2 approved] by Daryl Bem, Patrizio E. Tressoldi, Thomas Rabeyron, Michael Duggan, first published: 30 Oct 2015, latest published: 29 Jan 2016, last updated: 23 Jul 2020, *F1000Research*.

> If you want to shatter the Western mental structures, the Western mind, so to speak, which is now permeating the whole earth in its materialist, dualistic philosophy, the way you do it is you take something that's supposed to be in the spirit world—because even in the West we can make allowance for the spirit world, we can study it through mythology, through religion, through imagination, through poetry—but the one unforgivable sin to the Western mind is when something that should be in the spirit world transgresses and shows up in the physical world. That traffic is the cardinal sin for the Western mind. So, it has great power to shatter the belief structure of the Western mind when that occurs.

In response to this perceived crisis, those who regard themselves as defenders of rationality often assume a caustic and partial disposition to dispel disruptive data. Winning becomes more important than proving. It is the antithesis of science.

For example, on January 8, 1979, theoretical physicist John Archibald Wheeler (1911–2008) stumbled in his effort to get the American Association for the Advancement of Science (AAAS) to expel the Parapsychological Association, a professional society for parapsychologists, which has been affiliated with the AAAS since 1969. In a question-and-answer period following Wheeler's address at the group's annual meeting—which included his paper "Drive the Pseudos Out of the Workshop of Science," reprinted in *The New York Review of Books* (May 17, 1979), a frequent venue for professional skeptics—the physicist falsely accused Rhine, then 83, of fraud as a student, noting "he started parapsychology that way." Although unchallenged at the Houston conference, which Rhine did not attend, the physicist stingily retracted his charge, accompanied by Rhine's response, in the July 13, 1979, issue of *Science* magazine: "Parapsychology—A Correction." If someone of Wheeler's stature loses ethical bearing and judgment in matters of parapsychology, consider how these problems beset ad hoc skeptics on Wikipedia and social media.

Cambridge biologist Rupert Sheldrake, in addition to his own research into psi phenomena, has proven determined and intrepid in responding to serial problems among professional skeptics. Sheldrake was named one of the top 100 Global Thought Leaders of the year by Switzerland's prestigious Duttweiler Institute. Yet today on Wikipedia he is called a purveyor of "pseudoscience" for his theories of biological resonance and psi. He has, for example, performed years-long studies on what we call animal instinct, including of dogs who appear aware of when their owners are headed home.* Although skeptics like to guffaw over such efforts, animal experiments are common fare in behavioral sciences. Yet Sheldrake's efforts to parse matters of instinct, a widely recognized if colloquially defined phenomenon, have encountered inquisitorial pushback of the likes suggested by Mack.**

I recognize that skeptics fear a wave of irrationality will be unleashed on the world if headlines start announcing, "Harvard Study Says ESP Is Real." Consequently, they strive against that day (although in various forms it has already come and gone). In any case, the stymied science I have described has easily cost us more than a generation of progress in parapsychology. We are at least thirty or forty years behind where we ought to be, dated from when the professional skeptical apparatus began to ramp up in the mid-1970s.

One real challenge for parapsychology—and addressing this is, I think, necessary to the field's next leap forward—is to arrive at a *theory of conveyance*. I believe the field needs a persuasive theoretical model that pulls together the effects and posits how information is transferred in a manner unbound by time, space, distance, linearity, and common sensory experience. Researchers have made preliminary steps in this direction. Advances are overdue.

---

* "A Dog That Seems to Know When His Owner Is Coming Home: Videotaped Experiments and Observations" by Rupert Sheldrake and Pamela Smart, *Journal of Scientific Exploration*, Vol. 14, No. 2, January 2000.

** The skeptics' opening salvo appeared in the paper "Can animals detect when their owners are returning home?: An experimental test of the 'psychic pet' phenomenon" by Richard Wiseman, Matthew Smith, and Julie Milton, *British Journal of Psychology*, September 1998. A general critique of the skeptical counter appears in "'Heads I Lose, Tails You Win', Or, How Richard Wiseman Nullifies Positive Results, and What to Do about It: A Response to Wiseman's (2010) Critique of Parapsychology" by Chris Carter, *Journal of the Society for Psychical Research*, 75, 2010, and an article "Richard Wiseman Denies Psychic Pet Phenomenon" by Rupert Sheldrake at sheldrake.org. For their part, the critics respond in "The 'Psychic Pet' Phenomenon: A Reply to Rupert Sheldrake" by Richard Wiseman, Matthew Smith, and Julie Milton, *Journal of the Society for Psychical Research*, 65, 2000. I realize that debates over psychical search can seem like an unending ball of twine, which they often are. As in the case of back-and-forth over Daryl J. Bem's precognition experiments, Sheldrake's studies of "morphic fields," and the ongoing reactions to J.B. Rhine's experiments, I consider this an intentional device: continual restatement of questioned or rebutted premises and claims to the point where reference material is muddied or a plethora of counterclaims gain cultural dominance, such as on Wikipedia.

In 1960, Warren Weaver, a highly regarded mathematical engineer and grant-making science foundation executive, uttered a semi-famous lament about ESP research at a panel discussion at Dartmouth College: "I find this whole field [parapsychology] intellectually a very painful one. And I find it painful essentially for the following reasons: I cannot reject the evidence and I cannot accept the conclusions."* Weaver caught hell for his statement; some colleagues questioned whether his judgment had slipped; a few others (including Dartmouth's president) privately thanked him for broaching the topic.

Weaver had toured Rhine's labs in early 1960. On February 22, he privately wrote Rhine to raise several issues. Near the top of his seven-page, single-spaced letter, Weaver made this point: "For if you could make substantial progress in analyzing, explaining, and controlling, then the problem of *acceptance* would be largely solved."** Rhine had long labored to demonstrate *effect*, Weaver wrote, but he now needed to describe *mechanics*. His letter continued:

> But for three main reasons—or at least so it seems to me—the problem of acceptance remains. First, these phenomena are so strange, so outside the normal framework of scientific understanding, that they are inherently very difficult to accept. Second, the attempts to analyze, understand, and control have not been, as yet, very successful or convincing. And third, unreasonable and stubborn as it doubtless appears to you, very many scientists are not convinced by the evidence which you consider is more than sufficient to establish the reality of the psi phenomena.

Rhine replied:

> The three main reasons you give in your analysis are recognizably correct. Had you been inclined at this point to go a step further into the intellectual background for these reasons, this might have been

* For Weaver's statement and its background, see *Unbelievable* by Stacy Horn (HarperCollins/Ecco, 2009).

** Weaver's letter and Rhine's reply are from the Parapsychology Laboratory Records, 1893–1984, Rare Book, Manuscript, and Special Collections Library, Duke University, Durham, NC.

> the point to draw upon the judgments of some of the philosophers and other commentators who have dealt with the problem of acceptance. There is an increasingly candid recognition of the difficulty as an essentially metaphysical one. Psi phenomena appear to challenge the assumption of a physicalistic universe.

Rhine was reluctant to draw theoretical conclusions from his findings. As his daughter, Sally Rhine Feather, wrote in a private communication to me of September 20, 2021: " I have never known him to have gone very far in this direction . . . But he was always so cautious at going beyond the data and had this aversion to philosophers who did so—except for the implications of the nonphysical nature of psi on which he actually speculated extremely broadly at times." She went on to quote from his 1953 book *New World of the Mind*: "It will be the task of biophysics and psychophysics to find out if there are unknown, imperceptible, extraphysical influences in nature that function in life and mind, influences which can interact with detectable physical processes."

In his response to Weaver, Rhine was referencing commonly accepted physical laws at the time. For psychical researchers today, studies in quantum theory, retrocausality, extra-dimensionality, neuroplasticity, string theory, and "morphic fields" that enable communication at the cellular level (the innovation of Rupert Sheldrake) suggest a set of physical laws that surpass the known and may serve as a kind of macroverse within which familiar mechanics are experienced. It was already clear in Rhine's era that extrasensory transmission could not be explained through a "mental radio" model, since, according to Rhine's tests and those of others, ESP is unaffected by time, distance, or physical barriers.

This returns us to the question: If the psi effect is real, *how does it work*? How does mentality exceed the obvious boundaries of sensory transmission?

Perhaps science overvalues theory. Nonetheless, I believe that it falls to each generation to venture a theory of phenomena in which it professes deep interest. That theory can ignite a debate—it can be thrown out and replaced, it can be modified—but I do not believe that researchers and motivated lay inquirers (like me) can eschew the task. For this reason, I attempted a theory of mind causation in the closing chapter of my 2018 book *The Miracle Club* entitled, "Why It Works."

Consider this: when you say the word *precognition*, it strikes many people as fantastical, as though we are entering crystal-ball territory. Why the incredulity? We already know, and have known for generations, that *linear time as we experience it is an illusion*. Einstein's theories of relativity, and experiments that have affirmed them, establish that time slows down in conditions of extreme velocity—at or approaching light speed—and in conditions of extreme gravity, like black holes. The individual traveling in a metaphorical spaceship at or near light speed experiences time slowing (not from their perspective but in comparison to those not at that speed), and this is not a mere thought exercise. Space travelers in our era, although they are obviously not approaching anywhere near that velocity, experience minute effects of time reduction.*

In short, linear time is a *necessary illusion* for five-sensory beings to get through life. Time is not an absolute. What's more, 90 years of work in quantum physics leads us to conclude that we face an infinitude of concurrent realities—not in possibility but in actuality—one of which we will localize or experience within our framework based upon perspective or when we look.

To switch tacks, string theory posits that all of reality is interconnected by vast networks of vibrating strings. Everything, from the tiniest particle to entire universes to other dimensions, is linked by these undulating strings. Hence something that occurs within another dimension not only affects what happens in the reality of the dimension that we occupy but signals an infinitude of events playing out in these other fields of existence, as in ours. We may even crisscross into these concurrent realities, occupying lives that are infinite in terms of the psyche and variable in dimensional occupancy. Experiencing data or events from other dimensions may also be extrapolated to UFO encounters or other anomalous phenomena—a topic to which I return in the closing chapter.

Perhaps an individual, either because he or she is uniquely sensitive at a given moment or experiences a reduction of sensory data while retaining awareness (as in the ganzfeld experiments), is capable of accessing information—or taking measurements—from other states or dimensions that exist along the theorized bands of

---

* E.g., see "Here's why astronauts age slower than the rest of us here on Earth" by Kelly Dickerson, *Business Insider*, August 19, 2005.

strings. We call these measurements precognition, telepathy, ESP, or psychokinesis, the last of which may be a form of pre-awareness or movement or both. But maybe that is simply *what finer measurement looks like*. It is possible that measurement not only informs but also (at least in certain cases) actualizes, localizes, and determines. *Measurement selects*. Perhaps if we gleaned what was actually going on, or exercised fuller capacities of sensation, the experience would prove overwhelming. We would be overcome with data. Hence, we may *need* a linear sense of time and a limited field of information in order to *navigate experience*.

And yet: given that we understand spacetime as flexible, is it really so strange, so violative of our current body of knowledge, that there exist *quantifiable exceptions to ordinary sensory experience*? As we document these exceptions, trace their arc, and replicate the conditions under which they occur, perhaps we approach what poet and mystic William Blake foresaw in 1790 in *The Marriage of Heaven and Hell*: "If the doors of perception were cleansed every thing would appear to man as it is: Infinite."

CHAPTER ELEVEN

The Occult Revival, Part II

The figure who most fully bridges pre- and post-World War II occultism is psychic and medical clairvoyant Edgar Cayce (1877–1945).

Although Cayce rose to prominence in the early part of the twentieth century, and died shortly before the war ended, his career and teachings underwent significant and renewed popularity in the postwar era. In both eras, Cayce's trance-based readings popularized a vast catalogue of occult topics, from astrology and numerology to alternative health and reincarnation, which enticed the public in new and accessible ways. Hence, Cayce is our pivot point in the shift of occultism from the Blavatsky-era to the current one.

Our story begins in 1910, which itself marked a changeover in Western spirituality. It saw the deaths of some of the key independent religious voices of the previous century, philosopher William James, Spiritualist prophet Andrew Jackson Davis, and Christian Science founder Mary Baker Eddy. Their deaths that year were mirrored by the rise to prominence of Cayce, a religious innovator who built upon the spiritual experiments of the nineteenth century to shape the New Age culture of the dawning one.

On October 9, 1910, the *New York Times* profiled the Christian mystic in an extensive article and photo spread, "Illiterate Man Becomes a Doctor When Hypnotized." At the time Cayce, then thirty-three, was struggling to make a living as a commercial photographer in his hometown of Hopkinsville, Kentucky, while delivering daily trance-based medical readings during which he would psychically diagnose and prescribe natural cures for the illnesses of people he had never met.

Cayce's method was to recline on a sofa or day bed, loosen his tie, belt, cuffs, and shoelaces, and enter a sleeplike trance; then, given only the name and location of a subject, the "sleeping prophet" was said to gain insight into the person's body and psychology. By the time of his death on January 3, 1945, Cayce had amassed a record of more than 14,300 clairvoyant readings for people across the nation, many of the sessions captured by stenographer Gladys Davis.

In the 1920s, Cayce's trance readings expanded beyond medicine (which remained at the core of his work) to include "life readings," in which he explored a subject's inner conflicts and needs. In these sessions, Cayce made references to astrology, karma, reincarnation, and number symbolism. Other times, he expounded on global prophecies, climate or geological changes, and the lost history of mythical cultures, such as Atlantis and Lemuria. Cayce had no recollection of any of this when he awoke, though as a devout Christian the esotericism of such material made him wince when he read the transcripts.

Contrary to news coverage, Cayce was not illiterate, but neither was he well educated. Although he taught Sunday school at his Disciples of Christ church and read through the King James Bible at least once every year, he had never made it past eighth grade of a rural schoolhouse. While his knowledge of Scripture was encyclopedic, Cayce's reading tastes were otherwise limited. Aside from spending a few on-and-off years in Texas unsuccessfully trying to use his psychical abilities to strike oil—he hoped to raise money to open a hospital based on his clairvoyant cures—Cayce rarely ventured beyond the Bible Belt environs of his childhood.

Since the tale of Jonah fleeing the word of God, prophets have been characterized as reluctant, ordinary folk plucked from reasonably satisfying lives to embark on missions that they never originally sought. In this sense, if the impending New Age—the vast culture of Eastern, esoteric, and therapeutic spirituality that exploded on the

Western scene in the 1960s and 70s—was seeking a founding prophet, Cayce could hardly be viewed as an unusual choice, but, historically, as a perfect one.

It was this Edgar Cayce—an everyday man, dedicated Christian, and uneasy mystic—whom New England college student and future biographer Thomas Sugrue encountered in 1927. When Sugrue met Cayce, the twenty-one-year-old journalism student was not someone who frequented psychics or séance parlors. Sugrue was a committed Catholic who had considered joining the priesthood. Deeply versed in world affairs and possessed of an iron determination to break into news reporting, Sugrue left his native Connecticut in 1926 for Washington and Lee University in Lexington, Virginia, which was then one of the only schools in the nation to offer a journalism degree. Sugrue later switched his major to English literature, in which he earned both bachelor's and master's degrees in four years.

As a student, Sugrue rolled his eyes at most paranormal claims or talk of ESP. Yet he met a new friend at Washington and Lee who challenged his preconceptions: the psychic's eldest son, Hugh Lynn Cayce. Hugh Lynn had planned to attend Columbia but his father's clairvoyant readings directed him instead to the oldline Virginia school. The institution counted George Washington as an early benefactor. Sugrue grew intrigued by his new friend's stories about his father, in particular the elder Cayce's theory that one person's subconscious mind could communicate with another's. The two freshmen enjoyed sparring intellectually and soon became roommates. While cautious, Sugrue wanted to meet the agrarian seer.

Edgar and his wife Gertrude, meanwhile, were laying new roots about 250 miles east of Lexington in Virginia Beach, a location the readings had also selected. The psychic spent the remainder of his life in the Atlantic coastal town, delivering twice-daily readings and developing the Association for Research and Enlightenment (A.R.E.), a still-active spiritual learning center.

Accompanying Hugh Lynn home in June 1927, Sugrue received a "life reading" from Cayce. In these psychological readings, Cayce was said to peer into a subject's "past life" incarnations and influences, analyze his character through astrology and other esoteric methods, and view his personal struggles and aptitudes. Cayce correctly identified the young writer's interest in the Middle East, a region where Sugrue later issued news reports on the founding of the modern state of Israel. But it wasn't until Christmas that Sugrue, upon receiving an intimate and uncannily accurate medical reading, became an all-out convert to Cayce's psychical abilities.

Sugrue went on to fulfill his aim of becoming a journalist, writing from different parts of the world for publications including *The New York Herald Tribune* and *The American Magazine*. But his life remained interwoven with Cayce's. Stricken by debilitating arthritis in the late 1930s, Sugrue sought help through Cayce's medical readings. From 1939 to 1941, the ailing Sugrue lived with the Cayce family in Virginia Beach, writing and convalescing. During these years of close access to Cayce, while struggling with painful joints and limited mobility, Sugrue completed *There Is a River*, the sole biography written of Cayce during his lifetime. When the book appeared in 1942 it brought Cayce national attention that surpassed even the earlier *New York Times* coverage.

Sugrue was not Cayce's only enthusiast within American letters. *There Is a River* broke through the skeptical wall of New York publishing thanks to a reputable editor, William Sloane, of Holt, Rinehart & Winston, who experienced his own brush with the Cayce readings. In 1940, Sloane agreed to consider the manuscript for *There Is a River.* He knew the biography was highly sympathetic, a fact that did not endear him to it. Sloane's wariness faded after Cayce's clairvoyant diagnosis helped one of the editor's children. Novelist and screenwriter Nora Ephron recounted the episode in an August 11, 1968, *New York Times* article. "I read it," Sloane told Ephron. "Now there isn't any way to test a manuscript like this. So I did the only thing I could do." He went on:

> A member of my family, one of my children, had been in great and continuing pain. We'd been to all the doctors and dentists in the area and all the tests were negative and the pain was still there. I wrote Cayce, told him my child was in pain and would be at a certain place at such-and-such a time, and enclosed a check for $25. He wrote back that there was an infection in the jaw behind a particular tooth. So I took the child to the dentist and told him to pull the tooth. The dentist refused—he said his professional ethics prevented him from pulling sound teeth. Finally, I told him he

> would have to pull it. One tooth more or less didn't matter, I said—I couldn't live with the child in such pain. So he pulled the tooth and the infection was there and the pain went away. I was a little shook. I'm the kind of man who believes in X-rays. About this time, a member of my staff who thought I was nuts to get involved with this took even more precautions in writing to Cayce than I did, and he sent her back facts about her own body only she could have known. So I published Sugrue's book.

Many journalists and historians since Sugrue have traced Cayce's life. Journalist and documentarian Sidney D. Kirkpatrick wrote the landmark record of Cayce in his 2000 biography *Edgar Cayce*. Historian K. Paul Johnson crafted a deeply balanced and meticulous scholarly analysis in his 1998 *Edgar Cayce in Context*. Intrepid scholar of religion Harmon Bro—who spent nine months in Cayce's company toward the end of the psychic's life—produced insightful studies of Cayce as a Christian mystic in his 1955 University of Chicago doctoral thesis (a groundbreaking work of modern scholarship on an occult subject) and later in the 1989 biography *Seer Out of Season*. While Harmon Bro died in 1997, his family has a long—and still active—literary involvement with Cayce. Bro's mother, Margueritte, was a pioneering female journalist in the first half of the twentieth century who brought Cayce national attention in her 1943 profile in *Coronet* magazine: "Miracle Man of Virginia Beach."

Sugrue's historical Edgar Cayce is the man who grew from being an awkward, soft-voiced adolescent to a national figure who never quite knew how to manage his fame—and less so how to manage money, often foregoing or deferring his usual $20 fee for readings, leaving himself and his family in a perpetual state of financial precariousness. In a typical letter from 1940, Cayce replied to a blind laborer who asked about paying in installments: "You may take care of the [fee] any way convenient to your self—please know one is not prohibited from having a reading . . . because they haven't money. If this information is of a divine source it can't be sold, if it isn't then it isn't worth any thing."

Sugrue also captured Cayce as a figure of deep Christian faith struggling to come to terms with the occult concepts that ran through his readings beginning in the early 1920s. This material extended to numerology, astrology, crystal gazing, modern prophecies, reincarnation, karma, and the story of mythical civilizations, including Atlantis and prehistoric Egypt. People who sought readings were intrigued and emotionally impacted by this material as much as by Cayce's medical diagnoses. What's more, in readings that dealt with spiritual and esoteric topics—along with the more familiar readings that focused on holistic remedies, massage, meditation, and natural foods—there began to emerge the range of subjects that formed the parameters of therapeutic New Age spirituality in the latter twentieth century.

Cayce did more than assemble a catalogue of the dawning New Age. The spiritual ideas running through his readings, combined with his own intrepid study of Scripture, supplied the basis for a universal approach to religion, which, in various ways, also spread across Western culture. This chapter of Cayce's life opened during his metaphysical explorations with an Ohio printer and Theosophist named Arthur Lammers. Cayce's collaboration with Lammers, which began in the autumn of 1923 in Selma, Alabama, marked a turn in Cayce's career from medical clairvoyant to esoteric philosopher.

Nursing his wounds after his failed oil ventures, Cayce had resettled his family in Selma, where he planned to resume work as a commercial photographer. He and Gertrude, who had long suffered her husband's absences and chaotic finances, enrolled their son Hugh Lynn, then sixteen, in Selma High School. The family, now including five-year-old Edgar Evans, settled into a new home and appeared headed for some measure of domestic normalcy. All this got upturned in September, however, when the wealthy printer Lammers arrived from Dayton. Lammers had learned of Cayce during the psychic's oil-prospecting days. He showed up at Cayce's photo studio with an intriguing proposition.

Lammers was both a hard-driving businessman and an avid seeker in Theosophy, ancient religions, and the occult. He impressed upon Cayce that the seer could use his psychical powers for more than medical diagnoses. Lammers wanted Cayce to probe the secrets of the ages: What happens after death? Is there a soul? Why are we alive? Lammers yearned to understand the meaning of the pyramids, astrology, alchemy, the "Etheric World," reincarnation, and the mystery religions of antiquity. He felt certain that Cayce's readings could part the veil.

After years of stalled progress in his professional life, Cayce was enticed by this new mission. Lammers urged Cayce to return with him to Dayton, where he promised to place the Cayce family in a new home and financially care for them. Cayce agreed, and uprooted Gertrude and their younger son, Edgar Evans. Hugh Lynn remained behind with friends in Selma to finish out the school term. Lammers' financial promises later proved elusive, and Cayce's Dayton years, which preceded his move to Virginia Beach, turned into another period of financial despair. Nonetheless, for Cayce, if not his loved ones, Dayton also marked a stage of unprecedented discovery.

Cayce and Lammers began their exploration at a downtown hotel on October 11, 1923. In the presence of several onlookers, Lammers arranged for Cayce to enter a trance and to give the printer an astrological reading. Whatever hesitancies the waking Cayce evinced over arcane subjects vanished while in his trance state. Cayce expounded on the validity of astrology even as "the Source"—what Cayce called the ethereal intelligence behind his readings—alluded to misconceptions in the Western model.

Toward the end of the reading, Cayce almost casually tossed off that it was Lammers' "third appearance on this [earthly] plane. He was once a monk." It was an unmistakable reference to reincarnation—exactly the type of insight Lammers had been seeking. In the weeks ahead, the men continued their readings, probing into Hermetic and esoteric spirituality. From a trance state on October 18, Cayce laid out for Lammers a whole philosophy of life, dealing with karmic rebirth, man's role in the cosmic order, and the hidden meaning of existence:

> In this we see the plan of development of those individuals set upon this plane, meaning the ability (as would be manifested from the physical) to enter again into the presence of the Creator and become a full part of that creation. Insofar as this entity is concerned, this is the third appearance on this plane, and before this one, as the monk. We see glimpses in the life of the entity now as were shown in the monk, in his mode of living. The body is only the vehicle ever of that spirit and soul that waft through all times and ever remain the same.

These utterances were, for Lammers, the golden key to the mysteries: a theory of eternal recurrence, or reincarnation, that identified human destiny as inner refinement through karmic cycles of rebirth, then reintegration with the source of Creation. This, the printer believed, was the hidden truth behind the Scriptural injunction to be "born again" so as to "enter the kingdom of Heaven."

"It opens up the door," Lammers told Cayce, as recounted by Sugrue. "It's like finding the secret chamber of the Great Pyramid." He insisted that the doctrine that came through the readings synchronized the great wisdom traditions: "It's Hermetic, it's Pythagorean, it's Jewish, it's Christian!" Cayce himself wasn't sure what to believe. "The important thing," Lammers reassured him, "is that the basic system which runs through all the mystery traditions, whether they come from Tibet or the pyramids of Egypt, is backed up by you. It's actually the right system . . . It not only agrees with the best ethics of religion and society, it is the source of them."

Lammers' enthusiasms aside, the religious ideas that emerged from Cayce's readings did articulate a compelling theology. Cayce's teachings sought to marry a Christian moral outlook with the cycles of karma and reincarnation central to Hinduism and Buddhism, as well as the Hermetic concept of the individual as an extension of the Divine. Cayce's references elsewhere to the causative powers of the mind—"the spiritual is the *life*; the mental is *the builder*; the physical is the *result*"*—melded his cosmic philosophy with tenets of New Thought, Christian Science, and mental healing. If there was an inner philosophy unifying the world's religions, Cayce came as close as any modern person to defining it.

Religious traditionalists could rightly object: just where are Cayce's "insights" coming from? Are they the product of a Higher Power or merely the overactive imagination of a religious outlier? Cayce himself wrestled with these questions. His response was that all of his ideas, whatever their source, had to square with Gospel ethics in order to be judged vital and right. Cayce addressed this in a talk that he delivered in his normal waking state in Norfolk, Virginia, in February of 1933, just before he turned fifty-six:

* From a Cayce reading of July 28, 1928.

> Many people ask me how I prevent undesirable influences entering into the work I do. In order to answer that question let me relate an experience I had as a child. When I was between eleven and twelve years of age I had read the Bible through three times. I have now read it fifty-six times. No doubt many people have read it more times than that, but I have tried to read it through once for each year of my life. Well, as a child I prayed that I might be able to do something for the other fellow, to aid others in understanding themselves, and especially to aid children in their ills. I had a vision one day which convinced me that my prayer had been heard and answered.

Cayce's "vision" has been described differently by different biographers. Sugrue recounted the episode occurring when Cayce was about twelve in the woods outside his home in western Kentucky. Cayce himself placed it in his bedroom at age thirteen or fourteen. One night, this adolescent boy who had spoken of childhood conversations with "hidden friends," and who hungrily read through Scripture, knelt by his bed, and prayed for the ability to help others.

Just before drifting to sleep, Cayce recalled, a glorious light filled the room and a feminine apparition appeared at the foot of his bed telling him: "Thy prayers are heard. You will have your wish. Remain faithful. Be true to yourself. Help the sick, the afflicted."* Cayce did not realize until years later what form his answered prayers would take—and even in his twenties it took him years to adjust to being a medical clairvoyant. As his new powers took shape, he labored to use Scripture as his moral vetting mechanism. Yet he consistently attributed his information to the "Source" and, as seen earlier, the "Akashic records" as described, albeit indirectly, by Blavatsky.

In his continued wish to square his ideas with Scripture, Cayce reinterpreted the ninth chapter of the Gospel of John, in which Christ heals a man who had been blind from birth, to validate ideas of karma and reincarnation. When disciples ask Christ whether it was the man's sins or those of his parents that caused his affliction, the master replies enigmatically: "Neither hath this man sinned, nor his parents: but that the works of God should be made manifest in him"

---

* *The Lost Memoirs of Edgar Cayce*, compiled and edited by A. Robert Smith (A.R.E. Press, 1997).

(John 9:3). In Cayce's reasoning, since the blind man was born with his disorder, and Christ exonerates both the man and his parents, his disability must be karmic baggage from a previous incarnation. Cayce made comparable interpretations of passages from Matthew and Revelation.

Neither Cayce nor Sugrue lived long enough to witness the full reach of Cayce's ideas. The psychic died at age sisty-seven in Virginia Beach shortly at the start of 1945, less than three years after *There Is a River* appeared. Sugrue updated the book that year. After struggling with years of illness, the biographer died at age forty-five on January 6, 1953, at the Hospital for Joint Diseases in New York.

The first popularizations of Cayce's work began to appear in 1950 with the publication of *Many Mansions*, a work on reincarnation and karma by Gina Cerminara, a longtime Cayce devotee. But it wasn't until 1956 that Cayce's name took full flight across the culture with the appearance of the mass bestseller *The Search for Bridey Murphy* by Morey Bernstein. Sugrue's editor Sloane, having since warmed to parapsychology, published both Cerminara and Bernstein.

Bernstein was an iconic figure. A Coloradan of Jewish descent and an Ivy League-educated dealer in heavy machinery and scrap metal, he grew inspired by Cayce's career and became an amateur hypnotist. In the early 1950s, Bernstein conducted a series of experiments with a Pueblo, Colorado, housewife who, while under a hypnotic trance, appeared to regress into a past-life persona: an early nineteenth century Irish country girl named Bridey Murphy. The entranced homemaker spoke in an Irish brogue and recounted to Bernstein comprehensive details of her life more than a century earlier. Suddenly, reincarnation or recurrence—an ancient Vedic concept about which Americans had heard little before World War II—was the latest craze, ignited by Bernstein, an avowed admirer of Cayce, to whom the hypnotist devoted two chapters in his book.

Also in the 1950s, Beat icon Neal Cassady introduced the Cayce readings to his literary circle, including Jack Kerouac, who was having none of it. In 1992, poet Allen Ginsberg recalled, "Jack Kerouac's interest in Buddhism began after he spent some time with Neal Cassady, who had taken on an interest in the local California variety of New Age spiritualism, particularly the work of Edgar Cayce. Kerouac mocked Cassady as a sort of homemade American 'Billy Sunday with a suit' for praising Cayce, who went into trance states of sleep and then read what were called the Akashic records, and gave medical advice to the petitioners who came to ask him questions with answers which involve reincarnation."*

In the following decade, California journalist Jess Stearn renewed interest in Cayce with his 1967 bestseller, *Edgar Cayce, The Sleeping Prophet*. With the mystic '60s in full swing and the youth culture embracing all forms of alternative or Eastern spirituality—from Zen to yoga to psychedelics—Cayce, while not explicitly tied to any of this, rode the new vogue. During this period, Hugh Lynn Cayce emerged as a formidable custodian of his father's legacy, shepherding to market a new wave of instructional guides based on the Cayce teachings, from dream interpretation to drug-free methods of relaxation to the spiritual uses of colors, crystals, and numbers. Cayce's name became a permanent fixture on the cultural landscape.

The 1960s and '70s also saw a new generation of channeled literature from higher intelligences such as Seth, Ramtha, and even the figure of Christ in *A Course in Miracles*. The last of these was a profound and enduring lesson series, channeled beginning in 1965 by Columbia University research psychologist Helen Schucman. A concordance of tone and values existed between Cayce's readings and *A Course in Miracles*. Cayce's devotees and the Course's wide array of readers discovered that they had a lot in common; members of both cultures blended seamlessly, attending many of the same seminars, growth centers, and metaphysical churches.

Likewise, congruency emerged between Cayce's world and followers of the Twelve Steps of Alcoholics Anonymous. Starting in the 1970s, Twelve-Steppers of various stripes became a familiar presence at Cayce conferences and events in Virginia Beach. Cayce's universalistic religious message dovetailed with the purposefully flexible references to a Higher Power in the "Big Book," *Alcoholics Anonymous*, written in 1939. AA cofounder Bill Wilson, his wife Lois, his confidant Bob Smith, and several other early AAs were deeply versed in mystical and mediumistic teachings—extending to Cayce.

In a recently unearthed piece of correspondence, Bill Wilson wrote to Hugh Lynn Cayce, on November 14, 1951: "Long an admirer

* "Negative Capability: Kerouac's Buddhist Ethic" by Allen Ginsberg, *Tricycle*, Fall 1992.

of your father's work, I'm glad to report that a number of my A.A. friends in this area [New York City], and doubtless in others, share this interest." He went on to comment revealingly about contacts that Hugh Lynn had proposed between the Cayce organization and AA:

> As you might guess, we have seen much of phenomenalism in A.A., also an occasional physical healing. But nothing, of course, in healing on the scale your father practiced it . . . At the present time, I find I cannot participate very actively myself. The Society of Alcoholics Anonymous regards me as their symbol. Hence it is imperative that I show no partiality whatever toward any particular religious point of view—let alone physic [sic] matters. Nevertheless I think I well understand the significance of Edgar Cayce and I shall look forward to presently hearing how some of my friends may make a closer contact.

All three works—the Cayce readings, *A Course in Miracles*, and *Alcoholics Anonymous*—demonstrated a shared sense of religious liberalism, an encouragement that all individuals seek their own conception of a Higher Power, and a permeability intended to accommodate the broadest expression of religious outlooks and backgrounds. The free-flowing tone of the therapeutic spiritual movements of the twentieth and early twenty-first centuries had a shared antecedent, if not a direct ancestry, in the Cayce readings.

Cayce's role as an occult catalyst made a particular impact on the popular culture. But other voices and figures emerged from rarer and less visible wells of thought—with equally lasting, if subtler, results.

Primary among them was British graphic artist, occultist, and writer Austin Osman Spare (1886–1956). Through Spare's experimentation with breaking structures, rejecting formalism, and seeking to alter reality as we experience it in fleshly forms (our only means of experiencing it, he reckoned), he devised an anti-system of externalizing will, creating a visual language for the nonrational, and harnessing magick in a way that required no belief in the extraphysical—or in anything other than results.

I earlier quoted French mind theorist Émile Coué, who ventured a juxtaposition that applies to Spare's way of thought: "The French mind prefers first to discuss and argue on the fundamentals of a principle before inquiring into its practical adaptability to every-day life. The American mind, on the contrary, immediately sees the possibilities of it, and seeks . . . to carry the idea further even than the author of it may have conceived."* This approach of radical application animated Spare. The artist was, in a sense, a prime example of William James's philosophy of pragmatism: theory is far secondary to outcome. Spare, like James, desired measurable, if not always repeatable, results.

Born to a working-class family—including a doting policeman father who nurtured his son's artistic gifts—Spare attained a spiral of off-and-on critical and gallery success as a painter and illustrator, but never enough to lift him from near-poverty, especially after losing his home in the Nazi bombing of London. According to rumor, the Fuhrer in 1936 asked Spare for a portrait to which the impoverished occultist replied, "If you are supermen let me be forever animal."**

Although Spare believed in the existence of a disincarnate world, one of the most remarkable aspects of his philosophy, emerging in nascence around 1904 while he was a teen, was his conditioned idealism. He later wrote,

> All emanations are through the flesh and nothing has reality for us without it. The soul is ever unknowable because we can only realize by finite form in Time-Space. So, whatever you attribute to the inconceivable is your Ego, as conceived. The mind and its great thought-stream determines everything and permits all things conceivable as possible."***

As the artist saw it, reality is as present as flesh and knowable only through its material experiences and agencies. This was a concern that also frustrated Kant and Hegel: that psyche, whatever its perceptions, is capable only of experiencing itself. Hence for Spare,

---

* *My Method, Including American Impressions* (Doubleday, Page & Company, 1923).

** *Austin Osman Spare: The Occult Life of London's Legendary Artist* by Phil Baker (2011, 2014 North Atlantic Books).

*** *The Formulae of Zos Vel Thanatos*, 1954.

the task of the occult operation is to bridge the gap between what he deemed *Kia*—an all-pervading lifeforce similar to Tao—and *Zos*—the manifestation of energy in self.

"Magic, for Spare, is about bypassing the ordinary mind and harnessing the innate abilities of one's subconscious," writes Jake Dirnberger in his excellent 2020 companion *The Pocket Austin Osman Spare*. This being so, the rational mind cannot perform the operation. Another language—symbolic, emotional, and primal—is required.

Spare discovered this bridging force as sexuality, symbol, and interruption of rationality. Around 1913, his insight delivered the artist to his most radical, practical, and enduring method: creation of a *sigil* (Latinate for "little sign"), a symbol of desire charged with sexual energy or transcending emotion, including ecstasy or fear. Spare's method was simplicity itself. You write a concise statement of your desire, generally no more than a short sentence; cross out duplicate letters; and assemble the remaining characters into an abstract symbol. Another method shared by author and magician Grant Morrison is to write your desire, cross out vowels, and then cross out repeating consonants. Devise your symbol from there.

"Turn that thing into a little image," Morrison says, ". . . and keep reducing it down until it looks magical. And there are no rules for this thing. Do it until looks magical. At that point you now have a sigil. A sigil will work—you can project desire into reality and change reality. It works."*

The most popular method for projecting desire onto your sigil was extrapolated by influential occultist Peter J. Carroll (b. 1953): The "charging" of a sigil involves reaching sexual climax over the symbol, usually through masturbation. Other methods of ecstasy are available, including meditation, drugs, and any kind of extrarational state, such as that brought on through dance or movement. But masturbation, due to obvious ease and pleasure, has carried the day.

Themes of sex, disincarnate beings, and occasional grotesqueries dominate many of Spare's finely wrought drawings. But he recounted one remarkable occult episode in which his will was concretized by fear for survival. In a story recounted by Spare's impeccable biographer Phil Baker, Spare said that as a young man,

---

* "Grant Morrison Disinfo Con Lecture Magick Terence Mckenna CHAOS MAGIK," October 28, 2015, YouTube.

> he had been staying in the country with some friends when he had gone out for a walk on his own. He became lost and it started to snow, and as night came down he realised he was in trouble. He was overcome with cold and exhaustion by the time a pony cart appeared, and a man helped him on board and took him to an inn. The door opened, and another man beckoned him to enter.
>
> Once inside, he was given the finest wine he had ever tasted. The snow stopped, the innkeeper showed him the way home, and it was only later that he began to wonder at the man's old-fashioned clothing. He thought perhaps this was how they dressed in the country. His friends had meanwhile been worried about him, and they insisted there was no inn where he described it. He could show them, he said, and the next day they followed the tracks of the pony cart to a snow-covered mound; all that remained of a building that had been demolished outside of living memory. And, as Spare's later investigations disclosed, there had been an inn on that very spot some three hundred years earlier.
>
> And yet the wine had been real enough, he could be sure about that. "Who knows," he said, "but that at some time in my youth, whilst fooling about with sigils, I did not at some time wish to taste wine such as the gods savoured?"

Lest this story be filed under "careful what you wish for . . . ," occultist Kenneth Grant (1924–2011), who served as a friend, curator, and occasional muse to Spare and Aleister Crowley, adds the broadened observation: "The wish had been materialized at a time when Spare's mundane consciousness had been nullified by fatigue and cold, yielding one of the most vivid occult experiences of his life."* In Spare's view, magick reaches us only through the agency of unbridled passion, a perspective in line, more or less, with J.B. Rhine, Carl Jung, and William James.

But why should any of this be? And, assuming the accuracy of the telling, what is actually occurring? There exist only theories, many borne of personal experience of the practitioner. In the final chapter, I describe my own wager of how emotionalized thought or perspective *selects* a localized experience from among infinite possibilities. This may be exactly what the charged sigil does. Or, if one believes that

* *Images and Oracles of Austin Osman Spare* (Muller, 1975).

Zos—the physical man—can function as a capillary for Kia—which can be compared to Schopenhauer's "light of speculative thought," Mesmer's "animal magnetism," Edward Bulwer-Lytton's "Vril," or Crowley's "True Will"—it follows that the sigil can serve as an instigator and targeting device. "Sigils are monograms of thought," Spare wrote, "for the summoning of energy."*

In the 1970s, Spare's work became associated with the term *chaos magick* as used by Carroll in his 1978 book *Liber Null.* Chaos magick represents a cutup and reassembling of self-selected techniques (or what I, in a slightly different fashion, call anarchic magick). Seen from the perspective of chaos theory, to which it is not directly related, chaos magick means that if you alter one particle of existence you necessarily alter everything; there exists complexity and determinism within apparent chaos, an insight that has its earliest roots in pre-Socratic philosopher Heraclitus (c. sixth century BC). It is impossible for an interconnected reality to reflect otherwise. Hence, the chaos practitioner *need not believe in any of the aforementioned concepts or in any form of extra-physicality.* One could view the sigil simply as an exotic element introduced into the coding of life. This novel coding could involve arousing the subconscious, which seeks out confirmations of perspective, suggestion, or, as Spare called it, "true belief." In this vein, chaos magick could be seen as a materialistic operation. This reflects the terrific *freedom from concept* in Spare's thought. "Spare was a self-willed, anarchic character who not only couldn't understand organization but distrusted it on principle," Baker writes. As someone who has been expelled from the garden of supposed alternative spiritual movements for queries deemed heterodox, I can more than sympathize.**

Science is a means of methodological replication. But because something does not repeat—could Spare ever again find his ghostly inn (if he ever did)?—doesn't mean it fails the test of reality. When asked whether ESP is *real*, experimenter J.B. Rhine would reframe the question to say instead that it *occurs*. Spare was prepared to believe in extraphysical phenomena, if not its repetition. "Many experiences I cannot reproduce and in some cases even re-vision," he acknowledged in *The Formulae of Zos Vel Thanatos.* He continued, "My impression

* *The Book of Pleasure (Self Love): Psychology of Ecstasy* (1913).

** See my essay "How It Feels to Be Blacklisted" in *Uncertain Places* (inner Traditions, 2022).

was that many [mediums] had experienced phenomena but that they had no control over them, and in trying to relive [the experience] and convince others they resorted to fraud."

I uncomfortably encountered a variant of this during my years in book publishing where some authors of paranormal-themed accounts would freely—and often without disclosure until pressed—use devices of composite characters, rearranged time-lines, or embellished (or even fabricated) events to convey what they *believed* true. I have seen this among channelers. One deceased author, noted earlier, even falsified a Nostradamus quatrain. "You must understand that there is an entertainment quality to this," he told me. "I do understand," I replied. "But not here." Because of the natural resistance to paranormal material given its exception to commonly observed experience, I consider the onus all the greater on the author exploring anomalies to deal plainly. Such an example appears, I believe, in Whitley Streiber's classic 1987 memoir of supernatural visitors and abduction, *Communion*.

Spare's release from form presented a distinct appeal to many post-war artists. "Art," writes Phil Baker, "has long been bound up with magic—from cave paintings, which seem to have had magical purpose, to William Burroughs's dictum that 'writing is about making it happen'—and this was more than usually the case with Spare."

In a sense, it was not Crowley but Spare who closed the final chapter on the Golden Dawn era, filled with so much effort, promise, and extraordinary figures, yet so wed to liturgy, memorization, and ceremony. "For this reason," Burroughs wrote, "I consider the Egyptian and Tibetan books of the dead, with their emphasis on ritual and knowing the right words, totally inadequate. There are no right words . . ."* For Burroughs and his immediate circle, form ultimately represented systems of control, apparent throughout all media and social structure.

Burroughs was frustrated by how, with few exceptions, dictatory exposition remained the chief style in writing. In 1959, painter Brion Gysin, encountering Burroughs in Paris (the two previously meet in

* *Ah Pook Is Here* (John Calder, 1979).

Tangier), crystalized the matter for him, observing: "Writing is fifty years behind painting." Together, the two men devised and popularized a method, or anti-method, for a process implicit in some earlier works of literature, notably T.S. Eliot's "The Waste Land," known as *cut-up*. The technique involved dicing up and rearranging a text, thus summoning an unknown, subliminal, or even oracular meaning. Burroughs summarized the matter in the 1978 book he coauthored with Gysin, *The Third Eye*:

> A friend, Brion Gysin, an American poet and painter, who has lived in Europe for thirty years, was, as far as I know, the first to create cut-ups. His cut-up poem, "Minutes to Go," was broadcast by the BBC and later published in a pamphlet. I was in Paris in the summer of 1960; this was after the publication there of *Naked Lunch*. I became interested in the possibilities of this technique, and I began experimenting myself. Of course, when you think of it, "The Waste Land" was the first great cut-up collage, and Tristan Tzara had done a bit along the same lines. Dos Passos used the same idea in "The Camera Eye" sequences in *U.S.A.* I felt I had been working toward the same goal; thus it was a major revelation to me when I actually saw it being done.

For Burroughs, cut-up offered not only a freedom from dominant literary form but a means of expression and perception that violated systemic boundaries of Western conditioning. Again, in *The Third Eye* he noted: "Either-or thinking just is not accurate thinking. That's not the way things occur, and I feel the Aristotelian construct is one of the great shackles of Western civilization. Cut-ups are a movement toward breaking this down."

This reflects a point from chapter two: the insufficiency or ill-suitedness of Aristotelian absolutes in dealing with the occult, which is based in the ineffable. Any thinker who rejects, prima facie, the extraphysical—itself a position of sentiment versus reason—cannot abide suspension of absolutes. Burroughs and Gysin, preceded by Eliot, offered an offramp from this way of thought in both artistic and intellectual efforts. But this should not imply a release from excellence. Again, Burroughs: "A page of Rimbaud cut up and rearranged will give you quite new images. Rimbaud images—real Rimbaud images—but new ones." And since our psyches are constantly receiving diffuse stimuli, cut-ups, the writer observed, "make explicit a psychosensory process that is going on all the time anyway."

How exactly does cut-up work as a magickal or oracular technique—by which I mean capacity to approach and participate in the "Third Mind"? During this writing, I decided to revisit a bowl of cut-up phrases that I keep on a mantlepiece. About a year earlier, when considering themes and titles for a book in progress, I wrote down and cut-up phrases or words that were meaningful to me and scattered them on the floor to see what would emerge. In an observation that intersects with the ideas of the Jung circle, Burroughs wrote, "Perhaps events are pre-written and pre-recorded and when you cut word lines the future leaks out."*

For my exercise, on January 29, 2023, I pulled words from the bowl and rearranged them: "Deity of Chaos." The remaining words were "Mind Force." It struck me as propitious that these terms appeared at the exact moment I was immersed in the section on chaos magick in this book. I reckon that the "Mind Force"—again, *light of speculative thought* or multivarious correspondences referenced in this book—is the "Deity of Chaos": the psyche takes in, assembles, and prioritizes endless impressions. Their stoppage means stoppage of life. These impressions are the alchemist's raw matter—they are, in a sense, *chaos*. The individual as creator— *as above, so below*—has some capacity to refine this material, bringing protean tendencies to bear. This is the circle of magick. My byway of exploration, and the forces which may momentarily flash within it, results from cut-up.

Cut-up may also reveal meanings not immediately apparent or directly stated. "This," writes Matthew Levi Stevens, "was an attitude he would extend increasingly to all communications, and eventually all relationships: an early tape-recording from the Beat Hotel has Burroughs and his conspirators discussing a 'creepy letter' which Gysin says he 'can't bear to hear again'—but it is explained that Burroughs 'is going to cut it up—then we'll hear what he's *really* saying!'"

n a different but related tack, this passage of dialogue appears in the 1977 Burroughs-Gysin book, *The Third Mind*:

* *The Magical Universe of William S. Burroughs* by Matthew Levi Stevens (Mandrake, 2014).

14. *You and Brion have described your collaborations over the years as the products of a "third mind." What's the source of this concept?*

BURROUGHS: A book called *Think and Grow Rich.*

GYSIN: It says that when you put two minds together . . .

BURROUGHS: . . . there is always a third mind . . .

GYSIN : . . . a third and superior mind . . .

BURROUGHS: . . . as an unseen collaborator.

GYSIN: That is where we picked up the title. Our book *The Third Mind* is about all the cut-up materials.

This passage suggests a truth worth pausing over, which is that highly experimental artists like Burroughs, Gysin, and later artist-musician Genesis P-Orridge, integrated into their work the essential ethic of cut-up—which is that valuable material doesn't necessarily reach you through ordinary or proscribed channels, including what are considered "serious" categories of literature.

As alluded, standards and measurement matter—there exist exemplary and piss-poor efforts in every field or genre—but to categorically reject any "type" of expression is to self-hobble. This is why I consider it insufficient to rank and thereby exclude modes of thought. For example, shunning the label "self-help," as Hill's mega-selling book can be aptly described, means cutting-off versus cutting-up impressions.

"Rejected stones" not infrequently conceal remarkable insights. One of Napoleon Hill's such insights—discussed more freely in the decades following his death in 1970—is "sex transmutation." This bit of unexpected magick bears examination.

Writing in 1937 in *Think and Grow Rich*, Hill observed that the urge toward sexuality is the creative impulse of life expressing itself through the individual. Hill also taught—in a lesson that corresponds to other ancient and modern traditions including Taoism and Tantra—that sexuality extends far beyond matters of intimacy and reproduction; *sexuality expresses itself in every facet of human creativity.*

Through this creative impulse we are driven to function as generative beings. Whenever you strive to actualize your visions in the world you are, Hill wrote, operating from this vital, life-building impulse.

Once you cultivate this awareness, Hill argued, you can *transmute* the sexual urge into improved performance, focus, and insight in matters of wealth, art, or anything on which you elect to focus. Like Spare's, Hill's method is enticingly simple. Also, like Spare's, it requires no belief—including in the terms used (call them metaphors)—only experience and result. The method works this way: *When you feel the sexual urge, redirect your thoughts and energies along the lines of a cherished task or project. Through the mental act of redirecting yourself from physical expression to creative expression you harness and place the sexual urge at the back of your efforts.* Doing so, Hill taught, adds vigor, creativity, and intellectual prowess to your work.

Hill did not call for celibacy or physical sublimation of sexuality. He underscored the importance of sex not only as a physical release but also for therapeutic and stress-reducing purposes, as well as a core part of intimacy. Rather, his point is that you are capable, at times of your choosing, to harness this innate life force to elevate your energies and abilities in a manner far beyond what you may consider possible.

Understanding sexuality as a supraliminal force squares with psychical researcher Frederic Myers' observation on the nature of genius. Toward the end of his life in 1901, the British scientist came to believe that genius, or remarkable inspiration and application of ideas, possessed an origin beyond the everyday mind. Myers called it the *supraliminal mind*, a precursor and adjunct to concepts of the unconscious and subconscious. In his posthumously published 1903 treatise *Human Personality and Its Survival of Bodily Death*, Myers wrote:

> Genius—if that vaguely used word is to receive anything like a psychological definition—should rather be regarded as a power of utilising a wider range than other men can utilise of faculties in some degree innate in all;—a power of appropriating the results of subliminal mentation to subserve the supraliminal stream of thought;—so that an "inspiration of Genius" will be in truth a *subliminal uprush*, an emergence into the current of ideas which the man is consciously manipulating of other ideas which he has not consciously originated, but which have shaped themselves beyond his will, in profounder regions of his being. I shall urge that there is

> here no real departure from normality; no abnormality, at least in the sense of degeneration; but rather a fulfilment of the true norm of man, with suggestions, it may be, of something *supernormal*;—of something which transcends existing normality as an advanced stage of evolutionary progress transcends an earlier stage.

In short, Myers saw genius as an interplay of subliminal/subconscious mind—a concept he helped establish—and a supraliminal mind, or what Hill termed Infinite Intelligence. In Myers' view, this interplay produces genius, a perspective in harmony with Hill's. Indeed, Hill ventured that figures considered geniuses, icons, or impresarios often rise to that level of excellence because sex transmutation is at the back of their efforts.

For geniuses, Hill used the arcane plural *genii.* Genii dates to Roman-Latin usage. It means not only intellectual prowess but also suggests the Roman meaning—updated by Myers—that genius itself is a gift bestowed by higher spirits or daemons. The same term appears as *jinn* or genie in Arab folklore and culture, again referencing a spirit capable of possessing the individual or bestowing supernatural power. This further suggests the collaborative intermingling Hill saw between numinous forces and individual striving . All of these post-war figures traced an arc of connection between ineffability, sexuality, and creativity.

In years of working with Hill's ideas, I have come across no passage or statement indicating his familiarity with or reference to any of the sex magick practices or progenitors I've referenced. But that the success coach—oddly enough—can be considered part of their cultural conversation is without doubt. This is one of many ways in which occult ideas were entering a new stage of populism. Terms and labels might be jettisoned or retooled but ideas that emerged through occult and mystical channels were finding their way into widely circulated books and programs.

It should be noted that Burroughs advocated research into practical applications of the sex energy concept of *orgone,* pioneered in the 1930s by Austrian-American psychoanalyst Wilhelm Reich (1897–1957). Although it can be reasonably asked whether Hill knew of Reich's work, especially given the corresponding timeline, I have found no such evidence.

I noted earlier that the initials of NASA's Jet Propulsion Laboratory, JPL, are sometimes said to synchronously signify *Jack Parsons Lives*, for its cofounder. Jack Whiteside Parsons (1914–1952) was, by all accounts, a brilliant scientist and rocket engineer, as well as one of the most storied, mythically fascinating, and remarkable occultists of the twentieth century.

The scion of Caltech reported his interest in magick from young age, writing in his ritualist memoir *The Book of Babalon* in 1946: "And I was shown myself as a boy of thirteen in this life, invoking Satan and showing cowardice when He appeared. And I was asked: 'Will you fail again?' and I replied 'I will not fail.'" He kept his vow. Parsons continued: "The awakening interest in chemistry and science prepared the counterbalance for the coming magical awakening, the means of obtaining prestige and livelihood in the formative period, and the scientific method necessary for my manifestation."

To distant appearances, there was an abiding normalcy to the handsome young scientist. He met his first wife, Helen Northrup, at a Los Angeles church dance in 1934; the two were married the following year before Jack turned twenty-one. But within the neat and orderly engineer beat a rebel's heart. During his work on rocket development at Caltech in the late 1930s, Jack grew interested in Marxism and fell in with clusters of both scientists and science-fiction aficionados who held Communist or Marxist beliefs, an association that later caused him considerable professional difficulty.

In the heady sunshine of Southern California, however, Jack's beliefs and interests returned to those that he nurtured as a youth. He and Helen were introduced to the still-living Aleister Crowley's philosophy of Thelema, and in early 1941 formally joined Pasadena's Agape Lodge, an American redoubt of Crowley's O.T.O. For Jack, Crowley's rituals provided a magickal blueprint that did not clash with science but, in fact, formed a correlative circuitry for the outpicturing of will; his magickal research confirmed his lifelong conviction that alchemy and ritual were themselves primeval forms of modern engineering, medicine, and mathematics. Jack was encouraged in these connections by the implications of quantum mechanics, which pointed toward the perceptual basis of reality and coexistence of different dimensions and intersections of time, a logic demanded by the thought models of scientist Erwin Schrödinger the previous decade.

In a sense, Parsons compares with another twentieth century inventor-seeker, alternating current (AC) pioneer Nicola Tesla (1856–1943). As Erik Davis observes in *TechGnosis*:

> . . . the reason that Tesla cuts such an enigmatic figure is that he seemed to possess an intuitive, visceral, almost supernatural knowledge of the electromagnetic mysteries, and investigators are still picking up the strings he left dangling. According to Tesla's own memoirs, his inventions sometimes popped into his head fully formed, as if he had simply downloaded the prototypes from the astral plane. The notion of a motor capable of generating alternating current—perhaps his most important invention—came to the young engineering student one day when he was strolling with a friend in a park in Budapest. Moved by the stunning sunset, Tesla recited a verse from, of all things, Goethe's *Faust*; in a moment "the idea came like a flash of lightning."

This last observation, aside from the evocative reference to Goethe's *Faust*, comports with Frederic Myers' previously described conception of genius.

The term *agape* is Greek for divine love—and the Pasadena O.T.O. lodge's activities encouraged open relationships, which led to Jack and Helen's marital undoing. While Helen was traveling in June 1941, Jack commenced an affair with her seventeen-year-old sister, Sara, also called Betty. Helen began an extramarital relationship of her own, with both couples sometimes intermingling at the communal home Jack maintained in Pasadena, dubbed the Parsonage.

During this period, Jack also became a valued correspondent to Crowley, not only because of his formidable intellect and high reputation within the Los Angeles circle ("Jack is one hell of a nice guy and a number-one rocket engineer," opined the otherwise skeptical science-fiction writer Robert Heinlein) but because the scientist was now dedicating a significant portion of his income to supporting the Great Beast in his later years and declining health at his boarding home outside of London.* Jack was also supporting Helen and her new partner, but the pressures of their simultaneous estrangement and domestic proximity proved too great, resulting in divorce in 1946.

Into this messy situation entered a man who would render it far messier still: science-fiction writer, demobilized Naval officer, and future founder of Scientology, L. Ron Hubbard (1911–1986).

Drawn to the bohemian and communal enclave of the Parsonage, Hubbard appeared at Jack's door in August of 1945. As artist Art Spiegelman wrote in a different context, "And here my troubles began." Hubbard took up residence with the Parsons circle. With his stories of wild adventure, intellectual intrigues, and boundless self-confidence, the garrulous fantasy writer immediately either repelled or attracted the home's denizens. Jack himself was smitten. His admiration for Hubbard was, at least outwardly, undaunted by the first of several shakeups the newcomer brought to the household: Hubbard quickly began an affair with Jack's erstwhile paramour Betty. Friends suspected that Jack was merely concealing his jealousy, which would have been considered a weakness with the Agape Lodge of which he had recently taken charge.

He enthusiastically shared news of his new friend in a letter to Crowley on January 26, 1946:

> About 3 months ago I met Capt. L. Ron Hubbard, a writer and explorer of whom I had known for some time. He is a gentleman, red hair, green eyes, honest and intelligent we have become great friends. He moved in with me about 2 months ago, and although Betty and I are still friendly, she has transferred her sexual affections to him. Although he has no formal training in Magick he has an extraordinary amount of experience and understanding in the field. From some of his experiences I deduce he is in direct touch with some higher intelligence, possibly his Guardian Angel. He is the most Thelemic person I have ever met and is in complete accord with our own principles. He is also interested in establishing the New Aeon [as foreseen in Crowley's *Book of the Law*], but for cogent reasons I have not introduced him to the Lodge. We are pooling our resources in a partnership which will act as a parent company to

* Heinlein is quoted from a 1949 letter in George Pendle's impressive 2005 biography of Parsons, *Strange Angel*.

> control our business ventures. I think I have made a great gain and as Betty and I are the best of friends there is little loss. I cared for her rather deeply but I have no desire to control her emotions, and I can I hope control my own. I need a magical partner. I have many experiments in mind.*

Still sharp in his wits, Crowley was immediately suspicious of this "honest and intelligent" gentleman of red hair and green eyes who so quickly and fully inserted himself into Parsons' intimacies and finances. Indeed, by the time he wrote Crowley, the trusting scientist had already begun collaborating with Hubbard on a series of magickal rituals he called the "Babalon Working," intended both to bring the jilted Parsons a new lover and—more importantly—to produce with her a "magickal child" or "moonchild" who would commence Crowley's Aeon of Horus written about in *The Book of the Law*.

First on his own at the Parsonage and later with Hubbard in the Mojave Desert, Parsons from early January to early March 1946 threw himself into the Babalon Working, named for the harbinger Crowley termed the "Scarlet Woman" in his prophetic work.

Parsons employed elements of Enochian magick as devised by John Dee. Dressed in robes, sporting a wand and swords, listening to Prokofiev's Second Violin Concerto, and possibly imbibing narcotics, Parsons consecrated magickal tablets with his own blood and semen. One night during Jack's rituals at the Parsonage, his ostensible friend Hubbard felt himself ethereally struck on the right shoulder; his adjoining arm remained paralyzed for the night. Other times, the home's electricity went out and other housemates reported bangs and furniture toppled. Windstorms came and went. As Jack recorded in *The Book of Babalon*:

> *January 5*. A strong windstorm began suddenly about the middle of the first invocation.
>
> *Jan. 6*. Invoked as before. Windstorm continued intermittently all day and night.
>
> *Jan. 7.* Invoked twice. Wind subsided. Used Prokofief [sic] Violin Concerto No. 2 as musical background.
>
> *Jan. 8*. Invoked twice, using blood.

* "The Babalon Working 1946: L. Ron Hubbard, John Whiteside Parsons, and the Practice of Enochian Magic" by Henrik Bogdan, *Numen*, 2016, Vol. 63, No. 1.

> *Jan. 9.* Invoked twice, replenishing material basis.
> *Jan 10.* Invoked twice. I retired about 11 pm, and was awakened at 12 pm by nine strong, rapid knocks. A table lamp at the opposite corner of the room was thrown violently to the floor and broken. There was no window in this corner, and no wind was blowing at the time. (Note. I have little experience with phenomena of this sort. Magically speaking, it usually represents "breaks" in operation there should be no phenomena but the willed result.)
> *Jan 11.* Invoked twice, using blood.
> *Jan 12.* Invoked twice, A heavy windstorm.
> *Jan 13.* Invoked twice, Windstorm continued.
> *Jan. 14.* The light system of the house failed about 9 pm. Another magician [Hubbard] who had been staying at the house and studying with me, was carrying a candle across the kitchen when he was struck strongly on the right shoulder, and the candle knocked out of his hand. He called us, and we observed a brownish yellow light about seven feet high in the kitchen. I banished [it] with a magical sword, and it disappeared. His right arm was paralyzed the rest of the night.
> *Jan 15.* Invoked twice. At this time the Scribe [Hubbard] developed some sort of astral vision, describing in detail an old enemy of mine of whom he had never heard, and later the guardian forms of Isis and the Archangel Michael. Later, in my room, I heard the raps again, and a buzzing metallic voice crying "let me go free." I felt a great pressure and tension in the house that night, which was also noticed by the other occupants. There were no other phenomena.

Parsonage residents thought Jack was attempting to summon a demon and could only speculate as to his purpose. But he took Hubbard, whom he named his "Scribe," into his confidence and soon his partnership. Jack further recorded,

> The feeling of tension and unease continued for four days. Then, on January 18, at sunset, while the Scribe and I were on the Mojave desert, the feeling of tension suddenly snapped. I turned to him and said, "it is done," in absolute certainty that the operation was accomplished. I returned home, and found a young woman answering the requirements waiting for me. She is describable as an air of fire type with bronze red hair, fiery and subtle, determined and

> obstinate, sincere and perverse, with extraordinary personality, talent, and intelligence.

That very day, a newcomer arrived at the Parsonage. It was a strikingly beautiful and self-possessed young artist named Marjorie Cameron (1922–1995), who had recently been demobilized from the WAVES, the volunteer women's brigade in World War II.

"Her arrival," wrote George Pendle, "coincided exactly with Parsons' return from the Mojave. He was overwhelmed by the magnetism between the two of them. In a letter to Crowley, Parsons declared, 'I have my elemental!'"

Their intimacies began almost immediately and lasted two weeks. Cameron became pregnant. Was this the seed of the sought-after magickal child? The couple would never entirely know as Cameron, unaware of Jack's full purposes, opted to abort the pregnancy with his consent and did so again later.* Spenser Kansa notes in his 2011 biography of Cameron, *Wormwood Star*: "Claiming his magickal invocation with Hubbard had succeeded, Jack suggested Babalon was already nesting somewhere on Earth in a human host, and would manifest in time to unleash her prophecy." The couple married on October 19, 1946.

Whatever satisfaction Parsons may have experienced from the Babalon Working was soon clouded by validation of Crowley's suspicions about Hubbard. Parsons' mentor had always expressed misgivings from afar about the two men's magickal workings. In April 1946, Crowley wrote his old confidant Karl Germer, "Apparently Parsons or Hubbard or somebody is producing a Moonchild. I get fairly frantic when I contemplate the idiocy of these goats."** Indeed, the Beast had attempted to warn Parsons earlier about his workmate and activities. On March 27, 1946, he wrote Jack,

> I am particularly interested in what you have written to me about the Elemental, because for some little while past I have been

---

* From *Sex and Rockets: The Occult World of Jack Parsons* by John Carter (Feral House, 1999), a valuable book written under a pseudonym.

** "The Occult Roots of Scientology? L. Ron Hubbard, Aleister Crowley, and the Origins of a Controversial New Religion" by Hugh B. Urban, *Nova Religio: The Journal of Alternative and Emergent Religions*, Vol. 15, No. 3, February 2012.

> endeavoring to intervene *personally* in this matter on your behalf. I would however have you recall [Eliphas] Lévi's aphorism, "the love of the Magus for such beings is insensate and may destroy him." It seems to me that there is a danger of your sensitiveness upsetting your balance. Any experience that comes your way you have a tendency to over-estimate . . . At the same time, your being as sensitive as you are, it behooves you to be more on your guard than would be the case with the majority of people.*

The aged magician was still relying on Jack financially and some evident self-interest appears in his letter: "Meanwhile you have neglected and bewildered those who are dependent on you, either from above or from below."

Whatever Crowley's motives, Jack regretted not heeding his counsel. The previous January, Jack had cofounded—and largely financed through his lifesavings of more than $20,000 (Hubbard invested less than $2,000)—a company with Hubbard and Betty called Allied Enterprises. Apparently, one of Hubbard's plans was to purchase and flip yachts at a profit. Crowley had no illusions. On May 22, 1946, he wired Germer: "Suspect Ron playing confidence trick—John Parsons weak fool—obvious victim—prowling swindlers."**

By July, Jack was dejectedly inclined to agree. He discovered that Hubbard and Betty had absconded to Miami with his money where they apparently set sights on the yacht-flipping scheme. Jack realized belatedly that the two were making off with his savings and going their own way. He feverishly wrote Crowley from the port city on July 26, 1946,

> Here I am in Miami pursuing the children of my folly [Hubbard and Betty]. I have them well tied up; they cannot move without going to jail. However I am afraid that most of the money has already been dissipated. I will be lucky to salvage 3,000-5,000 dollars. In the interim I am flat broke counting on my fare 2,000 miles from home—c'est la vie. An interesting incident—Hubbard attempted to escape me by sailing at 5 p.m. and I performed a full invocation to Bartzabel within the circle at 8 p.m. At the same

* Sutin, *Do What Thou Wilt* (2000).

** Carter (1999).

> time, as far as I can check, his ship was struck by the sudden squall off the coast, which ripped off his sails and forced him back to port, where I took the boat in custody. I am not greatly impressed, but it is interesting.*

Jack was referencing a ritual published by Crowley in 1910, "An Evocation of Bartzabel, the Spirit of Mars."

In the end, he recovered $2,900 and his former friends headed east, marrying in August. Hubbard, as Betty later discovered, was already bound in matrimony from earlier nuptials in 1933. He soon produced his 1950 manifesto *Dianetics* and pursued the religious empire of Scientology. As for Hubbard's part in the whole Parsons affair, his church later issued a statement explaining that the writer's activity was an undercover operation on behalf of military intelligence to break up the Parsons circle and save young Betty. As Hugh B. Urban noted in "The Occult Roots of Scientology?":

> In December 1969, Scientology published a statement in the [*London Sunday*] *Times* asserting that these rites did indeed take place but that Hubbard was sent in on a special military mission to break up this black magic group. This he successfully did, the church claimed, "rescuing" Betty and shutting down the occult operation:
>
> > Hubbard broke up black magic in America . . . [H]e was sent in to handle the situation. He went to live at the house and investigated the black magic rites and the general situation and found them very bad . . . Hubbard's mission was successful far beyond anyone's expectations . . . Hubbard rescued a girl they were using. The black magic group was dispersed and destroyed.

Scientology embarked on its own calico path, attracting, for a time, the interests of none other than William S. Burroughs. After official expulsion in January 1969 for "a condition of Treason," the Beat icon issued a statement that probably would have elicited the general sympathy of Parsons, writing in the *Los Angeles Free Press* on March 6, 1970:

* Bogdan (2016).

> Some of the techniques are highly valuable and warrant further study and experimentation. The E. Meter is a useful device . . . (many variations of this instrument are possible). On the other hand I am in flat disagreement with the organizational policy. No body of knowledge needs an organizational policy. Organizational policy can only impede the advancement of knowledge. There is a basic incompatibility between any organization and freedom of thought. Suppose Newton had founded a Church of Newtonian Physics and refused to show his formula to anyone who doubted the tenets of Newtonian Physics? All organizations create organizational necessities. It is precisely organizational necessities that have prevented Scientology from obtaining the serious consideration merited by the importance of Mr. Hubbard's discoveries. Scientologists are not prepared to accept intelligent and sometimes critical evaluation. They demand unquestioning acceptance.*

Leaving no doubt as to where he finally stood, Burroughs, a few months before his death, wrote in his journals of November 30, 1996, "I said: 'L. Ron Hubbard needs a knife in his gizzard.'"**

Soon after Parsons' Miami fiasco, Crowley, apparently losing faith in his protégé, removed him as head of the Agape Lodge. Jack had been disillusioned from all sides—*but not in the magickal workings themselves*. In a statement that could've come from the pen of Austin Osman Spare, he wrote Cameron the year they wed in 1946, "Only in the irrational and unknown direction can we come to wisdom again."*** On August 20 of that year, he wrote Crowley resigning from the O.T.O. Addressing his former master only as "Dear Aleister," Parsons noted, "I do not believe that the O.T.O., as an autocratic organization, constitutes a true and proper medium for the expression and attainment of these principles."

* Reprinted in *Ali's Smile: Naked Scientology* by William S. Burroughs (Expanded Media Editions, 1972, 1973, 1978).

** *Last Words: The Final Journals of* William S. *Burroughs* edited by James Grauerholz, Grove Press, 2000). Also see *Scientologist! William S. Burroughs and the 'Weird Cult'* by David S. Wills (Beatdom Books, 2021).

*** Carter (1999) here and following.

Jack remained philosophical about his betrayals, writing of himself in his 1948 essay "An Analysis by a Master of the Temple": "The final experience with Hubbard and Betty, and the O.T.O. was necessary to overcome your false and infantile reliance on others, although this was only partially accomplished at the time."

Undaunted in his explorations, Jack began producing more of his own literature—with a particular aim in sight. "Simplicity," he wrote Cameron, "has been the key to victory in all the idea wars and, at present, Magick does not have it. There is a skeleton in the Rights of Man [Crowley's brief Thelemic credo *Liber Oz*], and the coverings in the main literature. But the true body has never been shown forth."*

Indeed, had Parsons lived, I believe his great contribution to the study of magick, which he had only just started, would have been the fulfillment of this dictum of *simplicity*. One can see it emerging in the writing he produced around this time, much of which was published posthumously. In his essay "On Magick," he noted: "Magick is not created by man, it is a part of man, having its basis in the structure of his brain, his body and his nervous system in their relationships to his conceptual universe, the matrix of thought, and of speech, the mother of thought."** Sadly, his experiments were cut short when on June 17, 1952, he apparently blew himself up at age thirty-seven in his home lab while mixing commercial explosives for a Hollywood special effects company.

If the individual is innately magickal—that is, if perception and emotional conviction form the basis, or are least co-creators, of reality—could not magick itself be unmoored from ritual, rite, and liturgy, areas to which Crowley had dedicated immense effort? Rather than complex ritual, could magick be as near as the psyche itself?

"In its absolute basis," Parsons continued, "magick is a passion and a discipline which relates to the mystery of love . . . In its relative and applied basis, which is the root of all secret traditions of mankind, magick relates to the sacrament of sex and the mystery of the creative will." This observation fulfilled a wish of Spare, an artist he never knew, echoed by Jake Dirnberger in his 2020 *Pocket Austin Osman*

---

* Undated correspondence from Carter.

** *Freedom is a Two-Edged Sword and Other Essays* by Jack Parsons, edited by Cameron and Hymenaeus Beta (New Falcon Publications, 1989).

Spare: "Magic, for Spare, is about bypassing the ordinary mind and harnessing the innate abilities of one's subconscious."

Following Jack's death, Cameron emerged as a remarkable artist and actor, appearing in groundbreaking independent classic films and shorts including 1954's *Inauguration of the Pleasure Dome* by Kenneth Anger (1927–2023) along with 1956's *The Wormwood Star* and 1961's *Night Tide* by Curtis Harrington, the latter marking Dennis Hopper's first starring role in a feature. Each is a haunting, collaged masterpiece proffering themes and images that colored the culture in areas both popular and avant-garde. The artist appeared, as she would for the remainder of her life, under the mononym Cameron. She also emerged as an extraordinary painter, portraitist, and sketch artist, often dedicating herself to the occult themes she and Jack had worked with.

For her part, Cameron believed that Jack had been murdered, possibly by *anti-Zionists*: suffering under the cloud of McCarthyism and scandal over his magickal pursuits, the occultist had pondered migrating to the newfound state of Israel to regain access to the technology that his earlier Marxist associations (he was later more of a libertarian) had denied him.*

Jack wrote in his poem "King David":

> Not even for the tall and headstrong son
> Scowling and dark and beautiful, that lay
> Sprawling in blood upon the Hebron plain**

In future decades, as Parsons' reputation grew—he appeared as a background meme in *Twin Peaks*—readers wondered whether the Babalon Working might have proved an anarchic triumph, of sorts. Hugh B. Urban keenly noted in his *Magia Sexualis*,

> Many of Parsons's admirers have suggested that his Babalon Working may have had some real-world effects, that it had served to "crack open the Apocalyptic gateway and activate the cult forces

* On these theories, see Kansa (2011) and Pendle (2005).

** From *Songs for the Witch Woman* by John W. Parsons and Marjorie Cameron (Fulgur Esoterica, 2015).

> necessary for the upheaval of consciousness," as we see in the increasing chaos of war, disease, famine, and terrorism in the late twentieth century. On a somewhat less apocalyptic note, however, at least one of Parsons's many projects would later come to fruition. He had in fact planned to devise a new kind of pagan religion called "The Witchcraft"—an idea that was soon to come to pass with the rebirth of neo-pagan witchcraft in the mid-1950s.*

Indeed, around the time of Jack's incendiary 1952 demise, new stirrings brought this latter prognosis to life.

In a final note, make of it what thou wilt, Parsons' birthdate of October 2, 1914, is the same day that Charles Taze Russell, founder of the Jehovah's Witnesses, called the starting point of the events of Revelation.**

---

* Urban is quoting from Richard Metzger's 1998 essay, "John W. Parsons: Anti-Christ Superstar."

** As noted by Jack's biographer Carter. For a critical overview and links to primary documents, see "1914: Failed Watchtower Prophecy" at JWfacts.com.

CHAPTER TWELVE

Aquarius Dawning

Only in 1951 did Britain lift its last law against witches. The Witchcraft Act of 1735, dating in its earliest form to the mid-sixteenth century, was finally repealed due to lobbying efforts by English Spiritualists who, although organized into ecclesiastic churches, were sometimes harassed under its strictures.

Through this opening stepped iconic writer-seeker Gerald Gardner (1884–1964). Freed from fear of legal reprisals, Gardner fostered a revival, or reinvention, of witchcraft in England and soon other parts of the world.

An adventurous and well-to-do customs agent who spent most of his life in Borneo, British Malaya, Singapore, and other trading posts of the Empire, Gardner retired to the southern English coast in the late 1930s. He used retirement to deepen his study of folklore and tribal rites he encountered in the Far East. Back home, Gardner was touched by the work of Egyptologist Margaret A. Murray (1863–1963), who postulated the survival of an ancient "witch cult" in England and Western Europe in her influential 1921 study *The Witch-Cult in Western Europe*, which, in the wake of new interest, Oxford University Press reissued in 1962.

American folklorist Charles G. Leland (1824–1903) endorsed a similar idea at the turn of the century, describing enduring nature cults as *la vecchia religione* or "the old religion" in his 1899 book on Italian folk traditions, *Aradia, or the Gospel of the Witches*. Aradia, the daughter of Diana and Lucifer ("the god of the Sun and of the Moon . . . who was so proud of his beauty, and who for his pride was driven from Paradise") is a kind of Gnostic deity dispatched to earth by her mother where "who fain would study witchcraft in thy school." In the U.S., suffragist Matilda Gage (1826–1898) brought attention to mass killing of women during the Witch Craze, which she argued colored present religious attitudes toward women. As it happens, Gage's son-in-law was Theosophist and *Oz* author L. Frank Baum.*

And here Theosophy, as it often does, reenters the scene. In the late 1930s, Annie Besant's daughter, Mabel Besant-Scott (1870–1952), grew active in a movement in which her mother had been instrumental, Co-Freemasonry, an extant branch of the Freemasonry that accepts both men and women. Within the folds of Co-Freemasonry, Besant-Scott collaborated on developing a modern Rosicrucian fellowship on the southern coast of England. As part of its activities, Besant-Scott's Rosicrucian Fellowship of Crotona (named for Pythagoras's legendary school) organized a theater company to teach mystical themes through plays. The troupe's efforts lasted just one season from June to September 1938.

Despite its short theatrical run, the Besant-Scott group attracted a range of people in the southern coastal area with interests in occultism and folklore, including, in 1939, Gerald Gardner. Around this time, the retiree reported his initiation into a longstanding witch's coven, one that retained ancient nature-based rites and traditions. Their practices, Gardner said, survived centuries of violence, backlash, repression, and discontinuity.

After the war, Gardner discovered a new path and purpose. "The year 1946," historian Ronald Hutton writes, "in which he claimed to have met [Aleister] Crowley and decided to publicize the witch religion, seems to have represented a turning-point for him; and as in the case of the Rosicrucian Theatre, he seems to be telling us something

* "Baum never expected *The Wonderful Wizard of Oz* to be a best-seller. He published five other books in 1900, and probably had more hopes for *The Art of Decorating Dry Goods Windows and Interiors*." From *Upstate Caldron: Eccentric Spiritual Movements in Early New York State* by Joscelyn Godwin (State University of New York Press, 2011).

which has at least symbolic truth. By 1947 he was certainly embarked upon a course which he was to follow for the rest of his life."*

Spiritual and artistic history emerges from the right junction of individual to cultural moment. Gardner found his with the repeal of the anti-witchery law. In 1954, he published his slender, sprightly book *Witchcraft Today*. The volume laid out what he called surviving beliefs and rituals of the nature-based coven with whom he said he collaborated in the coastal woods. He called their initiates "Wica," loosely an Old English term for wise or clever folk.

Gardner claimed initiation in the British coastal town of Highcliffe through an elder he called only "Old Dorothy." In private, he identified "Old Dorothy" as Dorothy Clutterbuck (1880–1951), a wealthy area matriarch. His claim is unsubstantiated. In any case, he said their magickal circle met in the woods during the war to cast spells against Hitler, a clandestine effort also practiced by British occultist Dion Fortune, on whose London headquarters German bombs twice fell. Gardner's coastal coven is charmingly if indirectly reflected in the 1971 Disney vehicle *Bedknobs and Broomsticks*, with Angela Lansbury playing a witch anyone could love who magically repels a Nazi invasion of her British isle village.

Historians have challenged the existence of Gardner's New Forest coven. Indeed, it must be noted that religious retentions, which sometimes endure in adapted or co-opted forms, are profoundly difficult to maintain in any formal sense during extended periods of persecution and upheaval, either during American slavery or the centuries-long Witch Craze. Regardless, Gardner's 1954 volume set off waves felt around the world. During the 1960s, his term *Wica* morphed into *Wicca* in Britain and the United States, used by some adherents to name and reclaim the old faith. Prolific Angelo-American occultist Raymond Buckland (1934–2017), initiated into Gardnerian witchcraft in 1963, proved instrumental in bringing the craft to America. Gardner encouraged initiates to "hive off" and form new covens, thus spreading the movement.**

---

* On the career of Gerald Gardner, key sources include Hutton's *Triumph of the Moon* (Oxford University Press, 2001); *Drawing Down the Moon* by Margot Adler (Penguin/Arkana, 1997); *An ABC of Witchcraft* by Doreen Valiente (Phoenix Publishing, 1973); Gerald Gardner: *Witch* by J. L. Bracelin—widely considered Idries Shah, who is soon met—(Octagon Press, 1960); and an annotated edition of Gardner's 1954 *Witchcraft Today* (Citadel Press, 2004).

** *New Age Religion and Western Culture: Esotericism in the Mirror of Secular Thought* by Wouter J. Hanegraaff (State University of New York Press, 1998)

In the late 1950s, brilliant and confoundingly opaque Sufi teacher Idries Shah (1924–1996), born in British India, served as secretary, friend, and man Friday to Gardner. Ensconcing himself into Wiccan circles, Shah, author of the 1956 study *Oriental Magic*, seems to have used his association to begin building his own audience. Shah played a significant role in introducing Islamic mysticism and folk practice to the West, particularly through his 1964 classic *The Sufis*. In 1960, Shah started his own publisher, Octagon Press, where he promptly issued a biography of his mentor titled, *Gerald Gardner, Witch*, attributed to by J. L. Bracelin, a disciple of Gardner's (and later Shah's) who had introduced the men; but the book is universally acknowledged as the pseudonymous work of Shah himself.

In its early form, Gardner's distinctive new/old theology was borrowed and invented, perhaps half-dreamed up and half-grounded in a mélange of folklore and traditional practices. It was, above all, a new religion that matched the needs of the era.

Wicca was nature-based, sexually free (Gardner was a nudist), and female-affirming. By the late 1960s, its of message pagan revivalism spoke to hundreds of thousands of young people, including purveyors of a thriving Goddess movement into the following decade, which included a feminine deity and, sometimes, her male counterpart, the Horned God.

"While Wicca tends to look especially to the putative European witchcult (along the lines of Margaret Murray)," wrote Wouter J. Hanegraaff in *New Age Religion and Western Culture*, "the Goddess-worshipers are more interested in historical and archeological evidence for a prehistoric matriarchy centered on worship of the Goddess."

Wicca also became a popular choice among searching adolescents—Wiccan books for teens swelled into a subcategory of its own—for whom occult imagery and ritual (a tantalizing taboo within mainstream Christianity) proved an empowering statement. Amid the neopagan and Wiccan rival, the practice of modern Druidry—actually active since the early Romantic era—also grew more visible, varied, and widespread. Among the hallmarks of the neopagan faiths was the growth of an insider/outsider spiritual culture. While some seekers established, or in their view reestablished, formal orders and hierarchies, others proved unabashedly independent.

"If you are witch nobody has to teach you," Australian occult-themed artist and Pan revivalist Rosaleen Norton (1917–1979) told an interviewer. Explaining that she was born a witch, the artist said, "In my case it came naturally, and nobody has to teach me."* Persecuted under obscenity charges, the strikingly original visual artist and self-declared witch exited her worldly existence with the same independence she demonstrated within it, as recounted by historian Nevill Drury:

> Late in November 1979, Norton was taken to the Roman Catholic Sacred Heart Hospice for the Dying at Sydney's St. Vincent's Hospital, the end clearly in sight. Shortly before she died she told her friend Victor Wain, 'I came into this world bravely; I'll go out bravely.' Unrepentant in her worship of Pan, unfazed by all the crucifixes surrounding her in hospice, and a pagan to the end, she departed this life on 5 December 1979.

Wicca and neopaganism ranked among America's fastest-growing spiritual movements in the late twentieth and early twenty-first centuries, even gaining official recognition in the U.S. Armed Forces.

Starting in 1978, the U.S. Army's *Handbook for Chaplains* listed guidelines and descriptions for Wiccan practice, all written in remarkably fair and lucid language. "It is very important to be aware that Wiccans do not in any way worship or believe in 'Satan,' 'the Devil,' or similar entities," read a 2001 revision. ". . . Wiccans do not revile the Bible. They simply regard it as one among many of the world's mythic systems, less applicable than some to their core values, but still deserving of just as much respect as any of the others."

The guidelines specified October 31—called by traditional names of "Samhain, Sowyn, or Hallows"—as a major festival or "Sabbat" for Wiccans. The original Celtic holiday became bound up with the Christian "All Saints' Day" or "All Hallow's Eve" during the Middle Ages. But many early twenty-first century Wiccans and neopagans see the celebration as a deeply rooted veneration of nature and ances-

* *Stealing Fire from Heaven: The Rise of Modern Western Magic* by Nevill Drury (Oxford University Press, 2011).

tors. As the Army handbook ably explained, the festival is "a means of attunement to the seasonal rhythms of Nature."

In 1999, Wiccan service members gained the right of public worship at Fort Hood, Texas. President George W. Bush, then governor of Texas, opposed requests of Wiccans for a ceremonial circle on base grounds. "I don't think witchcraft is a religion," he told *Good Morning America*. "I would hope the military officials would take a second look at the decision they made." He wasn't the only one who complained. Reacting to Wiccan worship ceremonies at the base, Rep. Robert L. Barr (R-GA) wrote Fort Hood's commanding officer: "Please stop this nonsense now. What's next? Will armored divisions be forced to travel with sacrificial animals for Satanic rituals? Will Rastafarians demand the inclusion of ritualistic marijuana cigarettes in their rations?" He threatened legislation and hearings. The military's response was basically: cool your jets.

"We see more discrimination in the civilian world," a Fort Hood Wiccan Priestess, Marcy Palmer, then a six-year veteran of the military police, told *The Washington Post* in 1999. "The military is actually much more sensitive."* Female leadership grew distinctly noticeable in Wicca—due in part to the influence and example of popular American witch Starhawk, born Miriam Simos in 1951, who blended Wicca, Goddess worship, social justice, and environmentalism.

In 2005, the Pentagon counted religious affiliations in the Air Force and discovered more than 1,800 active-service, self-identified Wiccans within that branch. By 2007, in a further setback to the Bush Administration, the American Civil Liberties Union and Americans United for Separation of Church and State used twin lawsuits to compel the Department of Veterans Affairs to offer Wiccan believers a pentagram on tombstones. As of this writing in 2023, the VA features the pentagram, Druidic symbols, the Science of Mind insignia, and the "EK" symbol of Eckankar (a new religious movement rooted in Vedism) among its 98 "emblems of belief." The figure has grown precipitously since I started tracking it: thirty-eight in 2007 and sixty-five in 2017.

In 1990, a survey conducted by the City University of New York counted only a few thousand self-identified Wiccans in the U.S. By

---

* "Wiccan Controversy Tests Military Religious Tolerance" by Hanna Rosin, *Washington Post*, June 8, 1999. Also see "Use of Wiccan Symbol on Veterans' Headstones Is Approved" by Neela Banerjee, *New York Times*, April 24, 2007, and my "Halloween as a Religious Holiday? You Better Believe It, Soldier," *Big Think*, October 18, 2010.

2001, the same survey—with sharpened and expanded categories—counted 134,000 Wiccans, 33,000 Druids, and 140,000 Pagans. These numbers squared with a later survey from Trinity College which found that the number of Americans identifying with "New Religious Movements" (including Wicca, Spiritualism, New Age, and other categories) grew from 1.29 million in 1990 to more than 2.8 million in 2008, trends that have more or less continued depending on how survey questions are structured.

Notably, the witchcraft revival proved popular in the tech sector, echoing the precedent of Jack Parsons. Erik Davis observed in *TechGnosis*:

> In 1985, when the witch and NPR reporter Margot Adler was revising *Drawing Down the Moon*, her great social history of American Paganism, she conducted a survey of the community and discovered something that would surprise anyone teleported into the woolly Renaissance Faire atmosphere of your typical Pagan gathering: An "amazingly" high percentage of this willfully anachronistic bunch drew their paychecks from technical fields and the computer industry.*

If not quite Crowley and Parsons' New Aeon, the expansion of Wicca was difficult to imagine a few decades earlier.

The occult boom of the era fostered a mélange of popular how-to guides and also substantial and erudite works, such as Colin Wilson's 1971 study *The Occult*, which explored a vast range of occult history through the lens of modernist philosophy; Richard Cavendish's 1967 *The Black Arts*, a lively and learned survey that won the admiration of Nobel laureate Isaac Bashevis Singer; and, beginning in 1970, Cavendish's magisterial 24-volume encyclopedia *Man, Myth & Magic*, an illustrated omnibus of impeccable quality. Vintage copies are today among prized possessions in occult libraries.

Tabloid journalist Jess Stearn's 1967 bestseller *Edgar Cayce: The Sleeping Prophet* brought a rebound of attention to the medical clair-

* I witnessed a similar phenomenon when delivering a talk on ESP research in 2022 at a conference of tech entrepreneurs: about every third person I met professed interest in Aleister Crowley, and a smaller number in Neville Goddard.

voyant. Cayce's new vogue was followed by an array of channeled literature and teachings—channel was a term Cayce minted in the spiritual sense in the early 1930s—including the "Seth material" by poet Jane Roberts; the voice of 35,000-year-old Lemurian warrior/teacher Ramtha through J.Z. Knight; and the figure of Christ in the hugely popular series of lessons called *A Course in Miracles* by Helen Schucman, a Columbia University research psychologist. *A Course in Miracles* turned out to be far more substantive and complex than most casual readers were expecting. Hence, many looked to friendlier metaphysical works, such as the popularized *Course in Miracles* psychology of Gerald G. Jampolsky and Marianne Williamson or the explorations of channeling and past lives in the memoirs and screen adaptions of actress Shirley MacLaine.

Channeling as a field is critically polarizing and there exists no easy manner in which to summarize it. The communications emergent from channeled literature are of widely varied and diffuse quality—often categorizable only in the eyes and experience of the querent. Scholar of religion J. Gordon Melton surprised some readers and colleagues by issuing a serious and laudatory 1998 book-length treatise on J.Z. Knight and Ramtha, *Finding Enlightenment: Ramtha's School of Wisdom*. The work grew, in part, from an academic conference financially supported by the Ramtha School of Enlightenment (RSE).*

Referring to the books attributed to the discarnate being Seth, Joscelyn Godwin notes,

> Of all the channels of the later twentieth century Jane Roberts (1929–1984) is the most sophisticated and fascinating. She was a Skidmore-educated writer who tumbled into mediumship in 1963 while she and her artist husband, Robert Butts, were experimenting with a Ouija board. Many sessions had no more audience than the two of them, but gradually word got out, and a small group started meeting at the Buttses' apartment in Elmira, New York. For all her subsequent celebrity, Jane Roberts was content to live a modest, provincial life, never going on tour or exploiting her contact beyond the printed word.**

---

* "A Cozy Visit with Ramtha" by Siobhán Houston, *Gnosis* magazine, Winter 1999.

** *Atlantis and the Cycles of Time* (2011).

This brings us to most popular source of purported channeled or extraphysical communication in modern history: the barcoded, shrink-wrapped Ouija board, a device that bounded to renewed popularity in the 1960s.

Modern Ouija had its earliest beginnings as the "talking board," "alphabet board," or "witching board"—a homemade folk device popular among Northern Ohio Spiritualists as early as 1886.* In 1890, a group of Baltimore novelty manufacturers sought to create ownership over the homespun portal. The patent for a "Ouija or Egyptian luck-board" was filed on May 28, 1890, by Baltimore resident and attorney Elijah J. Bond, who assigned the rights to two city businessmen, Charles W. Kennard and William H. A. Maupin. The patent was granted on February 10, 1891, and so was born the Ouija-brand talking board.

The Kennard Novelty Company of Baltimore employed a teenage varnisher who helped run shop operations: the legendary William Fuld (1870–1927). By 1892, Charles W. Kennard's partners removed Kennard from the company amid financial disputes, and a separate patent—this time for an improved planchette (the little plank that slides around the board)—was filed by the nineteen-year-old Fuld. In years to come, Fuld took over the novelty firm and affixed his name to every board.

The beguiling name *Ouija*—alternately pronounced *wee-JA* and *wee-GEE*—remains a mystery. Kennard once claimed it was Egyptian for "good luck" (it's not). Fuld later said it was simply a marriage of the French and German words for "yes." An early investor claimed the board spelled out its own name. In any case, consumers loved it and competitors came and went (sometimes through the help of Fuld's aggressive trademark suits, including against his own brother Isaac).

By 1920, Ouija was so well known that artist Norman Rockwell painted a send-up of a couple using one—the woman dreamy and credulous, the man fixing her with a cloying grin—for a cover of *The Saturday Evening Post.* For manufacturer Fuld, though, all was strictly

* "A Mysterious Talking Board and Table Over Which Northern Ohio Is Agitated," *New York Daily Tribune*, March 28, 1886.

business. "Believe in the Ouija board?" he told a reporter. "I should say not. I'm no Spiritualist. I'm a Presbyterian—been one ever since I was so high." In 1920, the *Baltimore Sun* reported that Fuld, by his own "conservative estimate," had pocketed an incredible $1 million from sales.*

For all its commercial reach, Ouija remained a family business. In a creepy denouement, William Fuld died on February 24, 1927, after tumbling from the roof of his Baltimore factory. The fifty-six-year-old manufacturer was supervising the replacement of a flagpole when an iron support bar gave way and he fell three stories backward. Fuld's children took over his business. Soon, however, bigger opportunities came rapping. Following World War II, novelty manufacturing shed its slightly disreputable, carnival-style reputation and became a more mainstream business. American toy giants eyed the enduring curio. In a move that placed an instrument from the age of Spiritualism into playrooms across America, toy manufacturer Parker Brothers bought rights to Ouija for an undisclosed sum in 1966. The next year, Parker sold more than two million Ouija boards—topping sales of its most popular game, Monopoly.

Ouija has legendary scare status in pop culture. Less known is its surprising literary pedigree. Poets Sylvia Plath and Ted Hughes wrote haunting and darkly prophetic passages about their experiences with Ouija. "Fame will come," the board tells Sylvia in Ted's 1957 poem, "Ouija," ". . . And when it comes you will have paid for it with your happiness, your husband, and your life." The poet took her life in early 1963 after Ted's abandonment.

In 1976, American poet James Merrill published—and won the Pulitzer Prize for—an epic poem that recounted his experience, with partner David Jackson, of using a Ouija board from 1955 to 1974. His work, *The Book of Ephraim*, was later combined with two other Ouija-conjured epic poems and published in 1982 as *The Changing Light at Sandover.* First employing a manufactured board and then a homemade one—with a teacup in place of a planchette—Merrill and Jackson encountered a world of spirit "patrons" who described for them a sprawling and profoundly involving creation myth. In Merrill's

---

* "William Fuld Made $1,000,000 on Ouija but Has No Faith in It," *Baltimore Sun*, June 4, 1920.

hands, it became poetry steeped in the epic tradition, in which myriad characters—from W. H. Auden, to lost friends and family members, to a ghostly Greek muse/interlocutor called Ephraim—walk on and off stage.

"It is common knowledge—and glaringly obvious in the poems, though not taken seriously by his critics—that these three works, and their final compilation, were based on conversations . . . through a Ouija board," wrote John Chambers in his 1997 analysis of Merrill in *The Anomalist.* Critic Harold Bloom, in a departure from others who avoided the question of the work's source, called the first of the Sandover poems "an occult splendor."

What may be Ouija's most remarkable legacy appears in the nation of Vietnam. It is a case-in-point of unintended consequences. In the late nineteenth and early twentieth centuries, Catholic missionaries to colonial Indochina created a Latinized version of the Vietnamese language. Vietnamese Spiritualists discovered that the Ouija board proved surprisingly adaptable to the Westernized phonetics.

Though use of Ouija beginning in the early 1920s, a Vietnamese civil servant working for the French colonial administration, Ngô Văn Chiêu, received tenets of a faith called Caodaism, roughly, "religion of the high palace." It was a mélange of Eastern traditions—from Taoism to Buddhism to Hinduism—combined with Vietnamese folk traditions and the ideas of French Spiritists, particularly teacher and writer Allan Kardec (1804–1869) and poet and novelist Victor Hugo (1802–1885), himself a habitué of séances.

So closely was Ouija associated with Caodaism that Graham Greene in his 1955 novel *The Quiet American* lampooned the Vietnamese faith as "prophecy by planchette."

As it happens, Caodaism possessed a defiant politics. It was militantly anticommunist and maintained a private army that sided against the Vietcong, first with French forces until their defeat in 1954 and then with American forces until their withdrawal in 1973 and up to fall of Saigon in 1975. The Caodai militia ranked among the U.S.'s long-running allies in the conflict. After the war, the religion fled underground. Newly emergent in the twenty-first century, Caodaism claims up to eight million followers worldwide and ranks as Vietnam's third-largest faith, after Buddhism and Catholicism.*

The 1960s also exposed Westerners to Native American shamanism—or a certain variant of it. A stocky Latin UCLA graduate student named Carlos Castaneda (1925–1998) ignited mass interest in the wisdom of a mysterious, and many said invented, Yaqui Indian medicine man in his 1968 bestseller, *The Teachings of Don Juan* and a series of sequels. .

In the following decade, critics and some disappointed readers heaped scorn upon the elusive Castaneda when the logistics and circumstances of his Don Juan books failed to hold up under scrutiny. Even Castaneda's own background as a globe-trotting Brazilian was exposed as invention. He was the Peruvian son of a jeweler. As some readers discovered, however, the books' true value did not appear by dissecting the realness of Don Juan or heading southwest in search of magic mushrooms or a Native American teacher. Rather, Castaneda's writings made most sense to readers who already had a commitment to a religious or wisdom tradition and understood his books as allegories on that path. The resonances, some found, were remarkable.

In that vein, I want to reproduce a short dialogue between Carlos his mythical mentor from his first book. It may strike you, as it has some, as possessed of indelible depth and resonance, regardless or perhaps in spite of source. It opens with Carlos's question to Don Juan:

> "Is there a special way to avoid pain?"
>
> "Yes, there is a way."
>
> "Is it a formula, a procedure, or what?"
>
> "It is a way of grabbing onto things. For instance, when I was learning about the devil's weed I was too eager. I grabbed onto things the way kids grab onto candy. The devil's weed is only one of a million paths. Anything is one of a million paths [un camino entre cantidades de caminos]. Therefore you must always keep in mind

* Historical information on Caodaism appears in Ralph B. Smith's two-part study, "An Introduction to Caodaism," *Bulletin of the School of Oriental and African Studies of the University of London*, Vol. XXXIII (1970). Other sources include "Cultural Intrusions and Religious Syncretism: The Case of Caodaism in Vietnam" by Graeme Lang, *Working Papers Series* No. 65, Southeast Asia Research Centre (July 2004); and "Vietnam's Cao Dai Sect Flourishing Amid Hollywood Endorsement," Agence France-Presse, June 3, 2001.

> that a path is only a path; if you feel you should not follow it, you must not stay with it under any conditions. To have such clarity you must lead a disciplined life. Only then will you know that any path is only a path, and there is no affront, to oneself or to others, in dropping it if that is what your heart tells you to do. But your decision to keep on the path or to leave it must be free of fear or ambition. I warn you. Look at every path closely and deliberately. Try it as many times as you think necessary. Then ask yourself, and yourself alone, one question. This question is one that only a very old man asks. My benefactor told me about it once when I was young, and my blood was too vigorous for me to understand it. Now I do understand it. I will tell you what it is: Does this path have a heart? All paths are the same: they lead nowhere. They are paths going through the bush, or into the bush. In my own life I could say I have traversed long, long paths, but I am not anywhere. My benefactor's question has meaning now. Does this path have a heart? If it does, the path is good; if it doesn't, it is of no use. Both paths lead nowhere; but one has a heart, the other doesn't. One makes for a joyful journey; as long as you follow it, you are one with it. The other will make you curse your life. One makes you strong; the other weakens you."

I was told a story by Michael Murphy, cofounder in 1962 of the Esalen Institute on the Pacific coast, one of the most significant growth centers to emerge in the new era of exploration, which included the popular and successful intentional community Findhorn in Scotland. Murphy said that in 1966, two years before Carlos's first book appeared, the author visited Esalen. The graduate student was seated in a circle talking with some of the institute's thoughts leaders. Murphy said that he noticed Carlos's narrative at the time was remarkably consistent to what he later related in his book. Gestalt therapist, Fritz Perls, infamous for his prickliness and confrontational manner, slapped Carlos on the knee and said, "Listen to me, young man! You're leading us into magic." Carlos turned on him and said, "You listen to *me*, old man. *This is real.*" Few people stood up to Perls.

Another portrait of Carlos reached me from philosopher Jacob Needleman. In the late 1960s, the author met with some people from the Gurdjieff work. Before leaving, he told them, "I've spoken to lots and lots of groups, and I don't really know what it is that you people are doing but you must be onto something—I've never addressed people that demonstrated such total attention." Carlos struck as eminently polite, likable, and poised. Not everyone encountered him that way. Some contemporaries remarked how Carlos left vastly different impressions: sometimes warm, sometimes diffident; some even swore witnessing him in bilocation.

This protean quality is something Carlos may have picked up from the ideas of mind-metaphysics teacher Neville Goddard (1905–1972). Born in 1905 in Barbados to an English family, the mononymous Neville arrived in New York in the early 1920s to study theater. His ambition for the stage faded by the early 1930s when, he said, he encountered an enigmatic, turbaned black man named Abdullah who tutored him in Scripture, number mysticism, Kabbalah, and Hebrew. The "hidden teacher" narrative was by now widely established in modern occultism. Whatever the source of Neville's education, his outlook not only reflected the most occultic edge of New Thought but also the philosophy's most intellectually stimulating expression, as considered later in this chapter.

In the mid-1950s, Carlos discovered Neville through an early love interest in Los Angeles, Margaret Runyan, who was among Neville's most dedicated students. A cousin of American storyteller Damon Runyon, Margaret wooed the stocky Latin art student Carlos at a friend's house, slipping him a slender Neville volume called *The Search,* in which she inscribed her name and phone number. The two became lovers and later, briefly, husband and wife.

Runyan spoke frequently to Carlos about Neville, but he responded with little more than mild interest—with one exception. In her memoirs, Runyan recalled Carlos growing fascinated when the conversation turned to Neville's discipleship under an exotic teacher:

> . . . it was more than the message that attracted Carlos, it was Neville himself. He was so mysterious. Nobody was really sure who he was or where he had come from. There were vague references to Barbados in the West Indies and his being the son of an ultra-rich plantation family, but nobody knew for sure. They couldn't even be sure about this Abdullah business, his Indian teacher, who was always *way back there* in the jungle, or someplace. The only thing you really knew was that Neville was here and that he might be back next week, but then again . . .

"There was," she concluded, "a certain power in that position, an appealing kind of freedom *in the lack of past* and Carlos knew it." [emphasis added]

In a nod to academic propriety, Carlos's first book *The Teachings of Don Juan* included in its closing third a long and tortuously worded "Structural Analysis." The book was, after all, published by the University of California Press as its author's master's thesis in UCLA's School of Anthropology. Most of Carlos's new legion of general readers probably perused a few pages of the labored analysis and deemed it "too academic" for them. And here the author may have been playing a *ludibrium* ("serious joke") on the culture. Some observers, including novelist Joyce Carol Oates, speculated that Carlos's obstruse postscript was a satire of academese—more parody than pedantry.

Amid the occult's entry to bestseller lists, toy aisles, and how-to guides, it could be fairly asked: were the "dark arts," or their most popular variants, growing domesticated? Not if Anton LaVey had anything to say about it. "There is always a risk to underestimate LaVey," writes sociologist Massimo Introvigne of modernity's best-known Satanist.*

On the evening of April 30, 1966—Walpurgisnacht, a Christian holiday that coincides with pagan rites of spring (sometimes considered the witches' sabbath)—the goateed San Franciscan shaved his head and declared the founding of the Church of Satan, designating 1966 "the Year One," *Anno Satanas*. In the Year Two, secular New York City novelist Ira Levin published his classic *Rosemary's Baby*—soon widely known for Roman Polanski's screen version—with coven leader Roman Castevet declaring at a New Year's celebration: "To 1966, The Year One." The die was cast.

With his founding of the Church of Satan, Anton became the first spiritual rebel to attain superstar status since Aleister Crowley. No one since Anton's death in 1997 has filled that role. New Agers and self-helpers have hit bestseller lists, run for president, and attracted millions of screen viewers. But no outsider occult figure—one unfit for weekend seminars or headset-wearing TED talks—has upended

* *Satanism: A Social History* (Brill, 2016).

our cultural assumptions, exposed moral hypocrisies, and embraced outcast iconography as he did.

LaVey was born Howard Stanton Levey in Chicago on April 11, 1930. From nearly that point forward, in true showman fashion—a designation he embraced—everything about LaVey's biography is either self-invented, from his playing the Devil in the 1968 screen version of *Rosemary's Baby*—a myth echoed in the press to this day—to his torrid affairs, including with Marilyn Monroe, or simply difficult to pin down, such as his background as a circus roustabout to his work as a crime-scene photographer for the San Francisco Police Department.

The widely repeated tale of his playing the Devil in *Rosemary's Baby* gained traction in 1969 when a *Wall Street Journal* article repeated the magician's plausible but invented claim, demonstrating—in a move that reflected Anton's trickster wiles—that you can get a major news outlet to affirm nearly anything if it is presented credibly enough.* The uncredited role of Satan was actually played by actor Clay Tanner (1931–2002) who appears in on-set photographs in his scaly Devil costume in the illustrated *This Is No Dream: Making Rosemary's Baby* by James Munn and Bob Willoughby (Reel Art Press, 2018).

In another oft-repeated tale, Anton said he acted as a technical advisor on set; I've found no supporting evidence for this and several crew interviews to the contrary. In a development that probably would have made Anton smile, he is credited as both Devil and tech advisor in his 1997 obituary in *Variety*. Anton is accurately credited as a technical advisor on the 1975 horror film *The Devil's Rain* in which he and then-partner Diane LaVey (née Hegarty) have small roles.

For all that, Howard Levey's alter ego Anton LaVey led an existence impressive enough for any ten public-facing figures. Indeed, once the thirty-six-year-old Western migrant (his parents relocated from Chicago when Anton was a teen) launched his counter-church, journalists thrilled to claims and exploits of the caped and sometimes horned-costumed man who seemed to resemble the mind's eye image

---

* For the reference, see "Strange Doings: Americans Show Burst of Interest in Witches, Other Occult Matters" by Stephen J. Sansweet, *Wall Street Journal*, October 23, 1969. The most recent repetition of the claim that I have seen in news media is "Did the Devil kill Jayne Mansfield?" by Helen O'Hara, *The Telegraph*, May 9, 2018.

of Mephistopheles. LaVey played His Satanic Majesty—this time for real—in director Kenneth Anger's 1969 short film *Invocation of My Demon Brother*, a movie that almost certainly, if more quietly, influenced as many filmmakers as Polanski's classic (its Moog soundtrack by Mick Jagger is minimalist splendor); in 1969 Anton published the perennially selling mass-market paperback *The Satanic Bible* that placed his byline in mall stores across the world; and at his peak hobnobbed with celebrities like Jayne Mansfield and Sammy Davis Jr.—the singer recounts his flirtation with Satanism with admirable candor in his 1989 memoir, *Why Me?*

Davis's earlier memoir, *Yes I Can* from 1965, shows up prominently in the screen version of *Rosemary's Baby*, at one point visibly read by its tragic heroine played by Mia Farrow. Davis did not come into contact with the yet-unborn Church of Satan until 1973, as recalled by Anton's widow Blanche Barton in *We Are Satanists: The History and Future of the Church of Satan* (2021). Davis gratefully accepted an honorary membership when Anton's one-time confederate Michael Aquino, who is reencountered, wrote the entertainer to praise his TV comedy film *Poor Devil*. On grimmer terms, Davis recounts at least titular introduction to Satanism through his barber and friend Jay Sebring, who was murdered along with Polanski's wife Sharon Tate and two housemates by followers of Charles Manson on August 9, 1969. The timing and circumstances of the murders pose endless rumors and speculations, the finest and most responsible treatment of which appears in director Jay Cheel's episode on *Rosemary's Baby* for the 2022 documentary series *Cursed Films II*.

In modern Left-Hand Path spirituality, if Aleister Crowley was Ancient Greece—deeply read, martial, and refined—Anton was Ancient Rome—given to intellectual borrowing, unfettered in conquest, and without restraint. And it worked.

In P.D. Ouspensky's 1949 record of his work with G.I. Gurdjieff, *In Search of the Miraculous*, the teacher observes: "truth can only come to people *in the form of a lie*." Indeed, Satan is sometimes called the Lord of Lies. In that sense, Anton was a Holy Liar. And yet—I pause over that designation. A lie implies malice—of which, critics be damned, his work is absent. Anton, like many popular artists, not only provoked but also mediated. He successfully brought decades of readers, including teen witches and goth kids, to ideals of protean self-creation when they might otherwise have had few accessible sources. As Alfred, Lord Tennyson put it in 1850 in his *In Memoriam A.H.H.*: "Truth embodied in a tale shall enter in at lowly doors."

Some readers, among them role-play gamers, tricksters, anarchic magickians, goths, metal heads, and a few credulous, took this principle further and crafted a full-throated (and often cohesive) religious scenario around horror eminence H.P. Lovecraft's (1890–1937) "Cthulhu Mythos," which forms the backstory of several of his tales, as well as the author's dramatized grimoire the *Necronomicon* ("Book of Dead Names"). The latter includes, among other versions, one intentional and long-selling "folly" edition, created in 1977 by imagineers at New York's defunct Magickal Childe bookstore.

Anton's *The Satanic Rituals*, the 1972 companion to his first book, features, among other Lovecraftian adaptations, the ceremonial "Call to Cthulhu." Erik Davis calls these "the first overtly Lovecraftian rituals to see print."* Davis continues:

> The word "fan" comes from *fanaticus*, an ancient term for a temple devotee, and Lovecraft fans exhibit the unflagging devotion, fetishism and sectarian debates that have characterized popular religious cults throughout the ages. But Lovecraft's "cult" status has a curiously literal dimension. Many magicians and occultists have taken up his Mythos as source material for their practice. Drawn from the darker regions of the esoteric counterculture—Thelema and Satanism and Chaos magic—these Lovecraftian mages actively seek to generate the terrifying and atavistic encounters that Lovecraft's protagonists stumble into compulsively, blindly or against their will.

That Lovecraft himself was sterile physicalist who disavowed mysticism of any sort only heightens the meta-experimentalism of revisioning his work into occult practice. Another anarchistic religion grew as an underground movement starting in the mid-sixties, Discordianism, communicated through its unholy text *Principia Discordia* and popularized in Robert Anton Wilson and Robert Shea's

* "Calling Cthulhu: H.P. Lovecraft's Magick Realism," *Gnosis* magazine, Fall 1995; I am quoting from an expanded version the author posted online.

1975 *Illuminatus! Trilogy*. Discordianism is a cut-up faith holding, with both whimsy and *why-not?* seriousness, that everything, from ancient gods to consumer culture to invented words, is at once meaningful and meaningless. It has a loose sister group in the satirical/sincere Church of the SubGenius. Discordianism's core value appears in Wilson's observation: "The idea that all ideas are partly true, partly false, and partly meaningless is partly true, partly false, and partly meaningless."*

Returning to Anton, the provocateur was probably the first modern who put forth Satanism as an ethical and religious philosophy. *The Satanic Bible* is, at its heart, a paean to individualism, and offers a set of ethics not much different from some of what William Blake explored in *The Marriage of Heaven and Hell*. Detractors assert that Anton's celebration of self-attainment lacks ethics. Not exactly. Reciprocity, loyalty, respect, and rejection of non-provoked violence form the Satanist's code. His core ethic could be defined as: *Thou shalt leave another alone*—unless intruded upon.

Other critics dismissed his mass-market paperback as a bastardization of Nietzsche and Ayn Rand, with occult frosting—to which a defender might reply: *so what?* Much religious and philosophical writing is syncretic, and I see LaVey's work as an effective popularization of those writers combined with his own shrewd insights into human nature. In his 2022 *Anton LaVey and the Church of Satan*, artist-author Carl Abrahamsson—Anton's finest chronicler—embraced rather than fled the critical refrain (something Anton would've smiled on), calling the Black Pope "America's own pop-Nietzsche."

To clarify Anton's outlook, he neither believed in nor worshipped Satan as a literal entity. Rather, he defined Satanism as the ethic of radical non-conformity and defiant selfhood. In his eyes, the Satanist is history's rebel, romantic, and iconoclast—but with a razor's edge of self-determination, captured in the statement famously (if loosely) attributed to street-fighting philosopher Ayn Rand: "The question isn't who is going to let me; it's who is going to stop me."

But Anton could not be called a Randian Objectivist, in the vein of the philosopher's ultra-individualism and utopian capitalism.

---

* *RAW Art* by Bobby Campbell (Weirdoverse, 2017)

Anton also believed in the power of rite and ritual, anathemas to the hyper-materialist Rand. Nor was Anton in line with the mystical and extraphysical outlook of his aesthetic antecedent Aleister Crowley. Anton's attitude toward metaphysics was ambiguous and creatively tense; he neither disavowed nor embraced them, often allowed colleagues latitude for their own approach, provided it didn't cross into mewling numinosity: his system had no room for chin-stroking but only for results. Anyone ponderous enough to ask, "What do you mean by results?" would quickly be shown the door at his San Francisco lair, the Black House.

I call his system *Positive Thinking Weaponized.* He took the principle of positive-mind philosophy—*thoughts are causative*—and wed it to a sense of theatricality, costume, and self-invention. Anton believed that well-wrought fantasy—heightened through real-life garb, designed surroundings, and even life-sized dolls (he was a philosophical pioneer of virtual reality)—was superior to settling for unsatisfying sexual relations or lame outer experiences. He termed his invented realms "total environments."

Anton's magick called for *self-awareness* of a kind rarely found in modern occult literature. In *The Satanic Bible* he wrote of the *Balance Factor*: "One of the magician's greatest weapons is knowing himself; his talents, abilities, physical attractions and detractions, and when, where, and *with whom!* . . . The aspiring witch who deludes herself into thinking that a powerful enough working will *always* succeed, despite a magical imbalance, is forgetting one essential tool: MAGIC IS LIKE NATURE ITSELF, AND SUCCESS IN MAGIC REQUIRES WORKING IN HARMONY WITH NATURE, NOT AGAINST IT."

Historian Stephen E. Flowers, Ph.D., adds in his 2012 *Lords of the Left-Hand Path* that LaVey's is *pragmatic magic*—"All elements in his magical system are there to act as triggers for certain psychological events." And further that the practitioner aims at "making only slight alterations in the right place at the right time to 'tip the balance' in one's favor."

Anton's approach to ritual was similar to Austin Osman Spare's. Rites could assume nearly any form—he used a potpourri of historical Satanic references, self-devised dramas, and sometimes an adapted system of the Enochian alphabet—but the nonnegotiable ingredients were *passion* and what might be called *creative forgetfulness.* Anton believed that a ritual or ceremony must immerse you in feeling *satisfied* that you have gained the thing wished for. In this regard, sexuality and self-sexuality were core tools in his rituals. Once you experience the longed-for sense of satedness, you drop the matter. "Burn every bit of desire out of your system," he wrote in his essay "Ravings from Tartarus" from his 1992 collection *The Devil's Notebook*, "and then, when you no longer care, it will come to you."

If you don't experience satisfaction, your fantasy or ritual must be performed again. Or you must find another way of diverting yourself from futile distraction with your aim. Rituals fail, he wrote, "Because it matters so much to you." Again, Anton:

> How can one avoid caring? There are many tricks which can be employed. Creativity is one. When you are in the process of creating something your brain must function on a creative level, not on a rote or repetitive one. Your mind cannot be possessed by one thing and yet entertain new thoughts—unless the object of your creation happens to be in the likeness of your obsession. Here we find an ideal combination, for if the hands can create a facsimile of the desired objective with such dexterity as to be convincing then it is as good as done.

As he suggests, the point of chaos magick, sigil work, and related techniques is to *bypass* the rational apparatus of the mind and allow the depths of the subconscious to perform. Another valuable hint for effective magickal practice appears in Anton's concept of *Erotic Crystallization Inertia* or ECI. In short, the practitioner peels back memory to determine the earliest instances of sexual arousal. In Blanche Barton's 1990 biography *The Secret Life of a Satanist*, ECI is described as the "point in time and experience in which a person's emotional/sexual fetishes are established."

ECI moments also harken to when the individual experiences key feelings of vitality, at-homeness, and conscious ease. This can occur in social situations and during tasks or efforts when you feel distinctly competent, seen, understood, capable—and hence powerful. He encouraged the recreation of these moments and settings in both personal rituals and general surroundings, further clarifying the notion of "total environment." This also means avoiding settings, people, and situations that detract from your sense of vitality. Relationships between parties who possess complementary ECIs can prove remarkably propitious and satisfying.

Understanding ECI provides a key help in working with both sigils and Napoleon Hill's previously explored practice of "sex transmutation." But there is more. Settings that evoke power, potency, and vitality appear to have measurable therapeutic benefits. In studies by Harvard psychologist Ellen Langer—the subject of controversy but their results never refuted—elderly subjects experienced physical and mental improvements—including increased strength and flexibility, recovered memory and cognitive function, and improved mood and vitality—when immersed in nostalgic settings populated with stimuli from their youth, including vintage books, music, and movies. In Langer's work, settings that evoke *feelings* of youth actually seem to summon the reappearance of youthful traits, extending even to improved eyesight.*

As some of Anton's students observed, the very act of "costumery" can evoke similar feelings of well-being. This implies dressing and comporting yourself in a manner that affirms idealized self-image. Too often our wished-for concepts of self are disrupted by therapeutic or spiritual truisms about what we are *supposed* to value, thereby short-circuiting authentic exploration or restricting it to familiar patterns. A more radical and, I believe, helpful approach is to trust your self-estimation, test it, and permit no one to summarily take it away. In other words: verify, not as a toothless truism but actually.

As I was completing this chapter, I heard from a thoughtful reader and freelance producer of reality shows, Leslie Spann, who offered an impromptu recollection that touches on this topic. This kind of propitious correspondence is not uncommon as I am wrapping a book. It appears with her permission:

> I worked on a weight loss show—the show was about eighteen-year-old kids who graduated from high school and were going off to college. These kids had been overweight all of their young lives and they were wanting to lose weight, with a personal trainer, before they started their "new" lives as college students. Long story

---

* See "What If Age Is Nothing but a Mind-Set?" by Bruce Grierson in *The New York Times Magazine*, October 22, 2014. Researchers often dispute older studies, such as Langer's 1981 aging study, based on newer standards of methodology. But this phenomenon affects our view of all past clinical work, as it will affect how future researchers view today's practices, since methods inevitably progress.

> short, I was working with one of the girls who had been told her whole life she had a "pretty face." This is something many overweight girls/women hear and most of them hate hearing it because it really means, "You have a pretty face. Too bad about your fat body though." While talking to this girl, I asked her why she *really* wanted to lose weight. We were in the presence of her parents and her trainer. Her trainer had been really frustrated with her because she wasn't "giving it her all" during her workouts. When I asked why she wanted to lose weight, she gave the standard answer many people give, "For my health." I said to her, "That's bullshit. You are eighteen years old and are tired of being told you have a pretty face. You want to be hot. That's what you dream about when you think about losing weight. It ain't because of your health, because you're eighteen for chrissakes. Of course you want to be hot! That is part of what someone who is eighteen and going off to college to start her life SHOULD want—and that is absolutely nothing to be ashamed of. Embrace that and really understand that there is ZERO shame in wanting to love the way that you look and feel in your body!"
>
> Well, this was transformative for her. Her whole face lit up and there was a palpable shift in her energy from then on. She was literally set free in that moment. She needed permission to want what she actually wanted—rather than to want the thing for the socially acceptable lame-ass reason. I tell you this because I feel like it's such a beautiful example of what I've heard you talk about . . . when you are discussing the power of being honest about what one wants in their deepest heart of hearts.

At the core of Anton's philosophy is clarity of aim, wish, or desire. I have observed that as you pursue your aim, you may find that friends and coworkers are always trying to distract you with media or events that interest them but not you. We can absorb and retain only so much. What appeals to you in media, as in company, usually involves expanding your sense of self. (Or, more plainly, your sense of power.) This cannot occur if you are bound to other people's agendas. Anton put it this way in his 1986 essay "Don't Recycle Your Brain" from his newsletter *The Cloven Hoof*:

> I refuse to partake of trendy or pop input. Not so much because it usually replaces valued old information, but because it will "medioc-

> ritize" me. It will dilute my special kind of knowledge bank (which has allowed me to remain unique) to a sort of common knowledge catchall. It will render me more adaptable to the common denominators of the herd, but much less adaptive as a role model to others. Rather than being possessed of data that gives me social distinction, I will be able to discuss the same movies, plays, singers, TV shows and stars, current events, sports, etc., as everyone else. Thus, I won't *look* like everyone else, but the moment I open my mouth, I'll *sound* like them.

Anton's principle is that new intake must be "augmentive" of your valued ideas, concepts, and techniques. This does not mean you shouldn't experience something wholly new; such a break provides fresh perspective from which to measure your ideas and thought forms. The point is you don't *give away* your attention to whatever comes along or whatever peer activity beckons. You view media, entertainment, social outings, design, clothing, and so on, as units that augment your aim, style, personhood, total environment—and power.

Author and magician Alan Moore has spoken eloquently about the connection between fiction, language, and magic.* Moore has mentioned—and I can affirm—that anyone who's been writing for a while has a file of extraordinary coincidences in which experience follows story. I expect this holds true across the arts in general. Hence, Anton's concept of "make believe" is powerful in ways we may not always suspect.

Before Anton LaVey founded the Church of Satan in 1966, there really was no cohesive Satanic tradition in Western culture. There were individuals, rebellious figures who made counter and esoteric readings of some of the foundational Western myths. Some of these very individualized readings appeared in Romantic literature and other variants. There were figures like French novelist J.K. Huysmans (1848–1907) and others who wrote about black masses and related things that were largely fanciful, although they might have picked them up from self-styled Satanists in some reaches of bohemian or fin de siècle culture.

* "Language, Writing and Magic," talk delivered September 6, 2016, YouTube.

But spiritual tradition requires liturgy, lineage, foundational literature, and, in some cases, a congregation. None of this has been true for Satanism although I do venture an esoteric historical reading in my *Uncertain Places*. Satanism is an anarchistic movement. With regard to elements like a black mass, there is no longstanding practice that extends back centuries or millennia, in the same way that we point to liturgical traditions in Buddhism, Islam, Judaism, or Christianity.

For the most part, charges of Satanism (in a negative sense) were directed by early church fathers against remaining pockets of paganism in late antiquity; the church wished to define religious holdouts—already on their way to vanquishment—as forces against which military and judicial power could be wielded. As the early church grew, and Christianity became Rome's officially sanctioned religion, the fading pagan powers were depicted as demonic (again, this was once a neutral term) and Satanic. They were described by labels they had never applied to themselves. Had pagan powers prevailed, they would have done the same thing to the early church. In matters of religion, at least, victors write the dominant history.

I must clarify a further historical point—one with a deep hold on contemporary pop culture: Satanism and cases of possession. Historian Massimo Introvigne provides a typically clarifying note:

> It could be said, in general, that Satanists seek the Devil, while the possessed claim they have been "found" by the Devil, whom normally they had not consciously sought. The Satanists *would like* to encounter the Devil, and some of them use specific rituals for calling or evoking him. On the contrary, the victims of spectacular demonic possessions have often been pious and devout Christians, very far away from the ideology and the activities of Satanists.

For several years recent to this writing, the Vatican has more than quadrupled the number of church-certified exorcists in the United States. The number has risen from about 12 to 50.* Church authorities generally blame this wave of demand on New Age culture, popularized occultism, Ouija boards, and so on. Another, probably likelier facet is entertainment. Horror is among the few movie genres that

---

* "Leading U.S. exorcists explain huge increase in demand for the Rite—and priests to carry them out" by Rachel Ray, *The Telegraph*, September 26, 2016.

coincide with belief due to congruency between many of its themes and spiritual or religious concepts, ranging from ghosts to after-death survival to demon possession.

Hence, the 1973 movie version of *The Exorcist*—one of the most talked-about films ever made and without which I doubt most people would even know the term *exorcism*—produced myriad spinoffs. How an idea goes viral remains mysterious but that perception and screen coincide is a given. Although less of an immediate blockbuster, the enduring classic *The Wicker Man*, released the same year as *The Exorcist*, about a Scottish island preserve of pagan practitioners, is widely considered one of the most historically authentic occult films ever made. *The Wicker Man* stands in polarity to *The Exorcist*, which takes a religiously condemnatory view of the occult. In more admiring terms, screenwriter Anthony Schaffer said in the 2021 documentary on folk horror, *Woodlands Dark and Days Bewitched*: "Paganism has a habit of surviving."

"Satanists seek the Devil," Introvigne wrote. What about the age-old myth of the rapacious seeker selling his soul, as explored in Marlowe's *Faust*? Many such stories populate folklore and literature. Among the most alluring was related by Baroque violinist Giuseppe Tartini (1692–1770). The composer's famously complex Violin Sonata in G minor, better known as the Devil's Trill Sonata, was, he said, played for him in a dream by Satan. To his agony, Tartini said that on waking he could reconstruct just a shadow of the original. A similar mythos of Satanic dispensation surrounds the career of virtuoso violinist Niccolò Paganini (1782–1840).

As yet another exhibit of Madame Blavatsky's omnipresence, the occultist adapted Tartini's narrative into a short story, "The Ensouled Violin," originally appearing in *The Theosophist* in January 1880 and in her posthumous 1892 collection *Nightmare Tales*. As it must, Blavatsky's horror tale has its own legend, which is that was cowritten, along with several other collaborations, by the hidden Cyprian adept called Master Hillarion.

One of the most popular modern iterations of soul-selling involves American bluesman Robert Johnson (1911–1938). As popular legend tells it, the guitarist met or conjured the devil at a crossroads and vowed to serve him in exchange for preternatural musical skills.

Although Johnson did record a song called "Crossroads," it was not about soul-selling but hitchhiking. But another blues master, Tommy Johnson (1896–1956), performed a similar—though more elusive—act of magick, recounted by his brother LeDell:

> If you want to learn how to make songs yourself, you take your guitar and you go to where the road crosses that way, where a crossroads is. Get there, be sure to get there just a little 'fore 12 that night so you know you'll be there. You have your guitar and be playing a piece there by yourself . . . A big black man will walk up there and take your guitar and he'll tune it. And then he'll play a piece and hand it back to you. That's the way I learned to play anything I want.*

Ledell does not specifically reference Tommy engaging in soul-selling or encountering Satan. Rather, Tommy drew upon a practice found in the Black magical tradition of hoodoo. Hoodoo references, especially to mojo bags, crossings, and spellwork, appear frequently in blues lyrics. Within the framework of hoodoo, Tommy, at least in his brother's account, was practicing a retention of Western and Central African magic in which a seeker summons a deific protector, sometimes in the form of Ellegua or Eshu, who guards the crossroads and dispenses wisdom and artistry, not dissimilar to the Hellenic gods Hermes or Mercury.

Where, finally, does the idea of selling your soul to Satan originate from, at least in the Western mind? The likeliest and earliest source is the Old Testament book Isaiah 28:15, in which nonbelievers are said to elude consequence by striking a deal with Dark Forces. It appears this way in a 1985 translation by the Jewish Publication Society (JPS):

> For you have said, "We have made a covenant with Death, Concluded a pact with *Sheol*. When the sweeping flood passes through, It shall not reach us; For we have made falsehood our refuge, Taken shelter in treachery."

Sheol references the Hebrew concept of the afterworld—sometimes translated *nether-world* as in JPS's 1917 translation—and is

* *Tommy Johnson* by David Evans (Studio Vista, 1971).

not synonymous with later concepts of Hell, the term appearing in the King James Bible. Although notions of a personified Satan had not fully taken shape in the biblical era, the idea of a maleficent pact spread among early Christians and probably formed the basis of "selling your soul."

In 1969, a searching and brilliantly heterodox U.S. Army officer—and specialist in psychological operations or PSYOP—entered Anton LaVey's orbit. This was Michael Aquino, whose efforts opened a new chapter in Satanism.

Aquino first briefly encountered LaVey in 1968 at the San Francisco premiere of *Rosemary's Baby*, the gelling agent for so much in modern Satanism. A recent graduate of UC Santa Barbara and commissioned officer, Aquino spent part of 1968 to 1969 at Fort Bragg with the 82nd Airborne Division and later as a PSYOP/Special Forces officer at the base's JFK Special Warfare Center.* In early 1969, the second lieutenant found himself questioning life's purpose. A study of existential philosophy had only deepened his despair and he was contemplating suicide.**

While on leave in March in San Francisco—where he was soon to be married—Aquino spotted an ad in the underground newspaper *Berkeley Barb* for a Satanic circle at Anton's Black House. Although the evening featured its share of garish theatrics, including a robed henchman stationed at the door (in actuality a lecturer in history at the University of San Francisco) and Anton's emergence from an Egyptian sarcophagus, the gathering itself featured ideas that spoke to the soldier-seeker. And then there was the figure of Anton himself: relaxed, self-assured, good humored, powerful but not arrogant, smiling not in a cruel fashion but "full of the purest metaphysical good humor," Aquino wrote. It was sealed: "I reached out and took the apple."***

"At that point," Aquino later wrote a friend—the same doorman at the Black House, "Anton LaVey said, 'Where there is no meaning,

---

* *Lords of the Left-Hand Path* by Stephen E. Flowers, Ph.D. (Inner Traditions, 1997, 2012).

** *Children of Lucifer: The Origins of Modern Religious Satanism* by Ruben van Luijk (Oxford University Press, 2016).

*** *The Church of Satan* by Michael A. Aquino, Sixth Edition, 2009—here and the two quotes following.

we *ourselves* can *create* it. Thus we are not creatures, but *creators: we* are gods.' It took me a long time to understand the full implications of such a hypothesis, but even in its most immediate sense it was a philosophical lifeline." Back at Fort Bragg, Aquino and his new wife ("a nominal Mormon") sent in their membership applications.

The erudite and enterprising Aquino was exactly who Anton wanted around him. The founder was loathe for the Church of Satan to become a reserve of nudniks and ne'er-do-wells. He insisted that the mark of a Satanist, versus a hapless "occultnik," entailed success in outer life. "Membership inquires continue to increase," Anton wrote Aquino in 1972, "but brain surgeons and Congressmen are still in short supply. Clearly increased membership per se will not elevate us beyond our present level but only hold us down."

Aquino proved his mettle not only organizationally but literarily. When returning to an active tour of duty in Vietnam in June 1969, Aquino brought with him a copy of Milton's *Paradise Lost*. In combat, Aquino's PSYOP job included "experiments to disorient Vietcong and North Vietnamese soldiers by using amplified sounds—sometimes complete with 'demonic screams'—blaring from helicopters flying over their heads," writes Stephen E. Flowers. When done with such tasks, the officer dedicated himself to Milton, which inspired a short and remarkable literary effort of his own, *The Diabolicon*.

Aquino's strangely precise and singular prose provides a haunting record of how he wrote his Satanic manifesto in battle. As Aquino puts it in his privately published, two-volume omnibus *The Church of Satan*:

> I had taken with me a copy of John Milton's epic *Paradise Lost*, which I considered then, as now, one of the most exalted statements of Satanism ever written. Satan is its true hero; its Christian moralisms are so pale and watery in comparison that I am surprised it and its author were not summarily burned upon its appearance in Cromwellian England. That it not only survived Puritan censorship but was actually lauded as a compliment to Christianity is yet another of those titanic ironies which have accompanied the Prince of Darkness on his tortuous journey across the eras of human civilization.
>
> As much as I admired *Paradise Lost*, I was annoyed at its ever-present, if pro forma bias. The die was loaded against Satan; he might put up a good fight, but in the end he was doomed to defeat.

> It was not so much that I wanted to see him triumph. Rather I felt that his power and position were equal to God's if not more potent, and I wanted to see a contest that would more accurately represent the struggle between the Powers of Darkness and those of Light.
>
> In early 1970 I took pen in hand and, during the moments when I was not occupied with military responsibilities [at the time I was based in the village of Lai Khe, directing PSYOP teams for the 1st Infantry Division], I began to write a restatement of certain themes from *Paradise Lost.* It was hardly an "ivory tower" meditation. I wrote in old, bombed-out buildings dating from the French occupation, in helicopters, in tents, and in the midst of underbrush . . . Part of the text of the "Statement of Beelzebub" had to be reconstructed from notes at one point when an incoming rocket blew a packet of papers [and the storage room holding them] to atoms. Often . . . I would be interrupted from my musings by the sudden necessity to dive for a sandbagged bomb shelter.
>
> Slowly but inevitably, however, the manuscript crept towards completion. I say "inevitably" because I began to develop a most peculiar feeling about it. As I wrote the sequential passages, I seemed to sense, rather than determine what they should say. And if I penned words or phrases that "didn't fit", I would experience continual irritation and impatience until I had replaced them with the "correct" combination. It was as though the text had a life of its own . . .

Aquino's statement should be kept handy by anyone who complains, "I don't have time to write." The officer completed his manuscript in March 1970 and sent it to Anton, who responded enthusiastically. (Aquino also wrote two of the Lovecraftian rites, "Ceremony of the Angles" and "The Call to Cthulhu," in *The Satanic Rituals.*)

The Diabolicon reinterprets the war in heaven from Revelation 12:7–10, which led to the expulsion of the Great Rebel and his legions. The concise *Diabolicon* re-visions, according to Aquino's insights, the friction between his gnostic view of a passive, hypocritical force of conformity—God and his legions—versus a radical, unbending individualism and wish for growth and development—Satan and his forces, who are fiercely committed to man's progress. With Anton's showmanship and vision, Aquino's literary efforts and organizational skills, national media at the beckon, and elbow-rubs with celebrities like Sammy Davis and Jayne Mansfield (Anton engineered mutually beneficial publicity photos with the bombshell actress), all seemed well in the Infernal Empire. But, as with nearly every community of belief, cracks emerged.

In May 1975, Aquino was editing an issue of *The Cloven Hoof* and read a draft article by Anton that made him double-take. The leader was offering to sell initiatory ranks from within the church. Aquino knew money was tight and proposed alternatives; but he considered sale of ranks dishonorable and corrupt. Anton had his own reasons both commercially and, possibly, linked to attracting *haves* versus *have-nots*. Whatever the case, the men clashed and in June Aquino resigned, taking the liberty of telling Anton that the church's "infernal mandate" was hereby withdrawn. Not only was Aquino leaving but he explained that the church, while serving as a preliminary vehicle, could no longer function under the "Will of Satan."

Was there any such *will*? And had Aquino any right to invoke it? The first question points to an underlying debate: whether Satanism is a strictly atheistic philosophy employing iconography and metaphor as symbols for self-development—or whether there are, in fact, extraphysical intelligences and dimensions in connection with the Satanic search. Current leaders of the Church of Satan emphasize the former; Aquino emphasized the latter. Where did Anton stand? Aquino claimed, based strictly on recollection, that in 1974 Anton revealed to him a written pact with Satan, suggesting literal belief in the Prince of Darkness. To my knowledge, no one else has seen this pact. The best I can surmise, based on Anton's nonbinary intellectual style, is that the church leader cracked open the door to either interpretation—I doubt theism versus atheism was a barbed-wire dividing line for him. There are longtime church members today who, at least in conversation, acknowledge the existence or possibility of the metaphysical.

Aquino stuck by his interpretation of the extraphysical side to Satanism, which he believed was a shared experience in the early circles:

> Satanists participating in rituals of Black Magic quickly became aware of an "interest" or "influence" in the atmosphere of the chamber that felt somehow alien to their own personalities. The pageantry and the oratory would fade into the background, and

> the participants would find themselves gripped in a sensory empathy so piercing, so powerful that it would leave them exhausted, drained, and shaken at the conclusion of the rite. It was not a chance occurrence, but an inevitable, recurring one. After such experiences participants were subdued, introspective, and disinclined to exchange comments on their feelings. There was perhaps even a slight feeling of embarrassment, as though one had somehow "slipped" from being a proper psychodramatic atheist.
>
> And Anton LaVey was himself the most familiar with this sensation. His behavior during a ritual was not that of an actor, nor of a megalomaniac, but rather of a High Priest in the sincere sense.

Feeling possessed of prophetic authority, Aquino that year crafted a new manifesto—*The Book of Coming Forth By Night*—and with it a new movement: The Temple of Set. Aquino said that the Great Rebel communicated to him that he no longer wished to be known by the adulterated Hebrew *Satan* but by his proper name *Set*, Egypt's god of storms and the desert, usurper and murderer of his brother Osiris, and sometime rival of Horus, alternately described as Set's nephew (the avenging son of Osiris and Isis) or brother. In at least one bas relief at the Egypt Museum in Cairo, Horus and Set are shown intertwining plants of Upper and Lower Egypt, thus uniting two lands, during the reign of Senusret I, c. 1971–1926 B.C. In Egyptian hieroglyph and symbol, Set appears with sharply protruding vertical ears, like twin bars, and a long, aardvark-like snout, his head perched upon a male human body. The deity is sometimes called the "Set animal"—a creature of unknown provenance.

In *The Book of Coming Forth by Night*, Set recalls deputizing Anton, now honorably deposed, to carry out his will: "Known as the Hebrew Satan, I chose to bring forth a Magus, according to the fashion of my Word. He was charged to form a Church of Satan, that I might easily touch the minds of men in this image they had cast for me. In the fifth year of the Church of Satan, I gave to this Magus my *Diabolicon* [delivered through Aquino], that he might know the truth of my ancient Gift to mankind, clothed though it might be in the myths of the Hebrews."

Set then describes manifesting to Aleister Crowley in 1904 through *The Book of the Law*, appearing to the magician as Horus, the deity's "Opposite Self." Crowley's work, potent but erratic, was felled by his "mindless destructiveness." Hence, *The Book of Coming Forth by Night* posits a modern lineage running from Crowley to Anton to Aquino, who is now charged with bringing the message of the Aeon of Set. *The Book of Coming Forth by Night* continues:

> The Satanist thought to approach Satan through ritual. Now let the Setian shun all recitation, for the text of another is an affront to the Self. Speak rather to me as a friend, gently and without fear. Do not bend your knee nor drop your eye, for such things were not done in my house at PaMat-et [the original priesthood center to Set in Upper Egypt]. But speak to me at night, because the sky then becomes an entrance and not a barrier. And those who call me the Prince of Darkness do me no dishonor.

To the second question I posed about whether Aquino possessed any *right* to invoke Satanic Will, I conclude only this: Virtually every religious movement in history begins with an individual's testimony of a purportedly greater vision. The evaluation of such a vision rests chiefly on its evocative persuasiveness, as well as the personal gravity of its messenger. In that vein, I rank Aquino among the primary theoreticians of any modern religious movement.

Rumors persist that Aquino attempted to conjure "the Devil" in Himmler's one-time redoubt, Wewelsburg castle in the Northern Rhine. Not exactly—but nor is the matter invention, either.

In October 1982, Aquino participated in a series of tours of European NATO installations. Later that month, through considerable personal effort, he located and entered the Renaissance-age castle, discovering Himmler's original ceremonial rooms. Historian Nevill Drury writes in *Stealing Fire from Heaven:*

> The specific links between the Setian philosophy and the magical practices of the esoteric Nazi group led by Heinrich Himmler are hard to identify but are nevertheless present. Although Aquino states very clearly that there are many aspects of the Nazi era that are repugnant to him, he is also convinced that the Nazis were able to summon an extraordinary psychic force which was misdirected—but need not have been.

In another of his two-volume omnibus editions (the Setian was nothing if not assiduous), the 2016 *Temple of Set*, Aquino reproduced his correspondence to Temple members explaining his intent "to summon the Powers of Darkness at their most powerful locus." The results of his "Wewelsburg Working" are opaque but I briefly quote one insight:

> Strengthen, exalt, and encourage the willful self, and you cannot avoid strengthening the natural instincts as well. No human being is free from these; they may be kept in check for years, but in eventual moments of stress, weakness, or stimulus they will break free. They may be either creative or destructive; this is not a mere "Jekyll/Hyde" scenario.

The passage highlights the intrinsic problem of actually *maintaining* any kind of Satanic order. Aquino observed that when a seeker is dedicated, unsentimentally and realistically, to self-development, whatever progress is experienced inclines him or her *less* toward an organization. As soon as members discover things of their own, they want to leave or become leaders themselves. In his social history, *Satanism*, Massimo Introvigne observes: "These problems, Aquino insisted, were not due to the personalities of the leaders or the members of the Church of Satan or the Temple of Set. They were due to the paradox that, the more an occult Satanist order is successful in strengthening self-consciousness, the more it sows the seeds of its own ruin by strengthening at the same time natural instinct."

Crowley's *Book of the Law* reads, "Success is thy proof: argue not; convert not; talk not over much!" The Left-Hand Path may finally entail solitary work.

In 1987, Aquino and his second wife Lilith faced a years-long period of agony, legal wrangling, and exoneration after being falsely accused of sexual abuse by the three-year-old daughter of a Presidio Army base clergyman during a flare up of "Satanic Panic" hysteria.

Investigators found that in the weeks of the claimed incident the Aquinos were not even in San Francisco but rather were living in Washington, D.C. No charges were filed. The Aquinos unsuccessfully attempted legal action against the girl's chaplain father and an Army psychiatrist who stoked the false claims. But the couple faced the barrier of gravitating between civilian and military law.

"Despite these setbacks," writes historian Gareth Medway, "the Aquinos were successful in legal actions against two books—Carl A. Raschke's *Painted Black* and Linda Blood's *The New Satanists*—that suggested they had been guilty. Both cases were settled out of court, and the Aquinos report themselves 'satisfied.'"* In an example of how these canards endure, a podcaster in 2021 attempted to play "gotcha" with me using *thirty-year-old* news coverage impugning Aquino, either unaware or unconcerned that the allegations were long since discredited.

In 1994, Aquino retired from the military as a lieutenant colonel and was awarded the Meritorious Service Medal. News of his death began circulating online in 2020. The Setian apparently intended to keep his passing private, at which he succeeded remarkably well in a digital age. According to San Francisco County records, the Temple of Set founder died at seventy-five on September 1, 2019.

Other organizations rumored to be "Satanic" came and went on the cultural scene. The most notorious—and misunderstood—was the Process Church of the Final Judgment, a group founded in England in 1966 by two excommunicated Scientologists. Again, suggesting that truth always beats fiction—and plenty of fiction swirled around the innovative sect—senior members of the Process Church in 1973 sublet the New York City apartment of actress Ruth Gordon, who played the busybody Satanic neighbor in *Rosemary's Baby*.**

The Process has been linked to everything from the Son of Sam serial killings in New York City in the 1970s to worldwide Satanic cult conspiracies—so that the facts, infinitely more benign but possessed of remarkable folds of their own, are difficult to discern in our era of digital burlesque, especially when lessons from Satanic Panic hysteria appear willfully lost on some commentators.

---

* *Lure of the Sinister: The Unnatural History of Satanism* by Gareth Medway (New York University Press, 2001).

** *Love, Fear, Sex, Death: The Inside Story of the Process Church of the Final Judgment* by Timothy Wyllie, edited by Adam Parfrey (Feral House, 2009).

The story begins in 1962, when Robert de Grimston Moor and Mary Ann MacLean met in the London branch of the Church of Scientology. Mary Ann, a former high-end call girl with a fiercely determined intellect, was already seen as a comer in church ranks, and quickly ascended to the position of auditor. Robert, a recently divorced dropout from architectural college, was a vulnerable seeker. The two immediately bonded and discovered their shared distaste for the personality cult around L. Ron Hubbard.*

The couple left the church in 1963, starting their own therapeutic organization, Compulsions Analysis, which combined Scientology methods with the developmental psychology of Alfred Adler (1870–1937). Scientology leadership soon branded the pair "squirrels"—people who use Scientology outside approved ranks—and in 1965 Hubbard declared the renegades "suppressive persons," the group's ultimate mark of Cain. That year, Mary Ann and Robert found that they and their clients possessed deep yearning for spirituality—and Compulsions Analysis became The Process. At Mary Ann's urging, Robert dropped his surname and went by the more alluring de Grimston.

Gathering a coterie of thirty followers and six German shepherds, the couple spent the next several years roaming the world with an eye on establishing an intentional community. It never took root in any one place. Their longest group-stay was about a month in summer-fall 1966 on an abandoned coastal estate in Mexico's Yucatan peninsula called Xtul ("The End"). While at Xtul, the group developed an apocalyptic and psychologized theology involving a three-part structure of deities that comport with human personality types: Lucifer, Jehovah, and Satan, the last of which possesses both lower and higher iterations. The three types are unified by the emissary and cosmic messenger of Christ.

One striking feature among writers and bloggers who spin tales of conspiracy around The Process, some of which are shortly considered, is near-total unfamiliarity with (or evident curiosity toward) the theology of the group, whose activities, real and imaginary, they

* Sources on The Process include Wyllie (2009), Introvigne (2016), and the one work of field scholarship on the group that is universally recognized for its quality, proximity, and reliability, *Satan's Power: A Deviant Psychotherapy Cult* by William Sims Bainbridge (University of California Press, 1978). Bainbridge, a sociologist, gained the group's trust and transparently joined for the purpose of documentation. In his highly readable monograph, Bainbridge alters proper names, referring to The Process as "The Power."

otherwise obsess over. Some of the Process Church's documents are obscure and difficult to find, others are available through online postings or in published editions. The FBI assembled a 171-page file on the group, chiefly composed of pages from Process magazines and newsletters. My theological interpretation is drawn in part from a rare 1970 church publication, *The Gods and Their People* recorded by Robert de Grimston.

In Process theology, every personality contains all three deific correspondences, with one dominant. The dominant strain has higher and lower iterations—but particularly the Satanic. The lower iteration of Satan is animalistic, violent, and lustful. Jehovah is punitive, loving, self-denying, legalistic, and strict. Lucifer is artistic, libertine, sensitive, and possessed of *joie de vivre*. The higher iteration of Satan is the force of radical selfhood, genius, magic, and mysticism. The figure of Christ is, as noted, unifying messenger. During the group's active years, Christ was variously emphasized in lesser or greater roles. Process theology was not a frozen block but underwent change and experiment.

Understanding, honoring, and integrating the Satanic and Luciferian elements were, without question, at the heart of The Process. Using his terminology for the group, Bainbridge wrote: "The Power was a Satanic cult, but *Satan* had a very special meaning for Powerites that no outsider could easily grasp." This is where most misunderstandings of The Process and Satanism in general arise from. Simplistic as it seems, many critics, both then and now, appear unable to fathom that a group or individual may be using a term *in a manner that differs from convention* or entertainment. In most such cases, critical surface assumptions are never once questioned or probed, sometimes with entire books, articles, or campaigns enacted based upon an observer's confidence that nothing more than a "familiar" or pop cultural definition of Satanism need be ventured. No matter how often The Process explained itself, for critics the needle never moved.

Although the bearded and handsome Robert was the group's public voice and face, most insiders viewed Mary Ann, who insisted on keeping in the background, as the visionary behind the curtain. Under the couple's leadership—and that of art director Timothy Wyllie—The Process embarked on an extraordinary series of publications and illustrated magazines so bracingly original in appearance (and often content) that it seems a gap in our understanding of 1960s counterculture that Process materials have not been made the subject of a gallery exhibit. (Publisher Feral House has admirably anthologized some of their illustrated material.)

The Process pursued direct provocation through aesthetics. Again Bainbridge:

> Powerites enjoyed projecting a wild image. Their black uniforms and red emblems excited cult members as much as they worried the general public. In its own imagination The Power was a Satanic cult. "Black is the color of the Bottomless Void to which the human race is doomed by its insistence upon a GODless compromise of living death. So Black we shall wear in mourning for the doom mankind has brought upon itself." Announcing themselves with such lurid rhetoric, the Beings of The Power stalked Europe and America in the late 1960s and early 1970s, dressed in sinister black uniforms with flowing cloaks, accompanied by huge Alsatian hounds and plagued by the vilest of rumors, bearing upon their chests the sign of the Devil, the red Mendes Goat badge.*

In the era of Vietnam, "Sympathy for the Devil," burgeoning witchcraft, and the underground aesthetics of Anton LaVey and Kenneth Anger, The Process seemed like the ultimate countercultural avatar of the Aquarian Age. No syrupy smelling incense, love beads, and Flower Power bromides—but hardcore aesthetics and foreboding pageantry. Celebrities, the magnetic lodestones of public titillation, grew intrigued—and The Process attracted queries, sometimes fleeting and other times more engaged, from an unlikely range of freethinkers from Mary Tyler Moore and Dick Van Dyke to Marianne Faithfull and Mick Jagger. The latter two appeared on covers of the church's magazine with one issue featuring an interview with Mick. In the late '60s, the group's street presence and chapters quickly grew, expanding to San Francisco, Southern California, New Orleans, New York City, Toronto, London, Munich, and Amsterdam. Their magazines proved

* I am stricter in my use of *cult* than Bainbridge. He writes, "I define *cult* as *a culturally innovative cohesive group oriented to supernatural concerns.*" Acknowledging colloquial usage and understanding, I define cult as an abusive and isolating community of belief. Hence, I call The Process a *sect.*

a hot street commodity; money and media attention flowed; membership expanded; and all seemed well. Until what Bainbridge calls "The Manson Disaster."

The cultural story around Charles Manson and The Process Church is at once confounding and simple, reflecting the Rorschach tendency of commentators, observers, and writers to believe what they wish, with sometimes-bounding leaps of supposition.

With the October 1969 arrest and sensationalized trials of Manson and members of the Manson Family, prosecutors and the media were eager to mine the sources behind Manson's worldview and the ritualistic-style killings. Rumors abounded that The Process was the source of Manson's ideology, if not a direct springboard and confederate. Prosecutor Vincent Bugliosi and others detected correspondences between Manson and Process theology. This is not out of the question, since Manson, although never a member or active participant, was in a position to encounter the influential street group during his days in San Francisco and Southern California. In the same manner that Manson imbibed and mutated ideas he detected in Beatles' lyrics, there is no reason to assume that The Process, then a source of countercultural fascination, would prove exempt.

How The Process handled the matter is controversial and questionable. In 1970, during Manson's trial in connection with the killings of Sharon Tate and housemates and Leno and Rosemary LaBianca, two members of The Process made an impromptu visit to prosecutor Bugliosi. They assured him that Manson had no connection to the group, that its leadership never met him, and, in any case, they opposed violence. They left Bugliosi with a stack of Process literature. He seemed satisfied. But Bugliosi wrote in his 1974 bestseller *Helter Skelter* that the following day the names of his two guests also "appeared on Manson's visitor's list. What they discussed is unknown. All I know is that in my last conversation with Manson, Charlie became evasive when I questioned him about The Process."

Manson's guests solicited from him (or perhaps transcribed) a short article on the nature of death, which they ran in their 1971 issue thematically titled *Death*. Manson's piece appeared opposite an interview on the subject with Catholic social critic Malcolm Muggeridge. Looking today at the modest layout of the page, with text columns and photographs of Manson and Muggeridge juxtaposed under the headline, "From Manson to Muggeridge (or the reconciliation of opposites)," it is difficult to view it as a source of high controversy—but the blowback proved extreme.

The Process was seen as a bloodthirsty cult in league with the culture's most fearsome image of social upheaval and murderous cruelty. Matters deepened later that year when musician and hippie literary eminence Ed Sanders published *The Family*, his take on the Manson circle, written with understandable umbrage at how Manson, as Sanders saw it, usurped, perverted, and smeared hippie rebelliousness.

But Sanders went a step too far. He dedicated a full chapter to The Process—"hooded snuffoids" and "a black-caped, black-garbed, devil-worshipping church"—asserting, by way of hearsay, supposition, and circumstance, spurious connection between the Church and Manson. The Process sued for libel and settled out of court in early 1972 requiring publisher, Dutton, to paste a *mea culpa* addendum inside its remaining stock and excise The Process chapter and other references from future editions. "A close examination," the addendum read, "has revealed that statements in the book about The Process Church, including those attributing any connection between The Process and the activities of Charles Manson . . . have not been substantiated."

In England, where libel laws place a higher burden on plaintiffs, The Process sued the British publisher—and lost. (Although the publisher did elect to reissue the book without the offending passages.) In this, several observers saw the group's unraveling. "Possibly the rot set in when we lost that English court case against the Ed Sanders book," Wyllie wrote, continuing:

> It was Mary Ann's idea not to demand a substantial sum in damages when we settled the American case. She would have wanted to impress people with how decent we were and how it wasn't about the money, but just about clearing the name of The Process. Presumably it was this miscalculation that encouraged the publisher in England to think we were rollovers—which turned out to be perfectly true.

In fact, The Process had to pay legal costs of the English press. "Out of the money we had scribbled off the streets for them, no less," Wyllie noted.

To Bainbridge, an even more pernicious cycle set in: the radical sect began *hedging*. Not only did it receive no money from publisher Dutton but, "In a meek attempt to assert its new, clean image, the cult inserted the following self-description in the press release [at the front of the book]: 'The Power is a religious organization devoted to spreading the word of Christ.'" Bainbridge noted ruefully:

> The Power was not responsible for Manson, but the controversy had a tremendous impact on the cult. Already committed to making peace with conventional society, already completely dependent on the good will of conventional society for its economic life, The Power was spurred to even greater attempts to clean up its image and downplay the Satanic aspect of its doctrines. St. Peter denied Christ and suffered for it; The Power would deny Satan and also suffer. To escape the dark halo of Satan, it would compulsively overfulfill the demands of Christ. To gain public support, it would first hide, then later abandon some of its most precious symbols and concepts, leaving a gnawing cultural void. Without Satan, what would distinguish The Power from all other religions?

Over de Grimston's objections, Process theology downplayed the Satanic, with signature black robes replaced by gray leisure-style suits, flying in the face of its own theology which saw grey as the name and color of conformity. Images of Mendes goats were discarded. Group members began looking like stage-costumed versions of the Osmonds—except for another innovation: large, gold-colored Star of David amulets decorated with the letters FF symbolizing the scrubbed group's new name, Foundation Church of the Millennium and then Foundation Faith of the Millennium.

In 1974, Robert and Mary Ann separated and he left the group. Before long, smiling members of Foundation Faith appeared in photographs with Alabama Governor George Wallace for a "faith healing" in his executive office. By 1982, remaining members of the group relocated to Utah where they created Best Friends, an ongoing and highly regarded animal shelter. As of 1993, the group became known as Best

Friends Animal Society. Mary Ann died in 2005 and, as of this writing, Robert lives quietly on Staten Island in New York City.

That would seem to suggest the end of The Process—but for an ongoing mythology. In 1987, New York journalist Maury Terry published his massive investigation into an alternative theory of the Son of Sam murders, *The Ultimate Evil*.

Terry, who died in 2015, maintained that David Berkowitz's victims were actually murdered by varied shooters who, along with Berkowitz, emanated from a vicious Satanic cult—The Process Church, a group, states the book's back cover copy, "whose deadly influence reaches across America, from New York City to Beverly Hills and countless towns in between . . . For today the Process is very much alive . . . and still killing." Stock images of Manson and Berkowitz adorned the front of the Bantam edition. Within are the author's ominous references to the Golden Dawn, Aleister Crowley, and Eliphas Lévi.

Reading Terry's book, I find it striking that this dogged researcher who spent decades pursuing his thesis demonstrated no instance, in a paperback of nearly 700 pages, of familiarity with, questions over, or curiosity toward Process theology or, in fact, any variant of Satanism beyond the pitchforks-and-sacrifices framing dominant in pop culture. Terry's connections between The Process and the Sam murders rest on distantly circumstantial symbols, conversations with sympathetic fellow travelers, and leaps of supposition greater than those ventured by Sanders.

Because Terry's work often functions as a resource for blogs and videos that posit Satanic connections behind sensational crimes (real or imagined), I want to quote Feral House publisher Adam Parfrey's (1957-2018) introduction to Wyllie's book:

> I first learned in 1987 that some of the conspiracy literature regarding The Process Church was either dishonest or was poorly fact-checked. After hearing a rumor that Robert de Grimston was listed in the Staten Island phone book under his given name Robert Moor, I called him up—that is, after certain hesitation. After all, Maury Terry's *The Ultimate Evil* informs us that de Grimston is a diabolical mystery man who had removed himself from the world at large to pursue the practice of evil. What was he doing so easily

reached in the phone book? And how confident could I be of Maury Terry's research if he couldn't even bother locating Robert de Grimston by calling the Information operator?

After dialing the listed Mr. Moor and hearing the phone answered by a polite man with a British accent, I was more than a bit surprised. Though he wasn't particularly happy to receive an unexpected phone call, Mr. Moor and I spoke for ten minutes about the conspiracy literature ("unbearable . . . a pack of lies"), and my appeal for him to tell his story ("I'll think about it").

Maury Terry reveals more about his experts on The Process Church within *The Ultimate Evil*:

> *I raised the subject of the dead German shepherds with Larry Siegel . . . Larry, twenty-seven, was a well-informed researcher and professional writer. He'd offered to spend some time checking into the occult, and was ready with an opinion.*
>
> *"You've heard of the Process, right? Well, the Process kept German shepherds."*

Here, a 27-year-old "researcher" speculates that since The Process Church took care of German shepherds, some sort of weird splinter group must be the ones massacring them à la the Son of Sam murders in the late '70s long after The Process Church folded and became The Foundation. Maury Terry further writes:

> *The Process, as far as is known, has now officially splintered, and its offspring—while still active—have gone underground. But before the Process divided, it spread seeds of destruction throughout the United States. Those spores were carried on winds of evil across the 1970s and into the present. The terror still reigns with far-flung subsidiary groups united by the sins of the father.*

It's strange to see these unsubstantiated assertions stated as fact, and repeated widely online as absolute proof. Coincidentally, Maury Terry's New York agent contacted Feral House in 2008 to publish a revised edition of *The Ultimate Evil*.

In 2021, Netflix ran a true-crime docuseries, *Sons of Sam: A Descent into Darkness*, based on Terry's book and at times critical of it. I was contracted for an interview but it got canceled during the Covid lockdown. I later sat for a taped interview for the series' official podcast; my comments were not aired.

From an occult and artistic perspective, The Process does have a fuller legacy. The group's strategies and aesthetics proved an influence on the highly inventive punk-arts-magick collective Thee Temple ov Psychick Youth or TOPY, founded in 1981 by a cohort of East London artists including Genesis and Paula P-Orridge, Derek Jarman, and Peter "Sleazy" Christopherson. TOPY functioned as a culturally and intimately exploratory movement dedicated to individual development, new modes of living, and experiments in artistic, musical, sexual, and bodily expression. The group placed considerable emphasis on chaos magick.

Among TOPY's most lasting legacies is how it explored the psychological and magickal effects of body art, adornment, and self-presentation, areas where cofounder Genesis P-Orridge (1950–2020) took inspiration from The Process. "Since the mid-'60s, my teenage years," the artist wrote in a contributed chapter to *Love, Sex, Fear Death*, "I have been profoundly obsessed with human behavior—whether there can be a system or discipline that is able to reprogram entrenched, inherited patterns of behavior." Genesis continued, "Parallel to this aesthetic and philosophical obsession has been an almost symbiotic series of similarities of problems and media issues that feel as if they are delivered like an advisory commentary of The Process."

For the dawning punk generation, Genesis explained, The Process held the promise of something not-yet-articulated: "The Process were the same group accused of being the 'Mindbenders of Mayfair' and later further alleged by the gutter press to have programmed the Manson Family, the Son of Sam and who knows what else. The Process became symbolic of the neo-hippie bogeyman! Anyone able to shatter society's complacency on such a deep level resonated with my own compulsive urge to strip away imposed behavioral patterns so that my life could be an unfolding, autonomous narrative written by my self-conscious choices."

In pioneering TOPY, P-Orridge pondered:

> What would happen if we created a paramilitary occult organization that shared demystified magickal techniques? Sleeve notes

> could become manifestos, a call to action and behavioral rebellion. Bit by bit we took this daydream more seriously. We examined The Process in particular for the 'best' in cult aesthetics. We needed an ideology, levels to achieve, secrets to reveal to those involved, symbols and uniforms, regalia and internal writings . . .
>
> TOPY's uniform combined gray priest shirts we bought at Roman Catholic suppliers with gray military-style trousers and combat boots. Embroidered patches in the vesica (vaginal) shape with a Psychick Cross and the number 23 were sewn on jackets and shirts to identify the TOPY community. We looked again at The Process and saw that the long hair and beards had a powerful impact once collected together en masse. The TOPY haircut had a long tail of hair at the back of the head, and then the rest of the head was shaved in reference to the ascetic spiritual disciplines. Ascetic and decadent, the contradictory eternal balance. The Psychick Cross was the most instantly effective strategy for generating the impression of a serious, focused, militant network. The Psychick Youth look was so strong that it seduced and attracted males and females to adopt it quickly. A handful of Psychick Youth dressed up had an immediate visceral impact far beyond what might be expected from such small numbers.

What strikes me, even with the passing of years and relative brevity of these passages, is the *sheer originality* of Genesis's observations. The gravest danger to the search is familiarity, certainty, repetition, and catechism. There exists a pernicious ease through which supposed alternative philosophies or outsider movements inadvertently mouth and internalize pervasive cultural reference points. Repetition by no means suggests an idea is wrong or flawed; but it often means it is *untested* or seen as a stopping point. In contrast Genesis wrote, "My lifelong search is for focused mutability, and to change the means of perception. To challenge every status quo as a matter of principle and never rest, never assume or imagine that the task of reinvention has a finite ending."

In that vein, I am further struck by how most alternative spiritual scenes summarily reject anything deemed challenging or violative within the "holistic" narrative. I write these words having been expelled from New Age centers, had talks cancelled, been subject to negative videos and podcasts solely for *thought explorations* deemed verboten, generally involving the Satanic themes explored in this chapter. What I have experienced is, however, trifling compared to those I admire:

> Just before I had taken my family away from East London to Brighton in 1988, we were thrust into the public eye on a national level when [a tabloid] . . . newspaper ran a vicious and sensational full-page article with the headline: "THIS VILE MAN CORRUPTS KIDS—DEMI-GOD FEEDS POP FANS ON SEX, SADISM, AND DEVIL RITES." We discovered we'd been under surveillance; casual and close friends and neighbors alike had been interrogated and bullied. Shades of "THE MINDBENDERS OF MAYFAIR" set off warning bells in my head! I had been officially declared an enemy of society, a wrecker of morals as well as civilization and a target for any unscrupulous journalist and nutcase on the street using outrage as an excuse for intolerance.
>
> A TOPY individual working in the local post office warned me that our mail was being opened and copied by the "authorities." Not long before this, Scotland Yard had raided Mr. Sebastian's tattoo and piercing studio, later charging him and several other men, none of whom ever knew each other, with being a "gay S&M porn ring." They were tried in the Old Bailey, usually reserved for serial killers, spies and the worst of the worst criminals . . . The case was tried by one judge, who eventually ruled piercing and tattooing a *criminal* act of grievous bodily harm, a charge immediately below manslaughter with a sentence of up to seven years. One poor man received three years in prison for piercing his own foreskin. Souvenir photos he got developed for himself alone were the damning evidence. All were found guilty, thus setting a legal precedent in Britain to prosecute anybody with a piercing or tattoo, or who created one! Suddenly, in 1991, my body, along with many of TOPY's, was illegal. It seems impossible now just 15 or so years later to believe this was true.

Amid myriad stresses, in winter 1991 the P-Orridge family journeyed with its two young daughters, Caresse and Genesse, on a personal relief mission to Nepal, distributing food, clothing, and clean water to the destitute. "Some days," P-Orridge wrote, "we fed 300 to 400 Tibetan refugees, lepers and beggars." This brief note warrants pausing over by observers who wonder why cultural outliers often display indifference to charges and prejudicial questions from defenders of probity: by whom are such defenders selected and by what personal standards or actions are their interrogatives valid? An authentic question is earned.

Some of the deepest trouble loomed directly ahead. In February 1992—on the day the P-Orridge family had planned to return home—an ominous fax arrived: "SERIOUS TROUBLE—CALL HOME IMMEDIATELY!" A swarm of Scotland Yard detectives from the Obscene Publications Squad had raided TOPY houses in London and Brighton, the latter the personal residence of the P-Orridges. Police seized original art, sigils, videos, archives, books, artifacts, sex toys, and private possessions.

In addition to a flood of tabloid media alleging "ritual abuse," that evening one of Britain's networks televised a one-hour "expose" of TOPY during a news program. It was an uninterrupted parade of Satanic Panic tropes, untruths, half-truths, and fabrication, including witnesses (later found to be mentally troubled and unconnected to TOPY) concealed in shadows alleging child sacrifices, live burials, at-home abortions, and mass murders in a manner surpassing even the most far-flung credibility. None of this matched any police records.

Within weeks, the media belatedly picked apart the special as a fundamentalist-inspired hatchet job with next-to-zero factchecking; the videos depicting "ritual abuse" were voluntary ceremonies and performance-art among TOPY members. No charges were filed. But the damage was done:

> I was advised that if we returned from Nepal, Scotland Yard would arrest me and hold me for questioning indefinitely, and take my two daughters into custody who would then likely be interrogated for evidence of child abuse. A false accusation of abuse usually led to your children being in the State's care for two or more years regardless of truth. We have never, to this day, been charged with anything. Nor has my seized archives and property been returned; in fact, Scotland Yard has implied it was all destroyed, for no legal reason.
>
> Our attorney told us in a frank phone call that our best course of action was to protect our children and go into exile, as someone at Scotland Yard had said off the record that they could not guarantee my physical safety if I returned.

The P-Orridges took refuge in Northern California with the help of LSD guru Timothy Leary. The strains drove the couple to divorce. Remaining in the U.S., Genesis continued working on various musical, occult, and artist fronts—pioneering cultural developments from raves to nonbinary sexuality—until dying from leukemia in 2020 at the start of the Covid pandemic.

The first major retrospective of Genesis's artwork, "We Are But One," appeared to positive reviews in 2022 at Brooklyn's Pioneer Works gallery As of this writing, a documentary on TOPY, "A Message from the Temple," is in production from filmmaker Jacqueline Castel, my partner.

As historian Massimo Introvigne observes, "Satanism is fueled, if not created, by anti-Satanism, much more than anti-Satanism is generated by a real prominence of Satanism."

Indeed, *anti-Satanism* is a far vaster ideology although possessed of a largely imaginary target. Even where self-identified Satanic organizations or intellects exist, their outlook and philosophy, as seen, are almost always misunderstood or mispresented. This is true of a more recent organization, The Satanic Temple, which uses innovative protests and legal challenges to defend First Amendment rights. A non-theistic group (although views of individual members may vary), the Temple is, by and large, a brilliantly conceived work of guerrilla theater on behalf of constitutional liberties and church-state neutrality.

Even magickal practitioners with no Satanic interests, such as magician Damien Echols, were caught in the web of 1980s–1990s Satanic Panic hysteria—sometimes with results almost impossible to fathom. In 1994, a teenaged Echols and two friends, known as the West Memphis Three, were tried and falsely convicted in Arkansas of triple homicide, which prosecutors depicted as a Satanic ritual murder. Echols was sentenced to death. After years of appeal and public outcry, with Echols incarcerated on death row, the three were finally freed in 2011. Space has allowed me to review only a few of the imprisonments, false accusations, and life-altering persecutions arising from Satanic Panic falsehoods in the media, legal system, and among self-appointed therapeutic experts, many of whom were found to plant, coerce, or otherwise encourage lurid and debunked testimonies from children or recovered memories from vulnerable adults.*

In fact, most of the myriad accusations of the 1980s and early 1990s were directed against people with no occult ties whatever: daycare workers, teachers, librarians, and happenstance pedestrians. By 1989, more than 50 such cases were underway in the U.S. legal system—involving literally thousands of unsubstantiated accusations of Satanic ritual abuse.** These allegations produced some of the longest-running criminal trials in American history—and all that the record finally bore out was that innocent lives of the accused were irreparably damaged.*** The most sensational and longest running case involved California's McMartin Preschool, of which journalist Heather Greene wrote in *Lights, Camera, Witchcraft* (Llewellyn, 2021):

> In 1983, accusations were made against owners and childcare workers at the McMartin Preschool in Manhattan Beach, California. They were accused of ritual child abuse, including sodomy, rape, and other forms of molestation. Stories circulated of animal sacrifice, secret tunnels, blood drinking, the placing of pentagrams on children's bottoms, and more. In 1984, 384 McMartin preschool children of the 400 interviewed were diagnosed as having been sexually abused. Arrests were made. Despite all early doubts as to the credibility of the children's testimonies and the legitimacy of various reports, the McMartin trial continued for seven years, becoming the most expensive and longest running criminal trial in American history.

All charges were dropped in 1990. And yet, despite myriad debunking, related canards endure in some of the episodes mentioned as well as in conspiracy narratives popularized by the QAnon movement in the early twenty-first century. The implications sometimes emerge on the geopolitical stage. In justifying his attempted annexation of four

---

* E.g., see "It's Time to Revisit the Satanic Panic" by Alan Yuhas, *New York Times*, March 31, 2021; "I'm Sorry" [the recantation of a former child witness] by Kyle Zirpolpo as told to Debbie Nathan, *Los Angeles Times*, October 30, 2005; and "Why Satanic Panic never really ended" by Aja Romano, Vox, March 31, 2021.

** Medway (2001).

*** E.g., see "The McMartin Preschool Abuse Trial: An Account" by Douglas O. Linder at Famous-Trails.com.

regions of Ukraine, Vladimir Putin announced in a speech of September 30, 2022, "The repression of freedom is taking on the outlines of a 'reverse religion,' of real Satanism," claiming that Western liberal outlooks on matters like gender identity amounted to a "denial of man."*

Amid sensational charges or waves of paranoia, it is always instructive to consider what schisms are concurrently playing out in a given society and how they are dealt with or digested. Very often, abuses in the mainstream or anxiety over cultural shifts are displaced onto scapegoats, real or imagined, on social fringes. The Satanic Panic of the 1980s seems to have arisen, at least in part, from anxiety over women entering the workplace, which in turn got projected onto daycare centers and workers. Similar projections were made against heavy metal musicians and fans who presented a convenient target for themes of adolescent suicide and despair.**

Indeed, the crisis that occurred concurrently with the 1980s Satanic Panic was a wave of unreported or underreported child abuse in mainstream institutions, most prominently the Catholic Church and the Boy Scouts of America. This was so much the case that in 2020 the Boy Scouts of America declared bankruptcy to defend itself against class action lawsuits from tens of thousands of claimants and survivors.*** Likewise, as of this writing more than thirty Catholic dioceses or organizations in the U.S. alone have declared bankruptcy for the same reasons.**** Similar events have played out, sometimes on a larger scale, in nations including France, Canada, and Germany.***** This is not "whataboutism"—it is the same issue: during the peak of the Satanic Panic, people with relatively no social power—daycare workers, counselors, teachers, heavy metal musicians, artists—were accused of crimes later proved fraudulent and non-existent. This

* "Putin's speech on annexation paints a stark picture of a face-off with the West" by Anton Troianovski, *New York Times*, September 30, 2022.

** E.g., for a sensational and spurious case against band Judas Priest see "Rock Group Cleared in Suicide Case," *Washington Post*, August 25, 1990.

*** See "Boy Scouts Of America Files For Bankruptcy As It Faces Hundreds Of Sex-Abuse Claims" by Laurel Wamsley and Wade Goodwyn, NPR Morning Edition and "U.S. judge signs off on $850 million Boy Scouts sex abuse settlement" by Maria Chutchian, Reuters, August 19, 2021.

**** See "Catholic Church Bankruptcies," The Meneo Law Group, AbuseLawsuit.com.

***** See "French report: 330,000 children victims of church sex abuse" by Sylvie Corbet, Associated Press, October 5, 2021; "Pope Francis vows to root out sexual abuse in Catholic Church after McCarrick report" by Nicole Winfield, Associated Press, November 11, 2020; and "Report finds 196 clerics abused minors in German diocese," Associated Press, June 13, 2022.

reflected an age-old cycle in which abuses and criminality within powerful quarters, sometimes precincts of social prestige, are dislodged onto outsiders who can do little to defend themselves. Historically, we've seen this occur in witch hunting, red scares, lynching, racism, Jew hatred, gay bashing, and mass arrests of nonviolent users and dealers in the War on Drugs.

The search for a hidden foe is a constant in human history. The Satanic Panic fit the impulse and to some degree still does. I wish space permitted greater justice to the lives of innocents caught in the stone-throwing; if there exist any victims of "sacrifice" in this narrative, it is them.

Through the work of a wide range of popular figures, including English theorists John Michell (1933–2009) and author-investigator Graham Hancock, the late twentieth and early twenty-first centuries saw renewed interest in questions of lost, primeval, or Atlantean civilizations, a theme appearing in the work of Madame Blavatsky, G.I. Gurdjieff, Edgar Cayce, and Manly P. Hall, among others.

The Platonic dialogues *Critias* and *Timaeus* familiarly expound upon a civilization called Atlantis; Plato's speakers record an advanced culture, drawing upon recollections of the legendary statesman, Solon, who was said to have visited Ancient Egypt, and who thus understood humanity's deepest origins. Plato's record says that this seafaring civilization grew so mighty and powerful that it committed the ultimate trespass: attacking Athens itself. The Athenians repelled Atlantean aggression, which ushered in the fall and disappearance of this once-hallowed empire.

In 1961—in what proved a fateful remark toward the end of his life—esoteric Egyptologist R.A. Schwaller de Lubicz (1887–1961) wrote that the "Sphinx whose leonine body, except for the head, shows indisputable signs of aquatic erosion," as translated in 1982 in his *Sacred Science* (Inner Traditions). The actuality of water erosion on the oldest portions of the monument could predate its timeline and, hence, that of Ancient Egypt. Ignited by Schwaller's comment, independent Egyptologist John Anthony West (1932–2018) extrapolated on the water-erosion thesis in his 1979 book *Serpent in the Sky*. About a decade later, West partnered with Yale-trained geologist Robert M.

Schoch to investigate the theory on a 1990 archeological expedition to Egypt. The following year, Schoch presented the water-erosion thesis, positing that water damage detected on the earliest portions of the Sphinx would predate the dawn of Egyptian civilization to 7,500 B.C. or as early as 10,000 B.C. In a coup of esoteric philosophy, the Schoch-West thesis formed the basis of an Emmy-winning and widely viewed 1993 network TV special, "Mystery of the Sphinx," hosted by Charlton Heston. The stage was set for mainstream consideration. But West, a mercurial man, never completed work on a book exploring the water-erosion thesis. When I got to know West in the years before his death, I pushed the brilliant but erratic man, unsuccessfully, to resume that work.

Today, academic archeologists (or at least those vocal on the matter) vociferously oppose the Schoch-West thesis. No archeologist, however, has directly contradicted it; i.e., no one has performed investigatory work on the monument that dispels the Schoch-West profiling. The most compelling (and oft-heard) argument is the absence of a single shard of pottery or piece of material evidence that *corroborates* the Schoch-West timeline. I brought this to the attention of West when he was living not far from me in the Hudson Valley region of New York. His counter was simply that further investigation is required; he and Schoch, he argued, pinpointed a vital piece of empirical evidence, which no one in the field has directly upended. There exist contradictory theories, of course, which also reference environmental and quarrying factors. These counter-theories, in my view, raise important points but remain tangential to the Schoch-West findings.

Observers may wonder: where is the rising generation of professors, grad students, and archeologists who want to review the Schoch-West research and directly check the evidence? This poses questions about the politics of academia and archaeology in the late twentieth and early twenty-first centuries.

First, it is extremely difficult to gain exploratory access to the Giza Plateau. Licensure is tightly regulated and expensive. Moreover, getting "green lit" for such a study from most Western universities is near-impossible. Schoch, who is on the faculty of the College of General Studies at Boston University, argued to me that if a graduate student or anyone in the field of archaeology expresses interest in exploring the water erosion thesis, it is career suicide. Most academics disdain the Schoch-West data because it indirectly undermines the timeline on which many have based their work. They would, of course, argue that they disdain it because it's pseudoscience, a disabling label that, in my estimation, requires the same level of evidence as its object. Science is methodology. If you haven't found flaws in methodology then you're arguing taste. In any case, the timeline is considered settled—and if you raise questions adjacent to it, you're seen as implicitly challenging the research on which many figures in the field built their reputations. Hence, licensing, funding, and approbation are absent.

There exists a geopolitical barrier, as well. Modern Egypt justly prides itself as the cradle of civilization. To some degree, this perception plays a nationalistic role in Egyptian life, as does custodianship of antiquities in many nations. Some government officials believe that any attempt to predate the timeline of Ancient Egypt strikes at the heart of the nation's heritage. I suggest a different perspective. If research posits that Egypt possesses deeper antiquity than the accepted timeline that prospect only enriches and fortifies the civilization's vintage. Many Egyptian officials see it differently. Their wariness is exacerbated by the "ancient alien" thesis, a topic unconnected to the Schoch-West report.

Among defining spiritual movements of the 1960s, '70s, and beyond was the New Age, which I define as a radically ecumenical culture of therapeutic spirituality.

In the mid-1970s, the monthly *New Age Journal* had solidified the name for this new spiritual movement, echoing the phrase once used by figures from William Blake and Warren Felt Evans to A.R. Orage and Alice Bailey. Many observers see Marilyn Ferguson's 1980 cultural manifesto *The Aquarian Conspiracy*, which celebrated new modes in lifestyle, politics, and spirituality from a holistic perspective, as the movement's informal declaration.

In practice, the New Age has a fitful relationship with the occult. Although wide-ranging in religious orientation, New Age centers, magazines, bookstores, and workshops tend to draw their boundaries within a Christian and Westernized Buddhist spiritual framework. Hence, concepts of light versus dark, white light, divine goodness, "Cosmic Christ," and generalized iterations of karma form the New

Age's compass points. Occultism as an outsider philosophy, versus its reprocessing through Tarot decks, popularized Kabbalah, and psycho-spiritual channeled messages, is not always a matching blood type for the New Age. Prometheus rules the occult; Gaia rules the New Age.

Inadvertently echoing William Dudley Pelley's "Star Guests" theme, some New Age religious expressions substituted extraterrestrial intelligences for unseen spiritual masters. "In the late 1960s . . . UFO research began to take on an occult character, giving credence to claims that UFOs can materialize out of invisibility and that their occupants can communicate telepathically with human 'contactees,' and to use regression hypnosis to elicit the experiences of the contactees," wrote Howard Kerr and Charles L. Crow in the 1983 monograph anthology, *The Occult in America* (University of Illinois Press).

Such a scenario could also echo themes from Gnosticism by positing superhuman forces, such as archons and angels by other names, vying for the fate of humanity. See in a certain light, UFO theorizing, or precincts of it, is a modern Gnosticism, with both secular and religious iterations. In the late 1950s to early 1960s, the founders of Scotland's highly regarded spiritual growth center Findhorn were so dedicated to their vision of psychic communication with extraterrestrials and imminent contact with visiting craft that they cleared their own landing site.*

Unforeseeable at that time, the international conversation around UFOs has both deepened and heightened to an unprecedented degree. This is attributable to the work of many figures and researchers but especially, as of this writing, to journalists Leslie Kean, Ralph Blumenthal, and Helene Cooper whose reportage in the *New York Times* from 2017 to 2019 brought to light a clandestine Pentagon program to track UFO or UAP (unidentified aerial phenomena) activity and validated Navy cockpit videos of engineered objects in extraordinary motion, including in later videos as submersibles.**

The scope of the UFO thesis, i.e., existence of engineered or natural phenomena and beings beyond known physicality, far surpasses

* "In Advance of Landing: The Findhorn Community" by Andy Roberts, *Magonia Magazine*, August 2005.

** E.g., see "Glowing Auras and 'Black Money': The Pentagon's Mysterious U.F.O. Program" by Helene Cooper, Ralph Blumenthal and Leslie Kean, December 16, 2017 and "'Wow, What Is That?' Navy Pilots Report Unexplained Flying Objects" by Helene Cooper, Ralph Blumenthal and Leslie Kean, May 26, 2019.

this book. But, as I suggested in my 2022 *Uncertain Places*, there is nascent convergence in conversation between UFO researchers, parapsychologists, and students of the occult or metaphysics. The reason for this, quite simply, involves the question of whether the most elusive of UFO/UAP phenomena—whatever it may be—poses questions of *interdimensionality* as much as *extraterrestrialism*. The former approach was popularized by computer scientist Jacques Vallée in his 1969 book *Passport to Magonia*.* Based on current understandings of reality and taking account of vastness of cosmic distances and known limits on velocity (excluding cosmic worm holes or other exotic models of travel), it may be *easier* to support the UFO thesis based on interdimensional versus extraterrestrial concepts.

Indeed, the convergence I propose suggests where occultism may be headed and what fields it may prove collaborative with, from exploration of entheogens to parapsychology to UFO studies to quantum theory. To venture this stage of inquiry requires stepping back before returning to it.

I noted earlier that today's spiritual search has entered an era of *individual experiment*, versus earlier stages of tutelage to great teachers and group experience, while excluding neither.

Historian Wouter J. Hanegraaff reasons that "the Way of Hermes was practiced in very small gatherings, probably not much larger than what we find in the texts themselves: one teacher and one to three pupils—hardly more."**

M. David Litwa observes in *Hermetica II* that French Dominican friar and scholar of Neoplatonism André-Jean Festugière (1898–1982) found "no trace in the Hermetic literature of ceremonies belonging to supposed believers in Hermes, nothing that resembles sacraments . . . There is no clergy, no appearance of hierarchical organization, no degrees of initiation . . . On the contrary . . . Hermeticism forthrightly expresses its loathing for material acts of worship."*** By choice and

* Also see "Five Arguments Against the Extraterrestrial Origin of Unidentified Flying Objects" by Jacques F. Vallée, *Journal of Scientific Exploration*, Vol. 4, 1990.

** *Hermetic Spirituality and the Historical Imagination* (Cambridge University Press, 2022)

*** It should be noted that, like all things Hermetic, analysis is unsettled. Discovery of Coptic Hermetica at Nag Hammadi in 1945 led some scholars, notably historian of Gnosticism Gilles Quispel (1916–2006), to assert the existence of secret initiatory lodges among Hermeticists.

practice, this may well be the position in which most seekers find themselves today. It is one I personally embrace, although I have spent fruitful years previously in group search.

I've noted that occultism itself is a revivalist movement of ancient religious forms, symbols, and practices. In strictest terms, occultism reclaims and adapts pre-Christian religious methods once prevalent in regions occupied by the armies of Alexander, i.e., Europe, the Mediterranean, Persia, and North Africa, whose cultural influence composes what we traditionally call the West. As such, occultism cannot properly be seen as *anything and everything* novel within the spiritual rubric nor every mystical expression generally.

Today, occultism runs increasingly parallel to how Hanegraaff and Festugière described Hermeticism: a culture of *small-scale* or *individual search* with few trappings of formalism.

Indeed, I find myself wondering whether current and expanding understanding of causative or extraphysical properties of thought, some of which we've already considered, may be indirectly reviving this traditional Hermetic model—but with two distinct wrinkles: 1) If one accepts, as I do, that the individual experiences extraphysical modes of existence—whether expressed in some degree of extrasensory perception (ESP), thought causation, or reality selection—it begs the question of whether what we call "magick" is even necessary. It may be that a warranted sense of extraphysical agency abrogates the need for formalism, liturgy, prayer, rite, and ritual. 2) If we loosen hold of concepts like angel, demon, jinn, spirit, tulpa, egregore, alien, and even the language of cryptozoology (e.g., alux, fairy, Bigfoot), it may be possible, at least theoretically, to consider whether persistently reported encounters with extraphysical or anomalous intelligences or beings, i.e., records, may reflect interdimensional experiences. Twentieth and twenty-first century findings and modeling have, in fact, done more to encourage than dismiss such gambits.

This query is aided by the insights of twentieth century mystic Neville Goddard. The mind-metaphysics teacher taught that what is called God in Scripture is nothing more than a symbolic rendering of the human imagination—and all you experience is an outpicturing of your mind's-eye imagery and emotive states selecting among a universe of concurrent, infinite realities. In a 1948 lecture series in Los Angeles, Neville told listeners: "Scientists will one day explain why there is a serial universe. But in practice, how you use this serial universe to change the future is more important."

It was not until several years later that quantum physicists began discussing the many-worlds theory, devised in 1957 by physicist Hugh Everett III (1930–1982). Everett was attempting to make sense of the extraordinary findings that had been occurring for about three decades in quantum mechanics. For example, scientists are able to demonstrate, through various interference patterns, that a subatomic particle occupies a wave state or state of superposition—that is, an infinite number of places—until a sentient observer or automatized device takes a measurement: it is only when measurement is taken that the particle collapses, so to speak, from a wave state into a localized state. At that point it occupies a definite, identifiable, measurable place. Before measurement is taken, however, the localized particle exists only in potential.

I am using language that sometimes raises objections. A critic wrote me: "The 'wave state' you describe is a wave function, which is descriptive of the particles' energy. That wave function, when squared mathematically gives you a probability of its spatial distribution. So, the wave function is a square root of a probability distribution." Yes and no. As my colleague Dean Radin points out, the "wave function is not about probabilities. It's much stranger than that. It's the square root of probability, which some distinguish from probability by calling what the wave function represents a 'possibility.'" In any case, the wave function describes a state as much as a formula.

Now, I have just about squeezed all of quantum physics into a couple of paragraphs. I consider it an accurate description, but obviously I am reducing huge complexities into the dimensions of a marble. I believe I am faithfully stating what has been observed in the last 90-plus years of particle experiments (as well as emerging experiments on larger objects, such as hydrogen molecules). We are seeing that on the subatomic scale matter does not behave as we are conditioned to expect.

Starting about twenty years previous to this writing, it became fashionable for New Agers and laypeople, like me, to place quantum theory at the back of cherished spiritual principles. It became equally fashionable for professional skeptics and mainstream journalists to pushback, crying *B.S.* and *sophistry.* That position, while still heard, has quieted. Not because skeptics have grown more pensive or attenuated to media-speak, but because the proposition of mind-over-matter, strange as it may seem, now resounds in debates on theoretical physics in mainline journals and magazines.

In 2009, I attended a presentation on the "quantum measurement problem" delivered by parapsychologist Dean Radin before an audience of scientists, social thinkers, and scholars of religion. I asked Radin to address the 800-pound gorilla in the room: If observation and perspective alter material on a micro level, in the world of waves and particles, might that say something about the legitimacy of the New Thought or mind-power thesis? "It's not complete bullshit," Radin replied. "There may be an inkling of something to it." Another physicist and longtime military researcher was also present. "As the resident skeptic," he said, "I concur."

Our understanding of matter in our macro world generally comes from measuring things through our five senses and experiencing them as singularities. There is one table. It is solid and definable. It is not occupying an infinite number of spaces. But contemporary quantum physicists have theorized that we may not normally see or experience superposition phenomena because of what is sometimes called *information leakage.*

This means we gain or lose data based on fineness of measurement. When you measure things with exquisitely well-tuned instruments, like a microscope, you see more and more of what is going on, i.e., actual reality. But when you pan the camera back, so to speak, your measurements coarsen and you see less and less of what is actually happening. To use the most basic example, to all ordinary appearances, a table is solid. The floor beneath your feet is solid. Where you are sitting is solid. But measuring through atomic-scale microscopes, we realize that if you go deeper and deeper, space appears within these objects. Particles make up the atom and still greater space appears. We do not experience that; we experience solidity. But no one questions that space prevails among particles composing an atom.

Furthermore, we possess decades of data demonstrating that when subatomic particles are directed at a target system, such as a double slit, they appear in infinite places at once until a measurement is made; *only then does locality exist.* But we fail to see this unless we are measuring things with comparative exactitude. Hence, what I am describing seems unreal based on lived experience—but it is actual.

In any event, my supposition is this: if particles appear in an infinite number of places at once until a measurement is taken; and if, as we know from studying the behavior and mechanics of subatomic particles, there exists an infinitude of possibilities; and if we know, as we have since the inception of Einstein's theories, that time is relative, then it is possible to reason—and it is almost necessary to reason—that linearity itself, by which we organize our lives, is *illusory*.

Linearity is a useful and *necessary* device for five-sensory beings to get through life; but it does not stand up objectively. Linearity is conceptual—a subjective interpretation of what is really going on. It is not reflected in Einstein's theory of relativity, which demonstrates that time slows for an object approaching the speed of light. (The individual traveling in a metaphorical spaceship at or near light speed experiences time slowing, not from their perspective but in comparison to those not at near light speed. And this is no mere thought exercise: space travelers in our era, although they are obviously approaching nowhere near that velocity, experience minute effects of time reduction.) Nor is linearity reflected in quantum mechanics, where particles appear in an infinitude of places and obey no orderly modality. Linearity is *not* replicated when measurement of a particle serves to localize the appearance or existence of the object.

This begins to clarify why Einstein famously wrote in a letter of March 1955: "People like us, who believe in physics, know that the distinction between past, present, and future is only a stubbornly persistent illusion."*

If we pursue this line of thought further—and this is where Everett's many-worlds theory comes into play—the very decision to take a measurement (or not take one) not only localizes a particle, but creates a past, present, and future for that particle. Hence, an observer's decision to log a measurement creates a *multidimensional reality* for the particle.

There exists debate over whether a *device* represents a method of measurement distinct from an *observer*, as well as whether the "collapse" from wave to particle results from an observer's individual psyche or "transpersonal mind behaving according to natural laws," as observed by Bernardo Kastrup, Henry P. Stapp, and Menas C. Kafatos

* "Fear of Nazis and Unpublished Work: Hebrew University Unveils 110 Albert Einstein Manuscripts" by Ofer Aderet, *Haaretz*, March 6, 2019.

in a May 29, 2018, *Scientific American* article "Coming to Grips with the Implications of Quantum Mechanics." The authors contend that "the boundaries of a detector are arbitrary" and this *transpersonal mind* "comprises but far transcends any individual psyche," a description similar to the Hermetic concept of *Nous* or an over-mind. The authors compellingly argue that even if a device is used for measurement—and thus localization—perception and intent, either of the individual, the meta-mind, or both, remains the determining force. (For those who think I'm exaggerating the implications of quantum mechanics, peruse this or any pertinent article—you will find, I believe, that I'm being conservative.)

Multidimensional reality is implied in the famous thought-experiment called Schrödinger's Cat. Twentieth century physicist Erwin Schrödinger (1887–1961) was frustrated with the evident absurdity of quantum theory, which showed objects simultaneously appearing in more than one place at a time. Such an outlook, he felt, violated all commonly observed physical laws. In 1935, Schrödinger sought to highlight this predicament through a purposely absurdist thought experiment, which he intended to force quantum physicists to follow their data to its ultimate degree.

Schrödinger reasoned that quantum data dictates that a sentient being, such as a cat, can be simultaneously alive and dead. Here is a variant of the Schrödinger's Cat experiment: a cat is placed into one of a pair of boxes. Along with the cat is a collar fitted with a device which, if exposed to an atom, releases a deadly poison. An observer then fires an atom at the boxes. The observer subsequently uses some form of measurement to check on which box the atom is in: the empty one, or the one with the cat and the poisoning device. When the observer goes to check, the wave function of the atom (the state in which it exists in both boxes) collapses into a particle function (the state in which it is localized to one box). Once the observer takes his measurement, convention says that the cat will be discovered to be dead or alive. But Schrödinger reasoned that quantum physics describes an outcome in which the cat is *both* dead and alive. This is because the atom, in its wave function, was, at one time, in either box, and either outcome is real.

Of course, all lived experience tells us that if the atom went into the empty box, the cat is alive; and if it went into the box with the cat and the poisoning device, the cat is dead. But Schrödinger, aiming to highlight the frustrations of quantum theory, argued that if the observations of quantum-mechanics experiments are right, you would have to allow for each outcome.

To take it even further, many-worlds theorists in the 1950s posited that if an observer waited some significant length of time—say, eight hours—before checking on the dead-alive cat, he would discover one cat that was dead for eight hours and another that was alive for eight hours (and now hungry). In this line of reasoning, conscious observation effectively manifested the localized atom, the dead cat, and the living cat—and *also manifested the past,* or in other words, created a history for both a dead cat and a living one. Both outcomes are true.

So, whatever a particle is doing, the very fact that an observer has chosen to take a measurement at that time, place, moment, and juncture creates a whole past, present, and future—an infinitude of outcomes. A divergent set of outcomes would exist if that measurement were never taken. A divergent set of outcomes would also exist if that measurement were taken one second later, or five minutes later, or tomorrow. And what is tomorrow? When particles exist in superposition until somebody takes a measurement, there is no such thing as tomorrow, other than subjectively.

Consider too: the cat, from its perspective, is local; the observer, from its perspective, is local—but both, in fact, are in a wave state or superposition. We can speak of them as concrete, singular beings only from their personal perspective. From the quantum perspective, they are infinite. Expanding on this idea, research physician Robert Lanza, adjunct professor at Wake Forest University School of Medicine, argues that death itself is ultimately a mental phenomenon: we "die" only insofar as an observer perceives demise; the consciousness of the "deceased" branches off into one of Everett's many worlds.* (This begs the question of *who* experiences these effects if there's no such thing as "one" person/life. I consider this in *Daydream Believer.*)

An adjunct set of possibilities appear in what is called string theory. String theorists attempt to explain the strange behavior of subatomic objects, as well as why such objects affect one another at distances, and why, as Isaac Newton observed, even macro-objects at

---

* "The Impossibility of Being Dead" by Robert Lanza, M.D., *Psychology Today,* November 11, 2020.

vast removes mirror each other's motions. String theory holds that all particles and all matter are not separate entities, but rather are part of vast, undulating networks of strings. When an object at one point in space affects another object, we are not seeing two distinct entities, but a unified string of objects. What's more, different dimensions and universes exist along these strings, so we may not always see the thing causing an effect. (I am deferring to language of causation, a typical Western formulation; another vista opens if one argues for correlation.) In string theory, all material and events are of one whole. We catch only hints of this through exquisitely fine measurement.

And what, finally, are our five senses but a technology by which we *measure* things? Are our five senses anything other than a biological technology, not necessarily different in intake from a camera, photometer, digital recorder, or microscope? So, it is possible that within reality—within this extra-linear, super-positioned infinitude of possibilities in which we are taking measurements—we experience things based on perspective. This is why in considering mind causation, or what is called New Thought, I use the term *select* rather than manifest.

It is entirely possible that we dwell in a world of unseen—or unknown—potentialities; they exist all around us, but we do not possess the instrumentation to measure such things. Our way of viewing the world is coarse and limited—even illusory. For example, linear time feels overwhelmingly persuasive. But, as seen, linearity itself is an illusion. We use it to organize life, but it is not real. Even knowing this, being able to understand this, being able to discuss this, does not necessarily impact our everyday experience of linearity.

But why not? Why does life seem so orderly? It is difficult to imagine that any of this quantum or string phenomena can be real in more than an abstract way or on the subatomic scale. William James, in his Gifford lectures in 1902, made an observation that speaks to this, which relates the spiritual to the physical. When a mystic sees something, James said, it is as if he is viewing it through a microscope. The mystic sees more and more of what is really going on because of his extreme sensitivity. If I look at a drop of water, all I see is a common drop. It is translucent; it feels like what I call "wet." But if I look at that same drop through a microscope, all kinds of things are revealed. There are single-cell organisms, there are bacteria, there are molecules moving around. The molecules are made up of atoms and other particles that are similarly moving around. All kinds of things are occurring that I do not normally see.

James contended that the mystic is always viewing things as though through a microscope. But when you pan the camera back, so to speak, you experience less and less of what is really happening. Without crediting James, this is what quantum physicists today call "information leakage," noted earlier. They respond to the apparent disparity between the particle world and our macro world by saying what James said about mysticism, which is that when you are measuring things with extremely fine and well-tuned instruments—including the psyche or senses—you are seeing more and more of what is really going on. But when your capacity for measurement coarsens, you lose data and see less and less of what is occurring. This can account for visionary experiences from St. Teresa of Ávila to Philip K. Dick.

In a 1960 essay, theoretical physicist Eugene Wigner spoke to the commonality, if not inevitability, of natural laws that do not necessarily square with one another: "Every empirical law has the disquieting quality that one does not know its limitations . . . Alternatively, it is possible that there always will be some laws of nature which have nothing in common with each other . . . It is even possible that some of the laws of nature will be in conflict with each other in their implications, but each convincing enough in its own domain so that we may not be willing to abandon any of them."* And further:

> It may be useful to illustrate the alternatives by an example. We now have, in physics, two theories of great power and interest: the theory of quantum phenomena and the theory of relativity. These two theories have their roots in *mutually exclusive* groups of phenomena. [emphasis added] Relativity theory applies to macroscopic bodies, such as stars. The event of coincidence, that is, in ultimate analysis of collision, is the primitive event in the theory of relativity and defines a point in space-time, or at least would define a point if the colliding panicles were infinitely small. Quantum theory has its roots in the microscopic world and, from its point of view, the event of coincidence, or of collision, even if it takes place between particles of no spatial extent, is not primitive and not at all sharply

* "The Unreasonable Effectiveness of Mathematics in the Natural Sciences," *Communications in Pure and Applied Mathematics*, vol. 13, No. I (February 1960).

> isolated in space-time. The two theories operate with different mathematical concepts . . . So far, the two theories could not be united, that is, no mathematical formulation exists to which both of these theories are approximations. All physicists believe that a union of the two theories is inherently possible and that we shall find it. Nevertheless, it is possible also to imagine that no union of the two theories can be found. This example illustrates the two possibilities, of union and of conflict, mentioned before, both of which are conceivable.

Hence, it is no argument against anomalous or paranormal events, or reports of such, to maintain that they violate natural laws. It could be said that we violate our own laws all the time, rarely fretting over implications. As H.P. Lovecraft put it in the opening line of his famed 1926 short story "The Call of Cthulhu": "The most merciful thing in the world, I think, is the inability of the human mind to correlate all its contents."

Under what circumstances might an individual experience such a violation? To recap, just as linear time is a device, just as particles exist in a wave state or state of superposition, it is possible that we live amidst an infinitude of events, including those we call anomalous, which we perceive only in fragments or at fleeting moments. Maybe the experience of extraordinary events, those that violate common observation and presumed lawful consistency, occur at moments of great awareness, sensitivity, or emotional investment; or perhaps at moments when ordinary thought patterns, for whatever reason, get interrupted, as in the formulas of Austin Osman Spare; or possibly there exist moments available to some individuals with aptitude for what we call ESP or intuition. It could be that at such times, the individual is capable of seeing what is really happening. Yet such individuals are sometimes smeared with terms like psychosis, crackpot, fraud, imagination, fantasy, or "confirmation bias." Materialists over-rely on confirmation bias and related concepts to disregard testimony. As noted, consistent testimony from varying sources forms a record and warrants consideration. Strident materialists, of course, fail to grasp that cognitive biases and prejudicial thinking are their own problems, too. None of what I've written suggests that those labels, judiciously applied, are always wrong; just that they're not always right.

If my hypothesis is correct—which is to say, in homiletic terms, you get what you're looking for—we're all in the same boat. Or as Robert Anton Wilson put it: "All perception is a gamble."* So, let us consider matters in an interdisciplinary way and try to determine the topography. We will not get anywhere, or at least not very quickly, if we dismiss, underfund, or effectively ban the so-called borderline sciences. Nor if we conceal online addiction, low emotional restraint, or even personality disorders behind vociferous skepticism, a malady of social media.

My summary framing is this: I believe we may be approaching a new way of understanding anomalies, including UFOs, near-death experiences, apparitional experiences, cryptozoology, and the discordant and non-linear data of ESP, precognition and retrocausality. It is possible that all of this testimony, replicable data, and experience could point to something of a non-materialist or extraphysical quality pertaining to interdimensionality and different intersections of time.

Astrophysicist Neil deGrasse Tyson sardonically asks to see an ashtray from attested UFO abductees. Maybe the reason we do not find more physical or DNA evidence of anomalies is that: a) they are unreal or b) persistently reported phenomena actually occur but do not necessarily conform to our five-sensory material lives. This returns us to the observation that Jacques Vallée made about UFOs possibly being some kind of interdimensional verity. There may exist an infinitude, or superposition, of events occurring always and everywhere, which we are capable of measuring or experiencing only intermittently, fractionally, or at periods of great sensitivity, in the same way that ESP or PK may manifest at highly receptive moments.

Neville implied that you could take a measurement by employing the emotive-visualizing forces of your imagination. This measurement, I aver, occurs within the infinitude of possible outcomes. The measurement localizes or actualizes the thing itself.

In the 1948 lectures quoted earlier, Neville noted:

> Man can prove the existence of a dimensionally larger world by simply focusing his attention on an invisible state and imagining that he sees and feels it. If he remains concentrated in this state, his present environment will pass away, and he will awaken in a dimen-

* "Maybe Logic: The Lives & Ideas Of Robert Anton Wilson," 2003, YouTube.

> sionally larger world where the object of his contemplation will be seen as a concrete objective reality. I feel intuitively that, were he to abstract his thoughts from this dimensionally larger world and retreat still farther within his mind, he would again bring about an externalization of time. He would discover that, every time he retreats into his inner mind and brings about an externalization of time, space becomes dimensionally larger. And he would therefore conclude that both time and space are serial, and that the drama of life is but the climbing of a multitudinous dimensional time block.

Once more, consider how foresightful Neville's ideas and language proved of the many-worlds theory. Aleister Crowley made a statement related to Neville's. Writing in the introduction to his 1904 received text *The Book of the Law*—published in a general edition in 1938—Crowley observed:

> Each of us has thus an universe of his own, but it is the same universe for each one as soon as it includes all possible experience. This implies the extension of consciousness to include all other consciousnesses. In our present stage, the object that you see is never the same as the one that I see; we infer that it is the same because your experience tallies with mine on so many points that the actual differences of our observation are negligible . . . Yet all the time neither of us can know anything . . . at all beyond the total impression made on our respective minds.

In bowing to Hermetic insights and empirical experience, I contend that even if awareness or consciousness is the ultimate arbiter of events, we still experience many different laws and forces within the physical framework we know. I used to say that we *live* under many different laws and forces; I'm not sure that's entirely right. But we *experience* diffuse laws and forces; and these experiences are hard-baked into us. Strike a stone and break a bone.

Hence, it stands to reason that even if emotive thought, perspective, and awareness are determinative of what reality gets concretized into our individual experiences, there persist, per Wigner, different laws playing out simultaneously. There are physical facts which also inform the nature of our experience within the framework we perceive. It could be that there are other frameworks in which our psyches are much freer. There may be frameworks in which we experience *fewer* laws and forces that seem to interrupt continuity between thought and experience. This may be among the results of successful occult practice or mystical insight.

We reify truth through system and doctrine. It may be that truths of human nature resound when they are less mediated—however aesthetically alluring, beautiful, and even objectively valuable are the constructs through which we experience them.

The Hermetic dialogue *Asclepius* tells us, "The world will be turned upside down, but oh, Egypt, Egypt, there will come a day when the gods are returned to their thrones and you are extolled in your glory once again." But in what form?

As seen in these pages, the occult—an imperfect, flawed, and rough-hewn vessel—has, through the efforts, travails, and uneven paths of its key intellects, both preserved and recreated an artery through which a dedicated few (and sometimes more) may discover fuller capacities of self, both uncommon and actual. It could be that we are entering a stage in which the vessel itself may be dissolvable through realization of the reality traversing it.

Or is it all imagination? Recall the words of Mesmer's student Charles d'Eslon: "It may indeed be entirely imagination. And if it is? Then imagination is a force as potent as it is little understood. Let us work with this mysterious imagination, let us use it to cure, let us learn more about it."

Try.

INDEX

C

ABOUT THE AUTHOR

MITCH HOROWITZ is a historian of alternative spirituality and one of today's most literate voices of esoterica, mysticism, and the occult. Mitch is the PEN Award-winning author of books including *Occult America, One Simple Idea, The Miracle Club, Daydream Believer, Uncertain Places, Practical Magick*, and *Happy Warriors. The Washington Post* says Mitch "treats esoteric ideas and movements with an even-handed intellectual studiousness that is too often lost in today's raised-voice discussions." *Filmmaker Magazine* calls him "a genius at distilling down esoteric concepts." He has discussed alternative spirituality on CBS Sunday Morning, Dateline NBC, NPR's *All Things Considered*, CNN, Vox/Netflix's *Explained*, VICE News, and seasons I and II of AMC Shudder's *Cursed Films*. Mitch hosted, cowrote, and produced a feature documentary about the occult classic *The Kybalion* directed by Emmy-nominee Ronni Thomas and shot on location in Egypt. The movie premiered as the #3 documentary on iTunes. Mitch plays a newscaster in the Paramount feature thriller *My Animal* directed by Jacqueline Castel, an official selection of the Sundance Film Festival. A former vice-president and executive editor at Penguin Random House, Mitch has written on alternative spirituality for *The New York Times, The Wall Street Journal, The Washington Post, Time, Politico,* and a wide range of 'zines and scholarly journals. Mitch's writing has called attention to the worldwide problem of violence against accused witches, helping draw notice to the human rights element of the issue. Mitch's books have been translated into French, Arabic, Chinese, Italian, Spanish, Korean, and Portuguese. His work is censored in China.

Printed in the USA
CPSIA information can be obtained
at www.ICGtesting.com
JSHW050224070923
47940JS00018B/325